Introduction to Business

Fourth Custom Edition—Humber College

D1359870

Taken from:

Keys to Success: Building Analytical, Creative, and Practical Skills,
Sixth Canadian Edition
by Carol Carter, Joyce Bishop, Sarah Lyman Kravits,
and Peter J. Maurin

Business Essentials, Sixth Canadian Edition
by Ronald J. Ebert, Ricky W. Griffin, Frederick A. Starke
and George Dracopoulos

Communicating in the Workplace
by Thomas Cheesebro, Linda O'Connor and Francisco Rios

Better Business, Canadian Edition
by Michael R. Solomon, Mary Anne Poatsy,
Kendall Martin and Kerri Shields

Strategic Analysis and Action, Eighth Edition
by Mary M. Crossan, Michael J. Rouse, Joseph N. Fry and J. Peter Killing

Cover Art: Courtesy of Photodisc/Getty Images, Digital Vision/Getty Images.

Taken from:

Keys to Success: Building Analytical, Creative, and Practical Skills, Sixth Canadian Edition
by Carol Carter, Joyce Bishop, Sarah Lyman Kravits, and Peter J. Maurin
Copyright © 2013, 2010, 2007, 2004, 2001, 1998 by Pearson Education Canada, Inc.
Published by Prentice Hall
Toronto, Ontario

Business Essentials, Sixth Canadian Edition
by Ronald J. Ebert, Ricky W. Griffin, Frederick A. Starke and George Dracopoulos
Copyright © 2012, 2009, 2006, 2003, 2000, 1997 by Pearson Education Canada, Inc.
Published by Prentice Hall

Communicating in the Workplace
by Thomas Cheesebro, Linda O'Connor and Francisco Rios
Copyright © 2010 by Pearson Education Canada, Inc.
Published by Prentice Hall

Better Business, Canadian Edition
by Michael R. Solomon, Mary Anne Poatsy, Kendall Martin and Kerri Shields
Copyright © 2013 by Pearson Education Canada, Inc.
Published by Prentice Hall

Strategic Analysis and Action, Eighth Edition
by Mary M. Crossan, Michael J. Rouse, Joseph N. Fry and J. Peter Killing
Copyright © 2013, 2009, 2005, 2002, 2000, 1997, 1992, 1989 by Pearson Education Canada, Inc.
Published by Prentice Hall

This special edition published in cooperation with Pearson Learning Solutions.

All trademarks, service marks, registered trademarks, and registered service marks are the property of their respective owners and are used herein for identification purposes only.

Pearson Learning Solutions, 501 Boylston Street, Suite 900, Boston, MA 02116
A Pearson Education Company
www.pearsoned.com

Printed in the United States of America

4 5 6 7 8 9 10 V0UD 18 17 16 15 14

000200010271690138

CG

 ISBN 10: 1-256-84056-4
ISBN 13: 978-1-256-84056-5

CONTENTS

part 1

Student Success

chapter 1

Learning How You Learn

Making the Most of Your Abilities

What Would You Do?

Think about this problem as you read, and consider how you would approach it. This chapter focuses on self-assessments to help you explore your learning strengths and challenges and how you interact with people. With this information, you can make practical decisions about work and study.

As a post-secondary student, author Joyce Bishop was confused by her spotty record—doing well in some classes but feeling totally lost in others, especially those that were lecture-based. She couldn't make sense of what she was hearing when she wasn't familiar with the information. If she read the material ahead of time, she could make visual pictures in her mind and look up concepts. This method helped, but there wasn't often time for it.

Joyce also had trouble in small classes, because she heard voices around her as much as she heard the instructor. She would borrow classmates' notes in exchange for typing their term papers. The notes and the typing helped her to retain information. Ultimately, finding that science classes were some-what less difficult than others, she majored in biology and managed to graduate.

Twelve years later, pursuing a master's in public health, Joyce was having trouble reading and her eye doctor was concerned about the stress it put on her eyes. He sent her to a centre that usually tests small children for learning disabilities. The therapist who tested her determined that Joyce processed language at a fourth-grade level, a condition that had not changed in her adult life. Guessing that she had not made it past the tenth grade, the therapist was shocked to hear that she was completing her master's degree. Joyce was beginning to understand what was behind so many years of mediocre grades and an intense struggle to learn. (To be continued . . .)

You don't have to have a learning disability to face learning challenges. For Joyce, taking part in adventure sports such as riding ATVs is a way to grow from taking a risk, just as she did when working through her disability. You'll learn more about Joyce, and revisit her situation, within the chapter.

In this chapter, you'll explore answers to these questions:

> Why explore who you are as a learner? p. 4

> What tools can help you assess how you learn and interact with others? p. 6

> How can you use your self-knowledge? p. 13

> How can you identify and manage learning disabilities? p. 20

MyStudentSuccessLab

Use these interactive tools to help you succeed in your course and career:
• Videos
• Exercises and applied activities
• Practice quizzes

STATUS *Check*

▶ *How aware are you of how you learn?*

For each statement, circle the number that feels right to you, from 1 for "not at all true for me" to 5 for "very true for me."

▶ I believe I can develop my skills and abilities through self-knowledge and hard work.	1 2 3 4 5
▶ I have a pretty clear idea of my strengths and abilities.	1 2 3 4 5
▶ I understand which subjects and situations make it more difficult for me to succeed.	1 2 3 4 5
▶ In my work in the classroom and out, I try to maximize what I do well.	1 2 3 4 5
▶ I recognize that being comfortable with the subject matter isn't necessarily enough to succeed in a course.	1 2 3 4 5
▶ I assess an instructor's teaching style and make adjustments so that I can learn effectively.	1 2 3 4 5
▶ I choose study techniques that tap into how I learn best.	1 2 3 4 5
▶ I try to use technology that works well with how I learn.	1 2 3 4 5
▶ I've taken a skills and/or interests inventory to help find a major or career area that suits me.	1 2 3 4 5
▶ I understand what a learning disability is and am aware of several different types of disabilities.	1 2 3 4 5

Each of the topics in these statements is covered in this chapter. Note those statements for which you circled a 3 or lower. Skim the chapter to see where those topics appear, and pay special attention to them as you read, learn, and apply new strategies.

REMEMBER: *No matter how well know yourself as a learner, you can improve with effort and practice.*

"Successfully intelligent people figure out their strengths and their weaknesses, and then find ways to capitalize on their strengths—make the most of what they do well—and to correct for or remedy their weaknesses—find ways around what they don't do well, or make themselves good enough to get by."

—Robert Sternberg

LEARNING STYLE
A particular way in which the mind receives and processes information.

Why explore who you are as a learner?

Have you thought about how you learn? Now, as you begin college or university, is the perfect time for thinking about how you learn, think, and function in the world. Thinking about thinking is known as *metacognition* (something you are building with each chapter-opening self-assessment). Building metacognition and self-knowledge will help you become a better student and decision maker because the more you know about yourself, the more effectively you can analyze courses, study environments, and study partners; self-knowledge can also help you come up with ideas as well as make practical choices about what, how, and where to study.

Use assessments to learn about yourself

Every person is born with a unique **learning style** and particular levels of ability and potential in different areas. These innate raw materials combine with effort and environment to create a "recipe" for what you can achieve. Part of that recipe is the way you perceive your strengths and challenges, which comes from many different sources and starts in childhood. Maybe your mother thinks you are "the funny one" or "the quiet one." A grade school teacher may have called you "a thinker," "a slacker," "a go-getter," or "shy." These labels—from yourself and others—influence your ability to set and achieve goals.

The danger in accepting a label as truth, as Sternberg did as a child is that it can put you in a fixed mindset and limit your potential. You are not simply stuck with what you've been given. Brain studies show that humans of any age are able to build new neuropathways and thereby learn new ideas and skills, supporting theories that intelligence can grow over time if you work to keep learning.

Picture a bag of rubber bands of different sizes. Some are thick, and some are thin; some are long, and some are short—*but all of them can stretch*. A small rubber band, stretched out, can reach the length of a larger one that lies unstretched. In other words, with effort and focus, you can grow whatever raw material you have at the start, perhaps beyond the natural gifts of someone not making any effort. Joyce's story illustrates just how far effort can stretch a person's natural abilities.

Ask yourself: Who am I right now? Where could I be, and where would I like to be, in five years? Assessments focused on how you learn and interact with others can help you start to answer these big questions. Assessments have a different goal than tests. Whereas a test seeks to identify a level of performance, an assessment, as professor and psychologist Howard Gardner puts it, is "the obtaining of information about a person's skills and (potentials) . . . providing useful feedback to the person."[1] You can think of an assessment as an exploration that, if honest, will reliably produce interesting and helpful information.

POTENTIALS Abilities that may be developed.

The assessments you will take in this chapter provide the questions that get you thinking actively about your strengths and challenges. (Learning disabilities—diagnosed, specific issues different from the learning challenges that all students face—are discussed at the end of the chapter.) As you search for answers, you will be gathering important information about yourself. With this information, you will be able to define your rubber band and get ready to stretch it to its limit.

Use assessments to make choices and to grow

There is much about yourself, your surroundings, and your experiences that you cannot control. However, self-knowledge gives you tools to choose how you respond to circumstances. Although you cannot control the courses you are required to take or how your instructors teach, for example, you can manage how you respond in each situation.

The two assessments in this chapter—Multiple Pathways to Learning and the Personality Spectrum—will give you greater insight into your strengths and weaknesses. The material after the assessments will help you think practically about how to maximize what you do well and compensate for challenging areas by making specific choices about what you do in class, during study time, and in the workplace.

Understanding yourself as a learner will also help you choose how to respond to others in a group situation. In a study group, classroom, or workplace, each person takes in material in a unique way. You can use what you know about how others learn to improve communication and teamwork.

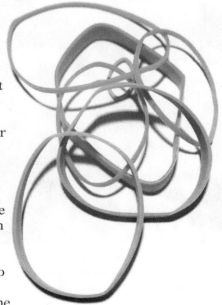

Remember: An assessment is simply a snapshot of where you are at a given moment. There are no "right" answers, no "best" scores. And because many educators are aware of research that shows the benefit of learning in a variety of ways—kind of like cross-training for the brain—they will often challenge you to learn in ways that aren't as comfortable for you.

As you complete this chapter's assessments, compare the experience to trying on new glasses to correct blurred vision. The glasses will not create new paths and possibilities, but they will enable you to see more clearly the ones in front of you. Furthermore, as you gain experience, build skills, and learn more, your learning patterns are apt to change over time. You may want to take the assessments again in the future to see whether your results are different.

What tools can help you assess how you learn and interact *with others?*

Many different tools can help you become more aware of how you think, process information, and relate to others. Some focus on learning preferences, some on areas of potential, and some on personality type. This chapter examines two assessments in depth. The first—Multiple Pathways to Learning—is a learning preferences assessment focusing on eight areas of potential, based on Howard Gardner's multiple intelligences (MI) theory. The second—the Personality Spectrum—is a personality-type assessment based on the Myers-Briggs Type Indicator and helps you evaluate how you react to people and situations.

Following each assessment is information about the typical traits of each **intelligence** or Personality Spectrum dimension. As you will see from your scores, you have abilities in all areas, though some are more developed than others.

INTELLIGENCE
As defined by Howard Gardner, an ability to solve problems or create products that are of value in a culture.

Assess your multiple intelligences with pathways to learning

In 1983, Howard Gardner changed the way people perceive intelligence and learning with his theory of multiple intelligences. Like Robert Sternberg, Gardner had developed the belief that the traditional view of intelligence—based on mathematical, logical, and verbal measurements that made up an intelligence quotient, or IQ—did not comprehensively reflect the spectrum of human ability. Whereas Sternberg focused on the spectrum of actions that help people achieve important goals, Gardner honed in on the idea that humans possess a number of different areas of natural ability and potential.

The theory of multiple intelligences

Gardner's research led him to believe that there are eight unique "intelligences," or areas of ability. These areas include the aptitudes traditionally associated with the term *intelligence*—logic and verbal skills—but go beyond, to encompass a wide range of potentials of the human brain.[2] These intelligences almost never function in isolation. You will almost always use several at a time for any significant role or task.[3]

Look at Key 1.1 for a description of each intelligence, along with examples of people who have unusually high levels of ability in each intelligence. Although few people will have the verbal-linguistic intelligence of William Shakespeare or the interpersonal intelligence of Oprah Winfrey, everyone has some level of ability in each intelligence. Your goal is to identify what your levels are and to work your strongest intelligences to your advantage.

Students drawn to the sciences may find that they have strengths in logical-mathematical or naturalistic thinking.
© iStockphoto

EACH INTELLIGENCE IS LINKED TO
SPECIFIC ABILITIES

INTELLIGENCE	DESCRIPTION	HIGH-ACHIEVING EXAMPLES
Verbal-Linguistic	Ability to communicate through language; listening, reading, writing, speaking	• Canadian author Margaret Atwood • Orator and American President Barack Obama
Logical-Mathematical	Ability to understand logical reasoning and problem solving; math, science, patterns, sequences	• Physicist Stephen Hawking • Mathematician Svetlana Jitomirskaya
Bodily-Kinesthetic	Ability to use the physical body skilfully and to take in knowledge through bodily sensation; coordination; working with hands	• Olympic gold-medalist skier Alexandre Bilodeau • Hockey superstar Sidney Crosby
Visual-Spatial	Ability to understand spatial relationships and to perceive and create images; visual art, graphic design, charts and maps	• Canadian graphic novelist Bryan Lee O'Malley • Movie director James Cameron
Interpersonal	Ability to relate to others, noticing their moods, motivations, and feelings; social activity, cooperative learning, teamwork	• Canadian media personality Marilyn Denis • Media philosopher Marshall McLuhan • "Me to We" co-founder, Canadian Craig Kielburger
Intrapersonal	Ability to understand one's own behaviour and feelings; self-awareness, independence, time spent alone	• Animal researcher Jane Goodall • Philosopher Marshall McLuhan
Musical	Ability to comprehend and create meaningful sound; sensitivity to music and musical patterns	• Canadian singer and musician Dallas Green • Composer Andrew Lloyd Webber
Naturalistic	Ability to identify, distinguish, categorize, and classify species or items, often incorporating high interest in elements of the natural environment	• Conservationist David Suzuki • Bird cataloguer John James Audubon

Different cultures value different abilities and therefore place a premium on different intelligences. In Tibet, mountain dwellers prize the bodily-kinesthetic ability of a top-notch Himalayan guide. In Detroit, automakers appreciate the visual-spatial talents of a master car designer.

Your own eight intelligences

Gardner believes that all people possess some capacity in each of the eight intelligences and that every person has developed some intelligences more fully than others. When you find a task or subject easy, you are probably using a more fully developed intelligence. When you have trouble, you may be using a less developed intelligence.[4]

Furthermore, Gardner believes your levels of development in the eight intelligences can grow or recede throughout your life, depending on your efforts and experiences. Although you will not become a world-class pianist if you have limited musical ability, for example, you still can grow what you have with focus and work. Conversely, even a highly talented musician will lose ability without practice. These examples reflect how the brain grows with learning and becomes sluggish without it.

A related self-assessment that you may have heard of, or have already taken, is the VAK or VARK questionnaire. VAK/VARK assesses learning preferences in three (or four) areas: visual, auditory, (read/write), and kinesthetic. The multiple intelligences (MI) assessment is this book's choice because it incorporates and expands on the elements of VAK/VARK, giving you a more comprehensive picture of your abilities. For further information about VAK/VARK, go to www.vark-learn.com or search online using the keywords "VAK assessment."

A note about auditory learners who learn and remember best through listening: auditory learning is part of two MI dimensions: *verbal intelligence* (hearing words) and *musical intelligence* (associating information with sounds and rhythms). If you tend to absorb information better through listening, try study suggestions for these two intelligences. Podcasts are especially helpful to auditory learners, and an increasing number of instructors are converting their lectures into digital format for downloading.

Use the Multiple Pathways to Learning assessment to determine where you are right now in the eight intelligence areas. Then look at Key 3.2 immediately following the assessment to identify specific skills associated with each area. Finally, the Multiple Intelligence Strategies grids in Chapters 2 through 3 will help you apply your learning styles knowledge to key post-secondary success skills and to specific areas of study.

Assess your style of interaction with the personality spectrum

Personality assessments help you understand how you respond to the world around you, including people, work, and school. They also can help guide you as you explore majors and careers.

The concept of dividing human beings into four basic personality types, as in the Personality Spectrum, goes as far back as Aristotle and Hippocrates, ancient Greek philosophers. Modern psychologist Carl Jung focused on personality **typology**, defining the following parameters:[5]

TYPOLOGY
A systematic classification or study of types.

▶ *An individual's preferred "world."* Jung said that extroverts tend to prefer the outside world of people and activities, whereas introverts tend to prefer the inner world of thoughts, feelings, and fantasies.

▶ *Different ways of dealing with the world, or "functions."* Jung defined four distinct interaction dimensions, which are used to different degrees: *sensing* (learning through what your senses take in), *thinking* (evaluating information rationally), *intuiting* (learning through an instinct that comes from many integrated sources of information), and *feeling* (evaluating information through emotional response).

Katharine Briggs and her daughter, Isabel Briggs Myers, developed an assessment based on Jung's typology, called the Myers-Briggs Type Inventory (MBTI; www.myersbriggs.org). One of the most widely used personality inventories in the world, it creates 16 possible types. David Keirsey and Marilyn Bates later condensed the MBTI types into four temperaments, creating the Keirsey Sorter (found at www.keirsey.com).

When author Joyce Bishop developed the Personality Spectrum assessment in this chapter, she adapted and simplified the Keirsey Sorter and MBTI material into four personality types—Thinker, Organizer, Giver, and Adventurer. Like the assessments on which it is based, the Personality Spectrum helps you identify the kinds of interactions that are most, and least, comfortable for you. As with the multiple intelligences, these results may change over time as you experience new things, change, and continue to learn. Key 1.3, on page 13, shows skills characteristic of each personality type.

MULTIPLE PATHWAYS TO LEARNING

Each intelligence has a set of numbered statements. Consider each statement on its own. Then, on a scale from 1 (lowest) to 4 (highest), rate how closely it matches who you are right now and write that number on the line next to the statement. Finally, total your results from each set of six questions. Enter your scores in the grid on page 10.

1. rarely　**2. sometimes**　**3. usually**　**4. always**

1. _____ I enjoy telling stories.
2. _____ I like to write.
3. _____ I like to read.
4. _____ I express myself clearly.
5. _____ I am good at negotiating.
6. _____ I like to discuss topics that interest me.
_____ **TOTAL for VERBAL-LINGUISTIC**

1. _____ I like math in school.
2. _____ I like science.
3. _____ I problem-solve well.
4. _____ I question how things work.
5. _____ I enjoy planning or designing something new.
6. _____ I am able to fix things.
_____ **TOTAL for LOGICAL–MATHEMATICAL**

1. _____ I enjoy physical activities.
2. _____ I am uncomfortable sitting still.
3. _____ I prefer to learn through doing.
4. _____ When sitting, I move my legs or hands.
5. _____ I enjoy working with my hands.
6. _____ I like to pace when I'm thinking or studying.
_____ **TOTAL for BODILY-KINESTHETIC**

1. _____ I use maps easily.
2. _____ I draw pictures/diagrams when explaining ideas.
3. _____ I can assemble items easily from diagrams.
4. _____ I enjoy drawing or photography.
5. _____ I do not like to read long paragraphs.
6. _____ I prefer a drawn map over written directions.
_____ **TOTAL for VISUAL-SPATIAL**

1. _____ I like doing a project with other people.
2. _____ People come to me to help settle conflicts.
3. _____ I like to spend time with friends.
4. _____ I am good at understanding people.
5. _____ I am good at making people feel comfortable.
6. _____ I enjoy helping others.
_____ **TOTAL for INTERPERSONAL**

1. _____ I need quiet time to think.
2. _____ I think about issues before I want to talk.
3. _____ I am interested in self-improvement.
4. _____ I understand my thoughts and feelings.
5. _____ I know what I want out of life.
6. _____ I prefer to work on projects alone.
_____ **TOTAL for INTRAPERSONAL**

1. _____ I listen to music.
2. _____ I move my fingers or feet when I hear music.
3. _____ I have good rhythm.
4. _____ I like to sing along with music.
5. _____ People have said I have musical talent.
6. _____ I like to express my ideas through music.
_____ **TOTAL for MUSICAL**

1. _____ I like to think about how things, ideas, or people fit into categories.
2. _____ I enjoy studying plants, animals, or oceans.
3. _____ I tend to see how things relate to, or are distinct from, one another.
4. _____ I think about having a career in the natural sciences.
5. _____ As a child, I often played with bugs and leaves.
6. _____ I like to investigate the natural world around me.
_____ **TOTAL for NATURALISTIC**

Source: Developed by Joyce Bishop, Ph.D., Golden West College, Huntington Beach, CA. Based on Howard Gardner, *Frames of Mind: The Theory of Multiple Intelligences*, New York: Harper Collins, 1993.

SCORING GRID FOR MULTIPLE PATHWAYS TO LEARNING

For each intelligence, shade the box in the row that corresponds with the range where your score falls. For example, if you scored 17 in bodily-kinesthetic intelligence, you would shade the middle box in that row; if you scored a 13 in visual-spatial, you would shade the last box in that row. When you have shaded one box for each row, you will see a "map" of your range of development at a glance.

A score of 20–24 indicates a high level of development in that particular type of intelligence, 14–19 a moderate level, and below 14 an underdeveloped intelligence.

	20–24 (HIGHLY DEVELOPED)	14–19 (MODERATELY DEVELOPED)	BELOW 14 (UNDERDEVELOPED)
Verbal-Linguistic			
Logical-Mathematical			
Bodily-Kinesthetic			
Visual-Spatial			
Interpersonal			
Intrapersonal			
Musical			
Naturalistic			

Key 1.2 | PARTICULAR **ABILITIES AND SKILLS** ARE ASSOCIATED WITH EACH INTELLIGENCE

Verbal-Linguistic	• Remembering terms easily • Mastering a foreign language • Using writing or speech to convince someone to do or believe something
Logical-Mathematical	• Recognizing abstract patterns • Using facts to support an idea and generating ideas based on evidence • Reasoning scientifically (formulating and testing a hypothesis)
Bodily-Kinesthetic	• Having a strong mind–body connection • Controlling and coordinating body movement • Using the body to create products or express emotion
Visual-Spatial	• Recognizing relationships between objects • Representing something graphically • Manipulating images
Interpersonal	• Seeing things from others' perspectives • Noticing moods, intentions, and temperaments of others • Gauging the most effective way to work with individual group members
Intrapersonal	• Accessing one's internal emotions • Understanding feelings and using them to guide behaviour • Understanding self in relation to others
Musical	• Sensing tonal qualities • Being sensitive to sounds and rhythms in music and in spoken language • Using an understanding of musical patterns to hear music
Naturalistic	• Categorizing something as a member of a group or species • Understanding relationships among natural organisms • Being deeply comfortable with, and respecting, the natural world

PERSONALITY SPECTRUM

STEP 1   Rank-order all four responses to each question from most like you (4) to least like you (1) so that for each question you use the numbers 1, 2, 3, and 4 one time each. Place numbers on the lines next to the responses.

4. most like me   3. more like me   2. less like me   1. least like me

1. I like instructors who

   a. _____ tell me exactly what is expected of me.

   b. _____ make learning active and exciting.

   c. _____ maintain a safe and supportive classroom.

   d. _____ challenge me to think at higher levels.

2. I learn best when the material is

   a. _____ well organized.

   b. _____ something I can work with hands-on.

   c. _____ about understanding and improving the human condition.

   d. _____ intellectually challenging.

3. A high priority in my life is to

   a. _____ keep my commitments.

   b. _____ experience as much of life as possible.

   c. _____ make a difference in the lives of others.

   d. _____ understand how things work.

4. Other people think of me as

   a. _____ dependable and loyal.

   b. _____ dynamic and creative.

   c. _____ caring and honest.

   d. _____ intelligent and inventive.

5. When I experience stress, I usually

   a. _____ do something to help me feel more in control of my life.

   b. _____ do something physical and daring.

   c. _____ talk with a friend.

   d. _____ go off by myself and think about my situation.

6. I would probably not be close friends with someone who is

   a. _____ irresponsible.

   b. _____ unwilling to try new things.

   c. _____ selfish and unkind to others.

   d. _____ an illogical thinker.

7. My vacations could be described as

   a. _____ traditional.

   b. _____ adventuresome.

   c. _____ pleasing to others.

   d. _____ a new learning experience.

8. One word that best describes me is

   a. _____ sensible.

   b. _____ spontaneous.

   c. _____ giving.

   d. _____ analytical.

STEP 2   Add up the total points for each letter.

TOTAL FOR   a. ____ Organizer   b. ____ Adventurer   c. ____ Giver   d. ____ Thinker

STEP 3   Plot these numbers on the brain diagram on page 12.

SCORING DIAGRAM FOR PERSONALITY SPECTRUM

Write your scores from page 11 in the four coloured squares just outside the brain diagram—Thinker score at top left, Giver score at top right, Organizer score at bottom left, and Adventurer score at bottom right.

Each square has a line of numbers that go from the square to the centre of the diagram. For each of your four scores, place a dot on the appropriate number in the line near that square. For example, if you scored 15 in the Giver spectrum, you would place a dot between the 14 and 16 in the upper right-hand line of numbers. If you scored a 26 in the Organizer spectrum, you would place a dot on the 26 in the lower left-hand line of numbers.

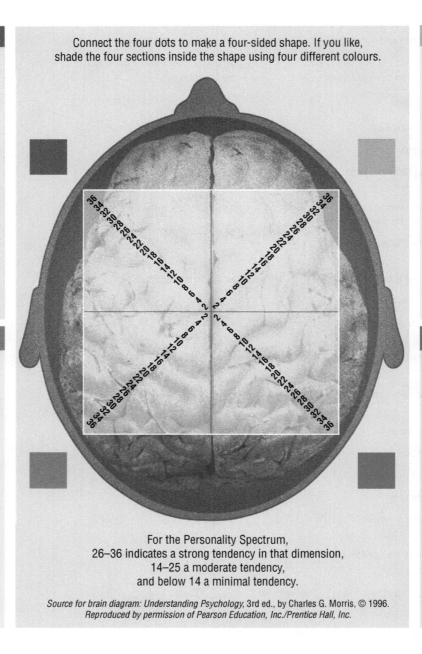

THINKER

Technical
Scientific
Mathematical
Dispassionate
Rational
Analytical
Logical
Problem Solving
Theoretical
Intellectual
Objective
Quantitative
Explicit
Realistic
Literal
Precise
Formal

GIVER

Interpersonal
Emotional
Caring
Sociable
Giving
Spiritual
Musical
Romantic
Feeling
Peacemaker
Trusting
Adaptable
Passionate
Harmonious
Idealistic
Talkative
Honest

ORGANIZER

Tactical
Planning
Detailed
Practical
Confident
Predictable
Controlled
Dependable
Systematic
Sequential
Structured
Administrative
Procedural
Organized
Conservative
Safekeeping
Disciplined

ADVENTURER

Active
Visual
Risking
Original
Artistic
Spatial
Skilful
Impulsive
Metaphoric
Experimental
Divergent
Fast-paced
Simultaneous
Competitive
Imaginative
Open-minded
Adventuresome

Connect the four dots to make a four-sided shape. If you like, shade the four sections inside the shape using four different colours.

For the Personality Spectrum,
26–36 indicates a strong tendency in that dimension,
14–25 a moderate tendency,
and below 14 a minimal tendency.

Source for brain diagram: Understanding Psychology, 3rd ed., by Charles G. Morris, © 1996. Reproduced by permission of Pearson Education, Inc./Prentice Hall, Inc.

PARTICULAR ABILITIES AND SKILLS ARE ASSOCIATED WITH EACH **PERSONALITY SPECTRUM** DIMENSION

Thinker	• Solving problems • Developing models and systems • Using analytical and abstract thinking
Organizer	• Being responsible and reliable • Being neat, organized, and detail-oriented • Following through on every aspect of a task
Giver	• Maintaining successful, close relationships • Making a difference in the world • Negotiating; promoting peace
Adventurer	• Being courageous and daring • Using hands-on problem solving • Possessing an active and spontaneous style

How can you use your self-knowledge?

In completing the assessments, you have developed a clearer picture of who you are and how you interact with others. Now, use this new picture to choose effective strategies for class, study time, the workplace, or technology.

Classroom choices

Most students have to complete a set of core curriculum courses, as well as whatever courses their majors require. As you sign up for the sections that fit into your schedule, you may be asking, "Where are the choices in this situation?"

The opportunity for choice lies in how you interact with your instructor and function in the classroom. It is impossible for instructors to tailor classroom presentation to 15, 40, or 300 unique learners. As a result, you may find yourself in a great situation with one teacher and in a mismatch with another. Sometimes, the way the class is structured can have more of an effect on your success than the subject matter.

After several class meetings, you should be able to assess each instructor's dominant teaching styles (see Key 1.4) and figure out how to maximize your learning. As with learning styles, most instructors will demonstrate some combination of styles.

Although styles vary and instructors may combine styles, the word-focused lecture is still most common. For this reason, the traditional post-secondary classroom is generally a happy home for the verbal or logical learner and the Thinker and the Organizer. However, many students need to experience other modes in order to learn effectively. What can you do when your preferences don't match up with how your instructor teaches? Here are three suggestions:

▶ *Play to your strengths.* For example, a musical learner whose instructor delivers material in a random way might record lecture highlights digitally

INSTRUCTORS OFTEN PREFER
ONE OR MORE **TEACHING STYLES**

TEACHING STYLE	WHAT TO EXPECT IN CLASS
Lecture, verbal focus	Instructor speaks to the class for the entire period, with little class interaction. Lesson is taught primarily through words, either spoken or written on the board, in a slide show, on handouts, or via the text.
Lecture with group discussion	Instructor presents material but encourages class discussion.
Small groups	Instructor presents material and then breaks class into small groups for discussion or project work.
Visual focus	Instructor uses visual elements such as slide shows, diagrams, photographs, drawings, transparencies, and videos.
Logical presentation	Instructor organizes material in a logical sequence, such as by steps, time, or importance.
Random presentation	Instructor tackles topics in no particular order and may jump around a lot or digress.
Conceptual presentation	Instructor spends the majority of time on the big picture, focusing on abstract concepts and umbrella ideas.
Detailed presentation	Instructor spends the majority of time, after introducing ideas, on the details and facts that underlie them.
Hands-on presentation	Instructor uses demonstrations, experiments, props, and class activities to show key points.

Add a new dimension to your experience of a course, and your learning, by talking to your instructor outside of class time.
© ThinkStock

and listen to them on an MP3 player (be sure to check whether your instructor and school permit recording). Likewise, if you are a Giver with an instructor who delivers straight lectures, you should consider setting up a study group to go over details and fill in factual gaps.

▶ *Work to strengthen weaker areas.* A visual learner reviewing notes from a structured lecture could use logical-mathematical strategies such as outlining notes or thinking about cause-and-effect relationships within the material. An Organizer, studying for a test from notes delivered by an instructor with a random presentation, could organize material by using tables and timelines.

▶ *Ask your instructor for help.* If you are having trouble with coursework, communicate with your instructor or teaching assistant through email or during office hours. This is especially important in large lectures in which you are anonymous unless you speak up. A visual learner, for example, might ask the instructor to recommend graphs, figures, or videos that illustrate the lecture.

student profile

Hongman Xu
Seneca College, Toronto, Ontario

About me:

I'm a mother of two and am originally from Jiujiang, a small and famous city in China. My mother and father are doctors. I have two sisters. Everyone in my family graduated from university in China. When my husband and I immigrated to Canada, I had 10 years of work experience in China but no idea of how to be a student in Canada. I'm enrolled in Seneca's International Transportation and Customs diploma program.

I plan to start my own customs brokerage company in the future.

What I focus on:

When I was younger, my dreams didn't include being a mature college student struggling with math in Canada. While it might be a common stereotype that Asians are good at math, it wasn't the case with me. I struggled. When I faced troubles in my studies, I was able to go to my professor for help. I also used both the textbook and online quizzes, which helped me practise over and over again. These were very useful for me and helped me study. Online studying was also helpful when my kids got sick and I couldn't get to class.

I also read the textbook step by step, a bit at a time, which helped me use what little time I had more effectively. Extra help from my professor, online quizzes, and the textbook were the keys for my success in accounting classes.

What will help me in the future:

Being able to overcome my struggles with math and accounting will help me reach my dream of starting my own customs brokerage firm. Succeeding in those classes has taught me that any problem can be solved with hard work. It's given me the confidence to succeed.

No instructor of a diverse group of learners can provide exactly what each student needs. However, adjusting to instructors' teaching styles builds flexibility that you need for career and life success. Just as you can't hand-pick your instructors, you will rarely, if ever, be able to choose your work colleagues or their ways of working or interacting with others.

A final point: Some students try to find out more about an instructor by asking students who have already taken the course or by looking up comments online. Be careful with investigations like this. You may not know or be able to trust an anonymous poster. Even if you hear a review from a friend you do trust, every student–instructor relationship is unique, and an instructor your friend loved may turn out to be a bad match for you. Prioritize the courses that you need, and know that you will find a way to make the most of what your instructors offer, no matter who they are.

Maximize Your Classroom Experience

Using what you know about yourself as a learner and about your instructors' teaching styles this term, decide which classroom situation is the most challenging for you. Use this exercise to think analytically, creatively, and practically about the situation.

Course:_____ Instructor style:_____

Your analysis of the problem:_____

_____

Next, brainstorm at least three ideas about actions you can take to improve the situation:

1._____

2._____

3._____

Finally, choose one action and put it to practical use. Briefly note what happened. Were there improvements as a result?

Study choices

Start now to use what you have learned about yourself to choose the best study techniques. For example, if you tend to learn successfully from a linear, logical presentation, you can look for order (for example, a *chronology*—information organized sequentially according to event dates—or a problem–solution structure) as you review notes. If you are strong in interpersonal intelligence, you can try to work in study groups whenever possible.

When faced with a task that challenges your weaknesses, use strategies that boost your ability. For example, if you are an Adventurer who does *not* respond well to linear information, you can apply your strengths to the material—for example, through a hands-on approach. Or you can focus on developing your area of weakness by trying skills that work well for Thinker-dominant learners.

When you study with others, you and the entire group will be more successful if you understand the different learning styles in the group, as in the following examples.

▶ An Interpersonal learner could take the lead in teaching material to others.

▶ An Organizer could coordinate the group schedule.

▶ A Naturalistic learner might organize facts into categories that solidify concepts.

Look at Keys 1.5 and 1.6 for study strategies that suit each intelligence and Personality Spectrum dimension. Because you have some level of ability in each area and because there will be times that you need to boost your ability in a weaker area, you may find useful suggestions under any of the headings. Try different techniques. Pay close attention to what works best for you—you may be surprised at what is useful, as Joyce was about how typing helped her retain information.

CHOOSE STUDY TECHNIQUES TO
MAXIMIZE EACH INTELLIGENCE

Key 1.5

Verbal-Linguistic	• Read text; highlight selectively • Use a computer to retype and summarize notes • Outline chapters • Recite information or write scripts/debates
Logical-Mathematical	• Organize material logically; if it suits the topic, use a spreadsheet program • Explain material sequentially to someone • Develop systems and find patterns • Analyze and evaluate information
Bodily-Kinesthetic	• Move while you learn; pace and recite • Rewrite or retype notes to engage "muscle memory" • Design and play games to learn material • Act out scripts of material
Visual-Spatial	• Develop graphic organizers for new material • Draw mind maps/think links • Use a computer to develop charts and tables • Use colour in notes to organize
Interpersonal	• Study in a group • As you study, discuss information over the phone or send instant messages • Teach someone else the material • Make time to discuss assignments and tests with your instructor
Intrapersonal	• Reflect on personal meaning of information • Keep a journal • Study in quiet areas • Imagine essays or experiments before beginning
Musical	• Create rhythms out of words • Beat out rhythms with your hand or a stick while reciting concepts • Write songs/raps that help you learn concepts • Write out study material to fit into a wordless tune you have on a CD or MP3 player; chant or sing the material along with the tune as you listen
Naturalistic	• Break down information into categories • Look for ways in which items fit or don't fit together • Look for relationships among ideas, events, and facts • Study in a natural setting if it helps you focus

Technology choices

Technology is everywhere these days. You see it in social settings as people communicate using email, text messaging, and social networking sites on the Internet. It also plays a significant role in academic settings, where you may encounter any of the following:

▶ Instructors who require students to communicate via email

▶ Courses that have their own websites, where you can access the syllabus and connect with resources and classmates

▶ Textbooks with corresponding websites that you can, or are required to, use to complete assignments that you email to your instructor

CHOOSE STUDY TECHNIQUES TO MAXIMIZE EACH PERSONALITY SPECTRUM DIMENSION

Key 1.6

Thinker	• Convert material into logical charts, flow diagrams, and outlines • Reflect independently on new information • Learn through problem solving • Design new ways of approaching material or problems
Organizer	• Define tasks in concrete terms • Use a planner to schedule tasks and dates • Organize material by rewriting and summarizing class or text notes • Create, or look for, a well-structured study environment
Giver	• Study with others in person, on the phone, or via instant messages • Teach material to others • Seek out tasks, groups, and subjects that involve helping people • Connect with instructors, advisors, and tutors
Adventurer	• Look for environments or courses that encourage non-traditional approaches • Find hands-on ways to learn • Use or develop games or puzzles to help memorize terms • Fight boredom by asking to do something extra or perform a task in a more active way

For some with extensive know-how, technology comes easily. For others, knowing their strengths and challenges as learners can help them make decisions about how to approach technology. Are you strong in the logical-mathematical intelligence or Thinker dimension? Working with an online tutorial may be a good choice. Are you an interpersonal learner? Find a tech-savvy classmate to help you get the hang of a new technology. An Adventurer may want to just dive in and try out the features of a book or course website in a random way. Know yourself, and make choices that can best help you demystify technology and get you up to speed.

Workplace choices

Knowing how you learn and interact with others will help you work more effectively and make better career planning choices. How can an employee or job candidate benefit from self-awareness?

Better performance and teamwork

When you understand your strengths, you can find ways to use them on the job more readily. For tasks that take you out of your areas of strength, you will be more able to compensate and get help. In addition, you will be better able to work with others effectively. For example, a Giver might help new hires adjust to the people and environment. Or a team leader might offer an intrapersonal team member the chance to take material home to think about before a meeting.

MULTIPLE INTELLIGENCES MAY OPEN DOORS TO **MAJORS AND INTERNSHIPS**

INTELLIGENCE	CONSIDER MAJORING IN	THINK ABOUT AN INTERNSHIP AT A
Verbal-Linguistic	• Communications • Marketing • English/literature • Journalism • Foreign languages	• Newspaper or magazine • Public relations/marketing firm • Ad agency • Publishing house • Network TV affiliate
Logical-Mathematical	• Math • Physics • Economics • Banking/finance • Computer science	• Law firm • Consulting firm • Bank • Information technology company • Research lab
Bodily-Kinesthetic	• Massage or physical therapy • Kinesiology • Construction engineering • Sports medicine • Dance or theatre	• Sports physician's office • Physical or massage therapy centre • Construction company • Dance studio or theatre company • Athletic club
Visual-Spatial	• Architecture • Visual arts • Multimedia designs • Photography • Art history	• Photo or art studio • Multimedia design firm • Architecture firm • Interior design firm • Art gallery
Interpersonal	• Education • Public relations • Nursing • Business • Hotel/restaurant management	• Hotel or restaurant • Social service agency • Public relations firm • Human resources department
Intrapersonal	• Psychology • Finance • Computer science • Biology • Philosophy	• Accounting firm • Biology lab • Pharmaceutical company • Publishing house • Computer or Internet company
Musical	• Music • Music theory • Voice • Composition • Performing arts	• Performance hall • Radio station • Record label or recording studio • Children's music camp • Orchestra or opera company
Naturalistic	• Geology • Zoology • Atmospheric sciences • Agriculture • Environmental law	• Museum • National park • Environmental law firm • Zoo • Geological research firm

Better career planning

Exploring ways to use your strengths in school will help you make better choices about what jobs or careers will suit you. For most college and university students, internships and majors are more immediate steps on the road to a career. A strength in one or more intelligences might lead you to particular internships and majors that may make sense for you.

Key 1.7 links majors and internships to the eight intelligences. This list is by no means complete; rather, it represents only a fraction of the

INTERNSHIPS
Temporary work programs in which a student can gain supervised practical experience in a job and career area.

available opportunities. Use what you see here to inspire thought and spur investigation. If something from this list or elsewhere interests you, consider looking for an opportunity to "shadow" someone (follow the person for a day to see what he or she does) to see if the more significant commitments of internships and majoring make sense for you.

Although all students have areas of strength and weakness, challenges diagnosed as learning disabilities are more significant. These merit specific attention. Focused assistance can help students with learning disabilities manage their conditions and excel in school.

How can you identify and manage learning disabilities?

Some learning disabilities create reading problems, some produce difficulties in math, some cause issues that arise when working with others, and some make it difficult for students to process the language they hear. The following information will help you understand learning disabilities as well as the tools people use to manage them.

Identifying a learning disability

The Learning Disabilities Association of Canada (LDAC) defines *learning disabilities* as "a number of disorders which may affect the acquisition, organization, retention, understanding, or use of verbal or non-verbal information. Learning disabilities result from impairments in one or more processes related to perceiving, thinking, remembering, or learning."[6]

How can you determine whether you should be evaluated for a learning disability? According to the LDAC, persistent problems in any of the following areas may indicate a problem:[7]

▶ Oral language (listening, speaking, understanding)

▶ Reading (word recognition, comprehension)

▶ Written language (spelling, writing)

▶ Mathematics (computation, problem solving)

Details on specific learning disabilities appear in Key 1.8. For an evaluation, contact your school's learning centre or student health centre for a referral to a licensed professional. Note that a professional diagnosis is required in order for a person with a learning disability to receive government-funded aid.

Managing a learning disability

If you are diagnosed with a learning disability, valuable information is available—information that it took Joyce until graduate school to obtain. Maximize your ability to learn by managing your disability.

▶ *Find information about your disability.* Search the library and the Internet—try LDAC at www.ldac-acta.ca or LD Online at www. ldonline.org. If you have an individualized education program (IEP)—a

WHAT ARE **LEARNING DISABILITIES** AND HOW DO YOU RECOGNIZE THEM?

Key 1.8

DISABILITY OR CONDITION	WHAT ARE THE SIGNS?
Dyslexia and related reading disorders	Problems with reading (spelling, word sequencing, comprehension) and processing (translating written language to thought or the reverse)
Dyscalculia (developmental arithmetic disorders)	Difficulties in recognizing numbers and symbols, memorizing facts, understanding abstract math concepts, and applying math to life skills (time management, handling money)
Developmental writing disorders	Difficulties in composing sentences, organizing a writing assignment, or translating thoughts coherently to the page
Dysgraphia (handwriting disorders)	Disorder characterized by writing disabilities, including distorted or incorrect language, inappropriately sized and spaced letters, or wrong or misspelled words
Speech and language disorders	Problems with producing speech sounds, using spoken language to communicate, and/or understanding what others say
LD-related social issues	Problems in recognizing facial or vocal cues from others, controlling verbal and physical impulsivity, and respecting others' personal space
LD-related organizational issues	Difficulties in scheduling and in organizing personal, academic, and work-related materials

Source: LD Online: LD Basics, www.ncld.org/content/view/445/389/, 2009.

document describing your disability and recommended strategies—read it and make sure you understand what it says.

▶ *Seek assistance from your school.* Speak with your advisor about getting a referral to the counsellor who can help you get specific accommodations in your classes. The following services are mandated by law for students who are learning disabled:

- Extended time on tests
- Note-taking assistance (for example, having a fellow student take notes for you)
- Assistive technology devices (MP3 players, tape recorders, laptop computers)

Tips for Learning Online

- *Share.* If you're comfortable, share your personality and learning style with others via Facebook or the course learning management system (LMS). You'll be able to connect with students whose weaknesses are your strengths and vice versa. Collaboratively, you'll be able to offer one another advice.

- *Explore your LMS.* Most LMSs are flexible and user-friendly. For example, if you are a Giver, participate in online discussion forums in which you have the opportunity to seek out other students who may need your help.

- *Build an online support network.* Using your favourite social networking sites, locate others with similar learning disabilities for support.

- Modified assignments
- Alternative assessments and test formats

Other services that may be offered include tutoring, study skills assistance, and counselling.

▶ *Be a dedicated student.* Show up on time and pay attention in class. Read assignments before class. Sit where you can focus. Review notes soon after class. Spend extra time on assignments. Ask for help.

▶ *Build a positive attitude.* See your accomplishments in light of how far you have come. Rely on support from others, knowing that it will give you the best possible chance to succeed.

Case *Wrap-up*

What happened to Joyce? Dr. Bishop now understands how her learning disability, auditory processing disorder, causes problems with understanding words she hears. Seeing how her strengths in visual-spatial, logical-mathematical, and bodily-kinesthetic intelligence served her well in science studies, she chose to study strategies for those strengths and over time earned her master's and doctorate degrees. Now a tenured psychology professor at Golden West College in California, Dr. Bishop has won Teacher of the Year twice at her school. She teaches both in-person and online courses and trains other teachers in online teaching strategies. She manages the challenges of her learning disability while pursuing her intention to learn throughout her life.

What does this mean for you? Getting perspective on strengths and weaknesses isn't just for those with diagnosed learning disabilities. Dr. Bishop got her wake-up call from an eye doctor and a therapist. Who can provide an outside perspective for you? Find someone who knows you well enough to have an opinion about you and who you believe will be honest and constructive. Tell this person ahead of time that you are looking for perspectives about what you do well and what challenges you. Prepare by making a short list of your three strongest and three weakest qualities. After receiving the outside perspective, compare it to your list. What matches up? What surprises you?

What effects go beyond your world? Broaden your knowledge of learning disabilities so you avoid inaccurate assumptions about people and learn how to support them in reaching their potential. Go to www.ldonline.org and read the section titled "LD Basics." Then browse the articles at www.ldonline.org/indepth/adults to focus more closely on how adults with learning disabilities navigate school, work, and life. Finally, think about an assumption you may have made regarding someone with whom you live, work, or go to school. Address your possibly false idea by approaching that person with an open mind from this point forward, looking for strengths as well as working reasonably with challenges (and maybe even helping the person to combat them). With every person who develops a more positive attitude and understanding perspective about those with learning disabilities or other challenges, the world becomes that much more of a supportive and productive place.

Successful Intelligence *Wrap-up*

HERE'S HOW YOU HAVE BUILT SKILLS IN CHAPTER 1:

ANALYTICAL THINKING	CREATIVE THINKING	PRACTICAL THINKING
> You analyzed your levels of ability in the multiple intelligences.	> Reading about the assessments may have inspired new ideas about your abilities and talents.	> In the in-text exercise, you took action to improve a classroom experience.
> You examined how you relate to people and the world around you.	> In the in-text exercise, you brainstormed ideas about how to improve a situation with an instructor.	> Reading Keys 1.5 and 1.6 gave you practical study strategies relating to each intelligence and Personality Spectrum dimension.
> In the in-text exercise, you examined how an instructor's teaching style affects how you learn.	> Seeing in Key 1.7 how intelligences relate to majors and internships may have inspired thoughts about your major and job plans.	> Reading the material on learning disabilities offered practical ways to investigate and address any learning disability you may have.

Word *for* Thought

In the language of the **Yoruba**, an ethnic group living primarily in West Africa, *oruko lonro ni* (oh-roo-ko lon-ro ni) translates as "names affect behavior."[8] Think of this as you work to break through the confines of the names and labels that you give yourself or that others give you. Put learning styles information to work as a tool to learn more, not a box into which to fit yourself.

Building Skills for
Post-Secondary, Career, and Life Success

Steps to Success

Link How You Learn to Your Coursework and Major

Apply what you know about yourself to some future academic planning.

STEP 1 BUILD BASIC SKILLS. On paper or on a computer, summarize yourself as a learner in a paragraph or two. Focus on what you have learned about yourself from the chapter assessments.

    Done? Check here. _____

STEP 2 TAKE IT TO THE NEXT LEVEL. Schedule a meeting with your academic advisor.

    Name of advisor: _____

    Office location/contact information: _____

    Time/date of meeting: _____

Give the advisor an overview of your learning strengths and challenges, based on your summary. Ask for advice about courses that might interest you and majors that might suit you. Take notes. Based on your discussion, name two courses to consider in the next year:

    1. _____

    2. _____

STEP 3 MOVE TOWARD MASTERY. In your mind, project both of those courses ahead in time. What majors might each of them lead you toward? Based on those courses, name two majors to investigate:

    1. _____

    2. _____

Finally, create a separate to-do list of how you plan to explore one course offering and one major. Set a deadline for each task. And keep in mind that if you are having trouble choosing a major because of uncertainty about a career direction, you can see an advisor in the career centre for guidance.

Teamwork

Create Solutions Together

IDEAS ABOUT PERSONALITY TYPES

Goal: To learn more about personality types—your own and others'.

Time on task: 25 minutes: 5 minutes to settle into groups, 10 minutes for group work, 10 minutes to share

Instructions: Divide into groups according to the four types of the Personality Spectrum—Thinkers in one group, Organizers in another, Givers in the third, and Adventurers in the fourth. Students whose scores point to more than one type can join whichever group is smaller. With your group, brainstorm about the following aspects of your type:

1. The strengths of this type

2. The struggles, or stressful aspects, of this type

3. Career areas that tend to suit this type

4. Career areas that are a challenge for this type

5. Challenges for this type in relating to the other three Personality Spectrum types

If there is time, each group can present this information to the entire class to boost understanding and acceptance of diverse ways of relating to information and people.

Writing

Build Intrapersonal and Communication Skills

Record your thoughts on a separate piece of paper, in a journal, or electronically.

EMOTIONAL INTELLIGENCE JOURNAL

Your interactions with others. With your Personality Spectrum profile in mind, think about how you generally relate to people. Describe the type(s) of people that you tend to get along well with. How do you feel around these people? Then describe the types that tend to irk you. How do those people make you feel? Use your emotional intelligence to discuss what those feelings tell you and how you can adjust your mindset or take action to create the best possible outcome in interactions with people with whom you just don't get along.

REAL-LIFE WRITING

Ask an instructor for support. Reach out to an instructor for a course that clashes with your learning style—in terms of the material itself, the style in which it is presented, or the way the classroom is run. Draft a friendly and respectful email requesting help that describes how you perceive yourself as a learner and details the issue you are having with the material or coverage. Include any ideas you have about how the instructor might be able to help you.

When you are done, make something happen: Send it and follow through on the response you receive.

Personal Portfolio

Prepare for Career Success

SELF-PORTRAIT

21st Century Learning Building Blocks
- Creativity and Innovation
- Initiative and Self-Direction

Complete the following on separate sheets of paper or electronically (if you can use a graphics program).

Because self-knowledge helps you make the best choices about your future, a self-portrait can be an important tool in your career exploration. Use this exercise to synthesize everything you have been exploring about yourself into one comprehensive "self-portrait." Design your portrait in think link (mind map) style, using words and visual shapes to describe your dominant multiple intelligences, Personality Spectrum dimensions, values, abilities and interests, personal characteristics, and anything else that you have discovered through self-exploration.

A *think link* is a visual construction of related ideas, similar to a map or web, representing your thought process. Ideas are written inside geometric shapes, often boxes or circles, and related ideas and facts are attached to those ideas by lines that connect the shapes (see the note-taking section in Chapter 3 for more about think links).

If you want to use the style shown in Key 1.9, create a "wheel" of ideas coming off your central shape. Then, spreading out from each of those ideas (interests, values, and so forth), draw lines connecting the thoughts that go along with that idea. Connected to "Interests," for example, might be "singing," "stock market," and "history."

You don't have to use the wheel image, however. You might instead want to design a tree-like think link, a line of boxes with connecting thoughts, or anything else you like. Let your design reflect who you are, just as your writing does. You may want to look back at it at the end of the term to see how you have changed and grown from the self-image you have today.

Social Networking

HELP OTHERS GET TO KNOW YOU

As you are building your self-knowledge, help viewers of your LinkedIn profile get to know you as well. Sign in to your LinkedIn account and click on "Edit Profile." Look for "Summary" and click "Add Summary." Fill in the two areas provided:

- Professional Experience & Goals (If you don't have any professional experience, you can fill in Goals only. Remember, too, that you can include experience from internships, work study, apprenticeships, and so on.)
- Specialties (In conjunction with talking about what you do well, you may want to consider including information related to learning styles—that you are highly visual, for example, or a strong organizer.)

In addition, go to the "Personal Information" section and fill in any of the following that you choose to have visible on your profile:

- Phone
- Address
- IM
- Birthday
- Marital status

Finally, you may choose to post a photo. Use only a respectable-looking picture. Click on "Edit Profile," and then on "Add Photo" underneath the photo icon. The program will direct you to upload a photo.

THIS IS AN EXAMPLE OF
A SELF-PORTRAIT

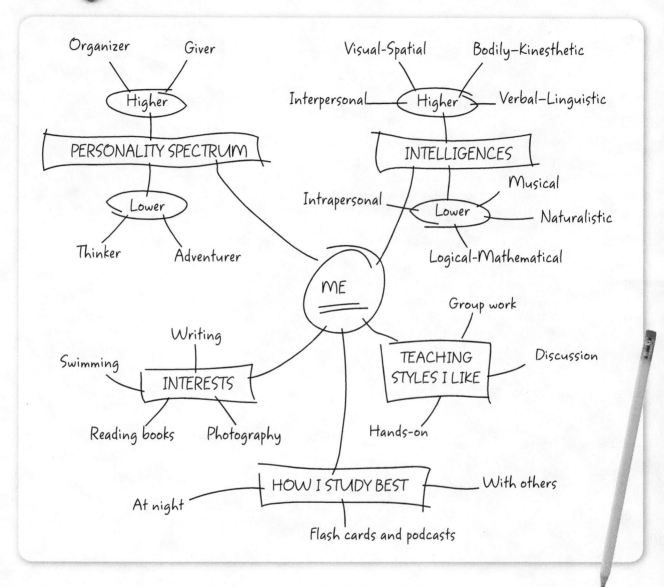

chapter 2

Reading and Information Literacy

Learning from Print and Online Materials

What Would You Do?

Think about this problem as you read, and consider how you would approach it. This chapter focuses on reading in ways that help you take in information comprehensively, analyze it critically, and decide what to remember. It can help you with any reading struggle you need to address on your path to success.

Gary Montrose had no idea why he struggled in public school, and neither did his family or teachers. He was the first to sit down during spelling bees and the last to turn in class exams, even though his hard work got him elected student council president while in high school. His guidance counsellor told him that he "wasn't college or university material" and should consider going straight into a job at the local Lockheed assembly plant.

Determined to persevere, Gary enrolled in college and put his nose to the grindstone. After two years he was able to transfer to university, but the confusing struggle remained, damaging his self-confidence and requiring survival strategies developed through experience. He avoided courses with in-class timed exams—an absolute terror—and looked for classes featuring papers he could write on his own time. He gave up 90 percent of a normal college student's social life and spent hours "unpacking" textbooks by reading the table of contents, chapter headings, tables, and charts. Knowing he was unlikely to complete any reading assignment without support, he needed to develop an idea of the scope of a book.

Despite graduating with high honours and a double major, Gary still lived with his "big secret," terrified about how slowly he read and wrote. Hoping for advice on what type of work he could successfully pursue, he went to the career centre while in graduate school, where a series of tests showed he was functioning at a seventh-grade reading level. From those results he learned that he had a reading disability called dyslexia that causes difficulty with recognizing and understanding words. He began to see why he needed to put in so much extra time and effort to appear normal to the outside world. (To be continued . . .)

Gary's ability to move out of his comfort zone has turned learning into an adventure that he continues as a worldwide traveller. You'll learn more about Gary, and revisit his situation, within the chapter.

In this chapter, you'll explore answers to these questions:

> What sets you up for reading comprehension? p. 30

> How can SQ3R improve your reading? p. 33

> What strategies help with specific subjects and formats? p. 44

> How can you be an information literate reader and researcher? p. 50

> How can you respond critically to what you read? p. 54

MyStudentSuccessLab

Use these interactive tools to help you succeed in your course and career:
• Videos
• Exercises and applied activities
• Practice quizzes

STATUS *Check*
▶ *How developed are your reading
and information literacy skills?*

For each statement, circle the number that feels right to you,
from 1 for "not at all true for me" to 5 for "very true for me."

▶ I make choices about when and how I read that help me boost focus and comprehension.   1 2 3 4 5

▶ I preview a text before studying it by skimming and scanning front matter, chapter elements,
and back matter for clues about content and organization.   1 2 3 4 5

▶ I develop questions to guide me before I begin to read.   1 2 3 4 5

▶ I practise reciting what I've learned from the reading by working with a study partner, taking notes,
using flash cards, or using some other study technique.   1 2 3 4 5

▶ I use text note taking and highlighting to turn my texts into study tools.   1 2 3 4 5

▶ I have a process for reading onscreen assignments and articles.   1 2 3 4 5

▶ I prioritize my reading assignments so that I focus on what is most important.   1 2 3 4 5

▶ When I get a research or writing assignment, I go first to general references for an overview.   1 2 3 4 5

▶ I don't just rely on the Internet for research—I also consult library materials.   1 2 3 4 5

▶ I evaluate every Internet source for signs of bias, validity, credibility, and reliability.   1 2 3 4 5

*Each of the topics in these statements is covered in this chapter. Note those statements for which you circled a 3 or
lower. Skim the chapter to see where those topics appear, and pay special attention to them as you read, learn, and
apply new strategies.*

REMEMBER: **No matter how developed your reading and information literacy skills are,
you can improve with effort and practice.**

"Successful intelligence is most
effective when it balances all
three of its analytical, creative,
and practical aspects. It is more
important to know when and how
to use these aspects of successful
intelligence than just to have
them."

—Robert Sternberg

What sets you up for
reading comprehension?

Post-secondary reading assignments—textbook chapters or other
materials—are often challenging, requiring more focus and new strategies to understand the material fully. In exchange for your extra effort,
though, you stand to receive a broad and deep range of information
and knowledge. Working hard to understand material in introductory-
level texts also provides a more solid foundation for your understanding in advanced courses. Finally, if you are open to them, the new
worlds reading reveals can bring you great satisfaction and even joy.

On any given day, you may have a variety of reading assignments,
such as the following:

▶ An 18-page text chapter on the contributions made by Aboriginal peoples
(Canadian history)
▶ An original research study on the relationship between sleep deprivation
and the development of memory problems (psychology)
▶ A review of *The Sentimentalists* by Johanna Skibsrud, winner of the 2010
Giller Prize (Canadian literature)

▶ A technical manual on the design of computer antivirus programs (computer science—software design)

To face this challenge, it's helpful to use specific reading techniques. Before you open a book or log onto your computer, how can you get ready to make the most of your reading?

Define your reading purpose

The first step in improving your reading comprehension is to ask yourself *why* you are reading particular material. With a clear purpose, you can decide how much time and effort to expend on your assignments. Key 2.1 shows four common reading purposes. Depending on what your instructor expects, you may have as many as three reading purposes for one assignment, such as understanding, critical evaluation, and practical application.

Use the class syllabus to help define your purpose for each assignment. For example, if the syllabus shows that inflation is the topic of your next economics class lecture, read the assigned chapter with that focus in mind: mastering the definition of inflation, evaluating historical economic events that caused inflation, and so on. And keep open the possibility that any reading assignment with purposes 1, 2, or 3 may also bring you purpose 4—enjoyment.

Take an active and positive approach

Many instructors spend little or no time reviewing reading in class because they expect you to complete it independently. How can you approach difficult material actively and positively?

▶ *Start with a questioning attitude.* Consider such questions as, How can I connect the reading to what I already

If you look carefully at your schedule, you may find useful segments of time in between classes. Try using such time for reading assignments.
© Spencer Grant/Photo Researchers

ESTABLISH WHY YOU ARE READING A GIVEN PIECE OF MATERIAL

Key 2.1

WHAT'S MY PURPOSE?	EXPLANATION
1. To understand	Read to comprehend concepts and details. Details help explain or support general concepts, and concepts provide a framework for details.
2. To evaluate analytically	Read with an open mind as you examine causes and effects, evaluate ideas, and ask questions that test arguments and assumptions. Evaluation develops a level of understanding beyond basic information recall (see pages 127–132 for more on this topic).
3. For practical application	Read to find information to help reach a specific goal. For instance, when you read a lab manual for chemistry, your goal is to learn how to do the lab experiment.
4. For pleasure	Read for entertainment, such as "The Hockey News" website or a mystery or romance novel.

know? Look at the chapter headings and ask yourself questions about what the material means and why it is being presented in this way.

▶ *Look for order.* Use SQ3R and the critical reading strategies introduced later in this chapter to discover patterns, logic, and relationships. Text cues—how the material is organized, outlines, bold terms, and more—help you anticipate what's coming next.

▶ *Have an open mind.* Be careful not to prejudge assignments as impossible or boring or a waste of time before you begin.

▶ *Plan for multiple readings.* Don't expect to master challenging material on the first pass. Get an overview of key concepts on the first reading. Use later readings to build your understanding, relate information to what you know, and apply information elsewhere. Gary accepted multiple readings as necessary to his success.

▶ *Get help.* If material is tough to understand, consult resources—instructors, study group partners, tutors, related texts, and websites—for help. Build a library of texts in your major and minor areas of study and refer to them when needed.

Choose the right setting

Where, when, and with whom you study has a significant effect on your success.

▶ *Choose locations that work.* Know yourself and choose settings that distract you least—in your room at home, at a library, outdoors, in an empty classroom, anywhere that works. Your schedule may restrict your choices. For example, if you can study only late at night when the libraries are closed, you will probably have to work at home; if you spend a good deal of your day commuting, mass transit may be your best study spot. Evaluate how effectively you focus. If you spend too much time being distracted at a particular location, try someplace different.

▶ *Choose times that work.* Pay attention to your body's natural rhythms, and try to read during times when you tend to be most alert and focused. For example, although night owls are productive when everyone else is sleeping, morning people may have a hard time reading late at night. The times you choose depend, of course, on what your schedule allows.

SECONDARY SOURCES
Other writers' interpretations of primary source documents.

PRIMARY SOURCES
Original documents, including academic journal articles and scientific studies.

Learn to concentrate

Even well-written college and university textbooks may require a lot of focus, especially when you encounter complex concepts and new terms. Even greater focus is often necessary when assignments are from **primary sources** rather than **secondary sources.** When you focus your attention on one thing and only one thing, you are engaged in the act of *concentration*. The following active-learning methods can help maintain focus as you study. Many involve tapping into your emotional and social intelligence.

▶ *Deal with internal distractions.* When worries come up, such as to-do list items for other projects, write them down to deal with later. Sometimes you may want to take a break to deal with what's bothering you. Exercise may help, or music may relieve stress; a snack can reduce hunger.

▶ *Structure your work session.* Set realistic goals and a specific plan for dividing your time. Tell yourself, "I'm going to read 30 pages and then go online for 30 minutes."

▶ *Manage family obligations.* Set up activities or child care if you have kids. Tell your children, if they are old enough to understand, what your education will mean to them and to you.

▶ *Plan a reward.* Have something to look forward to. You deserve it!

The strongest motivation to concentrate comes from within. When you see the connection between what you study and your short- and long-term goals, you will be better able to focus, to remember, to learn, and to apply.

Expand your vocabulary

As reading materials become more complex, your vocabulary influences how much you comprehend—and how readily you do so. When reading a textbook, the first "dictionary" to search is the end-of-book glossary that explains technical words and concepts. The definitions there are usually limited to the meanings used in the text. Standard dictionaries provide broader information, such as word origin, pronunciation, part of speech, synonyms, antonyms, and multiple meanings. Buy a standard dictionary and investigate websites such as Dictionary.com. The suggestions in Key 2.2 will help you make the most of your dictionary.

How can SQ3R improve your reading?

Reading may look like a one-way street in which you, the reader, take in words the author has written. However, it is intended as an interactive communication. The author communicates ideas to you and invites your response. How can you respond? One answer is provided in the SQ3R reading strategy, which stands for *Survey, Question, Read, Recite,* and *Review.*[1] This straightforward technique helps readers take in, understand, and remember what they read. It encourages you to fulfill your side of interactive communication by asking questions, marking key ideas, introducing your own connections, and more.

As you move through the stages of SQ3R, you will skim and scan your text. **Skimming** refers to the rapid reading of such chapter elements as section introductions and conclusions, boldface or italicized terms, pictures and charts, and summaries. The goal of skimming is a quick construction of the main ideas. In contrast, **scanning** involves a careful search for specific information. You might use scanning during the SQ3R review phase to locate particular facts.

Just like many strategies presented to you throughout your post-secondary career, SQ3R works best if you adapt it to your own needs. Explore techniques, evaluate what works, and then make the system your own. As you become

SKIMMING
Rapid, superficial reading of material to determine central ideas and main elements.

SCANNING
Reading material in an investigative way to search for specific information.

Use the word in the next 24 hours.

Not only does this demonstrate that you know how the word is used, but it also aids memorization.

Analyze word parts.

Many English words combine prefixes, roots, and suffixes. *Prefixes* are word parts added to the beginning of a root. *Suffixes* are added to the end of the root. The *root* is the central part or basis of a word around which prefixes and/or suffixes are added to produce different words. Recognizing these word parts can boost comprehesion.

Read beyond the first definition.

Then think critically about which meaning suits the context of the word in question and choose the one that makes the most sense.

dic·tio·nary

Pronunciation; \'dik-shə-,ner-ē, -,ne-rē\

Function: *noun*

Inflected Form(s): *plural* **dic·tio·nar·ies**

Etymology: Medieval Latin *dictionarium*, from Late Latin *diction-*, *dictio* word, from Latin, speaking

Date: 1526

1. A reference source in print or electronic form containing words usually alphabetically arranged along with information about their forms, pronunciations, functions, etymologies, meanings, and syntactical and idiomatic uses.

2. A book giving information on particular subjects or on a particular class of words, names, or facts, usually arranged alphabetically: *a biographical dictionary; a dictionary of mathematics.*

3. (*computing*) An associative array, a data structure where each value is referenced by a particular key, analogous to words and definitions in a physical dictionary.

Say and spell new words to boost recall.

Listen to the pronunciation on a hand-held electronic or online dictionary. Then practise writing the word to verify that you know the spelling.

Restate the definition in your own words.

When you can do this with ease, you know that you understand the meaning and are not merely parroting a dictionary definition.

---

familiar with the system, keep in mind that SQ3R works best with textbook-based courses such as science, math, social sciences, and humanities. SQ3R is not recommended for literature courses.

Step 1: Survey

Surveying, the first stage in SQ3R, is the process of previewing, or prereading, a book before you study it. Compare it to looking at a map before starting a road trip; determining the route and stops along the way in advance will save time and trouble while you travel. Gary made extensive use of the survey tools that most textbooks provide, including elements such as the following that provide a big picture overview of the main ideas and themes.

■ *Front matter.* Skim the *table of contents* for the chapter titles, the main topics in each chapter and the order in which they will be covered, as well as special features. Then skim the *preface*, which is a personal note from the author that tells you what the book will cover and its point of view. For example, the preface for the American history text *Out of Many* states that it highlights "the experiences of diverse communities of Americans in the unfolding story of our country."[2] This tells you that cultural diversity is a central theme.

■ ***Chapter elements.*** Text chapters use various devices to structure the material and highlight content.

> ► *Chapter titles* establish the topic and often the author's perspective.

> ► *Chapter introductions* or *outlines* generally list objectives or key topics.

> ► *Level headings* (first, second, third), including those in question form, break down material into bite-size chunks.

> ► *Margin materials* can include definitions, quotations, questions, and exercises.

> ► *Tables*, *charts*, *photographs*, and *captions* illustrate important concepts *in a visual manner.*

> ► *Sidebars* or *boxed features* are connected to text themes and introduce extra tidbits of information that supplement the text.

> ► *Different styles* or *arrangements of type* (**boldface**, *italics*, underlining, larger fonts, bullet points, boxed text) can flag vocabulary or important ideas.

> ► *End-of-chapter summaries* review chapter content and main ideas.

> ► *Review questions and exercises* help you understand and apply content in creative and practical ways.

In Key 2.3, a typical page from the textbook *Psychology: An Introduction*, by Charles G. Morris and Albert A. Maisto, how many elements do you recognize? How do these elements help you grasp the subject even before reading it?

■ ***Back matter.*** Some texts include a *glossary* that defines text terms, an *index* to help you locate topics, and a *bibliography* that lists additional readings.

Step 2: Question

The next step is to ask questions about your assignment. Using the *questioning* process that follows leads you to discover knowledge on your own, making an investment in the material and in your own memory.

Ask yourself what you know

Before you begin reading, think about—and summarize in writing if you can—what you already know about the topic, if anything. This step prepares you to apply what you know to new material. Building on current knowledge is especially important in your major, where the concepts you learn from intro courses prepare you for the higher-level material in classes to come later on.

Write questions linked to chapter headings

Next, examine the chapter headings and, on a separate page or in the text margins, write questions linked to them. When you encounter an

Classical (or Pavlovian) conditioning The type of learning in which a response naturally elicited by one stimulus comes to be elicited by a different, formerly neutral stimulus.

Unconditioned stimulus (US) A stimulus that invariably causes an organism to respond in a specific way.

Unconditioned response (UR) A response that takes place in an organism whenever an unconditioned stimulus occurs.

Conditioned stimulus (CS) An originally neutral stimulus that is paired with an unconditioned stimulus and eventually produces the desired response in an organism when presented alone.

Conditioned response (CR) After conditioning, the response an organism produces when only a conditioned stimulus is presented.

you are experiencing insight. When you imitate the steps of professional dancers you saw last night on television, you are demonstrating observational learning. Like conditioning, cognitive learning is one of our survival strategies. Through cognitive processes, we learn which events are safe and which are dangerous without having to experience those events directly. Cognitive learning also gives us access to the wisdom of people who lived hundreds of years ago, and it will give people living hundreds of years from now some insight into our experiences and way of life.

Our discussion begins with *classical conditioning*. This simple kind of learning serves as a convenient starting point for examining what learning is and how it can be observed.

Classical Conditioning

How did Pavlov's discovery of classical conditioning help to shed light on learning?

Ivan Pavlov (1849–1936), a Russian physiologist who was studying digestive processes, discovered classical conditioning almost by accident. Because animals salivate when food is placed in their mouths, Pavlov inserted tubes into the salivary glands of dogs to measure how much saliva they produced when they were given food. He noticed, however, that the dogs salivated before the food was in their mouths: The mere sight of food made them drool. In fact, they even drooled at the sound of the experimenter's footsteps. This aroused Pavlov's curiosity. What was making the dogs salivate even before they had the food in their mouths? How had they learned to salivate in response to the sound of the experimenter's approach?

To answer these questions, Pavlov set out to teach the dogs to salivate when food was not present. He devised an experiment in which he sounded a bell just before the food was brought into the room. A ringing bell does not usually make a dog's mouth water but, after hearing the bell many times just before getting fed, Pavlov's dogs began to salivate as soon as the bell rang. It was as if they had learned that the bell signaled the appearance of food, and their mouths watered on cue even if no food followed. The dogs had been conditioned to salivate in response to a new stimulus—the bell—that would not normally have prompted that response (Pavlov, 1927). Figure 5–1, shows one of Pavlov's procedures in which the bell has been replaced by a touch to the dog's leg just before food is given.

Elements of Classical Conditioning

Generally speaking, **classical (or Pavlovian) conditioning** involves pairing an *involuntary* response (for example, salivation) that is usually evoked by one stimulus with a different, formerly neutral stimulus (such as a bell or a touch on the leg). Pavlov's experiment illustrates the four basic elements of classical conditioning. The first is an **unconditioned stimulus (US)**, such as food, which invariably prompts a certain reaction—salivation, in this case. That reaction—the **unconditioned response (UR)**—is the second element and always results from the unconditioned stimulus: Whenever the dog is given food (US), its mouth waters (UR). The third element is the neutral stimulus—the ringing bell—which is called the **conditioned stimulus (CS).** At first, the conditioned stimulus is said to be "neutral" with respect to the desired response (salivation), because dogs do not salivate at the sound of a bell unless they have been conditioned to react in this way by repeatedly presenting the CS and US together. Frequent pairing of the CS and US produces the fourth element in the classical conditioning process: the **conditioned response (CR).** The conditioned response is the behavior that the animal has learned in response to the conditioned stimulus. Usually, the unconditioned response and the conditioned

getAnalytical!

Survey a Text

Practice will improve your surveying skills. Start now with this book or another you are currently using.

Skim the front matter, including the table of contents and preface. What does this material tell you about the theme? About the book's approach and point of view?

_____

_____

_____

Are there unexpected topics listed in the table of contents? Are there topics you expected to see that are missing?

_____

_____

Now look at a typical chapter. List the devices that organize the structure and content of the material.

_____

_____

After skimming the chapter, what do you know about the material? What elements helped you skim quickly?

_____

_____

Finally, skim the back matter. What elements can you identify?

_____

_____

How do you plan to use each of the elements you identified in your text survey when you begin studying?

_____

_____

assignment without headings, divide the material into logical sections and then develop questions based on what you think is the main idea of each section. There are no "correct" questions. Given the same headings, two students could create two different sets of questions. Your goal in questioning is to begin to think critically about the material.

Key 2.4 shows how this works. The column on the left contains primary and secondary headings from a section of *Out of Many*. The column on the right rephrases these headings in question form.

Use Bloom's Taxonomy to formulate questions

Questions can seek different types of answers and may require different levels of analytical thinking to solve. To help you understand and use different types

CREATE QUESTIONS
FROM HEADINGS

HEADINGS	QUESTIONS
The Meaning of Freedom	What did freedom mean for both slaves and citizens in the United States?
Moving About	Where did African Americans go after they were freed from slavery?
The African American Family	How did freedom change the structure of the African American family?
African American Churches and Schools	What effect did freedom have on the formation of African American churches and schools?
Land and Labor After Slavery	How was land farmed and maintained after slaves were freed?
The Origins of African American Politics	How did the end of slavery bring about the beginning of African American political life?

USE BLOOM'S TAXONOMY TO
FORMULATE QUESTIONS
AT DIFFERENT COGNITIVE LEVELS

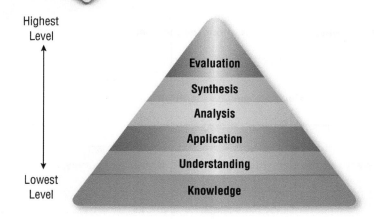

Highest Level

Evaluation
Synthesis
Analysis
Application
Understanding
Knowledge

Lowest Level

Verbs That Indicate Each Level

1. **Knowledge:** average, define, duplicate, label, list, memorize, name, order, recall, recognize, relate, repeat, reproduce, state.

2. **Understanding:** classify, describe, discuss, explain, express, identify, indicate, locate, recognize, report, restate, review, select, translate.

3. **Application:** apply, choose, demonstrate, dramatize, employ, illustrate, interpret, operate, practise, schedule, sketch, solve, use, write.

4. **Analysis:** analyze, appraise, calculate, categorize, compare, contrast, criticize, differentiate, discriminate, distinguish, examine, experiment, question, test.

5. **Synthesis:** arrange, assemble, collect, compose, construct, create, design, develop, formulate, manage, organize, plan, prepare, propose, set up, write.

6. **Evaluation:** appraise, argue, assess, attach, choose, compare, defend, estimate, evaluate, judge, predict, rate, score, select, support, value.

FOLLOW A QUESTION THROUGH
THE STAGES OF BLOOM'S TAXONOMY

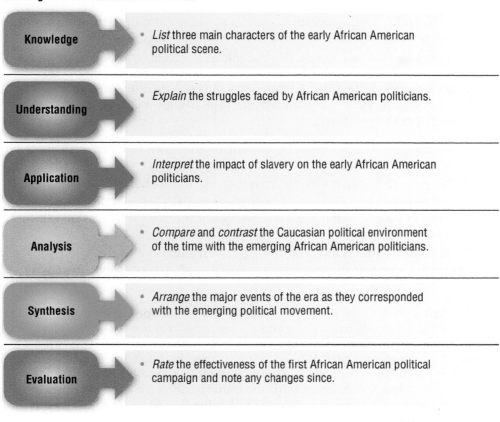

The Origins of African American Politics

Knowledge
- *List* three main characters of the early African American political scene.

Understanding
- *Explain* the struggles faced by African American politicians.

Application
- *Interpret* the impact of slavery on the early African American politicians.

Analysis
- *Compare* and *contrast* the Caucasian political environment of the time with the emerging African American politicians.

Synthesis
- *Arrange* the major events of the era as they corresponded with the emerging political movement.

Evaluation
- *Rate* the effectiveness of the first African American political campaign and note any changes since.

of questions, consider the system educational psychologist Benjamin Bloom developed based on the idea that deeper learning occurs when the effort to understand is more rigorous.[3] Although some questions ask for a simple recall, said Bloom, others ask for higher thinking levels.

Key 2.5 shows the six levels of questions identified by Bloom: knowledge, understanding, application, analysis, synthesis, and evaluation. It also identifies verbs associated with each level. As you read, use these verbs to create specific questions that will help you learn. For instance, if you were to continue Key 2.4's process of creating questions based on the headings from *Out of Many*, the questions would change based on the level specified by Bloom's Taxonomy. See Key 2.6 for an example.

Step 3: Read

Your text survey and questions give you a starting point for *reading*, the first R in SQ3R. Retaining what you read requires an active approach.

▶ *Focus on the key points of your survey.* Pay special attention to points raised in headings, in boldface type, in the chapter objectives and summary, and in other emphasized text.

▶ *Focus on your Q-stage questions.* Read the material with the purpose of answering each question. Write down or highlight ideas and examples that relate to your questions.

▶ *Create text tabs.* Place plastic index tabs or adhesive notes at the start of each chapter so you can flip back and forth with ease.

▶ *Mark up your text.* Write notes in the margins, circle main ideas, or underline supporting details to focus on what's important. For an ebook, use the "Insert comments" feature. These cues will boost memory and help you study for exams. Here are some tips for *annotating*—taking marginal notes on the pages of your text:

- Use pencil so you can erase comments or questions that are answered later.
- Write your Q questions in the margins next to text headings.
- Mark critical sections with marginal notations such as "Def." for definition, "e.g." for helpful example, "Concept" for an important concept, and so on.
- Write notes at the bottom of the page connecting the text to what you learned in class or in research. You can also attach adhesive notes with your comments.

▶ *Highlight your text.* *Highlighting* involves the use of special markers or regular pens or pencils to flag important passages. When working with ebooks, make note of the highlighting function, which allows you to overlay a colour on important text. When used correctly, highlighting is an essential learning technique. However, experts agree that you will not learn what to highlight unless you interact with the material through surveying, questioning, reciting, and reviewing. Use the following tips to make highlighting a true learning tool:

- *Develop a system and stick to it.* Decide whether you will use different colours to highlight different elements, brackets for long passages, or pencil underlining.
- *Consider using a regular pencil or pen instead of a highlighter pen.* The copy will be cleaner and may look less like a colouring book.
- *Mark text carefully if you are using a rented book or a book to be resold.* Use pencil as often as possible and erase your marks at the end of the class. Write on sticky notes that you can remove. Make copies of important chapters or sections for marking. If you are renting, check with the rental service to see what it permits.
- *Read an entire paragraph before you begin to highlight, and don't start until you have a sense of what is important.* Only then put pencil or highlighter to paper as you pick out the main idea, key terms, and crucial supporting details and examples.
- *Avoid overmarking.* Too much colour can be overwhelming. Try enclosing long passages with brackets and avoid underlining entire sentences, when possible.

Key 2.7, from an introductory business textbook describing the concepts of target marketing and market segmentation, shows how to underline and take marginal notes.

Chapter 10: Understanding Marketing Processes and Consumer Behavior · 297

How does target marketing and market segmentation help companies sell product?

■ TARGET MARKETING AND MARKET SEGMENTATION

Marketers have long known that products cannot be all things to all people. Buyers have different tastes, goals, lifestyles, and so on. The emergence of the marketing concept and the recognition of consumer needs and wants led marketers to think in terms of **target markets**—groups of people with similar wants and needs. Selecting target markets is usually the first step in the marketing strategy.

Target marketing requires **market segmentation**—dividing a market into categories of customer types or "segments." Once they have identified segments, companies may adopt a variety of strategies. Some firms market products to more than one segment. General Motors *(www.gm.com)*, for example, offers compact cars, vans, trucks, luxury cars, and sports cars with various features and at various price levels. GM's strategy is to provide an automobile for nearly every segment of the market.

In contrast, some businesses offer a narrower range of products, each aimed toward a specific segment. Note that segmentation is a strategy for analyzing consumers, not products. The process of fixing, adapting, and communicating the nature of the product itself is called *product positioning*.

Definitions

target market
Group of people that has similar wants and needs and that can be expected to show interest in the same products

← *GM eg*

market segmentation
Process of dividing a market into categories of customer types

GM makes cars for diff. market segments

How do companies identify market segments?

Identifying Market Segments

By definition, members of a market segment must share some common traits that affect their purchasing decisions. In identifying segments, researchers look at several different influences on consumer behavior. Three of the most important are *geographic, demographic,* and *psychographic variables*.

What effect does geography have on segmentation strategies?

Geographic Variables Many buying decisions are affected by the places people call home. The heavy rainfall in Washington State, for instance, means that people there buy more umbrellas than people in the Sun Belt. Urban residents don't need agricultural equipment, and sailboats sell better along the coasts than on the Great Plains. **Geographic variables** are the geographical units, from countries to neighborhoods, that may be considered in a segmentation strategy.

These patterns affect decisions about marketing mixes for a huge range of products. For example, consider a plan to market down-filled parkas in rural Minnesota. Demand will be high and price competition intense. Local newspaper ads may be

Buying decisions influenced by where people live

geographic variables
Geographical units that may be considered in developing a segmentation strategy

— good eg —
selling parkas in Minnesota

Thought
Geographical variables change with the seasons

Find the main idea

Understanding what you read depends on your ability to recognize *main ideas* and link other ideas to them. The main idea may appear in a topic sentence at the beginning of the paragraph followed by supporting details, or at the end of the paragraph with supporting details leading up to it. Sometimes, though, it is more difficult to figure out. When the main idea of a passage is unclear, use a three-step approach to decide what it is:[4]

1. *Search for the topic of the paragraph.* The topic of the paragraph is not the same as the main idea. Rather, it is the broad subject being discussed—for example, the late CEO of Apple Steve Jobs, hate crimes on campus, or binge drinking on campus.

2. *Identify the aspect of the topic that is the paragraph's focus.* If the general topic is Steve Jobs, the author may focus on any of thousands of aspects of that topic, such as his cofounding of Apple Computer in 1976; his role at Pixar, a computer animation company; or his involvement in the development of the iPod portable music player.

3. *Find what the author wants you to know about that specific aspect.* This is the main idea or topic sentence. Whereas the topic establishes the subject, a topic sentence narrows down the purpose of the paragraph into one or two focused statements. Thus, although the topic of the paragraph might be former Apple CEO Steve Jobs, the main idea, or topic sentence, might be "In his role as CEO of Apple, Steve Jobs oversaw the creation of the iPod portable music player, which changed the way the world listens to and purchases music."

Step 4: Recite

Once you finish reading a topic, stop and answer the questions you raised in the Q stage of SQ3R. Even if you have already done this during the reading phase, do it again now—with the purpose of learning and committing the material to memory by *reciting* the answers.

You can say each answer aloud, silently speak the answers to yourself, "teach" the answers to another person, or write your ideas and answers in note form. Whatever recitation method you choose, make sure you know how the ideas connect to one another and to the general concept being discussed.

Writing is often the most effective way to learn new material. Write responses to your Q-stage questions and use your own words to explain new concepts; save your writing as a study tool for review. Writing gives you immediate feedback: when it agrees with the material you are studying, you know the information. When it doesn't, you still need work with the text or a study partner.

Keep your learning styles in mind while exploring different strategies (see Chapter 1). For example, an intrapersonal learner may prefer writing, whereas an interpersonal learner may choose to recite answers aloud to a classmate. A logical-mathematical learner may benefit from organizing material into detailed outlines or charts, as opposed to a musical learner, who might chant information aloud to a rhythm.

Change the
CONVERSATION

Challenge yourself and your friends to ask—and answer—tough questions. Use the following to inspire discussion in pairs or groups.

▶ Understanding a text is essential to making good decisions, both in and out of the classroom. What other ways might reading skills impact your daily life?

▶ What steps do you take to ensure that you understand texts? Have those strategies worked for you so far? Why or why not?

▶ **CONSIDER THE CASE:** What step (or steps) from SQ3R were most helpful to Gary in dealing with his particular challenge? What step or steps do you think will be most helpful to you, and why?

get*Practical!*

Mark Up a Page to Learn a Page

Below, the text material in Key 2.7 continues. Read it and mark it up, highlighting concepts and taking marginal notes. Compare your efforts to those of your classmates to see how each of you approached the task and what you can learn from their methods.

298   Part IV: Understanding Principles of Marketing

effective, and the best retail location may be one that is easily reached from several small towns.

Although the marketability of some products is geographically sensitive, others enjoy nearly universal acceptance. Coke, for example, gets more than 70 percent of its sales from international markets. It is the market leader in Great Britain, China, Germany, Japan, Brazil, and Spain. Pepsi's international sales are about 15 percent of Coke's. In fact, Coke's chief competitor in most countries is some local soft drink, not Pepsi, which earns 78 percent of its income at home.

demographic variables
Characteristics of populations that may be considered in developing a segmentation strategy

Demographic Variables Demographic variables describe populations by identifying such traits as age, income, gender, ethnic background, marital status, race, religion, and social class. For example, several general consumption characteristics can be attributed to certain age groups (18–25, 26–35, 36–45, and so on). A marketer can, thus, divide markets into age groups. Table 10.1 lists some possible demographic breakdowns. Depending on the marketer's purpose, a segment can be a single classification (*aged* 20–34) or a combination of categories (*aged* 20–34, *married with children, earning* $25,000–$34,999). Foreign competitors, for example, are gaining market share in U.S. auto sales by appealing to young buyers (under age 30) with limited incomes (under $30,000). Whereas companies such as Hyundai *(www.hyundai.net)*, Kia *(www.kia.com)*, and Daewoo *(www.daewoous.com)* are winning entry-level customers with high quality and generous warranties, Volkswagen *(www.vw.com)* targets under-35 buyers with its entertainment-styled VW Jetta.[4]

psychographic variables
Consumer characteristics, such as lifestyles, opinions, interests, and attitudes, that may be considered in developing a segmentation strategy

Psychographic Variables Markets can also be segmented according to such **psychographic variables** as lifestyles, interests, and attitudes. Take, for example, Burberry *(www.burberry.com)*, whose raincoats have been a symbol of British tradition since 1856. Burberry has repositioned itself as a global luxury brand, like Gucci *(www.gucci.com)* and Louis Vuitton *(www.vuitton.com)*. The strategy, which recently resulted in a 31-percent sales increase, calls for attracting a different type of customer—the top-of-the-line, fashion-conscious individual—who shops at such stores as Neiman Marcus and Bergdorf Goodman.[5]

Psychographics are particularly important to marketers because, unlike demographics and geographics, they can be changed by marketing efforts. For example, Polish companies have overcome consumer resistance by promoting the safety and desirability of using credit rather than depending solely on cash. One product of changing attitudes is a booming economy and the emergence of a robust middle class.

TABLE 10.1

Demographic Variables

Age	Under 5, 5–11, 12–19, 20–34, 35–49, 50–64, 65+
Education	Grade school or less, some high school, graduated high school, some college, college degree, advanced degree
Family life cycle	Young single, young married without children, young married with children, older married with children under 18, older married without children under 18, older single, other
Family size	1, 2–3, 4–5, 6+
Income	Under $9,000, $9,000–$14,999, $15,000–$24,999, $25,000–$34,999, $35,000–$45,000, over $45,000
Nationality	African, American, Asian, British, Eastern European, French, German, Irish, Italian, Latin American, Middle Eastern, Scandinavian
Race	Native American, Asian, Black, White
Religion	Buddhist, Catholic, Hindu, Jewish, Muslim, Protestant
Sex	Male, female

When do you stop to recite? Waiting for the end of a chapter is too late; stopping at the end of one paragraph is too soon. The best plan is to recite at the end of each text section, right before a new heading. Repeat the question–read–recite cycle until you complete the chapter. If you fumble for thoughts, reread the section until you are on solid ground.

Step 5: Review

Reviewing, both immediately and periodically in the days and weeks after you read, will help you memorize, understand, and learn material. If you close the book after reading it once, chances are that you will forget almost everything, which is why students who read material for the first time right before a test don't tend to do too well. *Reviewing is your key to learning.*

Reviewing the same material in several sessions over time will also help you identify knowledge gaps. It's natural to forget material between study sessions, especially if it's complex. When you come back after a break, you can focus on where you need the most help.

Examine the following reviewing techniques (more on these in Chapter 4). Try them all, and use the ones that work best for you. Try using more than one strategy when you study—switching among several different strategies tends to strengthen learning and memory.

- ▶ Reread your notes. Then summarize them from memory.
- ▶ Review and summarize in writing the text sections you highlighted or bracketed.
- ▶ Rewrite key points and main concepts in your own words. Create written examples that will help solidify the content in your mind.
- ▶ Answer the end-of-chapter review, discussion, and application questions.
- ▶ Reread the preface, headings, tables, and summary.
- ▶ Recite important concepts to yourself, or record and play them back on an audio recorder.
- ▶ Listen to MP3 audio recordings of your text and other reading materials.
- ▶ Make flash cards with a word or concept on one side and a definition, examples, or other related information on the other. Test yourself.
- ▶ Quiz yourself, using the questions you raised in the Q stage.
- ▶ Discuss the concepts with a classmate or in a study group. Answer one another's Q-stage questions.
- ▶ Ask your instructor for help with difficult material.

Refreshing your knowledge is easier and faster than learning it the first time. Make a weekly review schedule and stick to it until you're sure you know everything.

GENERAL EDUCATION REQUIREMENTS Courses required for graduation in a variety of academic fields, including the humanities, social sciences, math, and science.

What strategies help with specific subjects and formats?

If your college or university has **general education requirements,** you may have to take a wide variety of courses to graduate. Knowing how to approach reading materials in different academic areas will help you learn.

*get**Creative!***

Use SQ3R to Make a Connection

For this exercise, partner up with someone in your class. To begin, each of you will write a mini-biography—approximately three to five paragraphs—answering the following questions:

▶ Where are you from?

▶ How would you describe your family?

▶ How have they influenced the student you are today?

▶ What three facts or ideas about yourself would you like someone else to know?

Include a title that reflects your biography as a whole. Also, for each paragraph in the middle (not the first or last), provide a title "header" that tells the reader what to expect in the paragraph (for example, "My Childhood in the Ottawa Valley," "Daytime Student, Nighttime Employee," and so on).

Once you're finished, read over what you've written for spelling, punctuation, and clarity. Switch papers with your partner and read his or her biography. Using SQ3R:

1. *Survey.* Scan your partner's paper for any words that stand out or phrases that seem important. Circle or highlight anything you notice right away.

2. *Question.* Thinking about what you learned from your survey, write questions in the margins. Your questions should reflect what you expect to learn as you read.

3. *Read.* Read through the biography. Make notes in the margins when you find answers to your Q-stage questions. Use your pen to circle or underline main ideas.

4. *Recite.* Discuss what you learned from the paper with your partner. How accurate was your comprehension of the biography? Were there any areas that were not clear or that you misunderstood? If so, what might help in those cases?

5. *Review.* Summarize the biography of your partner in writing for yourself. Be sure to note any important information that relates to getting to know your partner. If there is time, solidify your review by reciting the summary aloud in front of the class. Introduce your partner to the class as if he or she had just joined, focusing on the most interesting and unique information from the biography.

Finally, discuss the impact of using SQ3R with your partner. How did it affect your comprehension of the biography? What might you try differently next time?

Math and science

Math and science courses relate closely to one another, and almost all science courses require a base of math knowledge. Mathematical and scientific strategies help you develop thinking and problem-solving skills. In a world that is being transformed by new discoveries and technologies, a strong math and science background prepares you for tomorrow's jobs and can also help you create monthly budgets, choose auto insurance, understand illnesses, and more.

Math and science textbooks move *sequentially*. That is, your understanding of later material depends on how well you learned material in earlier chapters.

student profile

James Shields
University of King's College, Halifax, Nova Scotia

About me:

I grew up in Scarborough on the outer edge of the mega city. Toronto is a great city to live in; but, when I was growing up, it always seemed like a great looming presence. After high school, I was ready to move away and see what life was like at a different pace. Halifax is no small town but compared to Toronto it seemed like a different world, just the change I was looking for.

What I focus on:

As much as I love to read, when time gets tight and assignments pile up, I find that the first thing that falls off the to-do list is assigned readings. It doesn't take long, however, for that little lapse to snowball, and pretty soon everything suffers because of it. I am often disheartened, being the slow reader that I am, when the load is heavy and reading for pleasure becomes a thing of the past.

It took me a while to find a happy medium, but the first step was to find a good space.

It can either be in your home or at a nearby coffee shop, but find somewhere that feels comfortable, which you can identify with reading and stand for an extended period of time. The next step is to make a habit of spending at least some time there every day. Once it becomes routine, it will not feel like a chore and it will allow you to get out of the just-get-it-done mindset so that you can focus on the material and make sure that it registers. It is also important for me that I'm not worrying about other obligations during this time. Budgeting your time is key to staying on top of your workload, and the same principal applies to reading. If it is your designated time for reading, that should command your full attention, just as writing an exam or a paper requires your full focus and dedication.

What will help me in the workplace:

Identifying a work ethic with a workspace is not just useful at school. Making the transition from higher education to the workplace does not change the principal; it changes only the equation. The solutions can remain the same. Getting to work at 8:30 A.M. is easier some days than others, but I find that having a morning routine to help shake off the dew can put me in the right mindset for work. Similarly, organizing my workspace well and making it a comfortable place to spend the day makes a world of difference. Adding greenery, if possible, or books and little things from home that I can identify with a work environment allows me to focus on the task at hand regardless of whether I am feeling tired or anxious on my way out the door.

Keeping up with readings at school also means that I am well versed in the topics under consideration. When it comes to writing a paper or a test, completed readings can make the difference between careful, considered responses and grasping at straws. It doesn't take much to form habits, and once I started writing papers with an arsenal of material at my disposal, I found it impossible to write from a position of relative ignorance. This thoroughness has carried over into the workplace, giving me an instinct to understand all the facets of a task before embarking upon it. Not only does it improve the quality of my work, but it has propelled me past menial entry-level tasks to more interesting, challenging work, and I am happier for it.

Try the following strategies to get the most from your textbooks, and get extra help right away when you are confused.

■ *Interact with math material actively through writing.* Math textbooks are made up of problems and solutions. As you read, highlight important information and take notes on examples. Work out any missing problem steps on your pad or in the book. Draw sketches to help visualize the material. Try not to move on until you understand example problems and how they relate to the central ideas. Write down questions for your instructor or fellow students.

■ *Pay attention to formulas.* Math and science texts are filled with (formulas.) Focus on learning the main ideas behind each formula, and do problems to make sure your understanding sticks.

FORMULAS
General facts, rules, or principles usually expressed in mathematical symbols.

■ *Use memory strategies to learn science.* Science textbooks are packed with vocabulary specific to the field (for example, an environmental science text may refer to the *greenhouse effect*, *integrated waste management*, and the *law of limiting factors*). To remember what you read, use mnemonic devices, test yourself with flash cards, and rehearse aloud or silently (see Chapter 4).

Social sciences and humanities

Courses in the social sciences and humanities prepare you to be a well-rounded person, able and ready to fulfill your responsibilities to yourself, your family, and a free democracy. They also prepare you for 21st century jobs by focusing on critical thinking, civic and historical knowledge, and ethical reasoning. As you study these disciplines, look for themes with critical thinking as the foundation for your work. Build knowledge by using what you know to learn new material.

Themes

The National Council for the Social Studies (www.socialstudies.org) organizes the study of the social sciences and humanities under 10 themes, providing "umbrellas" under which you can group ideas that you encounter in different classes and reading materials:

▶ Culture
▶ Time, continuity, and change
▶ People, places, and environment
▶ Individual development and identity
▶ Individuals, groups, and institutions
▶ Power, authority, and governance
▶ Production, distribution, and consumption
▶ Science, technology, and society
▶ Global connections
▶ Ideals and practices of citizenship

   Look for these themes as you read, even if they are not spelled out. For example, as you read a chapter in a political science text on federal politics, you might think of the history of federal elections or how the Internet is changing electoral politics.

Think critically

Courses in the social sciences ask hard questions about ethics, human rights and freedoms, and personal and community responsibility, looking at these topics over time and in different cultures. Critical thinking will help you maximize learning and understanding as you ask questions about what you read, think of material in terms of problems and solutions, look for evidence in arguments, consider possible bias of the writers, and examine big-picture statements for solid cause-and-effect logic.

Literature

Even if you're not an English major, you will probably take one or more literature courses, which will expose you to books that allow you to experience other times and cultures and understand how others react to the problems of daily life. Additionally, the thoughts and emotions you experience in reaction to what you read give you the opportunity to learn more about yourself.

Literature courses ask you to look at different literary elements to find meaning on various levels. As you read, use critical reading skills to consider the various aspects.

- ▶ *Character.* How do characters reveal who they are? How are the main characters similar or different? How do a character's actions change the course of the story?
- ▶ *Plot.* How would you evaluate the power of the story? Did it hold your interest?
- ▶ *Setting.* How does the setting relate to the actions of the major and minor characters?
- ▶ *Point of view.* How are the author's views expressed through characters' actions?
- ▶ *Style.* How would you describe the writing style?
- ▶ *Imagery.* How does the author use imagery as part of the theme?
- ▶ *Theme.* What is the goal of the work? What is it trying to communicate?

Visual aids

Many textbooks use tables, charts, drawings, maps, and photographs—all types of visual aids—to show, clarify, or summarize information in a form that is easy to read and understand. Pay attention to these elements as you are reading—often they contain important information not found elsewhere. Visual learners especially may benefit from information delivered in a format other than chapter text.

Certain types of visual aids—word and data tables as well as charts/graphs (pie, bar, or line)—are designed to compare information and statistics that show the following types of information:

- ▶ *Trends over time.* For example, the number of computers with Internet connections per household in 2011 compared to 2002
- ▶ *Relative rankings.* For example, the sizes of the advertising budgets of four major companies
- ▶ *Distributions.* For example, student performance on standardized tests by geographic area
- ▶ *Cycles.* For example, the regular upward and downward movement of the nation's economy as defined by periods of prosperity and recession

Apply Different Intelligences to Concepts in Sociology

INTELLIGENCE	USE MI STRATEGIES TO BECOME A BETTER READER	APPLY MI READING STRATEGIES TO LEARN ABOUT SOCIAL GROUPS FOR YOUR INTRODUCTION TO SOCIOLOGY COURSE
Verbal-Linguistic	• Use the steps in SQ3R, focusing especially on writing Q-stage questions, summaries, and so on. • Make marginal text notes as you read.	• Summarize in writing the technical differences among social groups, categories, and crowds.*
Logical-Mathematical	• Logically connect what you are reading with what you already know. Consider similarities, differences, and cause-and-effect relationships. • Draw charts showing relationships and analyze trends.	• Create a table comparing and contrasting the characteristics of primary and secondary social groups.
Bodily-Kinesthetic	• Use text highlighting to take a hands-on approach to reading. • Take a hands-on approach to learning experiments by trying to recreate them yourself.	• Create an experiment that might turn a crowd of strangers into a social group joined together by a common problem.
Visual-Spatial	• Make charts, diagrams, or think links illustrating difficult ideas you encounter as you read. • Take note of photos, tables, and other visual aids in the text.	• Create a visual aid showing four primary mechanisms through which people with shared experiences, loyalties, and interests meet—for example, through school and business—and how initial contacts may lead to deep social group relationships.
Interpersonal	• Discuss reading material and clarify concepts in a study group. • Talk to people who know about the topic you are studying.	• Interview people who shared a difficult experience with a crowd of strangers—for example, people stuck in an elevator or on a train for an extended period—about how relationships changed as focus turned to a common problem.
Intrapersonal	• Apply concepts to your own life; think about how you would manage. • Try to understand your personal strengths and weaknesses to lead a study group on the reading material.	• After reading about the nature of primary groups, think about the nature of your personal family relationships and the degree to which family members are your key support system.
Musical	• Recite text concepts to rhythms or write a song to depict them. • Explore relevant musical links to the material.	• Listen to a rock concert that was performed in front of a live crowd. Then listen to the same music recorded in a studio. Think about performance differences that might link to the presence or absence of a crowd.
Naturalistic	• Tap into your ability to notice similarities and differences in objects and concepts by organizing reading materials into relevant groupings.	• Over the next few weeks, ask some close friends if you can have dinner with them and their families. After the visits, try to identify characteristics that all the families share. Create a chart to report your findings.

*For information on social groups, see John J. Macionis, *Sociology*, 11th ed., Upper Saddle River, NJ: Prentice Hall, 2007.

Online materials

Almost any student's success in college or university depends on being able to read both printed and onscreen material effectively. For some "digital natives" who have grown up with technology and the Internet, screen reading comes naturally and may even be preferable to reading text on paper. Others may prefer printed materials they can hold in their hands and write on. For either group, the goal is to get the most out of what you must read online.

Screen readers tend to focus on heads and subheads, bullet points, and visuals, scanning material for the important points instead of staying focused through long paragraphs or articles.[5] They may also develop what Web researcher Jakob Nielsen calls *F-pattern reading*—reading across the line at the beginning of a document, then reading less and less of the full width of the line as you move down the page, and only seeing the left-hand text by the time you reach the bottom of the document.[6]

Nielsen suggests making the most of screen reading by using a step-by-step process, which includes aspects of SQ3R:

1. *Skim through the article.* See whether it contains important ideas.

2. *Before reading in depth, save the article on your computer.* This gives you the ability to highlight and add notes, just as you would on a printed page.

3. *Survey the article.* Read the title, subtitle, headings, figures, charts, and tables.

4. *Come up with questions to guide your reading.* Ask yourself what general and specific information you want to learn from the article.

5. *Read the article in depth.* You have already judged that the material is important, so take it much slower than you would normally.

6. *Highlight and take notes.* Use the program's highlighter function and comment boxes.

7. *Print out articles you would rather study on paper.* Make sure the print-outs include your highlighting and notes.

8. *Review your notes.* Combine them with your class notes and those on your printed text.

Finally, your awareness that screen reading skills are different from those needed to read printed textbooks will help you shift gears when picking up a book. Textbooks require close, slow reading that may seem like walking through mud after spending time on the Internet.

How can you be an information literate reader and researcher?

Although many students' first instinct is to power up the computer and start jumping around on Google, there is a wealth of research resources at your fingertips. Many of the materials you'll find in a library have been evaluated by librarians and researchers and are likely to be reliable—a definite time saver when compared to the myriad of both credible and less-than-credible sources available online.

Map out the possibilities

To select the most helpful information for your research, you need to first know what is available to you. Sign up for a library orientation session. Familiarize yourself with the library resources shown in Key 2.8.

For a key advantage in any search for information, get to know a librarian. These professionals can assist you in locating unfamiliar or hard-to-find sources, navigating catalogues and databases, uncovering research shortcuts, and dealing with pesky equipment. Know what you want to accomplish before asking a question. At many schools, you can query a librarian via cellphone, email, or instant messaging.

Conduct an information search

To avoid becoming buried in the sheer magnitude of resources available, use a practical, step-by-step search method. Key 2.9 shows how you start wide and then move in for a closer look at specific sources.

When using virtual or online catalogues, you will need to adjust your research methods. Searching library databases requires that you use a *keyword search*—an exploration that uses a topic-related natural language word

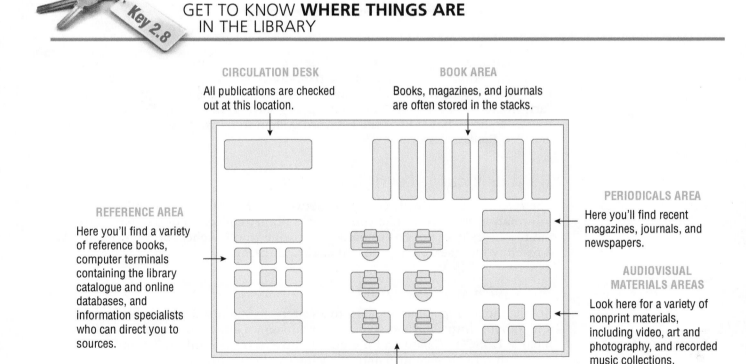

Key 2.8 GET TO KNOW **WHERE THINGS ARE** IN THE LIBRARY

CIRCULATION DESK
All publications are checked out at this location.

BOOK AREA
Books, magazines, and journals are often stored in the stacks.

REFERENCE AREA
Here you'll find a variety of reference books, computer terminals containing the library catalogue and online databases, and information specialists who can direct you to sources.

PERIODICALS AREA
Here you'll find recent magazines, journals, and newspapers.

AUDIOVISUAL MATERIALS AREAS
Look here for a variety of nonprint materials, including video, art and photography, and recorded music collections.

ELECTRONIC LIBRARY RESOURCES
Network systems allow access to online materials via computers. If your school has a wi-fi system, you can conduct research anywhere on campus.

USE A STEP-BY-STEP
SEARCH METHOD

Start with General Reference Works	Examples include encyclopedias, almanacs, dictionaries, and biographical references.
Move to Specialized Reference Works	Examples include encyclopedias and dictionaries that focus on a narrow field.
Use the Electronic Catalogue to Locate Materials	Search the library catalogue by author, title, or subject to learn where to locate specific books, periodicals, and journals. Most library catalogues are virtual and can be accessed by computers throughout the library. Ask a librarian for assistance, if needed.
Browse Through Relevant Books and Articles	Using your results from the catalogue search, dive in deeper by finding and accessing helpful information in books and articles related to your topic.

or phrase as a point of reference to locate other information. To narrow your topic and reduce the number of *hits* (resources pulled up by your search), add more keywords. For example, instead of searching through the broad category "art," focus on "French art" or, more specifically, "19th century French art." Key 2.10 shows how to use the keyword system to narrow searches with what is called *Boolean logic*.

Be a critical Internet searcher

The *Internet*, a worldwide computer network, can connect you to billions of information sources. Unlike your school's library collection or databases, Internet resources may not be evaluated by anyone who vouches for their quality. As a result, your research depends on critical thinking.

Start with search engines

Among the most popular and effective search engines are Google (www.google.ca) and Yahoo! (http://ca.yahoo.com). Search engines aimed at academic audiences include EBSCO's Canadian Reference Centre (www.ebscohost.com/public/canadian-reference-centre) and InfoMine (www.infomine.com). At these academic directories, someone has screened the sites and listed only those sources that have been determined to be reputable and regularly updated.

Additionally, your school may include access to certain nonpublic academic search engines in the cost of your tuition. Sites such as LexusNexus, InfoTrac, GaleGroup, and OneFile are known for their credibility in the academic world

PERFORM AN **EFFECTIVE KEYWORD SEARCH** WITH BOOLEAN LOGIC

IF YOU ARE SEARCHING FOR	DO THIS	EXAMPLE
A word	Type the word normally.	Aid
A phrase	Type the phase in its normal word order (use regular word spacing) or surround the phrase with quotation marks.	financial aid, "financial aid"
Two or more keywords without regard to order	Type the words in any order, surrounding the words with quotation marks. Use *and* to separate the words.	"financial aid" and "scholarships"
Topic A or topic B	Type the words in any order, surrounding the words with quotation marks. Use *or* to separate the words.	"financial aid" or "scholarships"
Topic A but not topic B	Type topic A first within quotation marks, and then topic B within quotation marks. Use *not* to separate the words.	"financial aid" not "scholarships"

as well as for their vast amounts of information. Check with your school's library to see how to access these sites.

Use a search strategy

The World Wide Web has been called "the world's greatest library, with all its books on the floor." With no librarian in sight, you need to master a practical Internet search strategy.

1. *Use natural language phrases or keywords to identify what you are looking for.* University of Michigan professor Elliot Soloway recommends phrasing your search in the form of a question—for example, What vaccines are given to children before age 5? Then he advises identifying the important words in the question (*vaccines, children, before age* 5) as well as related words (*polio, shot, pediatrics,* and so on). This will give you a collection of terms to use in different combinations as you search.[7]

2. *Use a search engine to isolate valuable sites.* Enter your questions, phrases, and keywords in various combinations to generate lists of hits. Vary word order to see what you can generate. If you get too many hits, try using fewer or more specific keywords.

3. *Skim sites to evaluate what seems most useful.* Check the synopsis of the site's contents, the content providers, and the purpose of the site. Does the site seem relevant, reputable, or biased in favour of a particular point of view? A site owned by a company will want to promote its new product rather than provide unbiased consumer information. Consider the purpose—a blog is apt to focus on opinion in contrast to an article in a scholarly journal, which is likely to focus on facts and research findings.

Much, although not all, research can be done using online databases. Get to know the databases and other resources that your school provides for you.
© Sarah Lyman Kravits

4. *Save, or bookmark, the sites you want to focus on.* Make sure you can access them again. You may want to copy URLs and paste them into a separate document.

5. *When you think you are done, start over.* Choose another search engine and search again. Different systems access different sites.

The limitations of Internet-only research make it smart to combine Internet and library research. Search engines can't find everything, in part because not all sources are in digital format. The Internet also prioritizes current information. Furthermore, some digital sources that are not part of your library's subscription offerings cost money. Finally, Internet searches require electricity or battery power and an online connection. Consider printing out Internet materials that you know you will need to reference over and over again.

Your need to be an effective researcher doesn't stop at graduation—especially in a workplace dominated by information and media. The skills you develop as you do research for school projects will serve you well in any kind of job that requires you to use the Internet and other resources to find and evaluate information.

How can you respond critically to what you read?

With anything you read—trade books, journal and newspaper articles, Internet documents, primary sources, and even textbooks that are supposed to be as accurate as possible—it is crucial to be a questioning reader who does not simply accept material as truth. Critical reading involves questioning, analysis, and evaluation. Think of the reading process as an archaeological dig. First, you excavate a site and uncover the artifacts. Then you separate out what you've found, make connections among ideas, and evaluate what is important. This process allows you to focus on the most important materials.

Different purposes engage different parts of critical reading. When you are reading to learn and retain information or to master a skill, you *focus on important information* (analyzing and evaluating how the ideas are structured, how they connect, and what is most crucial to remember). When you are reading to search for truth, you *ask questions to evaluate arguments* (analyzing and evaluating the author's point of view as well as the credibility, accuracy, reliability, and relevancy of the material).

Focus on important information

Before determining how to respond to something you've read, ask yourself what is important and what you have to remember. According to Adam Robinson, co-founder of the *Princeton Review*, "The only way you can effectively absorb the relevant information is to ignore the irrelevant information."[8] The following tips will help you determine what is most important to focus on as you study. Check to see whether the information does the following:

▶ Contains headings, charts, tables, captions, key terms and definitions, or an introduction or summary (for a textbook, check mid-chapter or end-of-chapter exercises)

  ▶ Offers definitions, crucial concepts, examples, an explanation of a variety or type, critical relationships or comparisons

- Sparks questions and reactions as you read
- Surprises or confuses you
- Mirrors what your instructor emphasizes in class or in assignments

When trying to figure out what to study and what to skim, ask yourself whether your instructor would expect you to know the material. If you are unsure and the topic is not on your syllabus, email your instructor and ask for clarification.

Ask questions to evaluate arguments

An *argument* refers to a persuasive case—a set of connected ideas supported by examples—that a writer makes to prove or disprove a point. Many scholarly books and articles, in print form or on the Internet, are organized around particular arguments (look for *claims*—arguments that appear to be factual but don't have adequate evidence to support them). Critical readers evaluate arguments and claims to determine whether they are accurate and logical. When quality evidence combines with sound logic, the argument is solid.

It's easy—and common—to accept or reject an argument according to whether it fits with your point of view. If you ask questions, however, you can determine the argument's validity and understand it in greater depth (see Key 2.11). Evaluating an argument involves looking at several factors:

- The quality of the (evidence) (facts, statistics, and other materials supporting an argument)
- Whether the evidence fits the idea concept
- The logical connections

> EVIDENCE
> Facts, statistics, and other materials that are presented in support of an argument.

Approach every argument with healthy skepticism. Have an open mind to assess whether you are convinced or have serious questions.

Evaluate every source

Evidence examination is important for all reading materials, but especially when you research on the Internet, because online resources vary widely in

Key 2.11 ASK QUESTIONS SUCH AS THESE TO **EVALUATE ARGUMENTS**

EVALUATE THE VALIDITY OF THE EVIDENCE	DETERMINE WHETHER THE EVIDENCE SUPPORTS THE CONCEPT
Is the source reliable and free of bias?	Is there enough evidence?
Who wrote this and with what intent?	Do examples and ideas logically connect?
What assumptions underlie this material?	Is the evidence convincing?
Is this argument based on opinion?	Do the examples build a strong case?
How does this evidence compare with evidence from other sources?	What different and perhaps opposing arguments seem equally valid?

USE THE CARS TEST TO DETERMINE
INFORMATION QUALITY ON THE INTERNET

CREDIBILITY	ACCURACY	REASONABLENESS	SUPPORT
Examine whether a source is believable and trustworthy.	*Examine whether information is correct—that is, factual, comprehensive, detailed, and up to date (if necessary).*	*Examine whether material is fair, objective, moderate, and consistent.*	*Examine whether a source is adequately supported with citations.*
What are the author's credentials? Look for education and experience, title or position of employment, membership in any known and respected organization, reliable contact information, biographical information, and reputation.	***Is it up to date, and is that important?*** If you are searching for a work of literature, such as Shakespeare's play *Macbeth*, there is no "updated" version. However, you may want reviews of its latest productions. For most scientific research, you will need to rely on the most up-to-date information you can find.	***Does the source seem fair?*** Look for a balanced argument, accurate claims, and a reasoned tone that does not appeal primarily to your emotions.	***Where does the information come from?*** Look at the site, the sources used by the person or group who compiled the information, and the contact information. Make sure that the cited sources seem reliable and that statistics are documented.
Is there quality control? Look for ways in which the source may have been screened. For example, materials on an organization's website have most likely been approved by several members; information coming from an academic journal has to be screened by several people before it is published.	***Is it comprehensive?*** Does the material leave out any important facts or information? Does it neglect to consider alternative views or crucial consequences? Although no one source can contain all of the available information on a topic, it should still be as comprehensive as is possible within its scope.	***Does the source seem objective?*** While there is a range of objectivity in writing, you want to favour authors and organizations who can control their bias. An author with a strong political or religious agenda or an intent to sell a product may not be a source of the most truthful material.	***Is the information corroborated?*** Test information by looking for other sources that confirm the facts in this information—or, if the information is opinion, sources that share that opinion and back it up with their own citations. One good strategy is to find at least three sources that corroborate one another.
Is there any posted summary or evaluation of the source? You may find abstracts of sources (summary) or a recommendation, rating, or review from a person or organization (evaluation). Either of these—or, ideally, both—can give you an idea of credibility before you decide to examine a source in depth.	***For whom is the source written, and for what purpose?*** Looking at what the author wants to accomplish will help you assess whether the text has a bias. Sometimes biased information will not be useful for your purpose; sometimes your research will require that you note and evaluate bias (such as if you were to compare the War of 1812 diaries from Canadian and American soldiers).	***Does the source seem moderate?*** Do claims seem possible, or does the information seem hard to believe? Does what you read make sense when compared to what you already know? While wild claims may turn out to be truthful, you are safest to check everything out.	***Is the source externally consistent?*** Most material is a mix of both current and old information. External consistency refers to whether the old information agrees with what you already know. If a source contradicts something you know to be true, chances are higher that the information new to you may be inconsistent as well.
Signals of a potential lack of credibility: Anonymous materials, negative evaluations, little or no evidence of quality control, bad grammar or misspelled words	***Signals of a potential lack of accuracy:*** Lack of date or old date, generalizations, one-sided views that do not acknowledge opposing arguments	***Signals of a potential lack of reasonableness:*** Extreme or emotional language, sweeping statements, conflict of interest, inconsistencies or contradictions	***Signals of a potential lack of support:*** Statistics without sources, lack of documentation, lack of corroboration using other reliable sources

Source: Robert Harris, "Evaluating Internet Research Sources," November 17, 1997, VirtualSalt (www.virtualsalt.com/evalu8it.htm).

reliability. In fact, your Internet research is only as strong as your critical thinking. Robert Harris, professor and Web expert, has developed an easy-to-remember system for evaluating Internet information called the *CARS test for information quality* (Credibility, Accuracy, Reasonableness, Support). Use the information in Key 2.12 to question any source you find as you conduct research. You can also use it to test the reliability of non-Internet sources.

Reading is the tool you will use over and over again to acquire information in school, on the job, and in life (to understand your Registered Retirement Savings Plan, to learn about local and world news, to understand the fine print in a cellphone contract). Develop the ability to read with focus, purpose, and follow-through, and you will never stop enjoying the benefits.

Case Wrap-up

What happened to Gary? With perseverance and support, Gary has become a health-care management and strategic planning consultant whose clients include Fortune 500 insurance companies. However, he lives every day with the challenge of dyslexia. Because of the time and effort he needs to read, he has spent most of his adult life working in small private offices or a home office. He can't read directions fast enough to avoid wrong turns on highways and often makes spelling mistakes. The support of his wife, Lynne, a gifted writer and public speaker, has proven essential in his struggle to persevere. Armed with today's knowledge about learning differences, Gary and Lynne tested their children early and often and were able to provide their son with an academic environment that addressed his reading challenges. With their support, he has developed a soaring sense of self-confidence—the kind that Gary still strives for.

What does this story mean for you? Learning to be a productive member of society, with the gifts you are born with or can develop, is the name of the game. It also helps to have an understanding support system. Nearly everyone has a "big secret"—or perhaps a "small secret"—that causes challenges in school or on the job. Whether a learning disability such as dyslexia, a negative attitude about a task such as reading or math, or some other obstacle, it gets in the way as you strive for success. Think about one secret that you have, and put it in writing. Then write the name of a person whom you trust to support you. Finally, talk with this person and begin to come up with ideas of how you will address and manage your secret.

What effects go beyond your world? Reading is the essential success skill for the 21st century information-focused workplace. The more the world's citizens know how to read, the more they will be able to lead productive and successful lives. To start exploring what is happening in the promotion of literacy, read about Room to Read at www.roomtoread.org and explore what this organization is doing to build schools, stock libraries, and support education. Click on the "Get Involved" tab to see how to support its initiatives. Perhaps you will want to get involved yourself—or, if not, look into ways you can support literacy in your community, at your college or university, or even within your own family. Be a part of the solution.

Successful Intelligence *Wrap-up*

HERE'S HOW YOU HAVE BUILT SKILLS IN **CHAPTER 2**:

ANALYTICAL THINKING	CREATIVE THINKING	PRACTICAL THINKING
> You explored the steps of SQ3R and learned how to utilize strategies to boost your understanding of written materials.	> You learned about innovative ways to improve comprehension by studying in a way suitable to your personal needs.	> You developed highlighting and note-taking skills to help you in recalling important information after reading.
> In the Get Analytical exercise, you tried surveying and skimming a text to become familiar with the application of SQ3R.	> The section on getting ready to comprehend what you read may have inspired creative ideas about study locations, times, and motivators.	> In the Get Practical exercise, you practised your highlighting abilities and learned new methods from other students.
> You explored the importance of evaluating online and hard-copy sources.	> In the Get Creative exercise, you wrote a short personal biography.	> You studied different strategies that can be used to master different subject areas.

Word *for* Thought

Reading college or university textbooks may feel at times like the disorientation implied by the **Japanese** word *yokomeshi* (yo-ko-meh-shee), which literally means "eating a meal sideways."[9] The word describes the Japanese learner's difficulty with a foreign language written horizontally, unlike Japanese script, which reads from top to bottom. You are not alone in trying to figure out what things mean. Keep your sense of humour and commit to the task, and it is likely to feel more comfortable over time.

Building Skills for
Post-Secondary, Career, and Life Success

Steps to Success

Study a Text Page

STEP 1 BUILD BASIC SKILLS. The following page is from the chapter "Groups and Organizations" in the sixth edition of John J. Macionis's *Sociology*.[10] Skim the excerpt. Identify the headings on the page and the relationships among them. Mark primary-level headings with a numeral 1, secondary headings with a 2, and tertiary (third-level) headings with a 3.

STEP 2 TAKE IT TO THE NEXT LEVEL. Analyze the headings and text.

Which heading serves as an umbrella for the rest?

_____

What do the headings tell you about the content of the page?

_____

_____

_____

_____

Name three concepts that seem important to remember.

1. _____

2. _____

3. _____

Based on the three concepts you pulled out, write three study questions that you can review with an instructor, a teaching assistant, or a fellow student.

1. _____

2. _____

3. _____

SOCIAL GROUPS

Virtually everyone moves through life with a sense of belonging; this is the experience of group life. A social group refers to *two or more people who identify and interact with one another*. Human beings continually come together to form couples, families, circles of friends, neighbourhoods, churches, businesses, clubs, and numerous large organizations. Whatever the form, groups encompass people with shared experiences, loyalties, and interests. In short, while maintaining their individuality, the members of social groups also think of themselves as a special "we."

Groups, Categories, and Crowds

People often use the term "group" imprecisely. We now distinguish the group from the similar concepts of category and crowd.

■ *Category.* A *category* refers to people who have some status in common. Women, single fathers, military recruits, homeowners, and Roman Catholics are all examples of categories.

Why are categories not considered groups? Simply because, while the individuals involved are aware that they are not the only ones to hold that particular status, the vast majority are strangers to one another.

■ *Crowd.* A *crowd* refers to a temporary cluster of individuals who may or may not interact at all. Students sitting in a lecture hall do engage one another and share some common identity as college classmates; thus, such a crowd might be called a loosely formed group. By contrast, riders hurtling along on a subway train or bathers enjoying a summer day at the beach pay little attention to one another and amount to an anonymous aggregate of people. In general, then, crowds are too transitory and impersonal to qualify as social groups.

The right circumstances, however, could turn a crowd into a group. People riding in a subway train that crashes under the city streets generally become keenly aware of their common plight and begin to help one another. Sometimes such extraordinary experiences become the basis for lasting relationships.

Primary and Secondary Groups

Acquaintances commonly greet one another with a smile and the simple phrase, "Hi! How are you?" The response is usually a well scripted, "Just fine, thanks, how about you?" This answer, of course, is often more formal than truthful. In most cases, providing a detailed account of how you are *really* doing would prompt the other person to beat a hasty and awkward exit.

Sociologists classify social groups by measuring them against two ideal types based on members' genuine level of personal concern. This variation is the key to distinguishing *primary* from *secondary* groups.

According to Charles Horton Cooley (1864–1929), a **primary group** is *a small social group whose members share personal and enduring relationships*. Bound together by primary relationships, individuals in primary groups typically spend a great deal of time together, engage in a wide range of common activities, and feel that they know one another well. Although not without periodic conflict, members of primary groups display sincere concern for each other's welfare. The family is every society's most important primary group.

Cooley characterized these personal and tightly integrated groups as primary because they are among the first groups we experience in life. In addition, the family and early play groups also hold primary importance in the socialization process, shaping attitudes, behaviour, and social identity.

Source: John J. Macionis, *Sociology,* 6th ed., p. 145, © 1997 Prentice-Hall, Inc. Reproduced by permission of Pearson Education, Inc., Upper Saddle River, NJ.

MOVE TOWARD MASTERY. Read the excerpt, putting SQ3R to work. Using a marker pen, highlight key phrases and sentences. Write short marginal notes to help you review the material later. After reading this page thoroughly, write a short summary paragraph.

_____

_____

_____

_____

Teamwork

Create Solutions Together

FORM A STUDY GROUP

Goal: To organize a study group with the intent of preparing for an upcoming event.

Time on task: 30 minutes; ongoing

Instructions: Get together with three or four members of your class with whom you would like to form a group. These are your study group members. Do the following at the group's first meeting:

- *Set a specific goal.* Create a weekly schedule for reaching your goal—to prepare for an upcoming test, for example. Write everything down and give everyone a copy.
- *Talk about the specific ways you will work together.* Discuss which of the following methods you want to try in the group: pooling your notes; teaching each other difficult concepts; making up, administering, and grading quizzes for one another; creating study flash cards; using SQ3R to review required readings. Set specific guidelines for how group members will be held accountable.

As an initial group exercise, try the following:

- *Review the study questions that you wrote for the* Sociology *excerpt in the previous exercise.* Each person should select one question to focus on while reading (no two people should have the same question). Group members should then reread the excerpt individually, thinking about their questions as they read and answering them in writing.
- *When you finish reading critically, gather as a group.* Each person should take a turn presenting the question, the response or answer that was derived through critical reading, and other thoughts. Other members may then add to the discussion. Continue until everyone presents a concept.

Over several weeks, evaluate the different methods as a group, singling out those that were most helpful. Then incorporate them into your ongoing study sessions.

Writing

Build Intrapersonal and Communication Skills

Record your thoughts on a separate piece of paper, in a journal, or electronically.

EMOTIONAL INTELLIGENCE JOURNAL

Reading challenges. Which current course presents your most difficult reading challenge? Describe what makes the reading tough—type of material, length of assignments, level of difficulty, or something else. What feelings come up for you when you read, and what effect do they have on your reading? Describe techniques you learned in this chapter that can help you get into a growth mindset to read productively.

REAL-LIFE WRITING

Ask for help.   Self-help plans often involve reaching out to others. Draft an email to your instructor describing the difficulties in your challenging course as well as the specific help you need to move to the next step. Make sure that your message is clear and accurate, your grammar, spelling, and punctuation are correct, and your tone is appropriate. (See Quick Start to College and University for guidelines on communicating with instructors.) *Whether or not you send the email is up to you.* In either case, writing it will help you move forward in your reading improvement plan.

Personal Portfolio

Prepare for Career Success

READING SKILLS ON THE JOB

21st Century Learning Building Blocks

- Information Literacy
- Media Literacy
- ICT (Information, Communications, and Technology) Literacy

Complete the following in your electronic portfolio or separately on paper.

Excellent reading skills are a requirement for almost every 21st century job. Employers expect that you will read independently to master new skills and keep up with change. Whether in print or electronic form, on-the-job reading will challenge you as does college or university reading. For example, sociology courses may involve reading textbooks, journals, and case studies, but actually working in the field requires that you keep on top of case reports, government regulations, court documents, and an unending stream of work-related emails.

Prepare yourself by honestly assessing your practical skills *right now*. Use the following list to rate your ability on a scale from 1 to 10, 1 being the lowest and 10 being the highest:

- Ability to concentrate, no matter the distractions
- Ability to use emotional triggers to learn and remember material
- Ability to define your reading purpose and use it to guide your focus and pace
- Ability to use specific vocabulary-building techniques to improve comprehension
- Ability to use every aspect of SQ3R to master content
- Ability to skim and scan
- Ability to use analytical thinking skills when reading
- Ability to use highlighting and notes to help you master content

For the two skill areas in which you rated yourself lowest, think about how you can improve. Make a problem-solving plan for each (you may want to use a flow chart like the one on page 151). Check your progress in one month and at the end of the term. Finally, write down how you anticipate using the reading skills you learned in this chapter in your chosen career.

Social Networking

INCLUDE YOUR EDUCATION

Information about your education is often important when networking for jobs. Sign in to your LinkedIn account and click on "Edit Profile." Then, click on "Education" and fill in the following:

- School name
- Degree (either attained or working toward)
- Field(s) of study
- Dates attended (Current students enter their graduation year.)
- Activities and societies
- Additional notes (Give any other information about your education that you think would be valuable to a contact or potential employer—awards, honours, details about your major, study abroad, and so on.)

If you have a previously earned degree at another institution, don't forget to fill in a separate Education field about that as well.

chapter 3

Listening and Note Taking

Taking In and Recording Information

What Would You Do?

Think about this problem as you read, and consider how you would approach it. This chapter introduces you to listening and note-taking skills that will help you successfully take in, and write down, knowledge that you can use.

Halfway through her first term in college, Maya Leanza is not feeling the connection she expected—neither to her coursework nor her school. She is working her way through a full load of core requirements, none of which really interests her. In fact, although she is not sure what her academic focus or major will be, after only half a term she is sure that it won't be in any of the departments of the courses she is taking now.

She and her study partner Ross have a once-a-week session on Tuesdays for their contemporary civilization class. When they met to prepare for the mid-term, they exchanged sets of notes as planned. Looking at hers, Ross said, "Maya, did you miss some of class? You have about half as many pages as I do, and I'm having trouble following your notes." Maya responded, "No, I was there the whole time. Honestly, Ross, I'm trying to listen but nothing sticks. I'm just done, and we still have seven weeks to go." "Well, is it okay if we study from my notes? The mid-term is Friday and I'm a little stressed," said Ross. Maya agreed, and they worked through Ross's notes and their textbook chapters for an hour.

When they were packing up, Ross said, "Maya, it's hard to get anywhere with this stuff unless you somehow believe it is important. Does it mean anything to you?" "I'm not sure," Maya said. "I feel like, what's the point?" "Well, try just thinking about why you are here," replied Ross. "Find some reason that will keep you going, even if it's just

'A degree will help me get a better job.'" Maya thought for a minute. "I'm not sure that's enough," she said. "I don't know what is enough, but I guess I'm wasting my time and money if I don't figure it out." (To be continued . . .)

Many students, at some point during college or university, feel disconnected from their coursework. You'll learn more about Maya, and revisit her situation, within the chapter.

In this chapter, you'll explore answers to these questions:

> How can you become a better listener? p. 66

> How can you improve your note-taking skills? p. 72

> What note-taking systems can you use? p. 76

> How can you take notes faster? p. 81

MyStudentSuccessLab

Use these interactive tools to help you succeed in your course and career:
- Videos
- Exercises and applied activities
- Practice quizzes

For each statement, circle the number that feels right to you, from 1 for "not at all true for me" to 5 for "very true for me."

▶ I know and understand the stages of listening.	**1 2 3 4 5**
▶ I arrive early for class prepared to absorb information by having read the required text ahead of time.	**1 2 3 4 5**
▶ I ask questions during lectures and listen for verbal clues to understand important information.	**1 2 3 4 5**
▶ I understand the differences between internal and external distractions and work to control my learning environment whenever possible.	**1 2 3 4 5**
▶ I use different note-taking systems depending on my instructor's teaching styles and the material being taught.	**1 2 3 4 5**
▶ I know how to use visuals in my notes to clarify tough concepts discussed in class.	**1 2 3 4 5**
▶ I believe that good preparation is a necessary first step toward taking comprehensive notes.	**1 2 3 4 5**
▶ I use strategies to make sense of and record large class discussions.	**1 2 3 4 5**
▶ I review notes within 24 hours of taking them.	**1 2 3 4 5**
▶ I use shorthand to take notes faster.	**1 2 3 4 5**

Each of the topics in these statements is covered in this chapter. Note those statements for which you circled a 3 or lower. Skim the chapter to see where those topics appear, and pay special attention to them as you read, learn, and apply new strategies.

REMEMBER: *No matter how developed your listening and note-taking skills are, you can improve with effort and practice.*

"Successfully intelligent people find their path and then pursue it, realizing that there will be obstacles along the way and that surmounting these obstacles is part of their challenge."

—Robert Sternberg

LISTENING
A process that involves sensing, interpreting, evaluating, and reacting to spoken messages.

How can you become **a better listener?**

The act of *hearing* is not the same as the act of **listening**. *Hearing* refers to sensing spoken messages and sounds from their source. You can hear all kinds of things and not understand or remember any of them. Listening, however, is a communication process that starts with hearing but also includes focused thinking about what you hear. Listening is a learnable skill that engages your analytical, creative, and practical thinking abilities and extends far beyond the classroom, enhancing your ability to relate with work and school colleagues, friends, and family.

Know the stages of listening

Listening is made up of four stages that build on one another: sensing, interpreting, evaluating, and reacting. These stages take the message from the speaker to the listener and back to the speaker (see Key 3.1).

▶ During the *sensation stage* (also known as *hearing*) your ears pick up sound waves and transmit them to the brain. For example, you are sitting in class and hear your instructor say, "The only opportunity to make up last week's test is Tuesday at 5:00 P.M."

THE **LISTENING PROCESS** MOVES MESSAGES ALONG A LISTENING LOOP

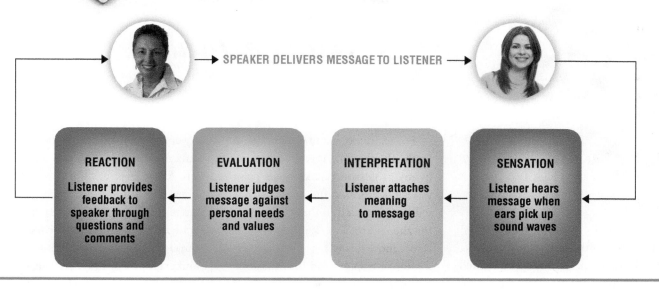

→ SPEAKER DELIVERS MESSAGE TO LISTENER →

REACTION	EVALUATION	INTERPRETATION	SENSATION
Listener provides feedback to speaker through questions and comments	Listener judges message against personal needs and values	Listener attaches meaning to message	Listener hears message when ears pick up sound waves

▶ In the *interpretation* stage, you attach meaning to a message. You understand what is said and link it to what you already know. You relate this message to your knowledge of the test, whether you need to make it up, and what you are doing on Tuesday at 5:00.

▶ In the *evaluation* stage, you evaluate the message as it relates to your needs and values. If the message goes against your values or does not fulfill your needs, you may reject it, stop listening, or argue in your mind with the speaker. In this example, if you need to make up the test but have to work Tuesday at 5:00, you may evaluate the message in an unfavourable way.

▶ The final stage of listening is a *reaction* to the message in the form of direct feedback. In a classroom, direct feedback often comes in the form of questions and comments. Your reaction, in this case, may be to ask the instructor whether she can schedule another test time.

You will become a better listener by learning to recognize and manage listening challenges and becoming actively involved with the material.

Become an active listener

On the surface, listening seems to be a passive activity. You sit back as someone else speaks. In reality, effective listening is an active process that involves the following factors.

■ *Be there.* Being an active listener requires that you show up on time—preferably a few minutes before class begins. Instructors often make important announcements in the first few minutes and may also summarize the last lecture.

Listening to other students can be as important as listening to instructors. These students may learn something useful from their fellow student's presentation.
© iStockphoto

student profile

Sarah Mocherniak
Acadia University, Wolfville, Nova Scotia

About me:

I am currently enrolled at Acadia University in the School of Business Administration. My school is located in Nova Scotia; however, I was originally born and raised in the Toronto area. I am bilingual. Throughout my years at Acadia, I have not only worked with students but also had the opportunity to gain an alumni perspective from working in the Office of Alumni Affairs. My friends and colleagues know me best as an upbeat social contributor.

What I focus on:

At the beginning of university I came across new, unexpected challenges. My biggest challenge was note taking. Certain strategies in particular work well for me.

For example, using either the textbook or online resources posted by my professor, I make notes prior to each lecture on the material that will be discussed in that class. During the lecture, I pick up on key terms more easily because I already know the background information. Using a different-coloured pen, I add examples and other details that are not given in the book. Preparing notes before I go to class gives me the opportunity not only to add key examples but also to listen to the professor without having to rush to get every note down.

When preparing for an exam, I expand on the idea above. I divide my page into two columns. The column on the left is for the terms, equation names, or theories. The column on the right is where I write down the definitions, actual equations, explanations, or examples given. This way, when I study, I can cover the right side of the page and quiz myself with the terms on the left. At the bottom of the two columns and at the end of each chapter's notes, I also have a section where I analyze and connect the terms. I go through the entire chapter's terms and examples to draw conclusions and summarize the main idea that the professor is trying to get across.

What will help me in the workplace:

It is important for me to always figure out how the material that I am learning in class relates or may relate to me in the future. Note taking in classes may not seem relevant for the future to some; however, it has shown to be extremely helpful in all of my jobs. For instance, knowing how to properly prepare ahead of time for a meeting and knowing how to pick up key points while in a meeting is extremely beneficial.

■ ***Set purposes for listening.*** Before every class, use your analytical intelligence to establish what you want to achieve, such as understanding a particular concept. Many instructors start a lecture with a statement of purpose, so listen carefully and write the purpose at the top of your notes to help you focus. If you read assignments and review previous notes before class, you may be able to follow along more easily. Come to class with ideas about how what you hear will help you achieve your goals. (This practice would help Maya make her purpose for listening more personal.)

■ *Focus on understanding.* Rather than taking notes on everything, record information only when you can say to yourself, "I get it!" If you miss important material, leave holes in your notes and return later. Your instructor may repeat the point you missed, or another comment may help you piece it together.

■ *Ask questions.* Active listeners ask analytical questions to clarify their understanding and to associate new ideas with what they already know. Questions such as "What is this part of?" or "How is it similar to yesterday's topic?" signal active involvement. Get into the habit of jotting down your questions and coming back to them during a discussion period so they don't interfere with listening.

Manage listening challenges

Sitting in your classes, you probably have noticed a variety of not-so-academic activities that interfere with listening. Some people may be texting or surfing the Internet; some may be talking or sleeping; and some might be daydreaming. In all of these cases, the students are probably not absorbing much—or any—of the information being provided by the instructor, and they may be distracting you from listening as well. Read on to see how to address these issues, and others, on your path to becoming a better listener.

Issue 1: Distractions that divide your attention

The common distractions that interfere with listening can be divided into *internal distractions* (worry, illness, fatigue, hunger, feeling too hot or too cold) and *external distractions* (chatting, computer use, any kind of movement or noise). Distractions such as these nip away at you while you're trying to pay attention.

Fix 1: Focus, focus, focus

First of all, tell yourself that you're in the class to learn and that you *really need* to know the material. You may even want to remind yourself of what you're paying to sit in this class. Find practical ways to minimize distractions.

► Sit near the front of the room.

► Move away from talkative classmates.

► Turn off your cellphone or put it on silent mode when in class.

► Get enough sleep to stay alert.

► Eat enough so you're not hungry—or bring small snacks, if allowed.

► Try to put your worries aside during class.

The often overwhelming pace of modern life leads students to *multitask* (do several things at once), under the impression that multitasking can help them accomplish goals effectively in less time. Although you may think you can handle distractions because you are used to multitasking, recent research shows that multitasking actually *decreases* both memory power and performance. In a study at Stanford University in the United States, low multitaskers actually outperformed high multitaskers on all tasks.[1] Try to keep your focus on one thing at a time.

Issue 2: Listening lapses

Even the most fantastic instructor can't make you listen. You and you alone can do that. If you decide that a subject is too difficult or uninteresting, you may tune out and miss what comes next, as Maya found out. You may also focus on certain points and shut out everything else. Either way, you run the risk of not being prepared and not making the most of your time.

Fix 2: An I-can-do-it attitude

► *Start with a productive mindset.* If the class is hard, that's all the more reason to pay attention. Instructors are generally more sympathetic to, and eager to help, students who've obviously been trying even when it's tough.

► *Concentrate.* Work to take in the whole message so you will be able to read over your notes later, combine your class and text notes, and think critically about what is important. Making connections between ideas can alleviate the difficulty of the material in some cases and boredom if you're familiar with the concepts.

► *Refocus.* If you experience a listening lapse, try to get back into the lecture quickly instead of worrying about what you missed. After class, look at a classmate's notes to fill in the gaps.

VERBAL SIGNPOSTS
Spoken words or phrases that call attention to information that follows.

► *Be aware.* Pay attention to ⟨**verbal signposts**⟩ to help organize information, connect ideas, and indicate what is important and what is not. See Key 3.2 for examples.

Issue 3: Rushing to judgment

It's common to stop listening when you hear something you don't like or don't agree with. You react, and then you focus on your emotions. Unfortunately, you can spend valuable class time thinking of all the reasons your instructor is wrong and miss everything else. The situation might not seem particularly bad that day, but when the test comes around, you may feel differently about having missed material.

Judgments also involve reactions to speakers themselves. If you do not like your instructors or have preconceived notions about their race, ethnicity, gender, physical characteristics, or disability, you may dismiss their ideas—and miss out on your opportunity to learn.

PAY ATTENTION TO
VERBAL SIGNPOSTS

Key 3.2

SIGNALS POINTING TO KEY CONCEPTS	SIGNALS OF SUPPORT
A key point to remember . . .	A perfect example, . . .
Point 1, point 2, etc. . . .	Specifically, . . .
The impact of this was . . .	For instance, . . .
The critical stages in the process are . . .	Similarly, . . .

SIGNALS POINTING TO DIFFERENCES	SIGNALS THAT SUMMARIZE
On the contrary, . . .	From this you have learned, . . .
On the other hand, . . .	In conclusion, . . .
In contrast, . . .	As a result, . . .
However, . . .	Finally, . . .

Fix 3: Recognize and correct your patterns

Although it can be human nature to stop listening when you react to a speaker or message, it can make listening a lot more difficult. College and university are about broadening your horizons and looking for what different people can teach you, even though they and their beliefs may differ from you and yours. So what do you do?

▶ *Recognize your pattern so you can change it.* When you feel yourself reacting to something said in a lecture, stop and take a moment to breathe. Count to 10. Take one more breath and see how you feel.

▶ *Know that you can't hear—and therefore can't learn anything from—others if you are filled with preconceived notions about them and their ideas.* Put yourself in their shoes; would you want them to stop listening to you if they disagreed, or would you want to be heard completely?

▶ *Stop it.* It's as simple as that. Listen with an open mind even when you disagree or have a negative reaction to an instructor. Being open to the new and different, even when it makes you a bit uncomfortable, is part of what education is about.

Issue 4: Partial hearing loss and learning disabilities

If you have a hearing loss or a learning disability, listening effectively in class may prove challenging. As discussed in Chapter 1, learning disabilities can come in a variety of forms, affecting different parts of cognition.

Fix 4: Get help

If you have a hearing loss, find out about available equipment. For example, listening to a taped lecture at a higher-than-normal volume can help you hear things you missed. Ask instructors whether or not digitized recordings are available for download to a computer or MP3 player. Meeting with your instructor outside of class to clarify your notes may also help, as will sitting near the front of the room.

If you have (or think you have) a learning disability, learn what services are available. Talk to your advisor and instructor about your problem, seek out a tutor, visit academic centres that can help (such as the writing centre, if you have a writing issue), scan your school's website, or connect to the office for students with disabilities. Know that you can succeed and that people are there to help you.

Issue 5: Comprehension difficulties for speakers of other languages

If English isn't your first language, listening and understanding material in the classroom can be challenging, requiring concentration, dedication, and patience. Specialized vocabulary, informal language, and the rate of speech can add to the challenge.

Fix 5: Take a proactive approach to understanding

Talk to your instructor as soon as possible about your situation. Recognizing a need early and meeting to discuss it keeps your instructor informed and shows your dedication. In some cases, your professor will give you a list of key terms to review before class. During class, keep a list of unfamiliar words and phrases to look up later; but, whenever possible, don't let these terms prevent you from understanding the main ideas. Focus on the main points of

*get*Analytical!

Discover Yourself as a Listener

Complete the following as you focus on your personal listening habits:

Analyze how present you are as a listener. Are you easily distracted, or can you focus well? Do you prefer to listen, or do you tend to talk?

_____

_____

When you are listening, what tends to distract you?

_____

_____

What happens to your listening skills when you become confused?

_____

_____

How do you react when you strongly disagree with something your instructor says—when you are convinced that you are right and your instructor is wrong?

_____

_____

Thinking about your answers, list two strategies from the chapter that will help you improve listening skills.

1. _____

2. _____

the lecture and plan to meet with classmates after class to fill gaps in your understanding. If, after several weeks, you're still having difficulties, consider enrolling in an English refresher course, getting a tutor, or visiting the campus advice centre for more assistance. Be proactive about your education.

Listening isn't always easy and it isn't always comfortable. As poet Robert Frost once said, "Education is the ability to listen to almost anything without losing your temper or your self-confidence." Keeping an open, engaged mind takes practice, but when excellent listening becomes second nature, you'll thank yourself for the work it took. Effective listening skills are the basis for effective note taking—an essential and powerful study tool.

How can you improve your note-taking skills?

Taking notes makes you an active class participant—even when you don't say a word—and provides you with study materials. What's on the line is nothing short of your academic success.

Class notes have two primary purposes: to serve as a record of what happened in class and to use for studying, alone and in combination with your text notes. Because it is virtually impossible to take notes on everything you hear, note taking encourages you to use your analytical intelligence to critically evaluate what is worth remembering. Exploring the strategies outlined next can help you prepare and take notes in class, review notes, and take notes on reading materials.

Prepare

Showing up for class on time is just the start. Here's more about preparing to take notes:

Good listening powers note taking. When taking notes in class, stop to listen to the information before deciding what to write down.
© iStockphoto

■ *Preview your reading material.* More than anything else you can do, reading assigned materials before class will give you the background to take effective notes. Check your class syllabi daily for assignment due dates and plan your reading time with these deadlines in mind.

■ *Review what you know.* Taking 15 minutes before class to review your notes from the previous class and your reading assignment notes for that day will enable you to follow the lecture from the start.

■ *Set up your environment.* Find a comfortable seat, away from friends if sitting with them distracts you. Use a separate notebook for each course, and start a new page for each class. If you use a laptop, open the file containing your class notes right away. Be ready to write (or type) as soon as the instructor begins speaking.

■ *Gather support.* In each class, set up a support system with one or two students so you can look at their notes after an absence. Find students whose work you respect, as Maya did with Ross.

■ *Choose the best note-taking system.* Take these factors into account to select a system that works best in each class:

▶ *The instructor's style* (which will be clear after a few classes). In the same term, you may have an instructor who is organized and speaks slowly, another who jumps around and talks rapidly, and a third who goes off topic in response to questions. Be flexible as you adapt.

▶ *The course material.* You may decide that an informal outline works best for a highly structured lecture and that a think link (discussed later in the chapter) is right for a looser presentation. Try one note-taking system for several classes and then adjust if necessary.

▶ *Your learning style.* Choose strategies that make the most of your strengths and compensate for your weaknesses.

Examples of various note-taking systems, and a more thorough discussion, appear later in the chapter.

Record information effectively during class

The following practical suggestions will help you record what is important in a format that you can review later:

get*Practical!*

Face a Note-Taking Challenge

Get set to take in and record information in your most difficult class.

Course name and date of class:

_____

Consult your syllabus, and then list what you have to read (text sections and/or other materials) before your next class:

_____

Where will you sit in class to focus your attention and minimize distractions?

_____

Which note-taking system is best suited for the class and why?

_____

_____

Write the phone numbers and email addresses of two classmates whose notes you can borrow if you miss a class or are confused about material:

_____

_____

▶ *Start a new page or section for each new topic,* especially if your instructor jumps from topic to topic during a single class.

▶ *Record whatever your instructor emphasizes* by paying attention to verbal and nonverbal cues.

▶ *Write down all key terms and definitions* so that you can refer back to them easily.

▶ *Note relevant examples, applications, and links to other material* when you encounter difficult concepts.

▶ *Ask questions.* If your instructor allows questions during class, ask them. Chances are several other students have similar queries. If your instructor prefers to answer questions at the end of class, keep a separate sheet of paper to jot down questions as you think of them.

▶ *Write down every question your instructor raises,* because these questions may be on a test.

▶ *Be organized, but not fussy.* Remember that you can always improve your notes later.

▶ *Leave blank spaces between points* to make it easy to see where one topic ends and another begins. (This suggestion does not apply if you are using a think link.)

▶ *Draw pictures and diagrams* to illustrate ideas.

▶ *Be consistent.* Use the same system to show importance—such as indenting, spacing, or underlining—on each page.

▶ *Record as much as you can if you have trouble understanding a concept.* Then leave space for an explanation and flag the margin with a large question mark. After class, try to clarify your questions by reading the text or ask a classmate or your instructor for help.

▶ *Consider that your class notes are only part of the picture.* You will learn best when you combine your text and class notes.

▶ *Go beyond the PowerPoint.* Increasingly, instructors are using computer software to present lectures in the classroom. Although it may be tempting to simply copy down what's written on the slide, realize that instructors usually show the main points, not the details that may be tested later. Take notes on what your instructor says about each main idea highlighted on a presentation slide.

Finally, don't stop taking notes when your class engages in a discussion. Even though it isn't part of the instructor's planned presentation, it often includes important information. Key 3.3 has suggestions for how to make the most of discussions.

Review and revise

By their very nature, class notes require revision. They may be incomplete in some places, confusing in others, and illegible in still others. That is why it is critical to review and revise your notes as soon as possible after class. This review will enable you to fill in gaps while the material is fresh, to clarify sloppy handwriting, or to raise questions.

If you can review your notes within 24 hours of taking them down in class, you are likely to reactivate and strengthen the new neural pathways you created when

IMPROVE YOUR NOTES
DURING CLASS DISCUSSION

- Listen to everyone; you never know when something important will be said.

- Listen for threads that weave through comments. They may signal an important point.

- Listen for ideas the instructor likes and for encouraging comments, such as "You make a great point" or "I like your idea."

- Take notes when the instructor rephrases and clarifies a point.

you learned the material. Waiting longer than 24 hours can result in losing the information you worked so hard to record. Reviewing and revising your class notes prepares you for the vital step of combining class and text notes.

Taking notes from a text

Taking notes while reading a text follows the same basic principles as taking notes in class, but with a bit of an SQ3R twist. Although you won't be asking as many probing questions of the material, you'll need your skills in observation, as well as in recording and reviewing, to make it a success.

You might take notes from a text when the book is a library copy or borrowed from a classmate—or when you don't have enough room to take notes in the margin. In that case, it's best to start by identifying what you want to get from the notes. Are you looking for the basic topics from a chapter? An in-depth understanding of a particular concept? Once you've decided on the need, then you can identify the method.

Revisit the note-taking methods listed earlier in the chapter. Different note-taking approaches work best for different situations. For instance, on the one hand, mind maps work well to understand broad connections, overall relationships, or how your text works in relation to your instructor's lecture. On the other hand, formal outlines can make sense of complicated information in a structured way that can provide clarity. Try different approaches to see which ones work for you.

What note-taking systems can you use?

Now that you have gathered some useful note-taking strategies, take a look at different approaches to note taking. As you read, keep some questions in mind:

▶ What class or type of instruction would this system be best suited for? Why?

▶ How could I make use of this system?

▶ Which system seems most comfortable to me?

▶ What system might be most compatible with my learning style strengths? Why?

Outlines

Outlines use a standard structure to show how ideas interrelate. *Formal outlines* indicate idea dominance and subordination with Roman numerals, uppercase and lowercase letters, and numbers. In contrast, *informal outlines* show the same associations but replace the formality with a system of consistent indenting and dashes.

When a lecture seems well organized, an informal outline can show how ideas and supporting details relate while also indicating levels of importance. Key 3.4 shows how the structure of an informal outline helps a student take notes on the topic of tropical rain forests. The multiple intelligences table in this chapter (see page 78) is designed to help harness different learning

AN **INFORMAL OUTLINE** IS USEFUL FOR TAKING NOTES IN CLASS

Tropical Rain Forests

What are tropical rain forests?
— Areas in South America and Africa, along the equator
— Average temperatures between 25° and 30°C
— Average annual rainfalls range between 250 to 400 centimetres
— Conditions combine to create the Earth's richest, most biodiverse ecosystem.
 – A biodiverse ecosystem has a great number of organisms coexisting within a defined area.
 – Examples of rain forest biodiversity
 – 2½ acres in the Amazon rain forest has 283 species of trees
 – a 3-square-mile section of a Peruvian rain forest has more than 1,300 butterfly species and 600 bird species.
 – Compare this biodiversity to what is found in the entire U.S.—only 400 butterfly species and 700 bird species

How are humans changing the rain forest?
— Humans have already destroyed about 40% of all rain forests.
 – They are cutting down trees for lumber or clearing the land for ranching or agriculture.
— Biologist Edwin O. Wilson estimates that this destruction may lead to the extinction of 27,000 species.
— Rain forest removal is also linked to the increase in atmospheric carbon dioxide, which worsens the greenhouse effect.
 – The greenhouse effect refers to process in which gases such as carbon dioxide trap the Sun's energy in the Earth's atmosphere as heat resulting in global warning.
— Recognition of the crisis is growing as are conservation efforts.

Source: Teresa Audesirk, Gerald Audesirk, and Bruce E. Byers. *Life on Earth*, 2nd ed., Upper Saddle River, NJ: Prentice Hall, 2000, pp. 660–662.

approaches for an earth science course. Specifically, the table will suggest different note-taking strategies you can use to study the topic of tropical rain forests.

When an instructor's presentation is disorganized, it may be difficult to use an outline. Focus instead on taking down whatever information you can as you try to connect key topics. The Cornell system and other note-taking methods discussed next can be beneficial in such situations.

From time to time, an instructor may give you a guide, usually in outline form, to help you take notes in class. This outline, known as *guided notes*, may be on the board, projected onto a screen, or in a handout that you receive at the beginning of class. Because guided notes are usually general and sketchy, you must fill in the details.

Cornell T-note system

The *Cornell note-taking system*, also known as the *T-note system*, consists of three sections on ordinary notepaper.[2]

▶ *Notes*, the largest section, is on the right. Record your notes here in whatever form you choose. Skip lines between topics so you can clearly see where a section begins and ends.

▶ The *cue column* goes to the left of your notes. Leave it blank while you read or listen, and then fill it in later as you review. You might insert keywords or comments that highlight ideas, clarify meaning, add examples, link ideas, or draw diagrams. Many students use this column to raise questions, which they answer when they study.

▶ The *summary* goes at the bottom of the page. Here you reduce your notes to critical points, a process that will help you learn the material. Use this section to provide an overview of what the notes say.

Apply Different Intelligences to Taking Notes in Earth Science

INTELLIGENCE	USE MI STRATEGIES TO IMPROVE YOUR NOTES	APPLY MI NOTE-TAKING STRATEGIES TO THE TOPIC OF TROPICAL RAIN FORESTS FOR AN EARTH SCIENCE COURSE
Verbal-Linguistic	• Rewrite your class notes in an alternate note-taking style to see connections more clearly. • Combine class and text notes to get a complete picture.	• Rewrite and summarize your reading and lecture notes to understand the characteristics of tropical rain forests.*
Logical-Mathematical	• When reviewing or rewriting notes, put information into a logical sequence. • Create tables that show relationships.	• Create a table comparing and contrasting the different species found in a typical rain forest.
Bodily-Kinesthetic	• Think of your notes as a crafts project that enables you to see "knowledge layers." Use coloured pens to texture your notes. • Study with your notes spread in sequence around you so that you can see knowledge building from left to right.	• Fill a tube with 4 metres of water to give you a physical sense of the annual rainfall in a rain forest. Or fill a bathtub with 25 centimetres of water and multiply by 16 to imagine rainfall totals. How would you react to living with so much rain? Take notes on your reaction.
Visual-Spatial	• Take notes using coloured markers or pens. • Rewrite lecture notes in think link format, focusing on the most important points.	• As part of your notes, create a chart that covers the types of vegetation that grow in a rain forest. Use a different-coloured marker for each plant species.
Interpersonal	• Try to schedule a study group right after a lecture to discuss class notes. • Review class notes with a study buddy. Compare notes to see what may have been missed.	• Interview someone you know who has visited a rain forest about what he or she saw, or interview a natural scientist at a museum about this environment. Use a different note-taking system for each person.
Intrapersonal	• Schedule some quiet time soon after a lecture to review and think about your notes. • As you review your notes, decide whether you grasp the material or need help.	• Think about the conflict between economic modernization and the preservation of rain forests in underdeveloped areas. Include your thoughts in your notes.
Musical	• To improve recall, recite concepts in your notes to rhythms. • Write a song that includes material from your class and text notes. Use the refrain to emphasize what is important.	• Use the Internet to find songs about the biodiversity of rain forests written by indigenous peoples who live in or near them. Then, use the song to remember key concepts. Take notes on what you find.
Naturalistic	• Notice similarities and differences in concepts by organizing material into natural groupings.	• If possible, visit a museum of natural history with exhibits of rain forests. Try to see common characteristics that make vegetation and species thrive in this environment. Take notes on your observations.

*For information on tropical rain forests, see Frederick Lutgens, Edward Tarbuck, and Dennis Tasa, *Foundations of Earth Science*, 5th ed., Upper Saddle River, NJ: Prentice Hall, 2008.

Create this note-taking structure before class begins. Picture an upside-down letter T as you follow these directions:

► Start with a sheet of 8½-by-11-inch lined paper. Label it with the date and lecture title.

► To create the cue column, draw a vertical line about 6.5 centimetres from the left side of the paper. End the line about 5 centimetres from the bottom of the sheet.

► To create the summary area, start at the point where the vertical line ends (about 5 centimetres from the bottom of the page) and draw a horizontal line that spans the entire paper.

Key 3.5 shows how the Cornell system is used in a business course.

THE **CORNELL SYSTEM** HAS SPACE FOR NOTES, COMMENTS, AND A SUMMARY

October 3, 2010, p. 1

Label a sheet of paper with the date and title of the lecture.

Understanding Employee Motivation

Why do some workers have a better attitude toward their work than others?

Purpose of motivational theories
— To explain role of human relations in motivating employee performance
— Theories translate into how managers actually treat workers

Some managers view workers as lazy; others view them as motivated and productive.

2 specific theories
— Human resources model, developed by Douglas McGregor, shows that managers have radically different beliefs about motivation.
— Theory X holds that people are naturally irresponsible and uncooperative
— Theory Y holds that people are naturally responsible and self-motivated

Maslow's Hierarchy

self-actualization needs (challenging job)
esteem needs (job title)
social needs (friends at work)
security needs (health plan)
physiological needs (pay)

— Maslow's Hierarchy of Needs says that people have needs in 5 different areas, which they attempt to satisfy in their work.
— Physiological need: need for survival, including food and shelter
— Security need: need for stability and protection
— Social need: need for friendship and companionship
— Esteem need: need for status and recognition
— Self-actualization need: need for self-fulfillment
Needs at lower levels must be met before a person tries to satisfy needs at higher levels.
— Developed by psychologist Abraham Maslow

Create the cue column by drawing a vertical line about 6.5 centi-metres from the left side of the paper. End the line about 5 centi-metres from the bottom of the sheet.

Two motivational theories try to explain worker motivation. The human resources model includes Theory X and Theory Y. Maslow's Hierarchy of Needs suggests that people have needs in 5 different areas: physiological, security, social, esteem, and self-actualization.

Create the summary area by starting where the vertical line ends (about 5 centimetres from the bottom of the page) and drawing a horizontal line across the paper.

Think links

A *think link*, also known as a *mind map* or *word web*, is a visual form of note taking that encourages flexible thinking. When you draw a think link, you use shapes and lines to link ideas with supporting details and examples. The visual design makes the connections easy to see, and shapes and pictures extend the material beyond words.

To create a think link, start by circling or boxing your topic in the middle of the paper. Next, draw a line from the topic and write the name of one major idea at the end of the line. Circle that idea. Then jot down specific facts related to the idea, linking them to the idea with lines. Continue the process, connecting thoughts to one another with circles, lines, and words. Key 3.6, a think link on the sociological concept "stratification," follows this structure.

Examples of think link designs include stair steps showing connected ideas that build toward a conclusion and a tree with trunk and roots as central concepts and branches as examples. Another type of think link called a jellyfish."

A think link may be difficult to construct in class, especially if your instructor talks quickly. If this is the case, transform your notes into think link format later when you review.

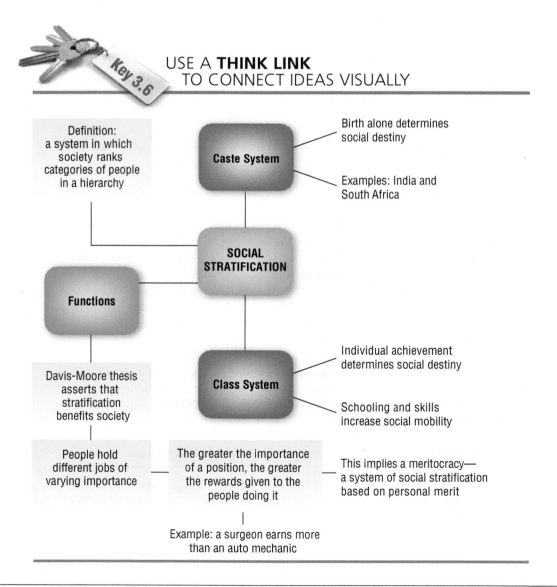

Key 3.6

USE A **THINK LINK**
TO CONNECT IDEAS VISUALLY

Definition: a system in which society ranks categories of people in a hierarchy

Caste System

Birth alone determines social destiny

Examples: India and South Africa

SOCIAL STRATIFICATION

Functions

Davis-Moore thesis asserts that stratification benefits society

People hold different jobs of varying importance

The greater the importance of a position, the greater the rewards given to the people doing it

Example: a surgeon earns more than an auto mechanic

Class System

Individual achievement determines social destiny

Schooling and skills increase social mobility

This implies a meritocracy— a system of social stratification based on personal merit

Charting method

Sometimes instructors deliver information in such quantities and at such speeds that taking detailed notes becomes nearly impossible. In such situations, when a lot of material is coming at you very quickly, the charting method might prove quite useful. It is also excellent for classes presented chronologically or sequentially.

To create charting notes, look ahead in your syllabus to determine the topics of the day's lecture. Then separate your paper into distinct columns, such as definitions, important phrases, and key themes. As you listen to the lecture, this will eliminate excessive writing, help you track dialogues that can be easy to lose, and provide quick memorization tools by splitting material into relevant categories. Shown is a partial set of charting notes for a history class:

Time Period	Important People	Events	Importance
1968–1972	Pierre Elliott Trudeau	October Crisis, "Just Society"	War Measures Act, Canada becomes officially bilingual, universal health care protected

Other visual strategies

Other strategies that help organize information are especially useful to visual learners, although they may be too involved to complete during class. Use them when taking text notes or combining class and text notes for review.

▶ *Pictures and diagrams.* Copy any and all diagrams from the board and feel free to adapt your own. Make complex concepts into images or cartoons. The act of converting material into a visual display will activate both your bodily-kinesthetic attributes as well as your visual intelligence.

▶ *Timelines.* Use a timeline to organize information into chronological order. Draw a vertical or horizontal line on the page and connect each item to the line, in order, noting the dates and basic event descriptions.

▶ *Tables.* Use the columns and rows of a table to organize information as you condense and summarize your class and text notes.

▶ *Hierarchy charts.* Charts showing an information hierarchy can help you visualize how pieces fit together. For example, you can use a hierarchy chart to show ranks within a government bureaucracy or levels of scientific classification of animals and plants.

How can you take notes faster?

> SHORTHAND
> A system of rapid handwriting that employs symbols, abbreviations, and shortened words to represent words and phrases.

Personal (shorthand) is a practical intelligence strategy that enables you to write faster. Because you are the only intended reader, you can misspell and abbreviate words in ways that only you understand. A risk of using shorthand is that you might forget what your writing means. To avoid this problem, review your notes shortly after class and spell out words that are confusing.

Another risk is forgetting to remove shorthand from work you hand in. This can happen when you use the same system for class notes as you do when talking to friends online. For example, when students take notes in text message shorthand they may be so accustomed to omitting capitalization and punctuation, using acronyms, and replacing long words with creative contractions that they may forget to correct their final work.

The suggestions that follow will help you master shorthand. Many will be familiar and, in fact, you may already use many of them to speed up your email and text messaging.

1. Use standard abbreviations in place of complete words.

w/, w/o	with, without	cf	compare, in comparison to
ur	you are	Ff	following
→	means; resulting in	Q	question
←	as a result of	gr8	great
↑	increasing	pov	point of view
↓	decreasing	<	less than
∴	therefore	>	more than
b/c	because	=	equals
≈	approximately	b&f	back and forth
+ or &	and	Δ	change
Y	why	2	to; two; too
no. or #	number	afap	as far as possible
i.e.	that is,	e.g.	for example
cos	change of subject	c/o	care of
Ng	no good	km	kilometres
p.	page	hx	history

2. Shorten words by removing middle vowels.

Prps = purpose
Lwyr = lawyer
Cmptr = computer

3. Substitute word beginnings for entire words.

Assoc = associate; association
Info = information
Subj = subject

4. Form plurals by adding *s* to shortened words.

Prblms = problems
Envlps = envelopes
Prntrs = printers

5. Make up your own symbols and use them consistently.

b/4 = before
4tn = fortune
2thake = toothache

6. Use standard or informal abbreviations for proper nouns such as places, people, companies, scientific substances, events, and so on.

BC = British Columbia
H_2O = water
Moz. = Wolfgang Amadeus Mozart

7. If you know that a word or phrase will be repeated, write it once and then establish an abbreviation for the rest of your notes. For example, the first time your political science instructor mentions the Iraq Study Group, the 2006 bipartisan commission that issued recommendations to the American president about the Iraq War, write the name in full. After that, use the initials ISG.

*get***Creative!**

Craft Your Own Shorthand

Now that you've read through some suggestions for shorthand, it's time to customize it to your needs.

Identify a class in which you take a lot of notes or one in which you would like to begin taking better notes.

_____

Next, write 10 terms that are used often in this class. For instance, if you were creating a list for your psychology class, you might include terms such as *Sigmund Freud, child development*, or *neuropsychology*.

_____

_____

_____

_____

_____

Finally, create a list of shorthand terms for the items you chose. Be creative but remember that they should be easy for you to remember and use. Thus, your shorthand should not be longer or more complex than the word itself. Use numbers, symbols, or even small images (such as a heart or smiley face). For the list of psychology terms, the shorthand might look like the following:

Sigmund Freud	=	**SigFrd**
Child development	=	**ChDev**
Neuropsychology	=	**nro-psych**

8. Write only what is essential. Include only the information nuggets you want to remember, even if your instructor says much more. Do this by paring down your writing. Say, for example, your instructor had the following to say on the subject of hate crimes.[3]

> After the terrorist attacks in the United States on September 11, 2001, law enforcement officials noted a dramatic shift in the nature of hate crimes. For the first time, replacing crimes motivated by race as the leading type of hate crime were crimes that targeted religious and ethnic groups and particularly Muslims.

Your shorthand notes might look something like this:

—After 9/11 HCs ▲ focus & targeted religious and ethnic groups, esp. Muslims
—Reduction of HC based on race

Tips for Learning Online

- *Take notes.* A variety of available technologies allow you to take online notes, just as you would mark up a regular textbook. You can highlight important passages and insert your own notes (or think links) within your online ebook.

- *Listen.* If your professors make their lectures available in podcast form, either on iTunes or on the school's learning management system (LMS), download and listen to them.

- Share. Using Google Docs, your school's LMS, or a Facebook page share notes with your classmates. This is useful if you miss a class or didn't quite understand the content of the lecture. While sharing notes is not a substitute for attending a class, it does offer a way to get caught up if you miss a class or two.

What happened to Maya? With Ross's help, Maya passed the mid-term. Afterwards, she found herself once again "there but not there" in her contemporary civilization class as well as others. Trying to find meaning in the coursework, she talked with her parents. Her mother commented that she was building incredible skills for life because not having much interest in the material meant that Maya needed extra motivation, commitment, and responsibility to get through it successfully. This comment awakened a sense of pride in Maya. Determined to improve during the remaining weeks, she concentrated on finding a note-taking system that made sense to her and deliberately used it in her classes. She found that the structure actually helped her pay more attention, and her increased focus helped her notice some ideas that interested her more than she had expected.

Case Wrap-up

What does this mean for you? Nearly every student has to fulfill core requirements as part of a degree program. Chances are that some—or even many—of the core courses you have to take will not be on your list of favourites. In many ways, this experience is a useful exercise for life, in which you will rarely be able to choose your favourite job, most desired co-workers, ideal neighbours, or perfect day-to-day schedule. Sure, sometimes you may find a way to enjoy a particular course, even if the material doesn't inspire you. You may make friends in the class, develop a good relationship with the instructor, or get motivated by the simple fact that passing the course moves you toward your goal of graduation. However, just getting through it with your GPA intact can teach you a useful skill—how to take something valuable away from any experience.

What effects go beyond your world? Searching for meaning in your coursework or your working life can mean more than just fulfillment for you. The more interested, committed, and fulfilled you are, the more the benefits radiate out from you and affect others. Read the article "Meaningful Work" located at www.psychologytoday.com/blog/the-meaning-in-life/200905/work-youre-meant-do-or-just-paid-do. Reflect on what kind of job might fulfill the three criteria for meaningful work (it must make sense to you, have a point or goal, and serve the greater good in some way). Brainstorm ideas for work that you believe would have positive effects on others, going beyond your needs for a steady paycheque and personal fulfillment.

Successful Intelligence*Wrap-up*

HERE'S HOW YOU HAVE BUILT SKILLS IN **CHAPTER 3**:

ANALYTICAL THINKING	CREATIVE THINKING	PRACTICAL THINKING
› You examined common challenges you face when listening.	› You developed new systems for note taking and how to apply them to your courses.	› You compiled practical tools for managing listening challenges.
› In the Get Analytical exercise, you analyzed your own listening skills to better understand your personal needs.	› In the Get Creative exercise, you brainstormed personal shorthand terms to speed up note taking.	› In the Get Practical exercise, you explored how to use note-taking systems in difficult situations.
› You explored note-taking systems and considered which would work best for you given certain locations and classes.	› You may have been inspired to think about new ways in which you might listen and receive information in classes.	› You learned shorthand techniques to add to your understanding of note-taking strategies.

Word*for*Thought

In **Swedish**, the word *lagom* (lagh-ohm) refers to the place between extremes, the spot that is neither too much nor too little, but just right.[4] Think of the quest for *lagom* as you work to improve listening and note-taking skills. You can never hope to take in and record every word your instructor says—and that's okay. You are aiming for "just right."

Building Skills for
Post-Secondary, Career, and Life Success

Steps to Success

Your Best Listening and Note-Taking Conditions

STEP 1 BUILD BASIC SKILLS. Think of a recent class in which you were able to listen and take notes effectively.

_____
_____
_____
_____

Describe the environment (course title, classroom setting, and so on):

_____
_____
_____

Describe the instructor's style (lecture, group discussion, Q and A):

_____
_____
_____

Describe your level of preparation and attitude toward the class:

_____
_____
_____
_____

Describe the note-taking style you generally use in the class and how effective it is for you:

_____
_____
_____
_____

Describe any barriers to effective listening that were present:

_____
_____
_____
_____

Now think of a recent class in which you found it *hard to listen* and *take notes*.

Describe the environment (course title, classroom setting, and so on):

_____
_____
_____
_____

Describe the instructor's style (lecture, group discussion, Q and A):

_____
_____
_____
_____

Describe your level of preparation and attitude toward the class:

_____
_____
_____
_____

Describe the note-taking style you generally use in the class and how effective it is for you:

_____
_____
_____
_____

Describe any barriers to effective listening that were present:

_____
_____
_____
_____

STEP 2 TAKE IT TO THE NEXT LEVEL. Examine the two situations. From what you notice, identify three conditions that seem, for you, to be crucial for effective listening and note taking:

1. _____

2. _____

3. _____

STEP 3 MOVE TOWARD MASTERY. Think about the more difficult listening and note-taking situation. For each of the three conditions you named, describe either how you can make sure that condition occurs or how you can compensate for it if it is out of your control.

1. _____

2. _____

3. _____

Teamwork

Create Solutions Together

TEAM UP TO TAKE NOTES

> *Goal:* To create a note-taking team.
>
> *Time on task:* One week; 30 minutes of review
>
> *Instructions:* In your most demanding course, form a study group with two classmates. Ask everyone to gather together a week's worth of class notes so that you can review and compare the different versions. Focus on the following:
>
> - Legibility (Can everyone read what is written?)
> - Completeness (Did you all record the same information? If not, why not?)
> - Organizational effectiveness (Does everyone get an idea of how ideas flow?)
> - Value of the notes as a study aid (Will this help everyone remember the material?)

What did you learn? Use your insights to improve personal note-taking skills. As a bonus, exchange contact information with the two students. Contact them to swap notes in the future or form a study group.

Writing

Build Intrapersonal and Communication Skills

Record your thoughts on a separate piece of paper, in a journal, or electronically.

EMOTIONAL INTELLIGENCE JOURNAL

Understanding your needs and making changes. Think about a situation when you've had trouble taking effective notes. Was it the teacher's pace? The subject matter of the class? How did you feel about the situation, and what did you do? After you describe the situation, find and write three note-taking strategies discussed in this chapter that could help you in the future. How might they help you create a more positive outcome?

REAL-LIFE WRITING

Determining the best method for you. Over the next week, commit to trying at least two different types of note-taking systems in your classes. If possible, choose a different method for each subject. Prepare for your method before entering the class by readying your notebook with the correct formatting. Try to complete your classes by using the new method. When the week is over, reflect on which style worked best for you and which would be the most beneficial going forward.

Personal Portfolio

Prepare for Career Success

LEARN MORE ABOUT CAREER SUCCESS

21st Century Learning Building Blocks

- Financial, Economic, Business, and Entrepreneurial Literacy
- Information Literacy
- Media Literacy

Complete the following in your electronic portfolio or separately on paper.

Put your listening and note-taking skills to work as you investigate what brings success in the workplace. Write down a few potential career areas that interest you.

1. _____

2. _____

3. _____

Next, visit an Internet website that hosts user-loaded videos such as YouTube.com. Perform a search for a career interview of your choice. You might try search terms such as "marketing interview," "what's it like to be a dental technician?" or "what does a movie producer do?" When you've found a usable video (keep in mind that you're looking for credible, realistic information), practise one of the note-taking techniques discussed in this chapter.

Watch the video once all the way through, concentrating on main points and overall themes. Then, watch it again focusing on filling in gaps, understanding key terms and concepts, and gathering interesting extras. Remember to use shorthand when necessary.

After you've watched the video twice and taken thorough notes, write a one-page summary of the career for your portfolio. Include important information discussed in the video, such as the training required, salary expectations, daily duties, and so on. Keep the summary in your portfolio for future career searches.

Social Networking

BUILD CONTACTS

Begin to build, or continue to build, your network on LinkedIn. Sign in to your account and click on "Add Connections." Find and contact 10 people in one of the following ways:

- Enter the name of someone you know in the "People" field at the top of the screen to see whether that person has a LinkedIn account. If he or she does, click on "Add to network" to invite them to join your network.
- Use the "See Who You Already Know on LinkedIn" feature to search your email contacts for people who have LinkedIn accounts.
- In the "Enter Email Addresses" box, enter the email addresses of people you want to invite to your network. Each will receive an invitation, regardless of whether they are already LinkedIn members.

Think carefully about who you want as part of your network. Consider family, friends, and co-workers. Choose people who you believe will help you move forward toward your goals, and who you think may have interesting and useful networks themselves.

chapter 4

Memory and Studying
Retaining What You Learn

What Would You Do?

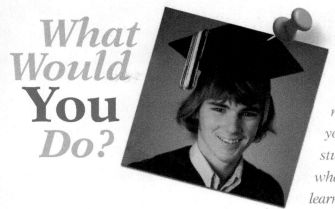

Think about this problem as you read, and consider how you would approach it. This chapter introduces you to how memory works and then helps you put your memory to work effectively as you study. Although it's easier to remember what you want to know, the strategies you learn will help you study materials no matter how you feel about them.

Norton Ewart struggled from fourth grade through high school. Overwhelmed by the work and the level of independence, he did the least amount of work possible and earned a C average. He enrolled in a liberal arts program out of a desire to please his parents. Uninterested in the coursework and not ready for the independence of post-secondary life, Norton hitchhiked home each weekend to work as a house painter and left school 10 weeks later. He then moved to his aunt's house in Colorado, where he skied black diamond runs, worked as a ski technician, and tried to figure out who he was and what he wanted.

After two years, Norton decided he wanted to return to college and moved back home. Thinking he might follow the family path of engineering, as had three generations before him, he decided to pursue a degree in math and science. Despite his new-found confidence and the fun state-of-the-art calculator his father had given him, Norton could not move on right away from his inconsistent study habits. He received Cs and Ds in calculus and physics courses during his first year.

Norton was behind, but for the first time he was determined to excel. He found himself enjoying the creativity and beauty of math and how the mind interacts with it. On the advice of an academic advisor, he spent a year in a civil technology program while retaking every calculus and physics course. Aware that he was more motivated when working with others, Norton put together a study group. His

group of fellow engineering students called themselves the "Engineering Defense League" and met daily to work through problems, drill one another on formulas and problem-solving steps, and experience the struggle together. (To be continued . . .)

Skiing and working gave Norton a sense of ownership of his success as well as a desire—and a reason—to get back to school. You'll learn more about Norton, and revisit his situation, within the chapter.

In this chapter, you'll explore answers to these questions:

> How does memory work? p. 92

> How can you remember what you study? p. 95

> What will help you remember math and science material? p. 107

> How can mnemonic devices boost recall? p. 109

> What study strategies help you put it all together? p. 113

MyStudentSuccessLab

Use these interactive tools to help you succeed in your course and career:
• Videos
• Exercises and applied activities
• Practice quizzes

STATUS *Check*

For each statement, circle the number that feels right to you, from
1 for "not at all true for me" to 5 for "very true for me."

▶ I know that not everything that I hear and read will necessarily stay in my memory for long—or at all.	**1 2 3 4 5**
▶ When I am studying, I try to choose what is most important to remember.	**1 2 3 4 5**
▶ Through trial and error, I have figured out study locations and times that work best for me.	**1 2 3 4 5**
▶ After a test or presentation is over, I retain much of what I had to know.	**1 2 3 4 5**
▶ I write, rewrite, and summarize information to remember it.	**1 2 3 4 5**
▶ I use flash cards and other active memory strategies to remember what I study.	**1 2 3 4 5**
▶ I create mnemonic devices with images and associations as memory hooks.	**1 2 3 4 5**
▶ I try to review material in several sessions over time rather than cram the night before a test.	**1 2 3 4 5**
▶ If I find myself looking up something over and over again, I make an effort to memorize it.	**1 2 3 4 5**
▶ I know how to study class and text notes effectively to prepare for tests.	**1 2 3 4 5**

Each of the topics in these statements is covered in this chapter. Note those statements for which you circled a 3 or lower. Skim the chapter to see where those topics appear, and pay special attention to them as you read, learn, and apply new strategies.

REMEMBER: *No matter how developed your memory and studying skills are, you can improve with effort and practice.*

"Successfully intelligent people are aware of the circumstances under which they are able to function at their best. They create those circumstances and then use them to their maximum advantage."

—Robert Sternberg

How does memory work?

Memory anchors all learning and performance—on tests as well as at work. The information you remember—concepts, facts, processes, formulas, and more—is the raw material with which you think, write, create, build, and perform day-to-day in school and out. Tasks ranging from high-level chemistry experiments to running a load of laundry through the washing machine all require you to retain and use information in your memory.

Memorization also gives you the tools to tackle higher-level thinking, such as in Chapter 2's discussion of Bloom's taxonomy (see pages 127–129). You need to recall and understand information before you can apply, analyze, synthesize, or evaluate it.

Through studying, you build your memory and use it to move toward your goals. This chapter provides a host of memory improvement techniques that you can make your own with a positive attitude and active involvement. The first step is exploring how memory works.

The information processing model of memory

Memory refers to the way the brain stores and recalls information or experiences that are acquired through the five senses. Although you take in thousands of

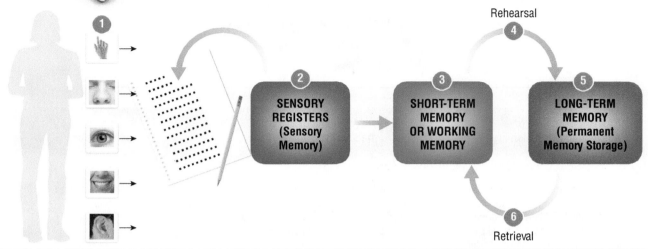

pieces of information every second—everything from the shape and colour of your chair to how your history text describes Sir John A. Macdonald's terms as prime minister—you remember few. Unconsciously, your brain sorts through stimuli and stores only what it considers important.

Key 4.1 illustrates how the brain forms lasting memories.

1. Raw information, gathered through the five senses, reaches the brain (for example, the tune of a song you're learning in your jazz ensemble class).

2. This information enters **sensory registers,** where it stays for only seconds. (As you play the notes for the first time, the sounds stop first in your auditory register.)

3. You then choose whether to pay attention to information in the sensory register. When you selectively look, listen, smell, taste, or feel the information, you move it into **short-term memory,** also known as *working memory*, which contains what you are thinking at any moment and from where information can be made available for further processing. (The part of the song that is your responsibility, for example, the clarinet solo, will likely take up residence in your working memory.) You can temporarily keep information in short-term memory through *rote rehearsal*—the process of repeating information to yourself or even out loud.

4. Information moves to **long-term memory** through focused, active rehearsal repeated over time. (As you practise the song in class and at home, your brain stores the pitch, rhythm, and tempo in your long-term memory, where you will be able to draw on it again.) Long-term memory stores everything you know, from the dates of both World Wars to the location of your elementary school. As shown in Key 4.2, long-term memory has three separate storage houses. There are no limits to how much information long-term memory can hold or how long it is held, but most people retain memories of personal experiences and procedures longer than concepts, facts, formulas, and dates.

When you need a piece of information from long-term memory, the brain retrieves it and places it in short-term memory. On test day, this enables you to

SENSORY REGISTER
Brain filters through which sensory information enters the brain and is sent to short-term memory.

SHORT-TERM MEMORY
The brain's temporary information storehouse, in which information remains for a limited time (from a few seconds to half a minute).

LONG-TERM MEMORY
The brain's permanent information storehouse, from which information can be retrieved.

Long-Term Memory

Storage of Procedural Memory	**Storage of Declarative Memory**	**Storage of Episodic Memory**
Storage for information about procedures, in other words, how to do things—ride a bike, drive a car, tie your shoes. It can take a while to develop these memories, but they are difficult to lose.	Memories of facts, concepts, formulas, and so on. These are relatively easy to learn, but are easy to forget without continual review.	Memories of events linked to personal experiences.

$$x = \frac{-b \pm \sqrt{b^2 - 4ac}}{2a}$$

choose the right answer on a multiple-choice question or prepare a fact-based argument for an essay question.

The movement of information in your brain, from short-term to long-term memory and then back again, strengthens the connections among neurons (brain cells). Learning happens and memories are built when neurons grow new dendrites and form new synapses. When you learn an algebra formula, for example, your brain creates new connections. Every time you review it, the connections get stronger.

Why you forget

Health issues and poor nutrition can cause memory problems. Stress is also a factor; research shows that even short-term stress can interfere with cell communication in the learning and memory regions of the brain.[1] *However, the most common reason that information fails to stay in long-term memory is ineffective studying*—not doing what you should to retain what you learn.

As Key 4.3 shows, retaining information requires continual review. You are still learning information 10 minutes after you hear it for the first time. If you review the material over time—after 24 hours, a week, a month, 6 months, and more—you will retain the knowledge. If you do not review, the neural connections will weaken, and eventually you will forget. For Norton, a combination of unfocused listening and reading and a lack of consistent studying made it tough for him to retain important information.

In a classic study conducted in 1885, researcher Hermann Ebbinghaus memorized a list of meaningless three-letter words such as *CEF* and *LAZ*. He then examined how quickly he forgot them.

REVIEWING IS ESSENTIAL FOR
MAINTAINING MEMORIES

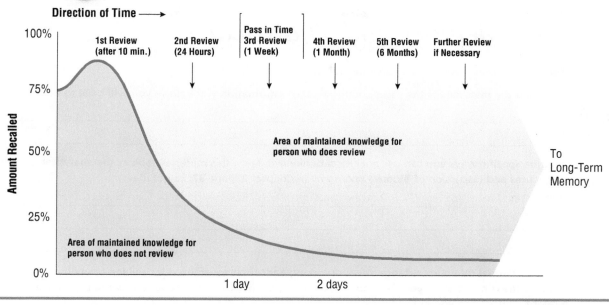

Direction of Time ⟶

1st Review (after 10 min.)	
2nd Review (24 Hours)	
Pass in Time 3rd Review (1 Week)	
4th Review (1 Month)	
5th Review (6 Months)	
Further Review if Necessary	

Amount Recalled

100%
75%
50%
25%
0%

Area of maintained knowledge for person who does review

Area of maintained knowledge for person who does not review

To Long-Term Memory

1 day   2 days

Source: From Tony Buzan, *Use Both Sides of Your Brain*, copyright © 1974, 1983, 1991 by Tony Buzan. Used by permission of Dutton, a division of Penguin Group (USA) Inc., and by kind permission of Tony Buzan, www.thinkbuzan.com.

Within one hour, he had forgotten more than 50 percent of what he had learned; after two days, he knew fewer than 30 percent of the memorized words. Although Ebbinghaus's recall of the nonsense syllables remained fairly stable after that, his experiment shows how fragile memory can be—even when you take the time and expend the energy to memorize information.[2]

Now that you know more about how memory works, get down to the business of learning how to retain the information you think is important and how to provide that information when you need it.

How can you remember what you study?

Whatever you study—textbooks, course materials, notes, primary sources—your goal is to anchor important information in long-term memory so that you can use it, for both short-term goals such as tests and long-term goals such as being an information technology specialist. To remember what you study, you need to carefully figure out and use what works best for you. One great way to do this is with *journalists' questions*—the six questions journalists need to answer to write an effective newspaper story.

1. *When, Where, Who.* Determine the times, places, and company (or none) that suit you.

2. *What, Why.* Choose what is important to study, and set the rest aside.

3. *How.* Find the specific tips and techniques that work best for you.

*get*Analytical!

Link Memory and Analytical Thinking

Identify your most interesting course this term.

Analyzing the material for the course, name a set of information you believe you will have to memorize:

_____

_____

Describe specific ways you can use analytical thinking to learn this material (look at the analytical thinking procedures and discussion of Bloom's taxonomy in Chapter 2, page 37, to get ideas):

_____

_____

_____

Will the material retain importance in your working and/or personal life after college or university? If so, describe the connection. If your first response is no, think more carefully about how the experience of learning it might be useful to you in the future.

_____

_____

When, where, and who: Choosing your best setting

Figuring out the *when*, *where*, and *who* of studying is all about self-management. You analyze what works best for you, create ideas about how to put that self-knowledge to work, and use practical thinking to implement those ideas as you study.

When

The first part of *When* is "How Much." Having the right amount of time for the job is crucial. One formula for success is the simple calculation you read about earlier in this book: *for every hour you spend in the classroom each week, spend at least two to three hours preparing for the class.* For example, if you are carrying a course load of 15 credit hours, you should spend at least 30 hours a week studying outside of class. Check your syllabus for the dates reading assignments are due, and give yourself enough time to complete them.

The second part of *When* is "What Time." If two students go over their biology notes from 8:00 to 9:00 A.M., but one is a morning person who went to bed at 11:00 P.M. and the other is a night owl who hit the sack around 2:00 A.M., you can guess who has a greater chance of remembering the information.

First, determine the time available to you in between classes, work, and other commitments. Then, thinking about when you function best, choose your study times carefully. You may not always have the luxury of being free during your peak energy times—but do the best you can.

The third part of *When* is "How Close to Original Learning." Because most forgetting happens right after learning, as you saw in Key 4.3, the review that helps you retain information most effectively happens close to when you first learn the material. If you can, review notes the same day you took them in class, make an organizer of important information from a text chapter shortly after you read it, or write a summary of a group study session within 24 hours of the meeting.

The final part of *When* is "When to Stop." Take a break, or go to sleep, when your body is no longer responding. Forcing yourself to study when you're not focused doesn't work.

The study location that works for you depends on your individual needs. This student has found he can concentrate best on his physical geology material if he reads it at a table in the library.
© Davis Barber/PhotoEdit

Where

Where you study matters. As with time, consider your restrictions first—there may be only so many places available to you, within a reasonable travel distance, and open when you have study time free. Also, analyze previous study sessions. If you spent more than 20 percent of your time blocking out distractions at a particular location, try someplace different.

Who

Some students prefer to study alone, and some in pairs or groups. Many mix it up, doing some kinds of studying—first reading, close reading, creating note sets—alone, and others—test review, problem sets—with one or more people. Some find that they prefer to study certain subjects alone and others with a group. For Norton, knowing he was going to work with others motivated him to be prepared, and sharing the work helped him learn.

Even students who study primarily alone can benefit by working with others from time to time. Besides the obvious benefit of greater communication and teamwork skills, group study enhances your ability to remember information in several ways:[3]

▶ Gets you to say what you know out loud, which solidifies your understanding

▶ Exposes you to the ideas of others and gets you thinking in different ways

▶ Increases the chance that all of the important information will be covered

▶ Motivates you to study in preparation for a group meeting

▶ Subjects you to questions about your knowledge, and maybe even some challenges, that make you clarify and build on your thinking

Instructors sometimes initiate student study groups, commonly for math or science courses, as peer-assisted study sessions or supplemental instruction. However, don't wait for your instructor—or for exam crunch time—to benefit from studying with others. As you begin to get to know students in your classes,

getPractical!

Answer Your Journalist's Questions

Think about a past study session that did not prepare you well for a test, and recall which strategies—if any—you used.

Now, plan a study session that will take place within the next seven days—one that will help you learn something important for one of your current courses. Answer the following questions to create your session:

When will you study, and for how long?

_____

Where will you study?

_____

Who will you study with, if anyone?

_____

What will you study?

_____

Why is this material important to know?

_____

How will you study it—what strategy (or strategies) do you plan to use?

_____

_____

How do you think the journalists' questions in this structure would have helped you get more from your previous study session?

_____

_____

The final step is putting this plan to work. Date you will use it: _____

start now to exchange phone numbers and email addresses, form groups, and schedule meetings. Here are some strategies for study group success:

▶ *Limit group size.* Groups of five or less tend to experience the most success.

▶ *Set long-term and short-term goals.* At your first meeting, determine what the group wants to accomplish, and set mini-goals at the start of the first meeting.

▶ *Determine a regular schedule and leadership rotation.* Determine what your group needs and what the members' schedules can handle. Try to meet weekly or, at the least, every other week. Rotate leadership among members willing to lead.

▶ *Create study materials for one another.* Give each person a task of finding a piece of information to compile and share with the group. Teach material to one another.

▶ *Share the workload and pool note-taking resources.* The most important factor is a willingness to work, not knowledge level. Compare notes with group members and fill in information you don't have.

▶ *Know how to be an effective leader.* The leader needs to define projects, assign work, set schedules and meeting goals, and keep people focused, motivated, and moving ahead.

▶ *Know how to be an effective participant.* Participants are "part owners" of the team process with a responsibility for, and a stake in, the outcome. Participants need to be organized, fulfill the tasks they promise to do, and stay open to discussion.

One final part of *Who* is dealing with "Who Might Be Distracting." You may have friends who want you to go out. You may have young children or other family members who need you. Think carefully about your choices. Do you want to head out with a group of friends you can see anytime, even if it compromises your ability to do well in an important course? Can you schedule your study time when your kids are occupied for an hour or so?

Tell your friends why studying is important to you. Friends who truly care about you are likely to support your goals. Tell your kids (if they are old enough to understand) what your education and eventual degree will mean to you—and to them. Children may be more able to cope if they see what lies at the end of the road. Key 4.4 shows some ways that parents or others caring for children can maximize their efforts.

MANAGE CHILDREN
WHILE STUDYING

STUDYING WITH CHILDREN	STUDYING WITH INFANTS
• **Keep them up-to-date on your schedule.** Kids appreciate being involved, even though they may not understand entirely. Let them know when you have a big test or project due and what they can expect of you.	• **Utilize your baby's sleeping schedule.** Study at night if your baby goes to sleep early or in the morning if your baby sleeps late.
• **Find help.** Know your schedule and arrange for child care if necessary. Consider offering to help another parent in exchange for babysitting, hiring a sitter, or using a daycare centre.	• **Make time in the middle.** Study during nap times if you aren't too tired yourself.
• **Utilize techonology.** You may be able to have a study session over the phone, through instant messaging, by email, or over social networking sites. Additionally, some sites offer tools that allow multiple users to work on a document or project remotely.	• **Talk to your baby.** Recite your notes to the baby. The baby will appreciate the attention, and you will get work done.
• **Be prepared and keep them active.** Consider keeping some toys, activities, or books that only come out during study time. This strategy will make the time special for children.	• **Keep them close.** Put your baby in a safe and fun place while you study, such as a playpen, motorized swing, or jumping seat.
• **Plan for family time.** Offset your time away from your children with plans to do something together such as watch a movie or go out for ice cream. Children may be more apt to let you study when they have something to look forward to.	

What and why: Evaluating study materials

Even if you had hours of study time and boundless energy, you would likely be overloaded if you studied every word and bit of information. Before you get ready to dive into your books and materials, engage your analytical thinking skills for a critical task: decide *what* to study by examining *why* you need to know it. Here's how to accomplish this:

▶ *Choose materials to study.* Put away materials or notes you know you do not need to review. Then examine what's left. Within textbooks or other materials, which chapters or sections are important to know for your immediate goal (for example, to study for an upcoming test) and why? Thinking about the Why highlights your purpose and can increase your focus.

▶ *Prioritize materials.* First of all, there's no point in spending the bulk of your study time reviewing material you already know well. Determine what you need the most work on, and study that first. Almost every student has more steam at the beginning of a study session than at the end; plus, fatigue or an interruption may prevent you from covering everything.

▶ *Set specific goals.* Looking at what you need to cover and the time available, decide what you will accomplish—for example, reading a specific section in a certain textbook, reviewing three sets of class notes, and creating a study sheet from both the book and your notes. Make a list for reference and check things off as you go.

▶ *Within the sections you study, separate main points from unimportant details.* Ask yourself, "What is the most important information?" Highlight only the key points in your texts, and write notes in the margins about main ideas.

How: Using study strategies

After figuring out the *When*, *Where*, *Who*, *What*, and *Why* of studying, focus on the *How* —the strategies that will anchor the information you need in your brain (Key 4.5). You may already use several of them. Try as many as you can, and keep what works.

Have purpose, intention, and emotional connection

If you can remember the lyrics to dozens of popular songs but not the functions of the pancreas, perhaps emotion is involved. When you care about something, your brain responds differently, and you learn and remember more easily.

To achieve the same results in school, try to create a purpose and will to remember by a kind of emotional involvement with what you study. For example, an accounting student might think of a friend who is running a small business and needs to keep his records in order—to pay bills on time, to record income, to meet tax payments. Putting himself in the position of his friend's accountant, the student connects learning accounting principles with making a difference in a friend's life.

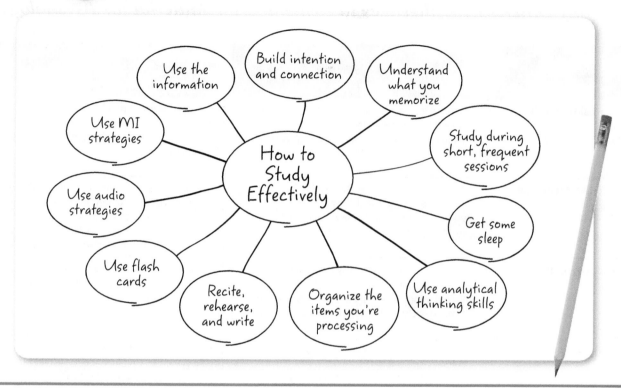

How to Study Effectively

- Use the information
- Build intention and connection
- Understand what you memorize
- Use MI strategies
- Study during short, frequent sessions
- Use audio strategies
- Get some sleep
- Use flash cards
- Recite, rehearse, and write
- Organize the items you're processing
- Use analytical thinking skills

Put your notes to work

It is common to let notes sit in a notebook unread until just before mid-terms or finals. Even the most comprehensive, brilliant notes won't do you any good if you don't refer back to them. Regularly reread your notes in batches (for example, every one or two weeks) to build your recall of information. As you reread, do the following:

▶ Fill in any gaps or get help with trouble spots.

▶ Mark up your notes by highlighting main ideas and key supporting points.

▶ Add recall or practice test questions in the margins.

▶ Add relevant points from homework, text, and lab work into your notes.

Understand what you memorize

It sounds kind of obvious—but something that has meaning is easier to recall than something that makes little sense. This basic principle applies to everything you study. Figure out logical connections, and use these connections to help you learn. For example, in a plant biology course, memorize plants in family groups; in a history course, link events in a cause-and-effect chain.

When you have trouble remembering something new, think about how the new idea fits into what you already know. A simple example: If you can't remember what a word means, look at the word's root, prefix, or suffix.

Apply Different Intelligences to Remembering Material for Psychology

INTELLIGENCE	USE MI STRATEGIES TO REMEMBER MORE EFFECTIVELY	APPLY MI MEMORY STRATEGIES TO THE TOPIC OF MOTIVATION AND EMOTION FOR A PSYCHOLOGY COURSE
Verbal-Linguistic	• Develop a story line for a mnemonic first; then work on the visual images. • Write out answers to practice essay questions.	• Answer learning objectives as though they were essay questions: "What are three types of needs?" "What are instinct approaches to motivation?" *
Logical-Mathematical	• Create logical groupings that help you memorize knowledge chunks. • When you study material in the middle, link it to what comes before and after.	• Group and compare the theories of emotion—the James–Lange theory, the Cannon–Bard theory, the Schachter–Singer cognitive arousal theory, the facial feedback hypothesis, and Lazarus's cognitive-mediational theory.
Bodily-Kinesthetic	• Re-enact concepts physically if you can to solidify them in memory. • Record information onto a digital recorder and listen as you walk between classes.	• Model facial expressions with another student and take turns guessing the emotion behind the expression.
Visual-Spatial	• Focus on visual mnemonics such as mental walks. • Use markers to add colour to the images you use in your mnemonics.	• Create a colourful mnemonic to remember maladaptive eating problems such as obesity, anorexia nervosa, and bulimia.
Interpersonal	• Do flash card drills with a study partner. • Recite important material to a study partner.	• Working with a study partner, recite and explain Maslow's hierarchy of needs to each other.
Intrapersonal	• Listen to an audio podcast that reviews test material. • Create vocabulary cartoons and test yourself on the material.	• Understand incentive approaches by considering what kind of external stimuli create incentive for you.
Musical	• Play music while you brainstorm ideas. • Create a mnemonic in the form of a musical rhyme.	• Write a rap that lists and explains the different approaches to understanding motivation.
Naturalistic	• Organize what you have to learn so you see how everything fits together. • Sit outside and go through your flash cards.	• Make a chart organizing explanatory details of the three elements of emotion—physiology, behaviour, and subjective experience.

*For information on motivation and emotion, see Saundra K. Ciccarelli and Glenn E. Meyer, *Psychology*. Upper Saddle River, NJ: Prentice Hall, 2006.

Knowing that the root *bellum* means "war" and the prefix *ante* means "before" will help you recognize that *antebellum* means "before the war."

Study during short, frequent sessions

You can improve your chances of remembering material by learning it more than once. A pattern of short sessions—say, three 20-minute study sessions—followed by brief periods of rest is more effective than continual studying with little or no rest. Try studying on your own or with a classmate during breaks in your schedule. Although studying between classes isn't for everyone, you may find that it can help you remember more.

In addition, scheduling regular, frequent review sessions over time will help you retain information more effectively. If you have two weeks before a test, set up study sessions three times per week instead of putting the final two days aside for hours-long study marathons.[4]

When you study for a test with a classmate, you can help each other understand difficult concepts as well as fill in the holes in each other's notes.
© Shutterstock

Get your body ready

Even though sleep may take a back seat with all you have to do in crunch times, research indicates that short-changing your sleep during the week impairs your ability to remember and learn, even if you try to make up for it by sleeping all weekend.[5] Sleep improves your ability to remember what you studied before you went to bed. So does having a good breakfast. Even if you're running late, grab enough food to fill your stomach.

Use analytical thinking skills

Analytical, or critical, thinking encourages you to associate new information with what you already know. Imagine you have to remember information about the signing of the Treaty of Versailles, which ended World War I. How can critical thinking help?

▶ Recall everything that you know about the topic.

▶ Think about how this event is similar to other events in history.

▶ Consider what is different and unique about this treaty in comparison to other treaties.

▶ Explore the causes that led up to this event, and look at the event's effects.

▶ Evaluate how successful you think the treaty was.

This critical exploration makes it easier to remember the material you are studying.

Organize the items you are processing

▶ *Divide material into manageable sections.* Master each section, put all the sections together, and then test your memory of all the material.

▶ *Use the chunking strategy.* **Chunking** increases the capacity of short-term and long-term memory. For example, though it is hard to remember these 10 digits—4808371557—it is easier to remember them in three chunks—480 837 1557. In general, try to limit groups to 10 items or fewer. The eight-day study plan in Key 4.6 relies on chunking.

> CHUNKING
> Placing disconnected information into smaller units that are easier to remember.

STUDY PLAN SUCCESS
DEPENDS ON A GOOD MEMORY

Key 4.6

DAY 8 (IN EIGHT DAYS, YOU'LL BE TAKING A TEST)

PLANNING DAY
- List everything that may be on the exam. (Check your syllabus and class notes; talk with your instructor.)
- Divide the material into four learning chunks.
- Decide on a study schedule for the next seven days—when you will study, with whom you will study, the materials you need, and so on.

DAY 7 (COUNTDOWN: SEVEN DAYS TO GO)

- Use the techniques described in this chapter to study chunk A.
- Memorize key concepts, facts, formulas, and so on that may be on the test.
- Take an active approach to learning: take practice tests, summarize what you read in your own words, and use critical thinking to connect ideas.

DAY 6 (COUNTDOWN: SIX DAYS TO GO)

- Use the same techniques to study chunk B.

DAY 5 (COUNTDOWN: FIVE DAYS TO GO)

- Use the same techniques to study chunk C.

DAY 4 (COUNTDOWN: FOUR DAYS TO GO)

- Use the same techniques to study chunk D.

DAY 3 (COUNTDOWN: THREE DAYS TO GO)

- Combine and review chunks A and B.

DAY 2 (COUNTDOWN: TWO DAYS TO GO)

- Combine and review chunks C and D.

DAY 1 (COUNTDOWN: ONE DAY TO GO)

PUT IT ALL TOGETHER: REVIEW CHUNKS A, B, C, AND D
- Take an active approach to review all four chunks.
- Make sure you have committed every concept, fact, formula, process, and so on to memory.
- Take a timed practice test. Write out complete answers so that concepts and words stick in your memory.
- Create a sheet with important information to memorize (again) on test day.

TEST DAY—DO YOUR BEST WORK

- Look at your last-minute study sheet right before you enter the test room so that difficult information sticks.
- As soon as you get your test, write down critical facts on the back of the paper.

Source: Adapted from the University of Arizona, "The Eight-Day Study Plan," http://ulc.arizona.edu/documents/8day_074.pdf.

▶ *Use organizational tools.* Rely on an outline, a think link, or another organizational tool to record material with logical connections among the elements (see Chapter 3 for more on note taking).

▶ *Be mindful when studying more than one subject.* When studying for several tests at once, avoid studying two similar subjects back-to-back. Your memory may be more accurate when you study history after biology rather than chemistry after biology.

▶ *Notice what ends up in the middle—and practise it.* When studying, you tend to remember what you study first and last. The weak link is likely to be what you study midway. Knowing this, try to give this material special attention.

Recite, rehearse, and write

Repetition is a helpful memory tool. The more you can repeat, and the more ways you can repeat, the more likely you are to remember. Reciting, rehearsing, and writing help you diversify your repetition and maximize memory.

When you *recite* material, you repeat key concepts aloud, summarizing them in your own words, to aid memorization. *Rehearsing* is similar to reciting but is done silently. *Writing* is reciting on paper. The following steps represent one way to benefit from these strategies:

▶ Focus as you read on *main ideas*, which are usually found in the topic sentences of paragraphs (see Chapter 2). Then recite, rehearse, or write the ideas down.

▶ Convert each main idea into a keyword, phrase, or visual image—something easy to recall that will set off a chain of memories, bringing you back to the original material. Write each keyword or phrase on an index card.

▶ One by one, look at the keywords on your cards and recite, rehearse, or write all the associated information you can recall. Check your recall against the original material.

These steps are part of the process of consolidating and summarizing lecture and text notes as you study—a key study strategy explored later in this chapter.

Reciting, rehearsing, and writing involve more than rereading material and then parroting words out loud, in your head, or on paper. Because rereading does not necessarily require involvement, you can reread without learning. However, you cannot help but think and learn when you convert text concepts into key points, rewrite main ideas as keywords and phrases, and assess what you know and what you still need to learn.

Use flash cards

Flash cards give you short, repeated review sessions that provide immediate feedback. Either find an online site on which you can create electronic flash cards or use the front of a 3-by-5-inch index card to write a word, idea, or phrase you want to remember. Use the back for a definition, explanation, example, or other key facts. Key 4.7 shows two flash cards used to study for a psychology exam.

The following suggestions can help you make the most of your flash cards:

▶ *Use the cards as a self-test.* As you go through them, create two piles—the material you know and the material you are learning.

▶ *Carry the cards with you and review frequently.* You'll learn the most if you start using cards early in the course, well ahead of exam time.

▶ *Shuffle the cards and learn the information in various orders.* This method will help you avoid putting too much focus on some items and not enough on others.

FLASH CARDS HELP YOU MEMORIZE IMPORTANT FACTS

Theory

- Definition: Explanation for a phenomenon based on careful and precise observations
- Part of the scientific method
- Leads to hypotheses

Hypothesis

- Prediction about future behaviour that is derived from observations and theories
- Methods for testing hypotheses: case studies, naturalistic observations, and experiments

▶ *Test yourself in both directions.* First, look at the terms and provide the definitions or explanations. Then turn the cards over and reverse the process.

▶ *Reduce the stack as you learn.* Eliminate cards when you know them well. As the pile shrinks, your motivation may grow. Do a final review of all the cards before the test.

Use audio strategies

Although audio strategies can benefit all students, they are especially useful if you learn best through hearing.

▶ *Create audio flash cards.* Record short-answer study questions by leaving 10 to 15 seconds blank after questions, so you can answer out loud. Record the correct answer after the pause to give yourself immediate feedback. For example, part of a recording for a writing class might say, "Three elements that require analysis before writing are . . . [10–15-second pause] . . . topic, audience, and purpose."

▶ *Use podcasts.* An increasing amount of information is presented in podcasts—knowledge segments that are downloadable to your computer or MP3 player. Ask your instructors if they intend to make any lectures available in podcast format.

Use learning styles strategies

Look back to your MI and Personality Spectrum assessments in Chapter 1. Identify your strongest areas and locate study techniques applicable for each. For example, if you scored high in bodily-kinesthetic, try reciting material aloud while standing or walking. Be open to trying something new—even if it sounds a little odd to begin with. Effective studying is about finding what works, often by any means necessary.

Use the information

In the days after you learn something new, try to use the information in every way you can. Apply it to new situations and link it to problems. Explain the material to a classmate. Test your knowledge to make sure the material is in long-term memory. "Don't confuse recognizing information with being able to recall it," says learning expert Adam Robinson. "Be sure you can recall the information without looking at your notes for clues. And don't move on until you have created some sort of sense-memory hook for calling it back up when you need it."[6]

What will help you remember math and science material?

The strategies you've just explored apply to all sorts of academic areas. However, recalling what you learn in math and science courses can demand particular attention and some specific techniques, as Norton really found out the second time around.

▪ **Review processes and procedures.** Much of math and science work involves knowing how to work through each step of a proof, a problem-solving process, or a lab experiment. Review your class notes as soon as possible after each class. Look at your notes with the textbook alongside and compare the lecture information to the text. Fill in missing steps in the instructor's examples before you forget them. You may want to write the instructor's examples in the text next to the corresponding topics.

▪ **Do problems, problems, and more problems.** Working through problems provides examples that will help you understand concepts and formulas. Plus, becoming familiar with a group of problems and related formulas will help you apply what you know to similar problems on other assignments and tests.

▪ **Fight frustration with action.** If you are stuck on a problem, go on to another one. If you repeatedly get a wrong answer, look at the steps you've taken and see whether anything doesn't make sense. If you hit a wall, take a break to clear your head. If you have done the assigned homework but still don't feel secure, do additional problems or ask for help.

▪ **Work with others.** Working with one or more classmates can be particularly helpful when trying to figure

---

Change the CONVERSATION

Challenge yourself and your friends to ask—and answer—tough questions. Use the following to inspire discussion in pairs or groups.

► All students experience the frustration of working hard to remember something that seems unimportant and irrelevant to their lives. How do you handle this? How should you handle it?

► What memorization techniques do you resist trying? Is it because they seem too unrelated to the information—or too goofy? What would you be willing to try out just to see whether it works?

► **CONSIDER THE CASE:** How do you respond when, like Norton, you have no interest in what you are studying? Do you attempt to find meaning, do the minimum, give up? How do the people in your life advise you to proceed—and what do you think of the advice?

TAKE A **MUSICAL APPROACH** TO MATH

"HOW MUCH IS THAT X IN THE EQUATION?"
(to the tune of "How Much Is That Doggie in the Window?")

How much is that **x** in the equation?
What value will make it be true?
To find the **x** and get the solution
The numbers attached we **undo.**

The **connector** is plus or minus seven,
To find **x** we have to **undo.**
Just write below both sides—make it even.
We **undo** to find the **x** value.

If multiply or divide is showing,
The **connector** tells what has been done.
To **undo** is where we still are going—
We're trying to get **x** alone.

Source: Reprinted with permission. Barbara Aaker, *Mathematics: The Musical,* Denver: Crazy Broad Publishing, 1999.

out math and science problems. Do as much homework as you can on your own, and then meet to discuss it and work through additional problems. Be open to other perspectives, and ask others how they arrived at answers, especially if they used different approaches. When the work is really tough, try to meet daily, as Norton's study group did.

■ *Focus on learning styles.* Use strategies that activate your strengths. A visual learner might draw pictures to illustrate problems, and an interpersonal learner might organize a study group. Musical learners might create songs describing math concepts. Barbara Aaker wrote 40 songs for her students at the Community College of Denver to help musical learners retain difficult concepts. Key 4.8 presents one of her algebra songs.

■ *Strive for accuracy.* Complete a step of an algebra problem or biology lab project inaccurately, and your answer will be incorrect. In class, the consequences of inaccuracy are reflected in low grades. In life, the consequences could show in a patient's health or in the strength of a bridge. Check over the details of your work and always try to get it exactly right.

Because many math and science courses require you to memorize sets and lists of information, one key tool is the *mnemonic device.* As you will see next, mnemonic devices create sense-memory hooks that are difficult to forget.

Craft Your Own Mnemonic

Create a mnemonic to help you remember some facts.

Identify a group of facts that you have to memorize—for example, the names of all the world's major religions or a series of elements in the periodic table.

_____

_____

Now create your own mnemonic to remember the grouping, using any of the devices in this chapter. Write the mnemonic here (or, if you need more space, use a separate sheet of paper).

_____

_____

_____

Describe your mnemonic. Is it focused on images or sounds—or both? Is it humorous, ridiculous, or colourful?

_____

_____

Considering your learning style preferences, describe why you think this particular device will help you retain the information.

_____

_____

_____

How can mnemonic devices **boost recall?**

Certain performers entertain audiences by remembering the names of 100 strangers or flawlessly repeating 30 ten-digit numbers. Although these performers probably have superior memories, they also rely on memory techniques, known as **mnemonic devices** (pronounced neh-MAHN-ick), for assistance. Mnemonics include visual images and associations and acronyms.

Mnemonics depend on vivid associations (relating new information to other information) that engage your emotions. Instead of learning new facts by *rote* (repetitive practice), associations give you a "hook" on which to hang these facts and retrieve them later. Mnemonics make information unforgettable through unusual mental associations and visual pictures.

Mnemonics take time and effort to create, and you'll have to be motivated to remember them. Because of this, use them

> MNEMONIC DEVICES
> Memory techniques that use vivid associations and acronyms to link new information to what you already know.

VISUAL IMAGES AID **RECALL**

Key 4.9

SPANISH WORD	DEFINITION	MENTAL IMAGE
carta	letter	A person pushing a shopping cart filled with letters into a post office.
dinero	money	A man eating lasagna at a diner. The lasagna is made of layers of money.
libro	book	A pile of books on a table at a library.

only when necessary—for instance, to distinguish confusing concepts that consistently trip you up. Also know that no matter how clever they are and how easy they are to remember, mnemonics usually do not contribute to understanding. Their objective is to help you memorize.

Create visual images and associations

Turning information into mental pictures helps improve memory, especially for visual learners. To remember that the Spanish artist Picasso painted *The Three Women*, you might imagine the women in a circle dancing to a Spanish song with a pig and a donkey (*pig-asso*). The best images involve bright colours, three dimensions, action scenes, inanimate objects with human traits, and humour.

As another example, say you are trying to learn some Spanish vocabulary, including the words *carta*, *dinero*, and *libro*. Instead of relying on rote learning, you might come up with mental images, such as those described in Key 4.9.

Use visual images to remember items in a list

With the *mental walk* strategy, you imagine storing new ideas in familiar locations. Say, for example, that on your next biology test you have to remember the body's major endocrine glands. To do this, think of your route to the library.

You pass the campus theatre, the science centre, the bookstore, the cafeteria, the athletic centre, and the social science building before reaching the library. At each spot along the way, you "place" a concept you want to learn. You then link the concept with a similar-sounding word that brings to mind a vivid image (see Key 4.10):

▶ At the campus theatre, you imagine bumping into actor Brad *Pitt* (pituitary gland).

▶ At the science centre, you visualize a body builder with bulging *thighs* (thyroid gland).

▶ At the campus bookstore, you envision a second body builder with his *thighs* covered in *mustard* (thymus gland).

▶ In the cafeteria, you bump into *Dean Al* (adrenal gland).

▶ At the athletic centre, you think of the school team, the Panthers—nicknamed the Pans—and remember the sound of the cheer "*Pans-R-Us*" (pancreas).

▶ At the social science building, you imagine receiving a standing *ovation* (ovaries).

▶ And at the library, you visualize sitting at a table taking a *test* that is *easy* (testes).

A **MENTAL WALK** HELPS YOU REMEMBER ITEMS IN A LIST

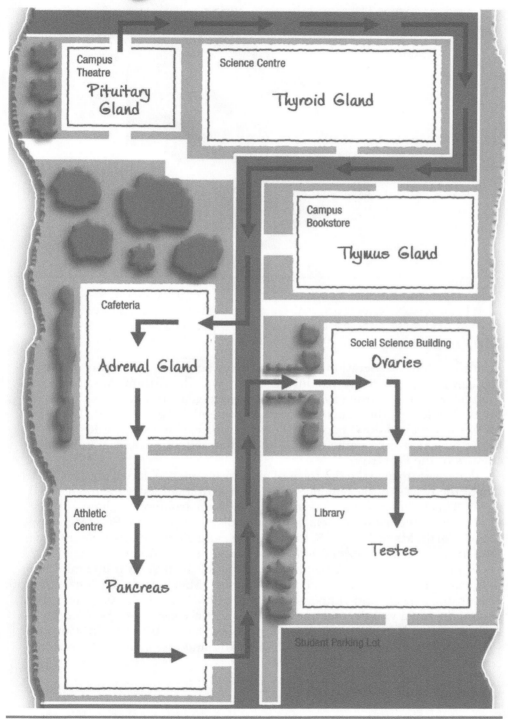

Campus Theatre — *Pituitary Gland*

Science Centre — *Thyroid Gland*

Campus Bookstore — *Thymus Gland*

Cafeteria — *Adrenal Gland*

Social Science Building — *Ovaries*

Athletic Centre — *Pancreas*

Library — *Testes*

Student Parking Lot

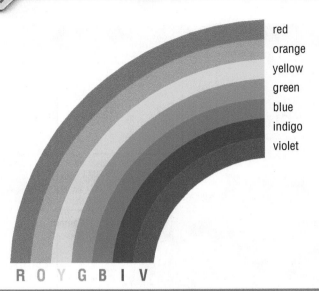

USE THIS ACRONYM TO REMEMBER THE COLOURS OF THE SPECTRUM

Key 4.11

red
orange
yellow
green
blue
indigo
violet

R O Y G B I V

Make acronyms

ACRONYM
A word formed from the first letters of a series of words created to help you remember the series.

Another helpful association method involves **acronyms.** In history class, you can remember the Allies during World War II—Britain, America, and Russia—with the acronym *BAR*. This example is a *word acronym*, because the first letters of the items you want to remember spell a word. The word (or words) spelled don't necessarily have to be real words. See Key 4.11 for an acronym—the name *Roy G. Biv* —that will help you remember the colours of the spectrum.

Other acronyms take the form of an entire sentence, in which the first letters of the words in the sentence stand for the first letters of the memorized terms. This is called a *list order acronym*. When astronomy students want to remember the list of planets in order of distance from the Sun (Mercury, Venus, Earth, Mars, Jupiter, Saturn, Uranus, and Neptune), they might learn the sentence *My very elegant mother just served us nectarines*.

Suppose you want to remember the names of the first six prime ministers of Canada. The first letters of their last names—Macdonald, Mackenzie, Abbott, Thompson, Bowell, and Tupper—together read *MMATBT*. To remember them, you might add a *y* to the end and create a short nonsense word—*mmatbty* — and remember it as the word *mmat-bity*. Since there are two *t* 's in your nonsense word, just remember that alphabetically, and historically, Thompson comes before Tupper.

Use songs or rhymes

Some of the classic mnemonic devices are rhyming poems that stick in your mind. One you may have heard is the rule about the order of *i* and *e* in spelling:

> Spell i before e, except after c, or when sounded like a as in neighbour and weigh.
> Four exceptions if you please: either, neither, seizure, seize.

Make up your own poems or songs, linking familiar tunes or rhymes with information you want to remember. For example, to continue our earlier example, if you wanted to remember the first names, as well as the last names, of the first six Canadian prime ministers—John, Alexander, John, John, Mackenzie, and Charles—you might set the names to the tune of "Happy Birthday," or any other musical tune you know.

Improving your memory requires energy, time, and work. It also helps to master SQ3R, the textbook study technique introduced in Chapter 2. By going through the steps in SQ3R and by using the specific memory techniques described in this chapter, you will be able to learn more in less time—and remember what you learn long after exams are over. These techniques will be equally valuable when you start a career.

What study strategies help you put it all together?

Especially in the later stages of review, strategies that help you combine and condense information are crucial. Such strategies help you relate information to what you know, connect information in new ways, and boost your ability to use it to think analytically and creatively, which is especially important for essay exams.

Create a summary of reading material

When you summarize main ideas in your own words, you engage analytical thinking, considering what is important to include as well as how to organize and link it together. To construct a summary, focus on the main ideas and examples that support them. Don't include your own ideas or evaluations at this point. Your summary should simply condense the material, making it easier to focus on concepts and interrelationships when you review.

Use the following suggestions for creating effective summaries:

- ▶ Organize your summary by subject or topic—a textbook chapter, for example, or an article.

- ▶ Before you summarize, identify the main ideas and key supporting details by highlighting or annotating the material.

- ▶ Wherever possible, use your own words. When studying a technical subject with precise definitions, you may have little choice but to use text wording.

- ▶ Try to make your writing simple, clear, and brief. Eliminate less important details.

- ▶ Consider creating an outline of your notes or the portion of the text so you can see how ideas relate to one another.

- ▶ Include information from tables, charts, photographs, and captions in your summary; these visual presentations may contain important information not written in the text.

- ▶ Combine word-based and visual note-taking forms that effectively condense the information, such as a concept map, timeline, chart, or outline.

- ▶ Use visual strategies such as a colour-coding system to indicate different ideas or different-coloured pens to indicate levels of importance for information.

student profile

Tia Nguyen
Ryerson University, Toronto, Ontario

About me:

I was born in Vietnam, in the city formerly known as Saigon. In the 1980s, my family and I escaped from Vietnam as refugees running from poverty and war. We arrived in Canada as immigrants when I was only three years old and my younger brother was learning to crawl. There was a lot of pressure on me because I was expected to do well in school and set an example for my younger brother. I struggled for a while, trying to figure out what I wanted to do before dedicating everything to my post-secondary education—I didn't want to waste time on the wrong program if I wasn't sure what I wanted to do. I decided to explore the work world to discover what options I had and what I'd enjoy doing. A few years ago, I decided to return to school and applied as a mature student. After being out of school for so long, the first semester at college was definitely a struggle for me. Three years later, I've obtained an advanced diploma in Business Administration—Marketing with honours from Seneca College. From there, I continued on as a direct-entry student to Ryerson University, where I'm working on obtaining a Bachelor of Commerce in Marketing Management with a minor in Finance. And I'm now sitting here writing about what student success means to me to encourage future post-secondary students—who knew?

What I focus on:

I am a visual learner. This learning style affected my study habits because I knew how important it was for me to attend every class. Being a visual learner meant that I needed to see the professor lecture and listen to his or her speech while watching visual presentations and words being written on the board. Sometimes, it's these exact visual memories that trigger a terminology, concept, or theory for me. Writing clear notes was helpful for me because sometimes during tests and examinations, I could recall images of sentences and paragraphs that I had written and could read them in my own script.

Recognizing my visual preference, to develop time-management skills, I invested in a huge wall calendar and notebook-size day planner. The wall calendar was organized, and entries were emphasized, with different colours to highlight important dates and grade percentages that I pulled directly from my course outline. While studying at my desk every night, I was reminded by my visual layout of the month of which days were going to be busiest and how far in advance I would need to begin certain assignments. And because I couldn't carry my enormous wall calendar around school—otherwise I might have!—I needed an 8½-by-11-inch planner for exactly the same purpose. It was a visual reminder, every moment of every day, of what I needed to do next.

Finally, during their in-class lectures, most professors will hint at what you can expect to see on class tests and final exams. If you listen carefully and take great notes, you can record these hints and then focus on these topics while studying. It'd be silly not to use this information to your advantage.

What will help me in the workplace:

My advice for students is to get started on things early! This will definitely help you in the workplace. Don't get into the habit of leaving things to the last minute. Post-secondary education is a great time for you to learn and master certain skills and habits that will help you find better jobs and keep them. On another note, be an active student and participate in events and programs that your institution offers. If you manage your time well, then you'll have more opportunities to get involved in your school's community. It's the extra experience and knowledge that you learn outside of the classroom that will help you in the work world.

Combine class and reading notes into a master set

Studying from either text or class notes alone is not enough; your instructor may present material in class that is not in your text or may gloss over topics that your text covers in depth. The process of combining class and text notes enables you to see patterns and relationships among ideas, find examples for difficult concepts, and much more. It takes time, but pays off enormously because it strengthens memory and offers a more cohesive and connected study tool.

Some students may prefer to act quickly, combining class and reading notes as close to that class meeting as possible so the material is fresh. Others may prefer to use this strategy nearer to mid-term or finals time.

Follow these steps to combine your class and text notes into a **master note set:**

> **MASTER NOTE SET**
> A complete, integrated note set that contains both class and text notes.

■ **Step 1: Focus on what's important by condensing to the essence.** Reduce your combined notes so they contain only main ideas and key supporting details, such as terms, dates, formulas, and examples. (Eliminating the repetition you are likely to find in your notes will also help reduce the material.) Tightening and summarizing forces you to critically evaluate which ideas are most important and to rewrite your notes with only this material. As you begin to study, move back and forth between the full set and the reduced set. Key 4.12 shows a comprehensive outline and a reduced key-term outline of the same material.

■ **Step 2: Recite what you know.** As you approach exam time, use the terms in your bare-bones notes as cues for reciting what you know about a topic. Many students assume that they know concepts simply because they understand what they read. This type of passive understanding doesn't necessarily mean that they can recreate the material on an exam or apply it to problems. Make the process more active by reciting out loud during study sessions, writing your responses on paper, making flash cards, or working with a partner.

■ **Step 3: Use critical thinking.** Now reflect on ideas in the following ways as you review your combined notes:

▶ Brainstorm examples from other sources that illustrate central ideas. Write down new ideas or questions that come up as you review.

▶ Think of ideas from your readings or from class that support or clarify your notes.

▶ Consider how your class notes differ from your reading notes and why.

▶ Apply concepts to questions at the ends of text chapters, to problems posed in class, or to real-world situations.

■ **Step 4: Create study sheets.** Putting your master notes in their shortest, most manageable (and portable) form, *a study sheet* is a one-page synthesis of all key points on one theme, topic, or process. Use critical thinking skills to organize information into themes or topics that you will need to know on an exam. On an individual study sheet, include the related lecture and text page references, a quick summary, possible questions on the topic, key terms, formulas, dates, people, examples, and so on.

■ **Step 5: Review and review again.** To ensure learning and prepare for exams, review your condensed notes, study sheets, and critical thinking questions until you know every topic cold.

Try to vary your review methods, focusing on active involvement. Recite the material to yourself, have a Q and A session with a study partner, or create and take a practice test. Another helpful technique is to summarize your notes in writing from memory after reviewing them. This process will tell you whether or not you'll be able to recall the information on a test.

Different Views of Freedom and Equality in the American Democracy

I. U.S. democracy based on 5 core values: freedom and equality, order and stability, majority rule, protection of minority rights, and participation.

   A. U.S. would be a "perfect democracy" if it always upheld these values.

   B. U.S. is less than perfect, so it is called an "approaching democracy."

II. Freedom and Equality

   A. Historian Isaiah Berlin defines freedom as either positive or negative.

      1. Positive freedoms allow citizens to exercise rights under the Constitution, including right to vote.

      2. Negative freedoms safeguard citizens from government actions that restrict certain rights, such as the right to assemble. The 1st Amendment restricts government action by declaring that "Congress shall make no law . . ."

   B. The value of equality suggests that all people be treated equally, regardless of circumstance. Different views on what equality means and the implications for society.

      1. Equality of opportunity implies that everyone has the same chance to develop inborn talents.

         a. But life's circumstances—affected by factors like race and income—differ. This means that people start at different points and have different results. E.g., a poor, inner-city student will be less prepared for college than an affluent, suburban student.

         b. It is impossible to equalize opportunity for all Americans.

      2. Equality of result seeks to eliminate all forms of inequality, including economic differences, through wealth redistribution.

   C. Freedom and equality are in conflict, say text authors Berman and Murphy: "If your view of freedom is freedom from government intervention, then equality of any kind will be difficult to achieve. If government stays out of all citizen affairs, some people will become extremely wealthy, others will fall through the cracks, and economic inequality will multiply. On the other hand, if you wish to promote equality of result, then you will have to restrict some people's freedoms—the freedom to earn and retain an unlimited amount of money, for example."*

KEY-TERM OUTLINE OF THE SAME MATERIAL

Different Views of Freedom and Equality in the American Democracy

I. America's 5 core values: freedom and equality, order and stability, majority rule, protection of minority rights, and participation.

   A. "Perfect democracy"

   B. "Approaching democracy"

II. Value #1—Freedom and equality

   A. Positive freedoms and negative freedoms

   B. Different views of equality: equality of opportunity versus equality of result

   C. Conflict between freedom and equality centres on differing views of government's role

*Larry Berman and Bruce Allen Murphy, *Approaching Democracy: Portfolio Edition*, Upper Saddle River, NJ: Prentice Hall, 2005, pp. 6–8.

What happened to Norton?   With increased effort and help from his study group, Norton did well in his courses the second time around and returned to the pre-engineering program, later transferring to Union College, where he graduated with a bachelor's in electrical engineering. He was hired by Hewlett-Packard after school and worked his way up to management over 20 years. One of several jobs there took him to Boeblingen, Germany, on international assignment for three years. His current work in the area of product management, defining high-tech products to address what the market wants and needs, combines his passion for engineering, business, and new technologies. He is still an expert skier and has learned to become just as successful in his personal life and career as he is when playing outdoors.

Case *Wrap-up*

What does this mean for you?   No student can spend every second of class time taking courses that are meaningful and inspiring. You will always experience different levels of motivation and interest for different courses. Your challenge is to find a way to do the work well when your interest doesn't provide the energy. Choose the course you are taking right now that interests you the least. Make three lists with the following headings: "Study Strategies That Can Help," "How I Will Use What I Learn in This Course," and "How I Will Reward Myself If I Persist in This Course." Then fill each list with as many items as you can. Refer to the lists whenever your focus or motivation begins to slip over the course of the term.

What effects go beyond your world?   Anywhere you turn, from your immediate neighbourhood to a country halfway around the world, you can find organizations looking for support. The demands of your everyday life may be so pressing that you cannot see how you will have the time to help out. Think about a person, place, thing, idea, or situation that has grabbed your attention and sparked your interest and emotion—your version of Norton's state-of-the-art calculator. Find an organization that relates to it and investigate to see how you can help in some small way. One action now, no matter how small, can help. Who knows? Maybe you can make time for more action in the future.

Successful Intelligence *Wrap-up*

HERE'S HOW YOU HAVE BUILT SKILLS IN CHAPTER 4:

ANALYTICAL THINKING	CREATIVE THINKING	PRACTICAL THINKING
❯ You analyzed why memory strategies work—and why people forget.	❯ You began thinking of places, times, and modes of studying that might suit you best.	❯ You explored strategies you can put to work to remember what you study, including specific strategies for math and science.
❯ You learned how analyzing your personal tendencies can help you design the most effective study plan.	❯ You considered different ways to use mnemonic devices to boost recall.	❯ You learned about how to create summaries of notes and text readings as well as helpful study sheets.
❯ In the Get Analytical exercise, you explored how analytical thinking will help you retain information for one of your courses.	❯ In the Get Creative exercise, you came up with your own mnemonic device for some information you need to remember.	❯ In the Get Practical exercise, you developed a study plan based on journalists' questions.

Word *for* Thought

Research shows that sleep helps solidify information in memory. In the Dyak language, spoken in **Borneo,** a figure called a *ngarong* (nn-ga-rawng) or "dream-helper" comes to sleepers and helps clarify ideas. Let your *ngarong* have a chance to do his or her good work—get some sleep.[7]

Building Skills for
Post-Secondary, Career, and Life Success

Steps to Success

Evaluate Your Memory

STEP 1 BUILD BASIC SKILLS.   Under each of these classifications of information in long-term memory, write down an example from your personal experience:

Episodic memory (events). Example: I remember the first time I conducted an experiment in chemistry class.

_____

_____

Declarative memory (facts). Example: I know that the party that wins the most seats in a federal election forms the next government in Canada.

_____

_____

Procedural memory (motion). Example: I know how to type without looking at the keyboard.

_____

_____

STEP 2 TAKE IT TO THE NEXT LEVEL.   Which type of information (events, facts, motion) is easiest for you to remember? Why?

_____

_____

_____

Which type of information is hardest for you to remember? Why?

_____

_____

STEP 3   MOVE TOWARD MASTERY.   Address the type of information you find *most difficult* to remember.

Name an example from your life of some information in this category that you need to be able to recall and use.

_____

_____

_____

Name two approaches from the chapter that you believe will help you strengthen it.

1. _____

2. _____

Now give both a try. Circle the one that worked best.

Teamwork

Create Solutions Together

ASSESS AND BUILD YOUR MEMORY POWER

>*Goal:* To improve your ability to remember.

>*Time on task:* 15 minutes

>*Instructions:* Gather as a class if there are fewer than 20 people, or divide into two groups if there are more. Proceed according to the following steps (you'll need a timer or a cellphone that can act as one):

>- Each person in your group should place at least one item on a table (try to avoid repeats). Try to reach a total of 15 items—from your backpack or bag, study area, home, or classroom—anything small enough to easily fit on the table. Find something that will cover them all—a jacket or newspaper, for example—and place it over the items. Let them stay covered for at least 10 minutes before beginning the activity. Alternatively, the instructor can gather 15 items ahead of time.
>- Allow one minute for everyone to look at the items, using the watch or cellphone timer.
>- When the time is up, cover the items. Each person should list as many items as possible on a sheet of paper.

Compare your lists to the actual items. Talk as a group about the results and about what you did and didn't remember. Describe your observations here.

_____

_____

_____

_____

_____

Now repeat the exercise by using a mnemonic device in the following steps:

- Talk as a group about ways to remember more items, considering different mnemonic devices or strategies. Together, choose a device or strategy to try.
- Create a new group of 15 items (if you can't swap out all of them, exchange as many as you can) and cover them.
- Uncover and allow one minute of observation as before, but focus on the mnemonic device as you look at the items.
- When time is up, cover again and make a new list.
- Think and talk about the difference between the two experiences. Write your findings here.

_____

_____

_____

_____

_____

_____

_____

_____

_____

_____

_____

_____

_____

Writing

Build Intrapersonal and Communication Skills

Record your thoughts on a separate piece of paper, in a journal, or electronically.

EMOTIONAL INTELLIGENCE JOURNAL

How feelings connect to study success.   Think about how you were feeling when you were most able to recall and use information in a high-stress situation—a test, a workplace challenge, a group presentation. What thought, action, or situation put you in this productive mindset that helped you succeed? Did you go for a run? Talk to your best friend? Take 30 minutes for yourself? Create a list of thoughts or actions that you can call on when you will be faced with a challenge to your memory and want the best possible outcome.

REAL-LIFE WRITING

Combining class and text notes.   Choose a course for which you have a test coming up in the next four weeks. Create a master set of notes for that course combining one week's classes and reading assignments (make sure it is material you need to know for your test). Your goal is to summarize and connect all the important information covered during the period.

Personal Portfolio

Prepare for Career Success

MEMORY AND NETWORKING

21st Century Learning Building Blocks

- Communication and Collaboration
- Social and Cross-Cultural Skills

Complete the following in your electronic portfolio or separately on paper.

Your ability to remember people you meet or interact with in the workplace—their names, what they do, and other relevant information about them—is an enormous factor in your career success.

Consider this scenario: You are introduced to your supervisor's new boss, someone who is in a position to help you advance in the company, and you both exchange small talk for a few minutes. A week later you run into him outside the building. If you greet him by name and ask whether his son is over the case of the flu he had, you have made a good impression that is likely to help you in the future. If you call him by the wrong name, realize your mistake, and slink off to work, you may have set up a bit of a hurdle for yourself as you try to get ahead.

Using what you know about memory strategies and what works for you, set up a system to record and retain information about people you meet whom you want to remember. For your system, decide on a tool (address book, set of notecards, electronic organizer, computer file), what to record (name, phone, email, title, how you met, important details), and how you will update the information. Choose a tool that you are most likely to use and that will be easy for you to refer to and update.

Tool of choice: _____

Information to record:

_____

When to record and how often to check or update:

_____

Get started by putting in information for all the people you consider to be important networking contacts at this point—family, friends, instructors and advisors, or work colleagues and supervisors. Make this the start of a database that will serve you throughout your career.

Social Networking

REMEMBER INFORMATION ABOUT YOUR CONTACTS

Use LinkedIn to connect with the list of important contacts you just developed. Sign in to your account and invite these people to join your network, using any of the methods from the Chapter 3 Social Networking exercise.

When at least three of these contacts have responded by joining your network, use the LinkedIn "My Connections" area to fill in helpful information about them that you want to remember.

- Click on "My Connections."
- Choose a name from your connections list and click on "View and edit details" beneath that person's name.
- Fill in any relevant information—phone, address, website, birthday, and notes about your contact with this person.

chapter 5

Analytical, Creative, and Practical Thinking

Solving Problems and Making Decisions

What Would You Do?

Think about this problem as you read, and consider how you would approach it. This chapter builds problem-solving and decision-making skills that will help you face challenges in college or university and beyond.

Ethan Gamal is carrying a 12-credit load this term toward his major in computer programming. He has been working part time at a local electronics store for his entire post-secondary career. It's difficult to keep up with both work and school, but he can't afford the tuition without the income.

Unfortunately, the chain that has employed him for the last three years is going into bankruptcy, and the consequences have hit home. Ethan has been notified that the store is closing in two weeks and all employees have been terminated. Trying to keep cash coming in, Ethan has applied for local jobs and uploaded some resumés to job websites, but he hasn't yet gotten any bites.

Ethan's friend and co-worker Adam talked it over with him as they sat in the backroom on a break. "Look at it this way: we'll both have more time to get schoolwork done. You know you've complained for weeks about being overloaded."

"What good is time to study if I can't pay tuition?" asked Ethan. "I was looking on the Internet and some experts said demand for computer programmers is going to drop a lot in the next decade. Great. Why bother to stick in this program if I won't even be able to find a job in a few years?"

"We're in the same boat," said Adam. "All of us need new jobs, and I've got to pay my own tuition just like you."

Ethan replied, "But you're headed toward an education major, and you're going to have job prospects. I don't know what to do, because there's nothing else I'm interested in. The truth is I'm ready to quit." (To be continued . . .)

Problems can come up suddenly and throw you off balance. You'll learn more about Ethan, and revisit his situation, within the chapter.

In this chapter, you'll explore answers to these questions:

> Why is it important to ask and answer questions? p. 126

> How can you improve your analytical thinking skills? p. 127

> How can you improve your creative thinking skills? p. 133

> How can you improve your practical thinking skills? p. 137

> How can you solve problems and make decisions effectively? p. 140

MyStudentSuccessLab

Use these interactive tools to help you succeed in your course and career:
• Videos
• Exercises and applied activities
• Practice quizzes

For each statement, circle the number that feels right to you,
from 1 for "not at all true for me" to 5 for "very true for me."

▶ I discover information, make decisions, and solve problems by asking and answering questions.	**1 2 3 4 5**
▶ I don't take everything I read or hear as fact; I question how useful, truthful, and logical it is before I decide whether I can use it.	**1 2 3 4 5**
▶ I look for biased perspectives when I read or listen because I am aware of how they can lead me in the wrong direction.	**1 2 3 4 5**
▶ Even if it seems like there is only one way to solve a problem, I brainstorm to think of other options.	**1 2 3 4 5**
▶ I try not to let the idea that things have always been done a certain way stop me from trying different approaches.	**1 2 3 4 5**
▶ When I work in a group, I try to manage my emotions and notice how I affect others.	**1 2 3 4 5**
▶ I think about different solutions before I choose one and take action.	**1 2 3 4 5**
▶ I spend time researching different possibilities before making a decision.	**1 2 3 4 5**
▶ I avoid making decisions on the spur of the moment.	**1 2 3 4 5**
▶ When I make a decision, I consider how my choice will affect others.	**1 2 3 4 5**

Each of the topics in these statements is covered in this chapter. Note those statements for which you circled a 3 or lower. Skim the chapter to see where those topics appear, and pay special attention to them as you read, learn, and apply new strategies.

REMEMBER: *No matter how developed your thinking skills are, you can improve with effort and practice.*

"Successfully intelligent people define problems correctly and thereby solve those problems that really confront them, rather than extraneous ones. . . . [They] carefully formulate strategies for problem solving. In particular, they focus on long-range planning rather than rushing in and then later having to rethink their strategies."

—Robert Sternberg

Why is it important to ask and answer questions?

What is thinking? According to experts, it is what happens when you ask questions and move toward the answers.[1] "To think through or rethink anything," says Dr. Richard Paul, director of research at the Center for Critical Thinking and Moral Critique, "one must ask questions that stimulate our thought. Questions define tasks, express problems and delineate issues. . . . [O]nly students who have questions are really thinking and learning."[2]

As you answer questions, you turn information into material that you can use to achieve goals. A *Wall Street Journal* article titled "The Best Innovations Are Those That Come from Smart Questions" relays the story of a cell biology student, William Hunter, whose professor told him that "the difference between good science and great science is the quality of the questions posed." Now a physician, Dr. Hunter asks questions about new ways to use drugs. His questions have helped his company reach the goal of developing a revolutionary product—a drug-coated mesh used to strengthen diseased blood vessels.[3]

■ **Know why you question.** To ask useful questions, you need to know why you are questioning. Start by defining your purpose: What am I trying to accomplish, and why? For example, if Ethan's purpose for questioning were to find another part-time job, that would generate an entirely different set of questions than if his purpose were to find another major. As you continue your thought process, you will find more specific purposes that help you generate questions along the way.

■ **Want to question.** Knowing why you are questioning also helps you want to think. "Critical-thinking skills are different from critical-thinking dispositions, or a willingness to deploy these skills," says cognitive psychologist D. Alan Bensley of Frostburg State University in Maryland. In other words, having the skills isn't enough—you also need the desire to use them.[4] Having a clear understanding of your goal can help you be more willing to work to achieve it.

■ **Question in different ways.**

▶ Analyze (How bad is my money situation?)

▶ Come up with creative ideas (How can I earn more money?)

▶ Apply practical solutions (Who do I talk to about getting a job on campus?)

When you need to solve a problem or make a decision, combining all three thinking skills gives you the greatest chance of achieving your goal.[5] This chapter will explore analytical, creative, and practical thinking first individually and then will show how they work together to help you solve problems and make decisions effectively. Asking questions opens the door to each thinking skill, and in each section you will find examples of the kinds of questions that drive that skill. Begin by exploring analytical thinking.

How can you improve your analytical thinking skills?

Analytical thinking is the process of gathering information, breaking it into parts, examining and evaluating those parts, and making connections for the purposes of gaining understanding, solving a problem, or making a decision.

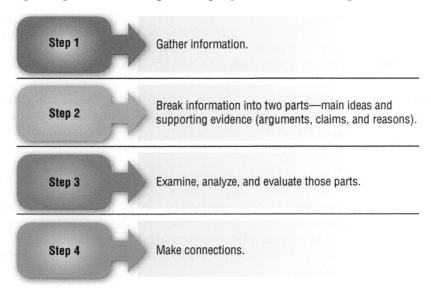

Step 1 → Gather information.

Step 2 → Break information into two parts—main ideas and supporting evidence (arguments, claims, and reasons).

Step 3 → Examine, analyze, and evaluate those parts.

Step 4 → Make connections.

Through the analytical process, you look for how pieces of information relate to one another, setting aside any pieces that are unclear, unrelated, unimportant, or biased. You may also form new questions that change your direction. Be open to them and to where they may lead you.

Gather information

Information is the raw material for thinking, so to start the thinking process you must first gather your raw materials. This requires analyzing how much information you need, how much time to spend gathering it, and whether it is relevant. Say, for instance, that you have to write a paper on one aspect of the media (TV, radio, Internet) and its influence on a particular group. Here's how analyzing can help you gather information for that paper:

▶ Reviewing the assignment terms, you note two important items: The paper should be approximately 10 pages and describe at least three significant points of influence.

▶ At the library and online, you find thousands of articles in this topic area. Analyzing your reaction to them and how many articles concentrate on certain aspects of the topic, you decide to focus your paper on how the Internet influences young teens (ages 13–15).

▶ Examining the summaries of six comprehensive articles leads you to three in-depth sources.

Many types of work, such as the elevation drawings this engineering student is working on, involve analytical thinking.
© Shutterstock

In this way, you achieve a subgoal—a selection of useful materials—on the way to your larger goal of writing a well-crafted paper.

Break information into parts

The next step is to search for the two most relevant parts of the information: the main idea or ideas (also called the (argument) or *viewpoint*) and the supporting evidence (also called *reasons* or *supporting details*).

ARGUMENT
A set of connected ideas, supported by examples, made by a writer to prove or disprove a point.

▶ *Separate the ideas.* Identify each of the ideas conveyed in what you are reading. You can use lists or a mind map to visually separate ideas from one another. For instance, if you are reading about how teens ages 13 to 15 use the Internet, you could identify the goal of each method of access they use (websites, blogs, instant messaging).

▶ *Identify the evidence.* For each main idea, identify the evidence that supports it. For example, if an article claims that young teens rely on instant messaging three times more than on emails, note the facts, studies, or other evidence cited to support the truth of the claim.

Examine and evaluate

The third step is by far the most significant and lies at the heart of analytical thinking. Examine the information to see whether it is going to be useful for your purposes. Keep your mind open to all useful information, even if it conflicts with your personal views. A student who thinks that the death penalty is wrong, for example, may have a hard time analyzing arguments that defend it or may focus her research on materials that support her perspective. Set aside personal prejudices when you analyze information.

The following four questions will help you examine and evaluate effectively.

Do examples support ideas?

When you encounter an idea or claim, examine how it is supported with examples or *evidence*—facts, expert opinion, research findings, personal experience, and so on (see Key 5.1 for an illustration). How useful an idea is to your work may depend on whether, or how well, it is backed up with solid evidence or made concrete with examples. Be critical of the information you gather; don't take it as truth without examining it.

For example, a blog written by a 12 year old may make statements about what kids do on the Internet. The word of one person, who may or may not be telling the truth, is not adequate support. However, a study of youth technology use by the Canadian Radio-television and Telecommunications Commission (CRTC) may be more reliable.

Is the information factual and accurate, or is it opinion?

A *statement of fact* is information presented as objectively real and verifiable ("The Internet is a research tool"). In contrast, a *statement of opinion* is a belief, conclusion, or judgment that is inherently difficult, and sometimes impossible, to verify ("The Internet is always the best and most reliable research tool"). When you critically evaluate materials, one test of the evidence is whether it is fact or opinion. Key 5.2 defines important characteristics of fact and opinion.

Do causes and effects link logically?

Look at the reasons given for a situation or occurrence (causes) and the explanation of its consequences (effects, both positive and negative). For example, an article might detail what causes young teens to use the Internet after school and

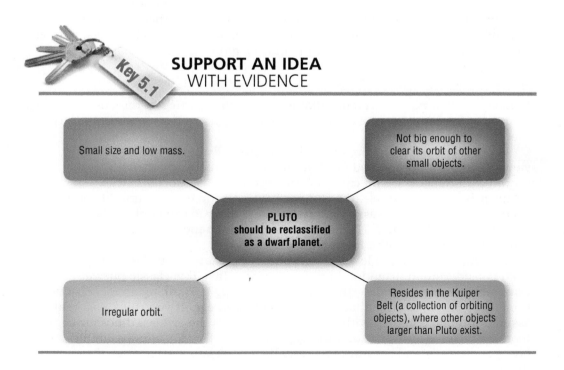

SUPPORT AN IDEA WITH EVIDENCE

Small size and low mass.

Not big enough to clear its orbit of other small objects.

PLUTO should be reclassified as a dwarf planet.

Irregular orbit.

Resides in the Kuiper Belt (a collection of orbiting objects), where other objects larger than Pluto exist.

EXAMINE HOW
FACT AND OPINION DIFFER

FACTS INCLUDE STATEMENTS THAT . . .	OPINIONS INCLUDE STATEMENTS THAT . . .
• **deal with actual people, places, objects, or events.** Example: "In 2002, the European Union introduced the physical coins and banknotes of a new currency—the euro—that was designed to be used by its member nations."	• **show evaluation.** Any statement of value indicates an opinion. Words such as *bad, good, pointless,* and *beneficial* indicate value judgments. Example: "The use of the euro has been beneficial to all the states of the European Union."
• **use concrete words or measurable statistics.** Example: "The charity event raised $50,862."	• **use abstract words.** Complicated words such as *misery* or *success* usually indicate a personal opinion. Example: "The charity event was a smashing success."
• **describe current events in exact terms.** Example: "Mr. Barrett's course has 378 students enrolled this semester."	• **predict future events.** Statements about future occurrences are often opinions. Example: "Mr. Barrett's course is going to set a new enrolment record this year."
• **avoid emotional words and focus on the verifiable.** Example: "Citing dissatisfaction with the instruction, seven out of the twenty-five students in that class withdrew in September."	• **use emotional words.** Emotions are unverifiable. Words such as *delightful* or *miserable* express an opinion. Example: "That class is a miserable experience."
• **avoid absolutes.** Example: "Some students need to have a job while in school."	• **use absolutes.** Absolute qualifiers, such as *all, none, never,* and *always,* often express an opinion. Example: "All students need to have a job while in school."

Source: Adapted from Ben E. Johnson, *Stirring Up Thinking.* New York: Houghton Mifflin, 1998, pp. 268–270.

the effects that this has on their family life. The cause-and-effect chain should make sense to you. It is also important that you analyze carefully to seek out *key* or *"root" causes*—the most significant causes of a problem or situation. For example, many factors may be involved in young teens' Internet use, including availability of service, previous experience, and education level of parents; but, on careful examination, one or two factors may be more significant than others.

Is the evidence biased?

BIAS
A preference or inclination, especially one that prevents even-handed judgment.

Evidence with a **bias** is evidence that is slanted in a particular direction. Searching for a bias involves looking for hidden perspectives or assumptions that lie within the material.

PERSPECTIVE
A characteristic way of thinking about people, situations, events, and ideas.

A **perspective** can be broad (such as a generally optimistic or pessimistic view of life) or more focused (such as an attitude about whether students should commute or live on campus). Perspectives are associated with **assumptions.** For example, the perspective that people can maintain control over technology leads to assumptions such as "Parents can control children's exposure to the Internet." Having a particular experience with children and the Internet can build or reinforce such a perspective.

ASSUMPTION
A judgment, generalization, or bias influenced by experience and values.

Assumptions often hide within questions and statements, blocking you from considering information in different ways. Take this classic puzzler as an example: "Which came first, the chicken or the egg?" Thinking about this question, most people assume that the egg is a chicken egg. If you think past that assumption and come up with a new idea—such as the egg is a dinosaur egg— then the obvious answer is that the egg came first. Key 5.3 offers examples of how perspectives and assumptions can affect what you read or hear through the media.

Key 5.3 DIFFERENT ARTICLES MAY PRESENT **DIFFERENT PERSPECTIVES** ON THE SAME TOPIC

Topic: *How teens' grades are affected by Internet use*

STATEMENT BY A TEACHING ORGANIZATION	STATEMENT BY A PR AGENT FOR AN INTERNET SEARCH ENGINE	STATEMENT BY A PROFESSOR SPECIALIZING IN NEW MEDIA AND EDUCATION
"Too much Internet use equals failing grades and stolen papers."	"The Internet allows students access to a plethora of information, which results in better grades."	"The effects of the Internet on young students are undeniable and impossible to overlook."

Examining perspectives and assumptions helps you judge whether material is *reliable*. The less bias you can identify, the more reliable the information.

After the questions: What information is most useful to you?

You've examined your information, looking at its evidence, validity, perspective, and any underlying assumptions. Now, based on that examination, you evaluate whether an idea or piece of information is important or unimportant, relevant or irrelevant, strong or weak, and why. You then set aside what is not useful and use the rest to form an opinion, possible solution, or decision.

In preparing your paper on young teens and the Internet, for example, you've analyzed a selection of information and materials to see how they apply to the goal of your paper. You then selected what you believe will be most useful in preparation for drafting.

Make connections

The last part of analytical thinking, after you have broken information apart, is to find new and logical ways to connect pieces together. This step is crucial for research papers and essays because it is where your original ideas are born—and it is also where your creative skills get involved (more on that in the next section). When you begin to write, you focus on your new ideas, supporting them effectively with information you've learned from your analysis. Use the following techniques to make connections.

■ *Compare and contrast.* Look at how ideas are similar to, or different from, each other. You might explore how different young teen subgroups (boys versus girls, for example) have different purposes for setting up pages on sites such as Facebook or Myspace.

When you think through something with others in a group, the variety of ideas gives you a better chance of finding a workable solution to a problem.
© iStockphoto

■ *Look for themes, patterns, and categories.* Note connections that form as you look at how bits of information relate to one another. For example, you might see patterns of Internet use that link young teens from particular cultures or areas of the country together into categories.

Come to new information ready to hear and read new ideas, think about them, and make informed decisions about what you believe. The process will educate you, sharpen your thinking skills, and give you more information to work with as you encounter life's problems. See Key 5.4 for some questions you can ask to build and use analytical thinking skills.

ASK QUESTIONS SUCH AS THESE TO **ANALYZE**

Key 5.4

To gather information, ask:	• What kinds of information do I need to meet my goal? • What information is available? Where and when can I get to it? • Of the sources I found, which ones will best help me achieve my goal?
To analyze, ask:	• What are the parts of this information? • What is similar to this information? What is different? • What are the reasons for this? Why did this happen? • What ideas, themes, or conclusions emerge from this material? • How would you categorize this information?
To see whether evidence or examples support an idea, ask:	• Does the evidence make sense? • How do the examples support the idea/claim? • Are there examples that might disprove the idea/claim?
To distinguish fact from opinion, ask:	• Do the words in this information signal fact or opinion? • What is the source of this information? Is the source reliable? • If this is an opinion, is it supported by facts?
To examine perspectives and assumptions, ask:	• What perspectives might the author have, and what may be emphasized or de-emphasized as a result? • What assumptions might lie behind this statement or material? • How could I prove—or disprove—an assumption? • How might my perspective affect the way I see this material?
To evaluate, ask:	• What information will support what I'm trying to prove or accomplish? • Is this information true or false, and why? • How important is this information?

Source: Adapted from www-ed.fnal.gov/trc/tutorial/taxonomy.html (Richard Paul, *Critical Thinking: How to Prepare Students for a Rapidly Changing World*, 1993) and from www.kcmetro.edu/longview/ctac/blooms.htm (Barbara Fowler, Longview Community College "Bloom's Taxonomy and Critical Thinking").

Pursuing your goals, in school and in the workplace, requires not just analyzing information but also thinking creatively about how to use what you've learned from your analysis.

How can you improve your creative thinking skills?

What is creativity?

▶ Some researchers define creativity as combining existing elements in an innovative way to create a new purpose or result (for example, after doctors noticed that patients taking Aspirin had fewer heart attacks, the drug was reinvented as a preventer of coronary disease).

▶ Others see creativity as the ability to generate new ideas from looking at how things are related (for example, noting what ladybugs eat inspired organic farmers to bring them in to consume crop-destroying aphids).[6]

▶ Still others, including Sternberg, define it as the ability to make unusual connections—to view information in quirky ways that bring about unique results (for example, using a weak adhesive to mark pages in a book, a 3M scientist created Post-it Notes).

To think creatively is to generate new ideas that may bring change. Even though some people seem to have more or better ideas than others, *creative thinking* is a skill that can be developed. Creativity expert Roger von Oech highlights mental flexibility. "Like race-car drivers who shift in and out of different gears depending on where they are on the course," he says, you can enhance creativity by learning to "shift in and out of different types of thinking depending on the needs of the situation at hand."[7]

The following tips will help you make those shifts and build your ability to generate and capture the ideas that pop up. Get in the habit of writing them down as you think of them. Keep a pen and paper by your bed, your smartphone in your pocket, a notepad in your car, or a recorder in your backpack so that you can grab ideas before they fade.

Brainstorm

(Brainstorming) is also referred to as *divergent thinking*: you start with a question and then let your mind diverge—go in many different directions—in search of solutions. Brainstorming is *deliberate* creative thinking. When you brainstorm, you generate ideas without thinking about how useful they are and evaluate their quality later. Brainstorming works well in groups because group members can become inspired by, and make creative use of, one another's ideas.[8]

One way to inspire ideas when brainstorming is to think of similar situations—in other words, to make *analogies* (comparisons based on a resemblance of things otherwise unlike). For example, Velcro is a product of analogy: after examining how burrs stuck to his dog's fur after a walk in the woods, the inventor imagined how a similar system of hooks and loops could make two pieces of fabric stick to each other.

When you are brainstorming ideas, don't get hooked on finding one right answer. Questions may have many "right answers"—answers that have degrees of usefulness. The more possibilities you generate, the better your chance of

BRAINSTORMING
Letting your mind wander to come up with different ideas or answers.

getAnalytical!

Analyze a Statement

Reread the case study that opens the chapter. Consider the statement below; then analyze it by answering the questions that follow.

There's no point in pursuing a career area that you love if it isn't going to earn you a living.

Is this statement fact or opinion? Why?

_____

_____

_____

What examples can you think of that support or negate this statement?

_____

_____

_____

_____

What perspective(s) are guiding this statement?

_____

_____

_____

_____

What assumption(s) underlie the statement? What negative effects might result from accepting these assumptions without investigation?

_____

_____

_____

_____

As a result of your critical thinking, what is your evaluation of this statement?

_____

_____

_____

_____

finding the best one. Ethan might brainstorm things he likes to do and people he admires, for example, and from those lists he may come up with ideas of other majors that he wants to investigate.

Finally, don't stop the process when you think you have the best answer—keep going until you are out of steam. You never know what may come up in those last gasps of creative energy.[9]

Take a new and different look

If no one ever questioned established opinion, people would still think the Sun revolved around the Earth. Here are some ways to change how you look at a situation or problem:

■ ***Challenge assumptions.*** In the late 1960s, conventional wisdom said that school provided education and TV provided entertainment. Jim Henson, a pioneer in children's television, asked, Why can't we use TV to educate young children? From that question, the characters of *Sesame Street*, and eventually many other educational programs, were born. Ethan might try to challenge his assumptions about what people with a computer programming major do in the workplace.

■ ***Shift your perspective.*** Try on new perspectives by asking others for their views, reading about new ways to approach situations, or deliberately going with the opposite of your first instinct.[10] Then use those perspectives to inspire creativity. For a political science course, for example, you might craft a position paper for a parliamentary candidate that goes against your view of that particular issue. For a fun example of how looking at something in a new way can unearth a totally different idea, look at the perception puzzles in Key 5.5.

USE **PERCEPTION PUZZLES** TO EXPERIENCE A SHIFT IN PERSPECTIVE

There are two possibilities for each image. What do you see? (See page 113 for answers.)

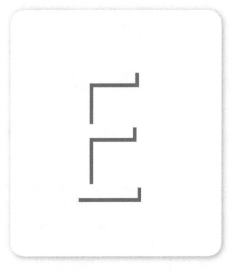

Activate Your Creative Powers

First, think about the past month; then, list three creative acts you performed.

1. To study, I _____

2. In my personal life, I _____

3. At work or in the classroom, I _____

Now think of a problem or situation that is on your mind. Brainstorm one new idea for how to deal with it.

_____

Write down a second idea—but focus on the risk-taking aspect of creativity. What would be a risky way to handle the situation? How do you hope it would pay off?

_____

_____

Finally, sit with the question—write down one more idea only after you have been away from this page for at least 24 hours.

_____

Keep these in mind. You may want to use one soon!

■ *Ask "what if" questions.* Set up imaginary environments in which new ideas can grow, such as What if I had unlimited money or time? For example, the founders of Seeds of Peace, faced with long-term conflict in the Middle East, asked, What if Israeli and Palestinian teens met at a summer camp in Maine so that the next generation has greater understanding and respect? What if follow-up programs and reunions strengthen friendships so that relationships change the politics of the Middle East? Based on the ideas that came up, they created an organization that helps teenagers from the Middle East develop leadership and communication skills.

Set the stage for creativity

Use these strategies to generate creative ideas:

■ *Choose, or create, environments that free your mind.* Find places that energize you. Play music that moves you. Seek out people who inspire you.[11]

■ *Be curious.* Try something new and different: Take a course outside of your major, listen to a new genre of music, read a book on an unfamiliar topic. Try something you don't think you will like to see whether you have misjudged your reaction. Seeking out new experiences will broaden your knowledge, giving you more raw materials with which to build creative ideas.[12]

■ *Give yourself time to "sit" with a question.* North American society values speed, so much so that we equate being quick with being smart.[13] In fact, creative ideas often come when you give your brain permission to "leave the job" for a while.[14] Take breaks when figuring out a problem—get some exercise, nap, talk with a friend, work on something else, do something fun. Even though he may not have the luxury of too much time, Ethan may benefit from sitting with the question of his major for as long as he can.

Take risks

Creative breakthroughs can come from sensible risk taking.

■ *Go against established ideas.* The founders of Etsy.com went against the idea that the North American consumer prefers cheap, conventional, mass-produced items. In 2005 they created an online company that allows artisans to offer one-of-a-kind, handmade products to the consumer. The site has also created a community of artists and connects each artist personally to his or her customers.

■ *Let mistakes be okay.* Open yourself to the learning that comes from not being afraid to mess up. When a pharmaceutical company failed to develop a particular treatment for multiple sclerosis, the CEO said, "You have to celebrate the failures. If you send the message that the only road to career success is experiments that work, people won't ask risky questions, or get any dramatically new answers."[15] If majoring in computer programming turns out not to be the best choice for Ethan, for example, he may find that what he considers a mistake was also a crucial voyage of self-discovery.

As with analytical thinking, asking questions powers creative thinking. See Key 5.6 for examples of the kinds of questions you can ask to get your creative juices flowing.

Creativity connects analytical and practical thinking. When you generate ideas, solutions, or choices, you need to think analytically to evaluate their quality. Then, you need to think practically about how to make the best solution or choice happen.

How can you improve your practical thinking skills?

You've analyzed a situation. You've brainstormed ideas. Now, with your practical skill, you make things happen.

Practical thinking—also called *common sense* or *street smarts*—refers to how you adapt to your environment (both people and circumstances), or shape or change your environment to adapt to you, to pursue important goals.

Change the **CONVERSATION**

Challenge yourself and your friends to ask—and answer—tough questions. Use the following to inspire discussion in pairs or groups.

▶ What problem(s) do you see others avoid?

▶ What happens as a result?

▶ **CONSIDER THE CASE:** What are the pros and cons of each of Ethan's available choices—to continue with his chosen major or to branch off into something new that seems like a better financial bet? What would you recommend for him?

ASK QUESTIONS SUCH AS THESE
TO **JUMP-START CREATIVE THINKING**

Key 5.6

To brainstorm, ask:
- What do I want to accomplish?
- What are the craziest ideas I can think of?
- What are 10 ways that I can reach my goal?
- What ideas have worked before and how can I apply them?

To shift your perspective, ask:
- How has this always been done—and what would be a different way?
- How can I approach this task or situation from a new angle?
- How would someone else do this or view this?
- What if . . . ?

To set the stage for creativity, ask:
- Where, and with whom, do I feel relaxed and inspired?
- What music helps me think out of the box?
- When in the day or night am I most likely to experience a flow of creative ideas?
- What do I think would be new and interesting to try, to see, to read?

To take risks, ask:
- What is the conventional way of doing this? What would be a totally different way?
- What would be a risky approach to this problem or question?
- What is the worst that can happen if I take this risk? What is the best?
- What have I learned from this mistake?

Another example: Your goal is to pass your first-year sociology course. You learn most successfully through visual presentations. To achieve your goal, you can use the instructor's slide-show presentations or other visual media to enhance your learning (adapt to your environment) or enrol in a heavily visual Internet course (change your environment to adapt to you)—or both.

Why practical thinking is important

Real-world problems and decisions require you to add understanding of experiences and social interactions to your analytical abilities. Your success in a sociology class, for example, may depend almost as much on getting along with your instructor as on your academic work. Similarly, the way you solve a personal money problem may have more impact on your life than how you work through a problem in an accounting course.

Keep in mind, too, that in the workplace you need to use practical skills to apply academic knowledge to problems and decisions. For example, although students majoring in elementary education may successfully quote child development facts on an exam, their career success depends on the ability to evaluate and address real children's needs in the classroom. Successfully solving real-world problems demands a practical approach.

Take a Practical Approach to Building Successful Intelligence

Look back at your Wheel of Successful Intelligence. Write here the skill area in which you most need to build strength:

_____

Write down two practical actions you can take that will improve your skills in that area. For example, someone who wants to be more creative could take a course focused on creativity; someone who wants to be more practical could work on paying attention to social cues; someone who wants to be more analytical could decide to analyze one newspaper article every week.

1. _____

_____

2. _____

Through experience, you build emotional intelligence

You gain much of your ability to think practically from personal experience, rather than from formal training.[16] What you learn from experience answers "how" questions—how to talk, how to behave, how to proceed.[17] For example, after completing several papers for a course, you may learn what your instructor expects—or, after a few arguments with a friend or partner, you may learn how to avoid topics that cause conflict.

Emotional intelligence gives you steps you can take to promote success. For example, when Ethan was let go from his job, he was angry about it. With effort, his response involved these practical and emotionally and socially intelligent actions:

▶ After he received the letter, *recognizing* his feelings

▶ Working to *understand* what his feelings and mindset told him about what he wanted and how he perceived the situation

▶ *Adjusting* his thinking to gain something out of a bad situation

▶ *Managing* his emotions by scheduling a meeting when he had calmed down, making his points at the meeting, keeping a productive goal in mind, and listening to what his supervisor said in response

▶ Politely requesting something related to his goal (such as a positive recommendation)

These emotionally intelligent actions make it more likely that Ethan's supervisor will be receptive and helpful and that there will be a positive outcome from the interaction.

Key 5.7

ASK QUESTIONS SUCH AS THESE TO ACTIVATE **PRACTICAL THINKING**

To learn from experience, ask:
- What worked well, or not so well, about my approach? My timing? My tone? My wording?
- What did others like or not like about what I did?
- What did I learn from that experience, conversation, event?
- How would I change things if I had to do it over again?
- What do I know I would do again?

To apply what you learn, ask:
- What have I learned that would work here?
- What have I seen others do, or heard about from them, that would be helpful here?
- What does this situation have in common with past situations I've been involved in?
- What has worked in similar situations in the past?

To boost your ability to take action, ask:
- How can I get motivated and remove limitations?
- How can I, in this situation, make the most of what I do well?
- If I fail, what can I learn from it?
- What steps will get me to my goal, and what trade-offs are involved?
- How can I manage my time more effectively?

If you know that social interactions are difficult for you, enlist someone to give you some informal coaching. Ask a friend to role-play the meeting with your instructor (your friend will act as if he is the instructor) and give you feedback on your words, tone, and body language. Or bring a friend with you to the actual meeting and talk later about how things went.

Practical thinking means action

Action is the logical result of practical thinking. Basic student success strategies that promote action—staying motivated, making the most of your strengths, learning from failure, managing time, seeking help from instructors and advisors, and believing in yourself—will keep you moving toward your goals.[18]

The key to making practical knowledge work is to use what you discover, assuring that you will not have to learn the same lessons over and over again. As Sternberg says, "What matters most is not how much experience you have had but rather how much you have profited from it—in other words, how well you apply what you have learned."[19]

See Key 5.7 for some questions you can ask in order to apply practical thinking to your problems and decisions.

How can you solve problems and make decisions **effectively?**

The best problem solvers and decision makers use their analytical, creative, and practical thinking skills together to solve problems and make decisions. Problem solving and decision making follow similar paths, both requiring you to identify and analyze a situation, generate possibilities, choose one, follow through on it, and evaluate its success. Key 5.8 gives an overview indicating the

SOLVE PROBLEMS AND MAKE DECISIONS BY
USING SUCCESSFUL INTELLIGENCE

PROBLEM SOLVING	THINKING SKILL	DECISION MAKING
Define the problem—recognize that something needs to change, identify what's happening, look for true causes.	**Step 1** Define	**Define the decision**—identify your goal (your need) and then construct a decision that will help you get it.
Analyze the problem—gather information, break it down into pieces, verify facts, look at perspectives and assumptions, evaluate information.	**Step 2** Analyze	**Examine needs and motives**—consider the layers of needs carefully, and be honest about what you really want.
Generate possible solutions—use creative strategies to think of ways you could address the causes of this problem.	**Step 3** Create	**Name and/or generate different options**—use creative questions to come up with choices that would fulfill your needs.
Evaluate solutions—look carefully at potential pros and cons of each, and choose what seems best.	**Step 4** Analyze (Evaluate)	**Evaluate options**—look carefully at potential pros and cons of each, and choose what seems best.
Put the solution to work—persevere, focus on results, and believe in yourself as you go for your goal.	**Step 5** Take Practical Action	**Act on your decision**—go down the path and use practical strategies to stay on target.
Evaluate how well the solution worked—look at the effects of what you did.	**Step 6** Analyze (Re-evaluate)	**Evaluate the success of your decision**—look at whether it accomplished what you had hoped.
In the future, apply what you've learned—use this solution, or a better one, when a similar situation comes up again.	**Step 7** Take Practical Action	**In the future, apply what you've learned**—make this choice, or a better one, when a similar decision comes up again.

process at each step. (Keys 5.10 and 5.11 show examples of how to map out problems and decisions effectively.)

Understanding the differences between problem solving and decision making will help you know how to proceed. See Key 5.9 for more information. Remember, too, that whereas all problem solving involves decision making, not all decision making requires you to solve a problem.

Solve a problem

The following strategies will help you move through the problem-solving process outlined in Key 5.8.

■ *Use probing questions to define problems.* Ask, What is the problem?

EXAMINE HOW **PROBLEMS AND DECISIONS** DIFFER

SITUATION	YOU HAVE A PROBLEM IF . . .	YOU NEED TO MAKE A DECISION IF . . .
Planning summer activities	Your low GPA means you need to attend summer school—and you've already accepted a summer job.	You've been accepted into two summer abroad internship programs.
Declaring a major	It's time to declare, but you don't have all the prerequisites for the major you want.	There are three majors that appeal to you and you qualify for them all.
Handling communications with instructors	You are having trouble following the lecture style of a particular instructor.	Your psychology survey course has seven sections taught by different instructors; you have to choose one.

And what is causing the problem? Engage your emotional intelligence. If you determine that you are not motivated to do your work for a class, for example, you could ask questions such as these:

▶ Do my feelings stem from how I interact with my instructor or classmates?

▶ Is the subject matter difficult? Uninteresting?

Chances are that how you answer one or more of these questions may help you define the problem—and ultimately solve it.

■ *Analyze carefully.* Gather information that will help you examine the problem. Consider how the problem is similar to, or different from, other problems. Clarify facts. Note your own perspective and look for others. Make sure your assumptions are not getting in the way.

■ *Generate possible solutions based on causes, not effects.* Addressing a cause provides a lasting solution, whereas "putting a Band-Aid on" an effect cannot. Say, for example, that your shoulder hurts when you type. Getting a massage is a helpful but temporary solution, because the pain returns whenever you go back to work. Changing your keyboard height is a lasting solution to the problem, because it eliminates the cause of your pain.

■ *Consider how possible solutions affect you and others.* What would suit you best? What takes other people's needs into consideration?

■ *Evaluate your solution and act on it in the future.* Once you choose a solution and put it into action, ask yourself, What worked that I would do again? What didn't work that I would avoid or change in the future?

What happens if you don't work through a problem comprehensively? Take, for example, a student having an issue with an instructor. She may get into an argument with the instructor, stop showing up to class, or take a quick-and-dirty approach to assignments. Any of these choices may have negative consequences. Now look at how the student might work through this problem by using analytical, creative, and practical thinking skills. Key 5.10 shows how her effort can pay off.

WORK THROUGH A PROBLEM
RELATING TO AN INSTRUCTOR

DEFINE PROBLEM HERE:	ANALYZE THE PROBLEM
I don't like my Sociology instructor	We have different styles and personality types—I am not comfortable working in groups and being vocal. I'm not interested in being there, and my grades are suffering from my lack of motivation.

Use boxes below to list possible solutions:

POTENTIAL POSITIVE EFFECTS	SOLUTION #1	POTENTIAL NEGATIVE EFFECTS
List for each solution: Don't have to deal with that instructor Less stress	Drop the course	List for each solution: Grade gets entered on my transcript I'll have to take the course eventually; it's required for my major
Getting credit for the course Feeling like I've honoured a commitment	**SOLUTION #2** Put up with it until the end of the semester	Stress every time I'm there Lowered motivation Probably not such a good final grade
A chance to express myself Could get good advice An opportunity to ask direct questions of the instructor	**SOLUTION #3** Schedule meetings with advisor and instructor	Have to face instructor one-on-one Might just make things worse

Now choose the solution you think is best—circle it and make it happen.

ACTUAL POSITIVE EFFECTS	PRACTICAL ACTION	ACTUAL NEGATIVE EFFECTS
List for chosen solution: Got some helpful advice from advisor Talking in person with the instructor actually promoted a fairly honest discussion I won't have to take the course again	I scheduled and attended meetings with both advisor and instructor and opted to stick with the course.	List for chosen solution: Still have to put up with some group work I still don't know how much learning I'll retain from this course

FINAL EVALUATION: Was it a good or bad solution?
The solution has improved things. I'll finish the course, and I got the chance to fulfill some class responsibilities on my own or with one partner. I feel more understood and more willing to put my time into the course.

student profile

Katie Hudgins
CDI College, Calgary, Alberta

About me:

I am a single mom of a child with special needs who has had a heart transplant. I have my Accounting and Payroll Administrator diploma and am currently working on my Business Administration Management diploma, both from CDI College in Calgary.

What I focus on:

Being a single mom of a child with special needs has a lot of challenges. My son has a suppressed immune system because of his heart transplant and needs to stay at home often to avoid infections. I also lost almost two months' worth of work time when my son had major surgery and was in the hospital. I had to rely on my own personal strength and determination to continue my studies while at the hospital and at home. I had to learn to balance taking care of my son's needs and my studies.

Being away from the school and teachers was a big challenge. The instructors at school were very understanding of my situation and I utilized the technology available to me to stay up to date. I used email almost daily to keep in touch with my teachers, to learn what was due, and to submit assignments.

Taking part in the ebook pilot program in which my textbooks were on an iPad was a very easy way for me to keep up with my work easily wherever I was. The ability to stay organized and keep to a schedule was paramount for me. I needed to know what was due at school and what the schedule was for my son and his doctors, as well as find the time to complete everything on time. Knowing that the goal of completing school was in the best interest for my son and myself kept me going. My motivation slipped quite a few times, but the ability to rely on the staff at my school made it possible. This support and encouragement got me through the rough times.

What will help me in the workplace:

For me, returning to school was a great challenge full of stress. I know that being able to meet tight deadlines and balance my responsibilities as a parent with a special needs child and my school responsibilities will help me meet work deadlines and balance my personal life and work. School was a great opportunity for me to learn that if I can handle these obligations while in school, then I will be able to handle them at work as well. Needing to stay organized to keep on track will help me while working in the high-stress working environments that many people face today. Also, technology played a huge part in my success and I will take the technology skills I learned with me to the workplace. School was stressful, but I now know that I can handle a busy schedule, and I look forward to continuing to balance my home life with a career.

Make a decision

As you use the steps in Key 5.8 to make a decision, remember these strategies:

■ ***Look at the given options—then try to think of more.*** Some decisions have a given set of options. For example, your school may allow you to major, double major, or major and minor. However, you may be able to brainstorm with an advisor to come up with more options, such as an interdisciplinary major. Consider similar situations you've been in or heard about, what decisions were made, and what resulted from those decisions.

■ ***Think about how your decision affects others.*** What you choose might have an impact on friends, family, and others around you.

■ ***Gather perspectives.*** Talk with others who have made similar decisions. If you listen carefully, you may hear ideas you haven't thought about.

■ ***Look at the long-term effects.*** As with problem solving, it's key to examine what happens after you put the decision into action. For important decisions, do a short-term evaluation and another evaluation after a period of time. Consider whether your decision sent you in the right direction or whether you should rethink your choice.

What happens when you make important decisions too quickly? Consider a student trying to decide whether to transfer schools. If she makes her decision based on a reason that ultimately is not the most important one for her (for example, close friends go to the other school), she may regret her choice.

Now look at how this student might make an effective decision. Key 5.11 shows how she worked through the analytical, creative, and practical parts of the process.

Keep your balance

No one has equal strengths in analytical, creative, and practical thinking. However, you think and work toward goals most effectively when you combine all three. Staying as balanced as possible requires that you analyze your levels of ability in the three thinking areas, come up with creative ideas about how to build areas where you need to develop, and put them to use with practical action. Above all, believe in your skills as a thinker.

"Successfully intelligent people," says Sternberg, "defy negative expectations, even when these expectations arise from low scores on IQ or similar tests. They do not let other people's assessments stop them from achieving their goals. They find their path and then pursue it, realizing that there will be obstacles along the way and that surmounting these obstacles is part of the challenge."[20] Let the obstacles come, as they will for everyone, in all aspects of life. You can face and overcome them with the power of your successfully intelligent thinking.

Tips for Learning *Online*

- *Brainstorm.* Online learning through a learning management system (LMS) is a great way for creative minds to brainstorm solutions to problems. Use chat rooms and forums to participate in class discussions. Creative people will not only offer their own opinions but also encourage others to participate.

- *Collaborate.* Using your course LMS or other social media (such as Google Docs), your team can work together on class projects online or by using mobile devices.

- *Consider the source.* Determining the credibility of any information found online is critical. Look for information about the author and owner of the website or document. A good place to start is the copyright information at the bottom of the page.

MAKE A DECISION ABOUT
WHETHER TO TRANSFER SCHOOLS

DEFINE PROBLEM HERE:	EXAMINE NEEDS AND MOTIVES
Whether or not to transfer schools	My father has changed jobs and can no longer afford my tuition. My goal is to become a physical therapist, so I need a school with a full physical therapy program. My family needs to cut costs. I need to transfer credits.

Use boxes below to list possible solutions:

POTENTIAL POSITIVE EFFECTS	SOLUTION #1	POTENTIAL NEGATIVE EFFECTS
List for each solution: No need to adjust to a new place or new people Ability to continue coursework as planned	Continue at the current university	List for each solution: Need to finance most of my tuition and costs on my own Difficult to find time for a job Might not qualify for aid
Some physical therapy courses available School is close so I could live at home and save room costs Reasonable tuition; credits will transfer	**SOLUTION #2** Transfer to the community college	No personal contacts there that I know of Less independence if I live at home No bachelor's degree available
Opportunity to earn tuition money Could live at home Status should be intact	**SOLUTION #3** Stop out for a year	Could forget so much that it's hard to go back Could lose motivation A year might turn into more

Now choose the solution you think is best—circle it and make it happen.

ACTUAL POSITIVE EFFECTS	PRACTICAL ACTION	ACTUAL NEGATIVE EFFECTS
List for chosen solution: Money saved Opportunity to spend time on studies rather than on working to earn tuition money Availability of classes I need	Go to community college for two years; then transfer to a four-year school to get a B.A. and complete physical therapy course work.	List for chosen solution: Loss of some independence Cannot receive a degree in physical therapy from the college Cannot receive a degree in physical therapy from the college

FINAL EVALUATION: Was it a good or bad solution?

I'm satisfied with the decision. It can be hard being at home at times, but my parents are adjusting to my independence and I'm trying to respect their concerns. With fewer social distractions, I'm really getting my work done. Plus the financial aspect of the decision is ideal.

What happened to Ethan? First of all, a savvy friend got him to look carefully at his short-term money situation. He realized that with his severance pay, even though it will only last a month, he can cover tuition expenses through the rest of the term. That will buy him time to think more carefully about what to do next. He also went back to the Internet to look at the 30 occupations anticipated to grow the most in the next five years. He noted that although programming is estimated to shrink, other related areas such as network systems and software engineering are looking good. He also reminded himself that a projection isn't necessarily going to come true. His mood began to turn more positive as he opened up his mind to other possibilities for how to use what he does well and has chosen to study.

Case Wrap-up

What does this mean for you? Think about the areas of study that interest you at this point. Look up any other articles you can find on career projections. Then write about where you stand. How does what you've read change, or reinforce, your educational and career goals?

What effects go beyond your world? The volatile job market is affecting workers from the bottom of the ladder to the top. Imagine you are the president of your university or college, speaking at graduation. What would you say to your graduating students to prepare them to successfully enter—and thrive in—today's workplace?

Successful Intelligence*Wrap-up*

HERE'S HOW YOU HAVE BUILT SKILLS IN **CHAPTER 5**:

ANALYTICAL THINKING	CREATIVE THINKING	PRACTICAL THINKING
> You explored the steps and parts of analytical thinking in the section on analytical thinking skills.	> You developed a detailed understanding of creative thinking as you read the section on creative thinking skills.	> You developed more specific ideas of how to apply your emotional intelligence.
> In the Get Analytical exercise, you honed your skills by analyzing a statement.	> In the Get Creative exercise, you brainstormed creative acts as well as new ideas about how to deal with a problem.	> In the Get Practical exercise, you generated practical ideas about how to improve your successful intelligence.
> You considered how to evaluate potential ideas and choices in the problem-solving and decision-making processes.	> You explored ways to brainstorm solutions and choices when solving a problem or making a decision.	> You explored practical ways to put solutions and choices to work when solving a problem or making a decision.

Word*for*Thought

A recently coined **Norwegian** verb—*kunnskaping* (kun-skahp-ping)—translates loosely as "knowledging," which can be read as developing knowledge and meaning that are useful in school and work (and more important than ever before in the global marketplace).[21] Work to develop the analytical, creative, and practical skills that can help you "knowledge" your way to success.

Building Skills for
Post-Secondary, Career, and Life Success

Steps to Success

Make an Important Decision

STEP 1 BUILD BASIC SKILLS. List the steps of the decision-making process.

_____

_____

_____

_____

STEP 2 TAKE IT TO THE NEXT LEVEL. Think about how you would put the decision-making process to work on something that matters to you. Write an important long-term goal that you have, and define the decision that will help you fulfill it. Example: "My goal is to become a nurse. My decision is about what to specialize in."

_____

_____

_____

_____

STEP 3 MOVE TOWARD MASTERY. Use a separate piece of paper to apply the decision-making process to your goal. Use the following steps to organize your thinking.

- *Examine needs and concerns.* What are your needs, and how do your values come into play? What is most needed in the health market, and how can you fulfill that need? What roadblocks might be involved? List everything you come up with. For example, the prospective nurse might list the following needs: "I need to feel that I'm helping people. I intend to help with the shortage of pre-natal or geriatric nurses. I need to make a good living."
- *Generate options.* Ask questions to imagine what's possible. Where might you work? What might be the schedule and pace? Who might work with you? What would you see, smell, and hear on your job? What would you do every day? List, too, all the options you know of. The prospective

nurse, for example, might list prenatal surgery, neonatal intensive care unit, geriatric nursing in a hospital or in a retirement community, and so on.

- *Evaluate options.* Think about how well your options will fulfill your needs. For two of your options, write potential positive and negative effects (pros and cons) of each.

Option 1: _____

Potential pros: _____

Potential cons: _____

Option 2: _____

Potential pros: _____

Potential cons: _____

- *Imagine acting on your decision.* Describe one practical course of action, based on your thinking so far, that you might follow. List the specific steps you would take. For example, the prospective nurse might list actions to help determine what type of nursing suits him best, such as interning, getting summer jobs, pursuing academic goals, and talking to working nurses.

An additional practical action is to go to an actual job site and talk to people. The prospective nurse might go to a hospital, a clinic, and a health centre at a retirement community. Get a feel for what the job is like day-to-day so that can be part of your decision.

Teamwork

Create Solutions Together

POWERFUL GROUP PROBLEM SOLVING

Goal: To experience problem solving as a group and to generate useful and relevant solutions.

Time on task: 30 minutes

Instructions: On a 3 × 5 card or a plain sheet of paper, each student in the class writes a school-related problem—this could be a fear, a challenge, a sticky situation, or a roadblock. Students hand these in without signing them. The instructor writes the list on the board.

Divide into groups of two to four. Each group chooses one problem to work on (try not to select the same problem that another group has chosen). Use the empty problem-solving flowchart (Key 5.12) to fill in your work.

Analyze: Define and examine the problem. As a group, look at the negative effects and state your problem specifically. Write down the causes and examine them to see what's happening. Gather information from all group members, verify facts, and go beyond assumptions.

Create: Generate possible solutions. From the most likely causes of the problem, derive possible solutions. Record all the ideas that group members offer. Each group member should choose one possible solution to evaluate independently.

Analyze: Evaluate each solution. In thinking independently through the assigned solution, each group member should (1) weigh the positive and negative effects, (2) consider similar problems, and (3) describe how the solution affects the causes of the problem. Will your solution work?

Get practical: Choose a solution. Group members then come together, share observations and recommendations, and take a vote: Which solution is the best? You may have a tie or want to combine two different solutions. Try to find the solution that works for most of the group. Then together come up with a plan for putting your solution to work.

To wrap up, think and write. What did you learn about problem solving from doing it in a group setting? Compared to problem solving by yourself, what was different, easier, harder, the same?

WORK THROUGH A PROBLEM BY USING THIS **FLOWCHART**

Key 5.12

DEFINE PROBLEM HERE:	ANALYZE THE PROBLEM

Use boxes below to list possible solutions:

POTENTIAL POSITIVE EFFECTS	SOLUTION #1	POTENTIAL NEGATIVE EFFECTS
List for each solution:		List for each solution:
	SOLUTION #2	
	SOLUTION #3	

Now choose the solution you think is best—circle it and make it happen.

ACTUAL POSITIVE EFFECTS	PRACTICAL ACTION	ACTUAL NEGATIVE EFFECTS
List for chosen solution:		List for chosen solution:

FINAL EVALUATION: Was it a good or bad solution?

Source: Based on a heuristic created by Frank T. Lyman Jr. and George Eley, 1985.

Writing

Build Intrapersonal and Communication Skills

Record your thoughts on a separate piece of paper, in a journal, or electronically.

EMOTIONAL INTELLIGENCE JOURNAL

Make a wiser choice. Think about a decision you made that you wish you had handled differently. Describe the decision and what feelings resulted from it. Then, describe what you would do if you could approach the decision again, thinking about a mindset and actions that might produce more positive feelings and a better outcome.

REAL-LIFE WRITING

Address a problem. Think about a problem that you are currently experiencing in school—it could be difficulty with a course, a scheduling nightmare, or a conflict with a classmate. Write a letter—to an advisor, instructor, friend, medical professional, or anyone else who may help—that asks for help with your problem. Be specific about what you want and how the person to whom you are writing can help you. After you finish, consider sending your letter via mail or email. Carefully assess the effect that it may have, and if you decide that it may help, send it. Be sure to have someone you trust review it for you before you send it.

Personal Portfolio

Prepare for Career Success

GENERATE IDEAS FOR INTERNSHIPS

21st Century Learning Building Blocks
- Financial, Economic, Business, and Entrepreneurial Literacy
- Leadership and Responsibility
- Communication and Collaboration

Complete the following in your electronic portfolio or separately on paper.

Pursuing internships is a practical way to get experience, learn what you like and don't like, and make valuable connections. Even interning in a career area that you don't ultimately pursue can build skills that are useful in any career. The creative thinking skills you've built will help you generate ideas for where you might intern at some point during your post-secondary career.

First, use personal contacts to gather information about career fields. List two people here:

People whom I want to interview about their fields/professions, and why:

1. _____   Field: _____

   Because: _____

2. _____   Field: _____

   Because: _____

Talk to the people you have listed and take notes.

Next, look up each of these fields at "Working in Canada" at www.workingincanada.gc.ca. Take notes and compare the fields based on what you've learned.

Finally, consult someone in your school's career office about local companies that offer internships. Get specific information about internship job descriptions, timing (during the term, in the summer), and whether there is any financial compensation.

Analyze what you have learned from your reading, your interviews, and career office information. Write here the field or fields in which you would like to intern and why, and describe what practical action you plan to take to secure an internship within the next two years:

_____

_____

_____

_____

_____

_____

_____

_____

_____

_____

Social Networking

ESTABLISH YOUR HISTORY

Broaden your profile with information about any work history you have. Sign in to your LinkedIn account and click on "Edit Profile." Fill in work information on the following (as applicable):

- Current (Click on "Current" and add information about your current employment: company name, job title, when you started working there, and description.)
- Past (Click on "Past" and add information about one or more past jobs: company name, job title, time period you worked at that job, and description.)

If you have a lean or non-existent work history, start thinking now about how to build that history while you are in school. Besides paid jobs in the workforce, other possibilities include internships, volunteering, and working on campus with faculty. Be sure to update your resumé and LinkedIn profile with work history as you build it.

■ ***Answers to perception puzzles on page 135:*** First puzzle: A duck or a rabbit. Second puzzle: Lines or a letter.

Study Tools: *Get Ready for Exams*

Start with a Study Plan and Schedule

Because some instructors may schedule exams early and often in the semester, begin right away to develop strategies for test success. Starting off on the right foot will boost your confidence and motivate you to work even harder. The saying that "success breeds more success" couldn't be more true as you begin college or university.

The material in this Study Tools is designed to help you organize yourself as you prepare for exams. As you learn to create a pretest study plan and schedule, you will also build your ability to use your time efficiently.

Decide on a study plan

Start your test preparation by deciding what you will study. Go through your notes, texts, related primary sources, and handouts, and set aside materials you don't need. Then prioritize the remaining materials. Your goal is to focus on information that is most likely to be on the exam. Use the test preparation tips and the material on studying your text in Chapter 4 to boost your effectiveness as you prepare.

Create a study schedule and checklist

Next, use the time-management and goal-setting skills from Chapter 6 to prepare a schedule. Consider all the relevant factors—your study materials, the number of days until the test, and the time you can study each day. If you establish your schedule ahead of time and write it in a planner, you are more likely to follow it.

A checklist like the one following will help you organize and stay on track as you prepare. Use a checklist to assign specific tasks to particular study times and sessions. That way, not only do you know when you have time to study, but you also have defined goals for each study session. Make extra copies of the checklist so that you can fill out a new one each time you have an exam.

Course: _____ Instructor: _____

Date, time, and place of test:_____

Type of test (is it a mid-term or a minor quiz?):_____

What the instructor said about the test, including the types of test questions, test length, and how much the test counts toward your final grade:

_____

_____

Topics to be covered on the test, in order of importance (information should also come from your instructor):

1. _____

2. _____

3. _____

4. _____

5. _____

Study schedule, including materials you plan to study (texts, class notes, homework problems, and so forth) and dates you plan to complete each:

MATERIAL   DATE OF COMPLETION

1. _____   _____

2. _____   _____

3. _____   _____

4. _____   _____

5. _____   _____

Materials you are expected to bring to the test (textbook, sourcebook, calculator, and so on):

_____

_____

_____

Special study arrangements (for example, plan study group meetings, ask the instructor for special help, get outside tutoring):

_____

_____

_____

Life-management issues (such as rearranging work hours):

_____

_____

_____

Source: Adapted from Ron Fry, *"Ace" Any Test*, 3rd ed., Franklin Lakes, NJ: Career Press, 1996. pp. 123–124.

Decide how well these techniques work for you

After you've used these studying and scheduling techniques to prepare for a few exams, answer the following questions:

- How did this approach help you organize your time before an exam?

_____

_____

- How did this approach help you organize your study material so that you remembered to cover every topic?

_____

_____

- Can you think of ways to change the checklist to improve your test-prep efficiency? If you can, list the ways here and incorporate them into the checklist.

_____

_____

_____

Self-Study Quiz

Circle or highlight the answer that seems to fit best.

1. **A *motivator* is**
   - A. the ability to achieve a goal.
   - B. progress toward a goal.
   - C. a decision to take action.
   - D. a want or need that moves a person to action.

2. **The direct benefits of responsibility include**
   - A. earning the trust of others at school, work, and home.
   - B. getting motivated to achieve study goals.
   - C. improved ability to plan strategically.
   - D. moving up at work.

3. **A *learning style* is**
   - A. the best way to learn when attending classes.
   - B. a particular way of being intelligent.
   - C. an affinity for a particular job choice or career area.
   - D. a way in which the mind receives and processes information.

4. **The best way to use learning style assessments is to see them as**
   - A. a reference point rather than a label; a tool with which to see yourself more clearly.

   - B. a road map for your life; a message that shows the paths you must take in order to be successful.
   - C. a lesson about group learning; a way to find the group of learners with whom you work best.
   - D. a definitive label for your working style; a clear-cut category where you fit.

5. **When choosing and evaluating your values, it is important to**
   - A. set goals according to what your friends and family value.
   - B. keep your values steady over time.
   - C. re-evaluate values periodically as you experience change.
   - D. set aside values that no one else seems to think are good for you.

6. **It is important to link daily and weekly goals with long-term goals because**
   - A. the process will help you focus on the things that are most important to you.
   - B. short-term goals have no meaning if they are not placed in a longer time frame.
   - C. the process will help you eliminate frivolous activities.
   - D. others expect you to know how everything you do relates to what you want to accomplish in life.

Fill in the blanks

Complete the following sentences with the appropriate word(s) or phrase(s) that best reflect what you learned in the chapters. Choose from the items that follow each sentence.

1. When you make a _____, you do what you say you will do. (initiative, motivation, commitment)

2. Showing _____ helps you take that first step toward a goal and respond to changes in your life. (motivation, initiative, integrity)

3. One way to look at learning style is to divide it into two equally important aspects: _____ and _____. (learning preferences/personality traits, verbal/visual, interests/abilities)

4. The best careers and majors/programs for you are ones that take into consideration your _____ and _____. (references/contacts, learning style/abilities, interests/abilities)

5. Your _____ is a philosophy outlining what you want to be, what you want to do, and the principles by which you live. (responsibility, mission, integrity)

6. Being _____ helps you cope with day-to-day changes and life changes. (organized, flexible, on time)

Essays

The following essay questions will help you organize and communicate your ideas in writing, just as you must do on an essay test. Before you begin answering a question, spend a few minutes planning (brainstorm possible approaches, write a thesis statement, jot down main thoughts in outline or think-link form). To prepare yourself for actual test conditions, limit writing time to no more than 30 minutes per question.

1. Discuss habits, both good and bad. What are the effects of each? Describe a useful plan for changing a habit that is having negative effects.

2. Define *values* and *value system*. How do values develop and what effect do they have on personal choices? How are values connected to goal setting? Give an example from your life of how values have influenced a personal goal.

chapter 6

Values, Goals, and Time

Managing Yourself

What Would You Do?

Think about this problem as you read, and consider how you would approach it. This chapter takes a closer look at your personal values, the goals you set reflecting those values, and how you manage your time to achieve those important goals.

Devonne Henley attended college as a part-time student for the past year and this term decided to take on a full load of courses. However, she is finding it difficult to manage her responsibilities. In sociology class the instructor, Ms. Cordoza, has assigned a group project focusing on the biggest problems the world is facing today. She has asked Devonne to stay after class to talk about it.

"Devonne, I know you haven't been able to make your group's first two meetings," she said, "and I want to make sure you don't let this project drop. How can I help?"

"I'm just swamped," Devonne replied. "I've got four other classes and I work weekends; I take care of my nephew every morning, and my schedule is just not working out."

"Is that the little guy you brought to class last week?" asked Ms. Cordoza.

"Yes, that's him. I'm sorry I had to do that," said Devonne.

Ms. Cordoza thought for a moment. "Look, you did keep him quiet so he didn't disturb the class. My issue is that you couldn't be present for the class while managing him. Class time is your time to get what you need from your education."

"You know, this project just doesn't make sense to me. We're supposed to be thinking through how to stop global warming, and I can't even turn in a paper on time or stay awake when I study," Devonne said.

"Listen, at the very least, you need a decent grade on this project," Ms. Cordoza responded. "But you might find out that world problems have more to do with you than you think. Can you make your group's next meeting this Friday at 1 p.m.?" (To be continued . . .)

Managing responsibilities is a challenge for almost every student. You'll learn more about Devonne, and revisit her situation, within the chapter.

In this chapter, you'll explore answers to these questions:

> Why is it important to know what you value? p. 160

> How do you set and achieve goals? p. 161

> How can you effectively manage your time? p. 168

MyStudentSuccessLab

Use these interactive tools to help you succeed in your course and career:
• Videos
• Exercises and applied activities
• Practice quizzes

STATUS *Check*

▶ *How developed are your self-management skills?*

For each statement, circle the number that feels right to you, from 1 for "not at all true for me" to 5 for "very true for me."

▶ I am aware of my values and beliefs.	**1 2 3 4 5**
▶ I have a system for reminding myself of what my goals are.	**1 2 3 4 5**
▶ I find ways to motivate myself when I am working toward a goal.	**1 2 3 4 5**
▶ When I set a long-term goal, I break it down into a series of short-term goals.	**1 2 3 4 5**
▶ I am aware of my time-related needs and preferences.	**1 2 3 4 5**
▶ I understand my time traps and have ways to avoid them.	**1 2 3 4 5**
▶ I know how to use the SMART approach to plan achievable goals.	**1 2 3 4 5**
▶ When I procrastinate, I know how to get back on track.	**1 2 3 4 5**
▶ I record tasks, events, and responsibilities in a planner of some kind and refer to it regularly.	**1 2 3 4 5**
▶ I understand how managing my time can help reduce my level of stress.	**1 2 3 4 5**

Each of the topics in these statements is covered in this chapter. Note those statements for which you circled a 3 or lower. Skim the chapter to see where those topics appear, and pay special attention to them as you read, learn, and apply new strategies.

REMEMBER: *No matter how effectively you set goals and manage time, you can improve with effort and practice.*

"Successfully intelligent people are well aware of the penalties for procrastination. They schedule their time so that the important things get done—and done well."

—Robert Sternberg

VALUES
Principles or qualities that you consider important.

Why is it important to know what you value?

You make life choices—what to do, what to believe, what to buy, how to act—based on your personal **values.** The choice to pursue a degree, for example, may reflect how a person values the personal and professional growth that come from a college or university education. If you like to be on time for classes, you may value punctuality. If you pay bills regularly and on time, you may value financial stability.

Values play a key role in your drive to achieve important goals and use your time wisely, helping you do the following:

▶ *Understand what you want out of life.* Your most meaningful goals will reflect what you value most.

▶ *Choose how to use your valuable time.* When your day-to-day activities align with what you think is most important, you gain greater fulfillment from them.

▶ *Build "rules for life."* Your values form the foundation for your decisions and behaviour throughout your life. You will return repeatedly to these rules for guidance, especially in unfamiliar territory.

▶ *Find people who inspire you.* Spending time with people who share similar values will help you clarify how you want to live while finding support for your goals.

How values develop and change

Your value system is complex, built piece by piece over time, and coming from many sources—such as family, friends, culture, media, school, work, neighbourhood, religious beliefs, and world events. These powerful external influences can so effectively instill values that you don't think about why you believe what you believe. However, you have a *choice* whether or not to adopt any value. Taking advantage of the power to choose requires evaluating values with questions such as the following:

▶ Where did the value come from?

▶ Is this value something from my family or culture that I have accepted without questioning, or have I truly made it my own?

▶ What other different values could I consider?

▶ What might happen as a result of adopting this value?

▶ Have I made a personal commitment to this choice? Have I told others about it?

▶ Do my life goals and day-to-day actions reflect this value?

Values are not set in stone any more than your thinking power is. Your values often shift as you grow. For example, Devonne may have begun to value her family more after her nephew was born. Life changes make it even more important to step back and think about what's truly important to you.

How values affect your life experience

Because what you value often determines the choices you make, it also shapes your life experiences. For example, the fact that you value education may have led you to college or university, a practical choice that will help you build skills and persistence, choose a major and career direction, find meaningful friends and activities, and achieve learning goals.

Another example is found on Canadian college and university campuses in the growing diversity of the student body, a diversity also increasingly seen in the working population. If you value human differences, you have taken an important step on the way to working successfully with people of various cultures, at various stages of life, and with various value systems both in post-secondary education and beyond.

Values become goals when you've transformed your beliefs into something tangible and long-lasting. Not every value becomes a goal, but every goal stems from your values.

How do you set and achieve goals?

When you set a (**goal**,) you focus on what you want to achieve and create a path that can get you there. Setting goals involves defining your aims in both long-term and short-term time frames. *Long-term* goals are broader objectives you

→ GOAL
An end toward which you direct your efforts.

get*Analytical!*

Explore Your Values

Rate each of the listed values on a scale from 1 to 5, 1 being least important to you and 5 being most important.

___ Knowing yourself	___ Being liked by others	___ Reading
___ Self-improvement	___ Taking risks	___ Time to yourself
___ Improving physical/mental health	___ Time for fun/relaxation	___ Lifelong learning
___ Leadership and teamwork skills	___ Staying fit through exercise	___ Competing and winning
___ Pursuing an education	___ Spiritual/religious life	___ Making a lot of money
___ Good relationships with family	___ Community involvement	___ Creative/artistic pursuits
___ Helping others	___ Keeping up with the news	___ Getting a good job
___ Being organized	___ Financial stability	___ Other

List your top three values:

1. _____

2. _____

3. _____

Now connect your values to educational goals. Choose one top value that is a factor in an educational choice you have made. Explain the choice and how the value is involved. Example: A student who values helping others chooses to study nursing.

_____

_____

want to achieve over a long period of time, perhaps a year or more. *Short-term* goals move you toward a long-term goal in manageable and achievable steps (see Key 6.1).

Establish your personal mission

Start with the biggest big picture: defining your *personal mission* can help you anchor your values and goals in a comprehensive view of what you want out of life. Think of a personal mission as your longest-term goal, within which all other long-term and short-term goals should fit.

Dr. Stephen Covey, author of *The Seven Habits of Highly Effective People*, defines a *mission statement* as a philosophy outlining what you want to be (character), what you want to do (contributions and achievements), and the principles by which you live (your values).[1] Defining your personal mission involves creating a mission statement. The following mission statement was written by Carol Carter, one of the authors of *Keys to Success*.

My mission is to use my talents and abilities to help people of all ages, stages, backgrounds, and economic levels achieve their human potential through fully

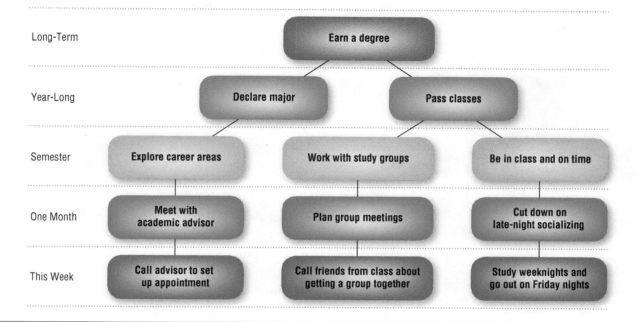

Key 6.1

GOALS REINFORCE ONE ANOTHER

Long-Term			Earn a degree		
Year-Long		Declare major		Pass classes	
Semester	Explore career areas		Work with study groups		Be in class and on time
One Month	Meet with academic advisor		Plan group meetings		Cut down on late-night socializing
This Week	Call advisor to set up appointment		Call friends from class about getting a group together		Study weeknights and go out on Friday nights

developing their minds and their talents. I aim to create opportunities for others through work, service, and family. I also aim to balance work with people in my life, understanding that my family and friends are a priority above all else.

How can you start formulating a mission statement? Try using Covey's three aspects of personal mission as a guide. Think through the following:

▶ *Character.* What aspects of character do you think are most valuable? When you consider the people you admire most, which of their qualities stand out?

▶ *Contributions and achievements.* What do you want to accomplish in your life? Where do you want to make a difference?

▶ *Values.* How do your values inform your life goals? What in your mission could help you live according to what you value most highly?

Because what you want out of life changes as you do, your personal mission should remain flexible and open to revision. Your mission can be the road map for your personal journey, giving meaning to your daily activities, promoting responsibility, and inspiring action. You will have a chance to craft a personal mission at the end of this chapter.

Goals take effort and planning to reach. This music producer spends days, and even weeks, adjusting equipment and recording tracks on the way to the production of just one song.
© UpperCut Images/Getty Images

Set long-term goals

What do you want your life to look like in 5 or 10 years? What degree do you want to earn? What job do you want? Where

student profile

Brandie Molley
Sprott-Shaw Community College, Penticton, British Columbia

About me:
I'm a mature student and a single mom.

What I focus on:
When I decided to go back to school, I really had no idea what I was signing up for! I was literally spinning in circles. Between trying to get my oldest off to school in the mornings, finding a childcare facility that was open the hours I was going to school for my youngest, and already attending school, I really wasn't sure I was going to make it. But somehow I have managed to juggle it all, and I have not yet missed a day of school.

I have learned how to make sure my time is well used. Being a single mom is hard, but when you decide to further your education it gets even harder. Making sure you get the proper amount of sleep is the key to being able to run all day and to making sure the kids stay on your timed schedule along with you. It's not always easy when there is only one of you and two of them; but, with enough energy and a schedule, everything that needs to be done gets done.

Sprott-Shaw makes going to school while caring for a family easier for me because classes don't start until later in the day. So when my oldest goes to school, after I drive a half-hour to my youngest son's daycare, I have plenty of time to study and get assignments finished before class starts. There are always computers open and classrooms available for studying. I was worried when I started that I was going to get behind, because, let's face it, if I had to do my homework or studying at home, it would never get done. Between kids screaming and dishes piling up, homework and studying is the last thing on my mind.

What will help me in the workplace:
Going to school has very much prepared me for the workforce and for working under tight timelines. I'll be using the lessons I have learned, such as scheduling everything I do as well as everything my sons do, making sure we all get good nights' sleeps, and most of all making sure I give myself extra time for "just in case" scenarios. My best advice to anyone who's feeling a little overwhelmed is take a deep breath, know that it will all be worth it in the end, and don't give up—a career is out there waiting for you.

do you want to live? How do you want to live your values and activate your personal mission? Answers to questions such as these help identify long-term goals.

Long-term goals are objectives that sit out on the horizon, at least six months to a year away. They're goals that you can imagine and maybe even visualize, reflecting who you are and what is important to you, but they're too far out for you to touch. The more you know about yourself, the better able you are to set and work toward meaningful long-term goals. One way to make long-term goals real is to put them in writing, as in the following example.

My goal is to build a business in which I, as a family doctor, create opportunities to expose young people in my community to the medical field.

A student two years away from graduation who is pursuing this long-term goal might establish the following supporting set of one-year long-term goals:

Design courses for the year to make sure I am on track for pre-med course completion. Find medical practices in the area that could serve as a model for my business. Research medical schools.

To determine your long-term goals, think about the values that anchor your personal mission. For someone who values health and fitness, for example, possible long-term goals might involve working for an organic food company or training as a physical therapist. Basing your long-term goals on values increases your motivation to succeed. The stronger the link between your values and your long-term goals, the happier, more motivated, and more successful you are likely to be in setting and achieving those goals.

Set short-term goals

Lasting from an hour or less to as long as several months, *short-term goals* narrow your focus and encourage progress toward long-term goals. If you have a long-term goal of graduating with a degree in nursing, for example, you may set these short-term goals for the next six months:

▶ I will learn the name, location, and function of every human bone and muscle.

▶ I will work with a study group to understand the musculoskeletal system.

These goals can be broken down into even smaller parts, such as the following one-month goals:

▶ I will work with onscreen tutorials of the musculoskeletal system until I understand and memorize the material.

▶ I will spend three hours a week with my study partners.

In addition to monthly goals, you may have short-term goals that extend for a week, a day, or even a couple of hours. To support your goal of regularly meeting with your study partners, you may set the following short-term goals:

▶ *By the end of today.* Text or email study partners to ask them when they might be able to meet.

▶ *1 week from now.* Schedule each of our weekly meetings this month.

▶ *2 weeks from now.* Have our first meeting.

▶ *3 weeks from now.* Type and distribute notes from first meeting; have second meeting.

Set up a SMART goal-achievement plan

At any given time, you are working toward goals of varying importance. First, decide which goals matter most to you and are most deserving of your focus. Then draw up a plan to achieve those goals, using the SMART system to make your goals <u>S</u>pecific, <u>M</u>easurable, <u>A</u>chievable, <u>R</u>ealistic, and linked to a <u>T</u>ime Frame.

▶ *Step 1.* Define an Achievable, Realistic goal. *What do you want?* Is it **achievable**—do you have the skill, ability, and drive to get there? Is it **realistic**—will the external factors (time available, weather, money, other people, and so on) help or hinder you? To develop an achievable, realistic goal, consider your hopes, interests, and abilities. Then reflect on how realistic it is, given your resources and circumstances. Write out a clear description of your goal.

▶ *Step 2.* Define a Specific path. *How will you get there?* Brainstorm different paths. Choose one; then map out its **specific** steps. Focus on behaviours and events that are under your control.

▶ *Step 3.* Link to a Time Frame. *When do you want to accomplish your goal?* Schedule steps within a realistic **time frame**. Create specific deadlines for each step you defined in Step 1. Charting your progress will help you stay on track.

▶ *Step 4.* Measure your progress. *What safeguards will keep you on track?* Will you record your progress in a weekly journal? Report to a friend? Use an alarm system on your smartphone to remind you to do something? Create a system to **measure** how well you are moving along.

▶ *Step 5.* Get unstuck. *What will you do if you hit a roadblock?* The path to a goal is often rocky and stressful. Anticipate problems and define **specific** ways to alter your plans if you run into trouble (stress management strategies are presented later in the chapter). Reach out to friends, family, and school personnel who can help you. Remind yourself of the benefits of your goal. Be ready to brainstorm other ideas if your plans don't work. The Get Creative activity will help you think your way past roadblocks.

▶ *Step 6.* Action time. Follow the steps in your plan until you achieve your goal.

See Key 6.2 for a way to apply this goal-setting plan to an important objective that nearly every college and university student will need to achieve—declaring a major or concentration (for the sake of simplicity, the term *major* will appear throughout the rest of the book).

Through the process of working toward your most important goals, you will often be thinking about how well you are using your time. In fact, being able to achieve any significant goal is directly linked to effective time management.

MAJOR or **CONCENTRATION** An academic subject area chosen as a field of specialization, requiring a specific course of study.

How can you **effectively manage your time?**

No matter how well you define the steps to your goals, you need to set those steps within a time frame to achieve them. Although the idea of "managing time" may seem impossible, time management can also be thought of as *behavioural management*—adjusting what you do so that you can meet your needs in the time you have available.

Everyone has only 24 hours in a day, and 8 or so of those hours involve sleeping (or should, if you want to remain healthy and alert enough to achieve your goals). You can't manage how time passes, but you *can* manage how you use it. Only by making active choices about your time can you hope to avoid

*get*Creative!

Find Ways to Get Unstuck

Think of a problem on which you tend to get stuck. It could be scheduling homework around extracurricular activities, finding time to hang out with friends, coming up with interesting career paths, or simply figuring out the theme of a literary work.

_____

_____

_____

Now come up with three reasonable ways to get unstuck. For example, if your issue is scheduling homework, one way to get unstuck might be to start your day earlier with a one-hour work session.

1. _____

2. _____

3. _____

Now that you've determined the most logical solutions, use a visual organizer to think outside of the problem-solving box. First, write your problem in the centre bubble. Then, begin filling in the surrounding bubbles with as many ideas as you can think of. Don't question their validity or whether or not they'll work; just keep writing until you've filled in every bubble with a possible solution.

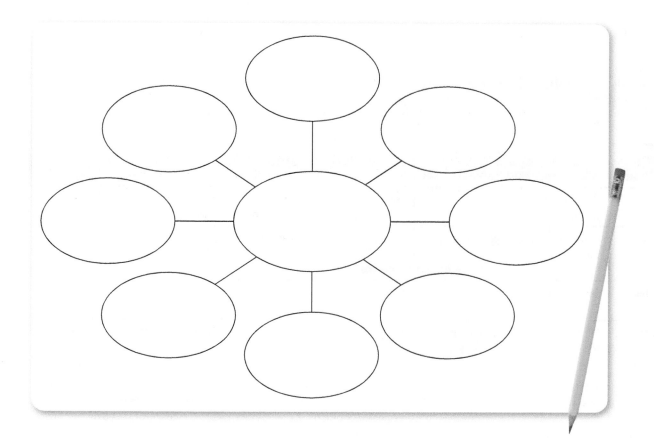

When you're finished, read through all of your creative solutions. Do any of them stick out to you? Find your two favourites and briefly describe how you might be able to use them next time you are faced with a similar situation.

_____

_____

_____

_____

_____

_____

_____

_____

You just got yourself unstuck. Consider using this method when faced with a tough problem. Thinking creatively can be an extremely productive (not to mention fun) way to solve any problem you may encounter.

WORK SMART TOWARD
AN IMPORTANT GOAL

Goal: To decide on a major.

SMART KEY	MEANING	EXAMPLE
Specific	Name exactly how you will achieve your goal.	I will read the list of available majors, meet with my academic advisor, talk with instructors, and choose a major by the deadline.
Measurable	Find ways to measure your progress over time.	I will set alarms on my smartphone to remind me of when I should have accomplished steps. I will ask my mom to check in to make sure I'm getting somewhere.
Achievable	Set a goal that your abilities and drive can handle.	I'm driven to declare a major because I want to earn my degree, graduate, and gain work-ready skills.
Realistic	Define a goal that is workable given the resources (time and money) and other circumstances.	Because I'm starting early and already know how the process works, I should have time to think through this carefully.
Time Frame	Set up a time frame for achieving your goal and the steps toward it.	I have a year until the deadline. I will read the catalogue in the next month; I will meet with my advisor by the end of the term; I will talk with instructors at the beginning of next term; I will declare a major by the end of next term.

that feeling of being swept along in time's swift tide that Devonne is experiencing. The first step in time management is to figure out your time profile and your preferences.

Identify your time profile and preferences

People have unique body rhythms and habits that affect how they deal with time. Some people are night owls who have lots of energy late at night. Others are early birds who do their best work early in the day. Some people are chronically late, whereas others get everything done with time to spare.

The more you're aware of your own time-related behaviours, the better able you'll be to create a schedule that maximizes your strengths and reduces stress. The following steps can help you get in touch with your own inner time clock:

■ **Create a personal time profile.** Ask yourself these questions: At what time of day do I have the most energy? The least energy? Do I tend to be early, on time, or late? Do I focus well for long stretches or need regular breaks? Your answers will help you determine your profile.

■ **Evaluate the effects of your profile.** Which of your time-related habits and preferences will have a positive impact on your success at school? Which are likely to cause problems? Which can you make adjustments for, and which will just require you to cope?

■ **Establish schedule preferences.** Based on the time profile you have developed, list your preferences—or even map out an ideal schedule as a way of illustrating them. For example, one student's preference list might read, "Classes bunched together on Mondays, Wednesdays, and Fridays. Tuesdays and Thursdays free for studying and research. Study time primarily during the day."

Next, build a schedule that takes your profile and preferences into account wherever possible. You will have more control over some things than others. For example, a student who functions best late at night may have more luck scheduling study time than class meeting times (unless he or she attends one of several schools that have begun to schedule late-night classes to handle an overload of students).

Build a schedule

Schedules help you gain control of your life in two ways: they provide segments of time for goal-related tasks and remind you of tasks, events, due dates, responsibilities, and deadlines.

Use a planner

A planner is a tool for managing your time. Use it to keep track of events and commitments, schedule goal-related tasks, and rank tasks according to priority. Time management expert Paul Timm says that "rule number one in a thoughtful planning process is: Use some form of a planner where you can write things down."[2]

There are two major types of planners. One is a book or notebook, showing either a day or a week at a glance, in which to note commitments. Some planners contain sections for monthly and yearly goals. The

Managing time effectively often means taking advantage of opportunities whenever they arise. This student, also a mother, fits schoolwork in during naptime.
© Michael Newman/PhotoEdit

other option is an electronic planner or mobile device such as an iPhone, iPad, or BlackBerry. Basic functions allow you to schedule days and weeks, note due dates, make to-do lists, perform mathematical calculations, and create and store an address book. You can also transfer information to and from a computer.

Though electronic planners are handy and have a large data capacity, they cost more than the paper versions, and they can fail due to software or battery problems. Analyze your preferences and options, and decide which tool you are most likely to use every day. A blank notebook, used conscientiously, may work as well for some people as a top-of-the-line smartphone. You might also consider online calendars, such as Google Calendar, which can "communicate" with your phone or other electronic planning device.

Keep track of events and commitments

Your planner is designed to help you schedule and remember events and commitments. A quick look at your notations will remind you when items are approaching. Your class syllabus is a crucial tool for keeping track of reading and homework assignments and test dates (see Key 6.3).

When you get your syllabi for the term, enter all relevant dates in your planner right away so you can prepare for crunch times. For example, if you see that

NOTE **DAILY AND WEEKLY** TASKS

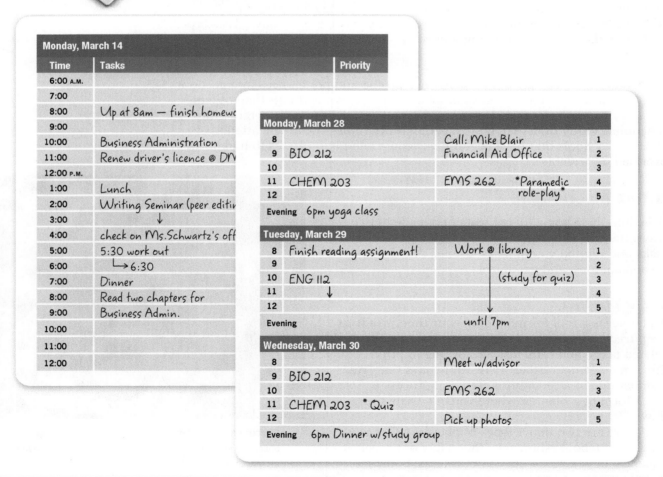

Monday, March 14		
Time	**Tasks**	**Priority**
6:00 A.M.		
7:00		
8:00	Up at 8am — finish homewo	
9:00		
10:00	Business Administration	
11:00	Renew driver's licence @ DN	
12:00 P.M.		
1:00	Lunch	
2:00	Writing Seminar (peer editin	
3:00	↓	
4:00	check on Ms.Schwartz's off	
5:00	5:30 work out	
6:00	↳6:30	
7:00	Dinner	
8:00	Read two chapters for	
9:00	Business Admin.	
10:00		
11:00		
12:00		

Monday, March 28		
8		Call: Mike Blair	1
9	BIO 212	Financial Aid Office	2
10			3
11	CHEM 203	EMS 262 *Paramedic	4
12		role-play*	5
Evening 6pm yoga class		

Tuesday, March 29		
8	Finish reading assignment!	Work @ library	1
9			2
10	ENG 112	(study for quiz)	3
11	↓		4
12			5
Evening	until 7pm	

Wednesday, March 30		
8		Meet w/advisor	1
9	BIO 212		2
10		EMS 262	3
11	CHEM 203 *Quiz		4
12		Pick up photos	5
Evening 6pm Dinner w/study group		

you have three tests and a presentation coming up all in one week, you may have to rearrange your schedule during the preceding week to create extra study time.

Among the events and commitments worth noting in your planner are the following:

▶ Test and quiz dates; due dates for papers, projects, and presentations

▶ Details of your academic schedule, including term and holiday breaks

▶ Club and organizational meetings

▶ Personal items—medical appointments, due dates for bills, birthdays, social events

▶ Milestones toward a goal, such as due dates for sections of a project

It's important to include class prep time—reading and studying, writing, and working on assignments and projects—in the planner. You should schedule at least two hours of preparation for every hour of class—that is, if you take 12 credits, you'll spend 24 hours or more a week on course-related activities in and out of class. It's tough to get that much studying in, especially if you are an athlete, a working student, or a parent. Situations like these demand creative time management and attention to your schedule.

Schedule tasks and activities that support your values and goals

Linking day-to-day events in your planner to your values and broader goals will give meaning to your efforts, bring order to your schedule, and keep you motivated. Planning study time for an economics test, for example, will mean more to you if you link the hours you spend to your goal of being accepted into business school and your value of meaningful employment. Here is how a student might translate his goal of entering business school into action steps over a year's time:

▶ *This year.* Complete enough courses to meet curriculum requirements for business school and maintain class standing.

▶ *This term.* Complete my economics class with a B average or higher.

▶ *This month.* Set up economics study group schedule to coincide with quizzes and tests.

▶ *This week.* Meet with study group; go over material for Friday's test.

▶ *Today.* Go over Chapter 1 in econ text.

The student can then arrange his time to move him in the direction of his goal. He schedules activities that support his short-term goal of doing well on the test and writes them in his planner. Achieving his overarching long-term goal of doing well in a course he needs for business school is the source of his motivation.

Before each week begins, remind yourself of your long-term goals and what you can accomplish over the next seven days to move you closer to them.

PRIORITIZE
To arrange or deal with in order of importance.

Additionally, every once in a while, take a hard look at your schedule to see whether you are spending time on what you most value. Key 6.3 shows parts of a daily schedule and a weekly schedule.

Make to-do lists and prioritize

Many people find it useful to create a daily or weekly to-do list and check off the items as they are completed. A to-do list can be useful on an especially busy day, during exam week, or at any other time that you anticipate being overloaded.

Making a list, however, is more than doing a "brain dump" of everything you have to do. You need to **prioritize** your list—code it, or organize it, according to how important each item is. Some people use numbers, some use letters, and some use different-coloured pens or, for electronic planners, highlighting and font colour tools. Prioritizing helps you focus the bulk of your energy and time on the most important tasks. Because many top-priority items (classes, work) occur at designated times, prioritizing helps you lock in these activities and schedule less urgent items around them.

Prioritizing isn't just for time management. You should also prioritize your long-term and short-term goals and the steps leading up to each. Keep these priorities alongside your daily lists so you can see how they influence one another. For instance, arriving at school a half-hour early so you can meet with an advisor influences your long-term goal of deciding on a major.

Whether it's a task or goal you're scheduling, set basic priority levels according to the following guidelines.

■ *Priority 1.* The most crucial items—you must do them. They may include attending class, working at a job, picking up a child from daycare, and paying bills. Enter Priority 1 items in your planner first, before scheduling anything else.

■ *Priority 2.* Important items but with flexibility in scheduling. Examples include library study time and working out. Schedule these around the Priority 1 items.

■ *Priority 3.* Least important items—the "nice to do" activities. Examples include phoning a friend or upgrading software for your iPod.

Plan and track

As you work on the tasks in your to-do lists and planner, follow these guidelines to stay focused on your goals:

▶ *Plan regularly.* Set aside a regular time each day to plan your schedule (right before bed, with your morning coffee, on your commute to or from school, or whatever time and situation works best for you). This regular planning reduces stress and prevents the hassle of forgetting something important.

▶ *Actively manage your schedule.* The most detailed planner won't do you a bit of good unless you look at it. Check your schedule at regular intervals throughout the day or week.

MARCH

SUNDAY	MONDAY	TUESDAY	WEDNESDAY	THURSDAY	FRIDAY	SATURDAY
	1 WORK	2 Turn in English paper topic	3 Dentist 2 pm	4 WORK	5	6
7 Frank's birthday	8 Psych Test 9 am WORK	9	10 6:30 pm Meeting @ Acad Ctr	11 WORK	12	13 Dinner @ Ryan's
14	15 English paper due WORK	16 Western Civ paper	17	18 Library 6 pm WORK	19 Western Civ makeup class	20
21	22 WORK	23 2 pm meeting, psych group	24 Start running: 3 km	25 WORK	26 Run 3 km	27
28 Run 5 km	29 WORK	30 Western Civ paper due	31 Run 3 km			

▶ *Use monthly and yearly calendars at home.* A standard monthly or yearly wall calendar is a great place to keep track of your major commitments. A wall calendar like the monthly calendar in Key 6.4 gives you the big-picture overview you need.

▶ *Work to stay motivated.* If you can get a task done ahead of time, get it done; it will help you avoid pressure later. Focus on your growth mindset, reminding yourself that achievement requires persistent effort.

▶ *Avoid time traps.* Stay away from situations that eat up time. Learn to say no when you just can't fit in an extra responsibility. Reduce time spent with anything that distracts you, such as your cellphone, social networking sites, or your Twitter account.

▶ *Schedule downtime.* It's easy to get so caught up in completing tasks that you forget to relax and breathe. Even a half-hour of downtime a day will refresh you and improve your productivity when you get back on task.

Confront procrastination

It's human, and common for busy students, to leave difficult or undesirable tasks until later. If taken to the extreme, however, procrastination can develop into a habit that causes serious problems. For example, procrastinators who

PROCRASTINATION
The act of putting off a task until another time.

Conquer Your Time Traps

Different people get bogged down by different time traps. What are yours? They could be productive activities, such as working out, or less productive activities, such as checking your email. Think of two common time traps that you encounter. For each, come up with two ways to say no graciously—to someone else, or even to yourself, as in the following example.

Time Trap: **Text messaging**

Response 1: **"I'll call you in an hour. I need to finish this paper."**

Response 2: **"I will respond to my text messages after I've read five pages."**

Your turn:

Time Trap: _____

Response 1: _____

_____

Response 2: _____

_____

Time Trap: _____

Response 1: _____

_____

Response 2: _____

_____

Choose one of the situations you just named and use one or both of your responses the next time the trap threatens your time. Afterwards, answer these questions:

How did the response affect your ability to take control of the situation? Did it help? Hurt? How?

_____

_____

_____

_____

What did the response teach you about your personal time traps? Do you find yourself needing to be stricter with your time? Why?

_____

_____

_____

_____

_____

don't get things done in the workplace may prevent others from doing their work, possibly losing a promotion or even a job because of it.

This excerpt from the Study Skills Library at California Polytechnic State University illustrates how procrastination can quickly turn into a destructive pattern.

> The procrastinator is often remarkably optimistic about his ability to complete a task on a tight deadline. . . . For example, he may estimate that a paper will take only five days to write; he has fifteen days; there is plenty of time, no need to start. Lulled by a false sense of security, time passes. At some point, he crosses over an imaginary starting time and suddenly realizes, "Oh no! I am not in control! There isn't enough time!"
>
> At this point, considerable effort is directed toward completing the task, and work progresses. This sudden spurt of energy is the source of the erroneous feeling that "I work well only under pressure." Actually, at this point you are making progress only because you haven't any choice. . . . Progress is being made, but you have lost your freedom.
>
> Barely completed in time, the paper may actually earn a fairly good grade; whereupon the student experiences mixed feelings: pride of accomplishment (sort of), scorn for the professor who cannot recognize substandard work, and guilt for getting an undeserved grade. But the net result is *reinforcement*: The procrastinator is rewarded positively for his poor behaviour ("Look what a decent grade I got after all!"). As a result, the counterproductive behaviour is repeated time and time again.[3]

People procrastinate for various reasons.

■ ***Perfectionism.*** According to Jane B. Burka and Lenora M. Yuen, authors of *Procrastination: Why You Do It and What to Do About It*, habitual procrastinators often gauge their self-worth solely by their ability to achieve. In other words, "an outstanding performance means an outstanding person; a mediocre performance means a mediocre person."[4] To the perfectionist procrastinator, not trying at all is better than an attempt that falls short of perfection.

■ ***Fear of limitations.*** Some people procrastinate to avoid the truth about what they can achieve. "As long as you procrastinate, you never have to confront the real limits of your ability, whatever those limits are," say Burka and Yuen.[5] A fixed mindset naturally leads to procrastination. "I can't do it," the person with the fixed mindset thinks, "so what's the point of trying?"

■ ***Being unsure of the next step.*** If you get stuck and don't know what to do, sometimes it seems easier to procrastinate than to make the leap to the next level of your goal.

■ ***Facing an overwhelming task.*** Some big projects create fear, as Devonne feels about her group project. If a person facing such a task fears failure, she may procrastinate to avoid confronting the fear. Get into your growth mindset and use the strategies to work through this or any other kind of fear, taking steps forward and knowing that you stand to learn something valuable.

Although it can bring relief in the short term, avoiding tasks almost always causes problems, such as a buildup of responsibilities and less time to complete them, work that is below par, the disappointment of others who depend

Change the
CONVERSATION

Challenge yourself and your friends to ask—and answer—tough questions. Use the following to inspire discussion in pairs or groups.

▶ What time-management issues do you see others face? How do they handle them?

▶ How do you handle similar situations? Do you think your approach is as good, better, or not as good? Why? What is the result?

▶ **CONSIDER THE CASE:** What do you think about Ms. Cordoza's suggestion that Devonne Henley become more involved in the project in order to find personal meaning? If you were the instructor, what would you add to convince Devonne?

on your work, and stress brought on by unfinished tasks. Particular strategies can help you avoid procrastination and its associated problems.

▶ *Analyze the effects.* What may happen if you continue to put off a task? Chances are you will benefit more in the long term if you face the task head-on.

▶ *Set reasonable goals.* Unreasonable goals intimidate and immobilize you. If you concentrate on achieving one small step at a time, the task becomes less burdensome.

▶ *Get started whether you "feel like it" or not.* Take the first step. Once you start, you may find it easier to continue.

▶ *Ask for help.* Once you identify what's holding you up, find someone to help you face the task. Another person may come up with an innovative method to get you moving again.

▶ *Don't expect perfection.* People learn by starting at the beginning, making mistakes, and learning from them. If you avoid mistakes, you deprive yourself of learning and growth.

▶ *Reward yourself.* Boost your confidence when you accomplish a task. Celebrate progress with a reward—a break, a movie, whatever feels like a treat to you.

Take a look at Key 6.5 to explore five major reasons that people waste time and procrastinate—and to learn how to take control of each.

TAKE CONTROL OF
TIME WASTERS

1. **Television**   It's easy to just keep flipping the channels when you know you've got something due.
   Take Control: Record favourite shows by using a digital video recorder or watch a movie instead. When your program of choice is over, turn off the TV.

2. **Commute**   Though not often something you can control, the time spent commuting from one place to another can be staggering.
   Take Control: Use your time on a bus or train to do homework, study, read assignments, or work on your monthly budget.

3. **Internet Browsing**   Currently, Internet misuse in the workplace costs companies almost $200 billion per year in lost productivity.
   Take Control: If you use the Internet for research, consider subscribing to RSS feeds that can alert you when relevant information becomes available. When using the Internet for social or personal reasons, stick to a time limit.

4. **Fatigue**   Being tired can lead to below-quality work that may have to be redone and can make you feel ready to quit altogether.
   Take Control: Determine a stop time for yourself. When your stop time comes, put down the book, turn off the computer, and go to bed. During the day when you can, take naps to recharge your battery.

5. **Confusion**   When you don't fully understand an assignment or problem, you may spend unintended time trying to figure it out.
   Take Control: The number one way to fight confusion is to ask. As the saying goes, ask early and ask often. Students who seek help show that they want to learn.

Be flexible

Change is a part of life. No matter how well you think ahead and plan your time, sudden changes—ranging from a room change for a class to a medical emergency—can upend your plans. However, you have some control over how you handle circumstances. Your ability to evaluate situations, come up with creative options, and put practical plans to work will help you manage changes.

Small changes—the need to work an hour of overtime at your after-school job, a meeting that runs late—can result in priority shifts that jumble your schedule. For changes that occur frequently, think through a backup plan ahead of time. For surprises, the best you can do is to keep an open mind about possibilities and rely on your internal and external resources.

When change involves serious problems—your car breaks down and you have no way to get to school, or you fail a class and have to consider summer school—use problem-solving skills to help you through (see Chapter 5). Resources available at your college or university can help you throughout this process. Your academic advisor, counsellor, dean, financial aid advisor, and instructors may have ideas and assistance.

Manage stress by managing time

If you are feeling (stress) in your everyday life as a student, you are not alone. Stress levels among post-secondary students have increased dramatically.[6] Stress factors for college and university students include adjusting to a new environment with increased work and difficult decisions, as well as juggling school, work, and personal responsibilities.

> STRESS
> Physical or mental strain or tension produced in reaction to pressure.

Dealing with the stress of post-secondary life is, and will continue to be, one of your biggest challenges. But here's some good news: *every time-management strategy in this chapter contributes to your ability to cope with stress*. Remember that stress refers to how you react to pressure. When you create and follow a schedule that gets you places on time and helps you take care of tasks and responsibilities, you reduce pressure. Less pressure, less stress.

Analyze, and adjust if necessary, the relationship between stress and your time-management habits. For example, if you're a night person with early classes and are consistently stressed about waking up in time, use strategies such as going to bed earlier a few nights a week, napping in the afternoon, exercising briefly before class to boost energy, or exploring how to schedule later classes next term. Reduce anxiety by thinking before you act.

The following practical strategies can help you cope with stress through time management.

■ *Be realistic about time commitments.* For example, many students attempting to combine work and school find that they have to trim one or the other to reduce stress and promote success. Overloaded students often fall behind and experience high stress levels that can lead to dropping out. Determine what is reasonable for you; you may find that taking longer to graduate is a viable option if you need to work while in school.

■ *Put sleep into your schedule.* Sleep-deprived bodies and minds have a hard time functioning, and research reports that one-quarter of all college and university students are chronically sleep deprived.[7] Figure out how much sleep you need and do your best to get it. When you pull an all-nighter, make sure you play catch-up over the days that follow. With time for relaxation, your mind is better able to manage stress, and your schoolwork improves.

■ *Actively manage your schedule.* The most detailed datebook page can't help you unless you look at it. Get in the habit of checking your planner at regular intervals throughout the day. Also, try not to put off tasks. If you can get something done ahead of time, get it done.

■ *Focus on one assignment at a time.* Stress is at its worst when you have five pressing assignments in five different classes all due in the next week. Focus on one at a time, completing it to the best of your ability as quickly as you can before moving to the next and the next until you're through.

■ *Check things off.* Each time you complete a task, check it off your to-do list, delete it from your electronic scheduler, or crumple up the sticky note. This physical action promotes the feeling of confidence that comes from getting something done.

Sometimes stress freezes you in place and blocks you from finding answers. At those times, remember that taking even a small step is a stress-management strategy because it begins to move you ahead.

Case Wrap-up

What happened to Devonne? After agreeing to give the problems-of-the-world assignment a try, Devonne made it to the next meeting and listened to what her group had researched so far about the problem of worldwide water shortages. She realized that though her own problems felt overwhelming, the effects of the lack of water—food shortages, people in need who tap the resources of others, widespread pollution—could touch her life as well. She felt a little more committed to the project and to attending meetings. As a bonus, Devonne connected with a group member who has a young son, lives nearby, and is home most mornings. She and Devonne discussed coming up with a schedule to trade off caring for the boys.

What does this mean for you? What is your take on the world's problems? Are you interested, or do you just pass right by that section of the news, perhaps because there is too much else on your mind? Explore the information about five large-scale issues at World's Biggest Problems (www.arlingtoninstitute.org/wbp/portal/home). Choose the one that interests you most and read the site's in-depth information about it. Write about your reaction: How do you think this problem touches—or could touch—your life directly? What can you do on a day-to-day scale that is manageable for you and might make a difference?

What effects go beyond your world? Project yourself 10 years into the future. You are using some of your best talents and passions, working in a field that is somehow involved in improving this same world problem. What is your job, and what are you doing? What does this imaginary self and job tell you about the academic and personal goals you are pursuing now?

Successful Intelligence*Wrap-up*

HERE'S HOW YOU HAVE BUILT SKILLS IN CHAPTER 6:

ANALYTICAL THINKING	CREATIVE THINKING	PRACTICAL THINKING
> As you read the section on goals, you broke down the goal-setting process into parts.	> You considered how to create a personal time profile.	> You explored the practical action of pursuing goals step by step.
> In the Get Analytical exercise, you explored your values and connected them to your educational goals.	> In the Get Creative exercise, you thought of innovative ideas to move past your toughest obstacles.	> In the Get Practical exercise, you identified your time traps and then thought of ways to say no in different situations.
> You thought about how who you are as a time manager affects your scheduling and procrastination habits.	> Exploring flexibility in time management showed you the role of creativity in the face of change.	> At the end of the chapter, you gathered practical techniques for managing stress.

Word*for*Thought

The **Spanish** word *paseo* (pah-say-oh) refers to a relaxed late-afternoon walk outdoors.[8] The relaxed pace of traditional life in many European countries holds a lesson for the overscheduled, harried student. Relaxation is crucial for stress management. Define your version of the paseo and make it a part of your life.

Building Skills for
Post-Secondary, Career, and Life Success

Steps to Success

Discover How You Spend Your Time

STEP 1 BUILD BASIC SKILLS. Everyone has exactly 168 hours in a week. How do you spend yours? Start by making guesses, or estimates, about three particular activities. In a week, how much time do you spend on the following?

_____ hours   Studying

_____ hours   Sleeping

_____ hours   Interacting with media and technology (computer, online services, cellphone, texting, video games, TV) for non-study purposes

Now, to find out the real story, record how you spend your time for seven days. The chart on the next pages has blocks showing half-hour increments. As you go through the week, write down what you do each hour, indicating starting and stopping times. Include sleep and leisure time. Record your actual activities instead of the activities you think you should be doing. There are no wrong answers.

After a week, add up how many hours you spent on each activity (round off to half-hours—that is, mark 15 to 44 minutes of activity as a half hour and 45 to 75 minutes as one hour). Log the hours in the boxes of the chart on page 183 by using tally marks, with a full mark representing one hour and a half-size mark representing a half-hour. In the third column, total the hours for each activity, and then add the totals in that column to make sure that your grand total is approximately 168 hours (if it isn't, go back and check your grid and calculations and fix any errors you find). Leave the "Ideal Time in Hours" column blank for now.

STEP 2 TAKE IT TO THE NEXT LEVEL. Take a look at your results, paying special attention to how your estimates of sleep, study, and technology time compare with your actual logged activity hours for the week. Use a separate sheet of paper or an electronic file to answer the following questions:

- What surprises you about how you spend your time?
- Do you spend the most time on the activities representing your most important values?
- Where do you waste the most time? What do you think that is costing you?
- On which activities do you think you should spend *more* time? On which should you spend *less* time?

TIME	MONDAY activity	TUESDAY activity	WEDNESDAY activity	THURSDAY activity
6:00 A.M.				
6:30 A.M.				
7:00 A.M.				
7:30 A.M.				
8:00 A.M.				
8:30 A.M.				
9:00 A.M.				
9:30 A.M.				
10:00 A.M.				
10:30 A.M.				
11:00 A.M.				
11:30 A.M.				
12:00 P.M.				
12:30 P.M.				
1:00 P.M.				
1:30 P.M.				
2:00 P.M.				
2:30 P.M.				
3:00 P.M.				
3:30 P.M.				
4:00 P.M.				
4:30 P.M.				
5:00 P.M.				
5:30 P.M.				
6:00 P.M.				
6:30 P.M.				
7:00 P.M.				
7:30 P.M.				
8:00 P.M.				
8:30 P.M.				
9:00 P.M.				
9:30 P.M.				
10:00 P.M.				
10:30 P.M.				
11:00 P.M.				
11:30 P.M.				
12:00 A.M.				
12:30 A.M.				
1:00 A.M.				
1:30 A.M.				
2:00 A.M.				

TIME	FRIDAY activity	SATURDAY activity	SUNDAY activity
6:00 A.M.			
6:30 A.M.			
7:00 A.M.			
7:30 A.M.			
8:00 A.M.			
8:30 A.M.			
9:00 A.M.			
9:30 A.M.			
10:00 A.M.			
10:30 A.M.			
11:00 A.M.			
11:30 A.M.			
12:00 P.M.			
12:30 P.M.			
1:00 P.M.			
1:30 P.M.			
2:00 P.M.			
2:30 P.M.			
3:00 P.M.			
3:30 P.M.			
4:00 P.M.			
4:30 P.M.			
5:00 P.M.			
5:30 P.M.			
6:00 P.M.			
6:30 P.M.			
7:00 P.M.			
7:30 P.M.			
8:00 P.M.			
8:30 P.M.			
9:00 P.M.			
9:30 P.M.			
10:00 P.M.			
10:30 P.M.			
11:00 P.M.			
11:30 P.M.			
12:00 A.M.			
12:30 A.M.			
1:00 A.M.			
1:30 A.M.			
2:00 A.M.			

Activity	Time Tallied Over One-Week Period	Total Time in Hours	Ideal Time in Hours
Example: Class	ꟷꟷꟷꟷ	16.5	
Class			
Work			
Studying			
Sleeping			
Eating			
Family time/child care			
Commuting/travelling			
Chores and personal business			
Friends and important relationships			
Telephone time			
Leisure/entertainment			
Spiritual life			
Other			

STEP 3 MOVE TOWARD MASTERY. Go back to the chart above and fill in the "Ideal Time in Hours" column. Consider the difference between actual hours and ideal hours. What changes are you willing to make to get closer to how you want to be spending your time? Write a short paragraph describing, in detail, two time-management changes you plan to make this term so that you are focusing your time more effectively on your most important goals and values.

Teamwork

Create Solutions Together

SET A SMART GOAL

> *Goal:* To utilize the SMART goal-setting system as a group.
>
> *Time on task:* 20 minutes
>
> *Instructions:* As a group, brainstorm important academic goals that can be accomplished within one year at school. Write your ideas on a piece of paper. From that list, pick out one goal to explore together.

Each group member takes two minutes alone to think about this goal in terms of the second goal achievement step on page 167—defining a *specific* strategy. In other words, answer the question: How would I do it? Each person writes down all the paths they can think of.

The group then gathers for everyone to share strategies. The group evaluates strategies and chooses one that seems achievable and realistic. Finally, as a group, brainstorm the rest of the goal achievement process, based on the chosen strategy or path:

- *Set a timetable.* When do you plan to reach your goal? Discuss different *time frames* and how each might change the path.
- *Be accountable.* What safeguards will keep you on track? Talk about different ways to *measure* your progress.
- *Get unstuck.* What will you do if you hit a roadblock? Brainstorm the roadblocks that could get in the way of this particular goal. For each, come up with ways to overcome the obstacle.

At the end of the process, you should have a wealth of ideas for how to approach one particular academic goal—and an appreciation for how many paths you could take to get there.

Writing

Build Intrapersonal and Communication Skills

Record your thoughts on a separate piece of paper, in a journal, or electronically.

EMOTIONAL INTELLIGENCE JOURNAL

How you feel about your time management. Paying attention to your feelings about how you spend time can be a key step toward making time-management choices that are more in line with your values. Think, and then write, about how your most time-demanding activities make you feel. What makes you happiest, most fulfilled, or most satisfied? What makes you most anxious, frustrated, or drained? What do these feelings tell you about your day-to-day choices? Describe how you could adjust your mindset, or make different choices, to feel better about how you spend your time.

REAL-LIFE WRITING

Examine two areas of academic specialty. Use your course catalogue to identify two academic areas that look interesting. Write a short report comparing and contrasting the majors in these areas, being sure to note GPA requirements, number of courses, relevance to career areas, campus locations, "feel" of the department offices, other requirements, and any other relevant characteristics. Conclude your report with observations about how this comparison and evaluation process has refined your thinking.

Personal Portfolio

Prepare for Career Success

EXPLORE CAREER GOALS THROUGH A PERSONAL MISSION

21st Century Learning Building Blocks

- Initiative and Self-Direction
- Creativity and Innovation
- Productivity and Accountability

Complete the following in your electronic portfolio or separately on paper.

No matter what employment goals you ultimately pursue, a successful career will be grounded in your personal mission in one or more ways.

First, write a draft of your personal mission. Refer to the list on page 163 to remind yourself of the elements of a personal mission statement. Use these questions to get you thinking:

1. You are at your retirement dinner. You have had an esteemed career in your chosen field. Your best friend stands up and talks about the five aspects of your character that have taken you to the top. What do you think they are?
2. You are preparing for a late-in-life job change. Updating your resumé, you need to list your contributions and achievements. What would you like them to be?
3. You have been told that you have one year to live. With family or close friends, you talk about the values that mean the most to you. Based on that discussion, how do you want to spend your time in this last year? Which choices will reflect what is most important to you?

After you have a personal mission statement to provide vision and motivation, take some time to think more specifically about your working life. Spend 15 minutes brainstorming everything that you wish you could be, do, have, or experience in your career 10 years from now—the skills you want to have, money you want to earn, benefits, experiences, travel, anything you can think of. List your wishes, draw them, depict them using cut-outs from magazines, or combine ideas—whatever you like best.

Now, group your wishes in order of priority. On paper or electronic pages labelled "Priority 1," "Priority 2," and "Priority 3," write each wish where it fits, with Priority 1 being the most important, Priority 2 the second most important, and Priority 3 the third.

Look at your priority lists. What do they tell you about what is most important to you? What fits into your personal mission, and what doesn't? Circle or highlight three high-priority wishes that mesh with your personal mission. For each, write down one action step you may have to take soon to make it come true.

You may want to look back at these materials at the end of the term to see what changes may have taken place in your priorities.

Social Networking

IDENTIFY YOURSELF

Sign in to your LinkedIn account and begin to build your profile. Click on "Edit Profile" and then click on the "Edit" mark next to your name. Fill in or edit this basic information:

- First and last name
- Display name (how you want it to appear to others viewing your profile)
- Professional "Headline" (how you identify yourself now—if you are not currently working, you may choose to identify yourself as a student and perhaps include your area of study)
- Country and zip/postal code
- Industry (if you are working)

chapter 7

Introduction to Presentation

"The best way to sound like you know what you're talking about is to know what you're talking about."

—Unknown

Learning Objectives

At the end of this chapter, you should be able to meet the following objectives:

> Identify the importance of informative presentations.

> Recognize the types of informative presentations.

> Analyze the audience of your informative presentation.

> Determine the specific purpose of your informative presentation.

> Formulate the central idea of your informative presentation.

Informative presentations are important

Stephen Eggleston, author of an article titled "Fear of Public Speaking" (2005), described his earliest experience facing an audience: "My first public humiliation came when, as a top-heavy mushroom in the second grade play, I fell off the stage. I hid for weeks. Kids are more cruel than any other species of animal, since they tell the truth. Surely I would never be a whole human being again. I might as well have died. Two days later, all of the other kids had forgotten the whole thing" (p. 1).

Eggleston's performance as a mushroom was just the first of many public presentations he was destined to give. Further in the article, he commented, "The real great awakening came quite a few years later when I realized that umpteen million years from now, when the sun grows to burn the Earth to a cinder, that stupid mushroom is not very important in the cosmic sense" (Eggleston, 2005, p. 1).

"I stopped worrying about what people would think about me when I realized how seldom people think about anyone but themselves. There is no real trick to public speaking; there is only confidence. If you cannot begin by having confidence in yourself, you must begin by having confidence in your message" (Eggleston, 2005, p. 1).

Eggleston went on to become a highly successful public speaker. "His seminars, keynotes and training programs on presentations, speaking, management,

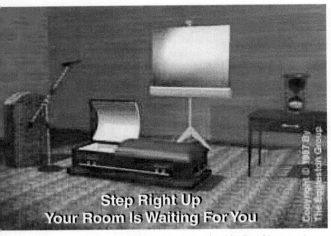

Step Right Up
Your Room Is Waiting For You

One of People's Greatest Fears Is of Public Speaking.
Source: The Eggleston Group.

quality, technology, and the Internet are popular among small business and Fortune 100 companies alike" (Eggleston, 2005, p. 3).

Although you may not have the opportunity to speak publicly on a regular basis, you will discover that in today's workplace, the ability to communicate effectively is one of the most important skills employees can possess.

Joe Grenier, representing Toastmasters International— a worldwide organization that teaches effective public speaking and leadership skills—commented that the work Toastmasters does "has never been more important."

"A lot of young people have spent a lot of time in front of the computer, and they don't have the social skills to make a presentation to a lot of people," said Grenier, a product support manager for Caterpillar, Inc., in Peoria, Illinois. "But as they go into the working world, many are being thrown into those roles. They need the skills, and they find themselves lacking" (Hogan, 2005, p. 1).

Not surprisingly, the kind of presentations Grenier is speaking about are more likely to intimidate you than other forms of communication, especially if you find your public speaking skills lacking. "According to *The Book of Lists,* the fear of speaking in public is the #1 fear of all fears. The fear of dying is #7! Over 41% of people have some fear or anxiety dealing with speaking in front of groups" (Laskowski, 1996, p. 1).

It is because of this prevalent fear of public speaking that an organization like Toastmasters International has become so popular (key 7.1). Toastmasters clubs meet in most major cities of the world at different times and locations during the week and offer a supportive and affordable way for those interested to practice their public speaking, leadership and communication skills. There are over 230,000 members in more than 11,500 clubs located in 92 countries throughout the world, and the organization is still growing." In *The Toastmasters International Guide to Successful Speaking,* authors Slutsky and Aun state that, "Over 3 million people have gone through the Toastmasters program. Clubs generally meet weekly." They also point out, "Some clubs meet inside an organization and are distinguished as corporate clubs, including IBM, Apple Computers, AT&T, Bank of America, Coca-Cola Co., Disneyland, Eastman Kodak, Hewlett Packard Co., Kraft, Inc., Rockwell International, Levi Strauss & Co., the United States Armed Forces, and hundreds of others" (Slutsky & Aun, 1997, pp. x–xi).

Slutsky and Aun go on to point out, "There is perhaps no greater skill that can help you build your career or business better than effective public speaking. Whether you're speaking to a small committee of ten decision makers or an arena filled with 10,000 future leaders, knowing how to present your point of view persuasively can make the difference between merely surviving or thriving in a vastly competitive environment" (Slutsky & Aun, 1997, p. 1).

Once you have been hired, the forms that your workplace communication can take are many and varied. These forms may include resolving a customer complaint, working collaboratively within a team, or asking for a raise. However, workplace communication is not limited to interpersonal or group settings alone. As Grenier pointed out, you may be expected to speak more formally by delivering presentations.

"I'm a little nervous ... you see,
I didn't expect to be thrown to the wolves."

TOASTMASTERS INTERNATIONAL LOGO
WWW.TOASTMASTERS.ORG

Informative speeches are one of the most common presentations you are likely to encounter in the workplace. Introducing a new product to potential customers, providing on-the-job training to a group of new employees, presenting a progress report for your team to several managers, or building company/community relations by addressing a local Rotary Club are all examples of informative presentations you might be called upon to make.

However, you might find yourself in a position to deliver an informative presentation outside of the workplace as well. Think for a moment about the classes you are currently taking that require informative presentations. Perhaps as a student in law enforcement, you must deliver an informative speech to your classmates on Homeland Security or crisis intervention; if you are enrolled in culinary management, you may deliver an informative speech on choosing fresh herbs to enhance meal preparation; as an interior design student, you may explain a room makeover that you created, complete with floor-cover samples and swatches of window treatment fabrics.

In addition, as a participant in community or church organizations, you might be called upon to speak informatively. For example, if you are a volunteer firefighter in your town, you may be asked to deliver fire prevention tips to local schoolchildren. Possibly you belong to a garden club where you present information on growing daylilies to other club members. You may be asked to teach a Sunday school class or offer a treasurer's report for the annual church picnic. You can see that informative speaking opportunities can come in many different forms, depending on your involvement in outside activities.

So that you can count yourself among those who are confident about speaking informatively in public, whether at work, at school, or in your community, the remainder of the chapter is designed to get you started. In the sections that follow, you will learn more about identifying types of informative presentations, selecting appropriate topics, analyzing your audience, determining your specific purpose, and formulating your central idea.

Determining the
specific purpose

Specific purposes identify the desired audience response at the conclusion of your speech. In other words, what do you want your listeners to know, think, or do after they have heard your presentation?

Although you do not actually state the specific purpose in the context of your speech, you use this statement to give direction to the development and organization of your information.

To be effective, a specific purpose statement should meet the following guidelines:

1. It should be a complete sentence.
2. It should contain only one key idea.
3. It should be stated in measurable terms.

Let's take a brief look at each of these guidelines.

Complete Sentence: Typically, specific purpose statements begin like this: "At the end of my speech, my audience will. . . ." Then you supply the desired audience response. For example, "At the end of my speech, my audience will be able to list the four steps for safe lifting (Key 7.2)." This statement is a complete sentence, unlike the following, "The four steps for safe lifting."

One Key Idea: You'll notice that the specific purpose stated previously has only one key idea that includes the steps required for safe lifting. If the speaker had stated, "At the end of my speech, my audience will be able to list the four steps for safe lifting and also identify several exercises for strengthening the back," he or she would have more than one key idea.

Measurable Terms: When you state your specific purpose in measurable terms, you ensure the likelihood of reaching your speaking goal. Notice how the next example fails to express the speaker's goal in measurable terms:

 **SAFE** LIFTING

Source: www.natasafety1st.org

"At the end of my speech, my audience will have a better understanding of safe lifting practices."

This example lacks measurable terms because the speaker would find it difficult to actually measure whether or not the audience understood safe lifting practices as a result of the speech. On the other hand, when the speaker states that the audience will "list" the four steps, now he or she has a strategy for assuring the audience's comprehension.

After you have phrased your specific purpose statement, you are ready to construct one of the most important elements of an effective presentation, your central idea, sometimes called the thesis.

Formulating the central idea

Think of the central idea as the core or foundation of your presentation. A central idea states, in a single sentence, the essence of the speech. It needs to be clear, concise, and focused for the audience. So important is this central idea that the effectiveness of the entire presentation is largely dependent upon it. It tells the audience what the speech is all about and prepares your listeners for the information that is to come. Here is an example: "You can take steps to protect yourself against identity theft" (Key 7.3). Notice that this central idea begins with the word "you." Phrasing a central idea in this way lets your audience know that the information is focused on them.

The central idea appears in the introduction of the speech, setting the stage for the audience and helping you to develop and organize the body of the presentation. In order to create a clear, concise central idea, you need to keep in mind the following criteria:

1. *A central idea must be expressed as a sentence.* In other words, central ideas cannot be stated as phrases or titles of a speech. Consider the following example: "How to Handle Customer Complaints." This is a phrase that could also serve as the title of a speech. However, it does not represent a sentence and is, therefore, not a central idea. Revised to form a central idea, it might sound something like this: "Handling customer complaints requires strong communication skills." As you can see in the latter example, the focus of the speech is much clearer. The audience now knows that the presentation will address the communication skills needed to handle customer complaints skillfully.

2. *A central idea should not be expressed as a question.* Questions such as "Do you know how to handle customer complaints?" might be used to arouse audience interest in the introduction of the speech, but like phrases or titles, questions do not set the stage for the specific information that is to follow.

3. *A central idea should contain only one key idea.* "Laptop computers are a convenience for business travelers, and they are also quite affordable." This example contains two key ideas. It attempts to address not only the convenience but also the affordability of laptops. You will do better to confine your presentation to a **single key idea**. In this case, you could eliminate the part about laptops' cost and deal solely with their convenience. If, however, you really wanted to cover both issues, you could rephrase the central idea to read: "Laptop computers offer several advantages for business travelers." With this revision, the central idea still has only one key idea, the advantages. Then

IDENTITY THEFT

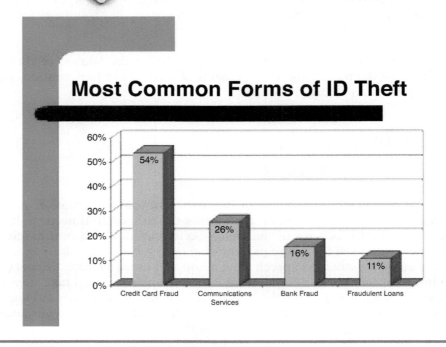

Most Common Forms of ID Theft

Credit Card Fraud	54%
Communications Services	26%
Bank Fraud	16%
Fraudulent Loans	11%

Source: http://www.ftc.gov/os/2000/07/images/idtheft6.gif.

in the body of the speech, you might include among those advantages convenience and affordability.

4. *A central idea consists of a subject and a focus.* The **subject** of a central idea represents who or what the speech is about. "Handling customer complaints requires strong communication skills" is a speech whose subject is handling customer complaints. The **focus**, on the other hand, represents the key idea of the speech. In other words, what do you wish to emphasize about the subject? With this example, the focus is on strong communication skills. The focus allows both you and your audience to predict the main points in the body of the speech.

Given this particular focus, you could safely assume that the rest of the speech will discuss the communication skills that employees need to handle customer complaints. It is also important that subjects and focuses be neither too general nor too specific. Consider this example: "Technological advances in the workplace have changed the way workers work." This central idea has a subject (technological advances) and a focus (changed the way workers work) that are both too general and, therefore, lack direction for both you and the audience. Consider this improved version: "Email systems have revolutionized the way workers communicate with each other."

Notice that both the subject and the focus have been sharpened. In contrast, a central idea that is too specific leaves you with no place to go. Take this example: "The view function on email allows workers to look at a document without actually opening it." Although this statement may be true, there is little more that you could say about this function.

5. *A central idea should be stated in the introduction and the conclusion.* In the introduction, you first attempt to capture listener interest and then state the central idea so your audience knows what to expect in the body of the presentation. The central idea is stated once again in the conclusion for two reasons. First, such restatement reinforces the importance of the information you have just shared with the audience. In addition, listeners remember most what they hear last. Including the central idea in the closing remarks helps to ensure that this idea will be remembered.

In summary, keep in mind that developing the skills required to deliver effective presentations can increase your confidence and success both personally and professionally. The process of analyzing your audience, selecting a topic, determining your specific purpose, and formulating your central idea will enable you to achieve a truly memorable presentation.

Developing main points

Kim began her semester as a new student at a local community college. After the first week or two, she found herself struggling to keep her life organized. Between a demanding class schedule with several hours of homework each night and her part-time waitress job at Pizza Heaven, she was having a hard time keeping track of all her responsibilities. Terry, a fellow classmate and friend, suggested that Kim invest in a personal electronic organizer. He told her that he had been using one for several months and was able to stay on top of his demands at school and work. Kim decided to follow Terry's advice and found that in a few weeks, she was feeling more in control of her life too.

Interestingly, if you are having trouble getting your life organized, you can actually hire someone to help you. The National Association of Professional Organizers provides this service. If you go to their website at www.napo.net/, you can access a list of select specialty services. The organization can help you organize your home, your time, your garage sale, or your public speaking.

Although you may not seriously consider hiring a professional to help you get organized, you will likely agree that being organized makes you more efficient, eliminates unnecessary stress, and enables you to enjoy what you do.

Just as in all areas of your life, organization can increase your effectiveness as a public speaker as well. Think for a moment about a few of the best speakers you have ever heard. These individuals might have been classroom teachers, motivational presenters, or experienced politicians. One skill they all probably had in common was the ability to organize their ideas clearly.

Your task as a speaker is the same—to take the information you have gathered for your speech and structure it in a way that will enable your listeners to follow along. The best place to begin is by identifying your main points.

Developing Main *Points*

- State main points in sentence form.

- Choose between three and five main points.

- Include only one idea for each main point.

- Establish a direct connection with the central idea.

- Make the main points parallel.

- Include balanced information in all main points.

Identify the main points

Once the central idea has been written, you can determine the main points for the body of the presentation. You will remember from Chapter 7 that a central idea contains a subject and a focus. The subject identifies your topic, and the focus states a key idea about your topic. Just as central ideas must meet these two criteria, main points have a set of criteria they must meet as well.

1. *State main points in sentence form.* This means that main points cannot be questions or phrases. When you express your main points as sentences, you take steps to ensure that you will be communicating a complete thought instead of a fragmented one. Let's say, for example, that your central idea states, "You can help save the life of a possible stroke victim by following three major steps."

Main Point A: *Have the victim repeat a simple sentence.* Notice that you are informing the audience what to do, as opposed to phrasing the main point as a question or fragment: Can the victim speak? (question) or Getting the victim to speak (phrase). These latter two examples are less clear than the first one.

2. *Choose between three and five main points.* Somehow three seems to be a magic number when it comes to main points in a speech. Audiences tend to remember multiples of three most easily. Of course for topics that are quite complex, you may need to incorporate additional main points. However, try not to use more than five. If you exceed five main points, your audience is likely to have more difficulty retaining the information you present.

3. *Include only one idea for each main point.* This third guideline is especially important to guarantee clarity in your speech. For instance, you wouldn't want to have Main Point A of your speech read like this: *Have the victim read a simple sentence, and see if the victim can stick out his or her tongue.* By combining two ideas, you are likely to create some confusion for your listeners. You would be better off dividing the two into separate main points.

4. *Establish a direct connection with the central idea.* The central idea of your speech serves as a predictor of your main points. When audience members hear that they can help a possible stroke victim by following three major steps, they will be primed for an explanation of those steps in the body of your speech. Consequently, you will want to make sure that all of your main points do, in fact, develop that central idea. Including a main point such as "Strokes occur for a variety of reasons" doesn't relate to the central idea and shouldn't be included in the speech.

5. *Make the main points parallel.* When main points are parallel, they are worded similarly. Take a look at the following example of parallel structure.

(CENTRAL IDEA): **Quality customer service is easy to provide.**

▶ **Main Point 1:** Quality customer service includes treating the customer with respect.

▶ **Main Point 2:** Quality customer service includes listening to customer needs.

▶ **Main Point 3:** Quality customer service includes providing customer satisfaction.

Notice how each of these three main points begins with the words "Quality customer service includes." This setup for your main points adds style to your speech, makes the information easier to remember, and creates coherence in your outline.

6. *Include relatively balanced information in all main points.* This final guideline suggests that all of your main points be developed with the same amount of information. For example, if you spend three minutes on your first main point and less than a minute on your last two, your main points probably lack balance. If one or two of your main points are quite short, perhaps you could find a way to combine them, or maybe you have to reconsider alternative main points. Just keep in mind that when you select main points for an audience, you are basically telling your listeners that all of the main points are equally important. You communicate that importance by keeping your points balanced.

Selecting a pattern of organization

As an informative speaker, you must make sure that the main points in the body of your presentation are logically organized. Numerous patterns of organization can be used to give presentations a coherent structure. Some of the most common patterns of organization for informative presentations are chronological, topical, or spatial. Let's examine each.

Chronological

Chronological patterns organize information in a time sequence. This pattern is typically used when the speaker is delivering a set of instructions, describing steps in a process, explaining a series of events that happened over time, or retracing history. You could use a chronological pattern to explain the steps for inserting a Foley catheter; you could use a time sequence to explain how a TASER X26 stops a suspect, or you could trace the decline of the labor movement in this country using a chronological pattern.

Topical

Topical patterns divide information into logical categories or groupings. This pattern classifies your main point by types or kinds. You may describe the options for office furniture as being traditional, contemporary, or eclectic, or you could report to company employees the various choices of health care coverage: traditional major medical, PPO, HMO, or self-insured. The order of your topical listing may be from the most common to the least common (as with household fires) or the most important to the least important (as with the responsibilities of an emergency room nurse).

A topical pattern may also work for your presentation on the three key elements of design, as you could discuss line, color, and texture in each of your main points. Another application for the topical pattern occurs when you discuss the types of job placements available to human services graduates by devoting a main point to social work, placement counseling, and community outreach careers.

Spatial

Spatial patterns organize ideas on the basis of physical location or how something is put together (Key 7.4). You may report the incidents of aggravated assaults by discussing crimes from the East Coast, the Midwest, and the West Coast. When you are asked to conduct a tour of your business, you will likely discuss the layout of the various departments within the company. When you introduce a new piece of machinery to a group of workers you will likely

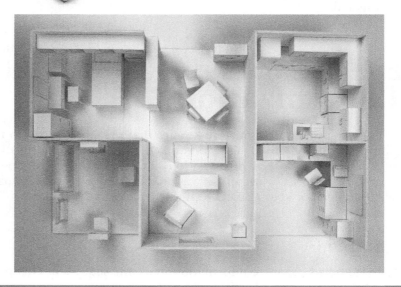

describe the machinery in terms of its component parts and their relationship to each other.

Creating the **outline**

Once you have developed your main points and determined the most appropriate pattern of organization, you are ready to create your outline. An outline provides the framework for putting all of your information together in a logical sequence. Although outlines can take a variety of forms, depending upon the nature of your subject and purpose, generally outlines consist of three primary parts: the introduction, the body, and the conclusion. The introduction captures your audience's attention and identifies the nature and purpose of your presentation. The body provides main points with the verbal and visual supporting information and evidence to make your presentation clear and convincing. The conclusion brings closure to the presentation by summarizing and providing appropriate closing comments. Let's look more closely at each part.

The introduction

The introduction acts as a preview for the remainder of the speech. You'll want to begin your presentation by capturing the audience's attention. Creating interest can be accomplished in several different ways. You may cite some startling facts, tell a brief story, ask a rhetorical question, use a quotation, refer to the audience and/or the occasion, or include appropriate humor. Whatever device you choose, the goal is the same—to motivate the audience to listen.

Here are some examples of attention-getting strategies you could use for a presentation on credit card debt among college students.

Startling Facts: A survey done by Nellie Mae, a lender of educational loans, found that "78% of undergraduates (aged 18–25) have at least one credit card. Ninety-five percent of the graduate students surveyed had at least one card. Undergraduates carried an average balance of $2,748 while graduate students carried an average balance of $4,776." In addition, "of the 78% of undergraduates with a card, 32% have four or more cards; 13% have credit card debt between $3,000–$7,000; and 9% have credit card debt greater than $7,000" (Holub, 2003–2004, p. 1).

Story: "WASHINGTON (CNN)—Before his recent graduation from college, Jason Britton confronted his mounting credit card bills, worked to pay off thousands of dollars in debt and got on with his life. Sean Moyer and Mitzi Pool took another path.

Your Speech Introduction Should Capture Audience Attention

Moyer, a University of Oklahoma junior, had earned the minimum wage as a part-time salesman and gift wrapper in a department store. Yet, by the time he hanged himself in his bedroom closet, he had 12 credit cards and had amassed $10,000 in debt on them. Moyer, who died in February 1998, still gets credit card offers in the mail, his mother told CNN.

"Pre-selected credit line of up to $100,000 from Chase (Manhattan Bank)," Jane O'Donnell said, reading off the envelope of a letter that arrived for her son last week. "He owed Chase when he died. And we get these at least once a month, so it never stops."

Pool had only three cards, but they were maxed out, and $2,500 is a heavy debt load for an 18-year-old. The University of Central Oklahoma freshman also hanged herself, her checkbook and credit card bills spread out on her dorm bed" (CNN.com, 2001 p. 1).

Rhetorical Question: How would you react if you received statements from several credit card companies stating that you had maxed your line of credit and owed $10,000?

Quote: "Georgetown University sociologist Robert Manning, who studied credit card debt among college students, maintains that marketing of the cards on campuses 'now poses a greater threat than alcohol or sexually transmitted diseases'" (CNN.com, 2001 p. 1).

Refer to Audience/Occasion: It's the start of another semester and a time of expenses for us as students. We have tuition

Greater Threat

to pay and textbooks to buy—in addition to covering other necessities like rent, food, and car insurance. No problem! We just take that little plastic card out of our wallets and charge our bills. Such an easy way out—that is, until the credit card statement arrives at the end of the month.

Humor:

Kids do the darnedest things.

For example, six-year-old Bennett Christiansen of Aurora, Illinois, managed to get his own credit card from Bank of America.

Amy Christiansen, the child's mother, said that all of her family members had been receiving offers of credit in the mail—including Bennett. For a bit of fun, she allowed Bennett to fill out and send in one of the applications addressed to him.

In a totally unexpected development, Bennett soon received a credit card with his name on it, even though he'd listed his birth date as 2002 and his income as $0. The child's card carried a $600 credit limit.

Bank of America insists that they do not target or give credit to minors, but Mrs. Christiansen was understandably concerned about the ease with which her child obtained his first credit card. She'd better stay on her toes; Bennett's 3-year-old sibling has also received offers of credit.

(Creditor Web, 2008, p. 1).

After you have captured the interest of your audience, you will want to show them that the information that follows in the body of your speech will be of value to them. In other words, let them know that what you have to say is worth their time and attention. You should try to show some tangible gain that will result for them such as saving time or money, enhancing health or safety, or increasing personal or career effectiveness. For the topic of credit card debt, you might tell your audience, "This presentation can help you avoid the devastating consequences of credit card debt that many college students experience." With a statement like this, it is a good bet that most of your listeners will want to hear more about your topic.

Third, you must state the central idea or thesis. A well-written central idea communicates the gist of the speech in a single sentence and lets the audience know what you hope to accomplish. A central idea for the subject of credit card debt could sound something like this: "Avoiding credit card debt is easier than you think." Now your audience is aware that they will learn about some simple ways to keep themselves out of debt.

Finally, you need to preview the main points that will be developed in the body of your speech. As stated earlier in this chapter, you should limit your main points to about three, and generally not more than five. Here is what you might say to preview your main points: "To avoid credit card debt, you need to limit your use to one card, cut back on your spending, and pay your account on time." Once these four steps have been accomplished, you are ready to move on to the body of the outline.

The body

The body of the outline contains your choice of main points, along with supporting material. Supporting material consists of information that makes your main points interesting, understandable, and believable. You could use explanations, examples, statistics, stories, testimonies, and comparisons. For now, keep in mind that it is a good idea to use several supports for each main point and to use a variety of different supports throughout your speech. For example, using only statistics in your speech is likely to bore your audience. However, if you also incorporate some inspiring stories, a few memorable quotes or testimonies from experts, and several imaginative comparisons, you will have a more balanced speech that keeps your audience involved.

It is also important for you to make a smooth connection between one main point and the next. This connection is made largely by the use of **transitions**—words or phrases that create a bridge between ideas. You've undoubtedly heard speakers say "first, next, then" to signal movement from one thought to another. Other examples of transitions include "in addition," "consequently," "therefore," "however," "finally," and so on. Besides the use of these common transitions, speakers may comment on how one main point relates to the next one.

For instance, a speaker might say, "Now that you understand the importance of proper lifting techniques, we will examine those techniques one step at a time." You should also know that transitions are used not only in the body but throughout the entire speech as well. In fact, they exist in all of the necessary parts of the outline. See Key 7.5 for examples of transition words.

The conclusion

The final part of the outline is the conclusion. This section contains three major parts: a summary of the main points, a restatement of the central idea, and memorable closing remarks. Although the conclusion represents the final

Key 7.5

TRANSITION TABLE

Transition words are like road signs. They help the listeners understand the direction of your thought. Here is a chart of example transition words you can use to guide your listeners through your presentations.

Above all	Finally	Meanwhile
Accordingly	First, Second, Third	Moreover
Actually	First and foremost	Next
Afterward	For instance, For example	No doubt
All things considered	For this reason	Of course
Another	From here on	On the other hand
Arguably	Furthermore	Otherwise
As a consequence	However	Paradoxically
As a matter of fact	In addition	Presently
As a result	In any case	Presumably
At any rate	In conclusion	Regrettably
At the same time	In fact	Similarly
At this point	In my opinion	Still
Be that as it may	In other words, as it were	Strangely enough
By, and, or	In the first place	Then
By and large	In the meantime	Therefore
By the same token	In the same way	Too, also
Consequently	Incidentally	Ultimately
Even so	Ironically	

Source: Wichita State University, College of Education.

Key 7.6 SKELETAL OUTLINE

I. Introduction
   A. Gain attention
   B. State need for information
   C. State central idea
   D. Preview of main points

II. Body
   A. First main point
      1. Verbal support
      2. Verbal support
      3. Verbal support
      Transition

   B. Second main point
      1. Verbal support
      2. Verbal support
      3. Verbal support
      Transition

   C. Third main point
      1. Verbal support
      2. Verbal support
      3. Verbal support

III. Conclusion
   A. Review main points
   B. Restate central idea
   C. Close memorably

portion of a presentation, do not underestimate its importance. The conclusion gives you a chance to review your key information one final time, as well as an opportunity to close the presentation memorably. Interestingly, some of the most noteworthy lines in famous speeches have occurred in the conclusion. In addition, research indicates that what audiences hear last, they remember most. Unforgettable conclusions are what bring audiences to their feet, motivate them to take action, and stir powerful emotions within their hearts.

After you have reviewed the main points and central idea, you can then end with a quotation, a brief illustration, a provocative question, a humorous anecdote, or a reference to an attention-getter that was used in the introduction. Most importantly, you should be brief and to the point, not allowing the conclusion to drag on. In addition, no new information should be introduced in this final portion of the speech. Key 7.6 shows a skeletal outline form.

In several of the upcoming chapters, you will learn more about putting together a successful presentation. Now that you have a better understanding of what it takes to organize an informative outline, you will be ready to select verbal and visual supports, gather information to develop your outline, and prepare for delivering your speech to a live audience.

VISUAL AIDS

Types of visual **supports**

Supporting materials that develop your presentation are not only verbal but may be visual as well. The inclusion of visual aids enables the audience to "see" what you are talking about. By coupling verbal and visual support, you can powerfully reinforce the information you are presenting (Key 7.7). For example, if you were trying to persuade co-workers to contribute to the United Way Campaign, you might use statistics to illustrate how the funds are allocated among various social agencies. However, if you incorporate a pie chart to visually divide the funds, the listeners would have a more memorable picture of the figures.

Visuals can be used in a variety of forms. Those forms include some of the following: objects or models, charts or graphs, lists or tables, photographs or diagrams.

Objects or models

As visual support, objects include real-life examples of your subject. For instance, musical instruments, mechanisms, tools, and even living creatures add realism and authenticity to your presentation. Objects can be an effective form of visual support when they are easily transported, skillfully manipulated, and clearly seen by your entire audience. In some situations, you may need to enhance the view of your object by projecting its image so others can see it more clearly.

When objects are not available or are too awkward for comfortable use, models of your subject can be effective visual supports. Scaled replicas, life-like reproductions, and miniature mock-ups are common types of models you could use. The 3D model shown in Key 7.8,

HEART MODEL

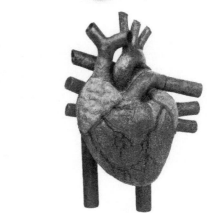

for example, is helpful for nursing students to understand the structure of the human heart. One website that offers life-like replicas for your presentation is 3-D-Models.com.

Charts or graphs

If you have numerical or statistical data to share with your audience, you can create charts or graphs. These visual supports summarize numerical data, show relationships, and describe trends. You can choose from several types of charts or graphs, such as bar, pie, line, column, etc. The statistics on drunk drivers (see Key 7.9) become clearer when presented with visual support in the form of a bar graph.

Lists or tables

Information presented in lists can include a series of examples in a bulleted list, steps of a process in a numbered sequence, or a list of reasons why you should vote for a referendum as found in a persuasive brochure. Lists help to simplify the information, reducing it to the kernels that are easy to remember.

Tables provide a summary of information that would take pages of text to explain. Data is presented in rows and columns in a clear, direct manner so that relationships, values, and categories are easily identified for your

Key 7.9   **DUI BAR** GRAPH

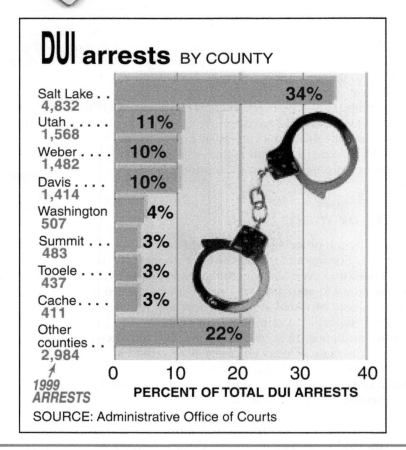

DUI arrests BY COUNTY

County	Arrests	Percent
Salt Lake	4,832	34%
Utah	1,568	11%
Weber	1,482	10%
Davis	1,414	10%
Washington	507	4%
Summit	483	3%
Tooele	437	3%
Cache	411	3%
Other counties	2,984	22%

1999 ARRESTS

PERCENT OF TOTAL DUI ARRESTS

0 10 20 30 40

SOURCE: Administrative Office of Courts

Source: Deseret News.

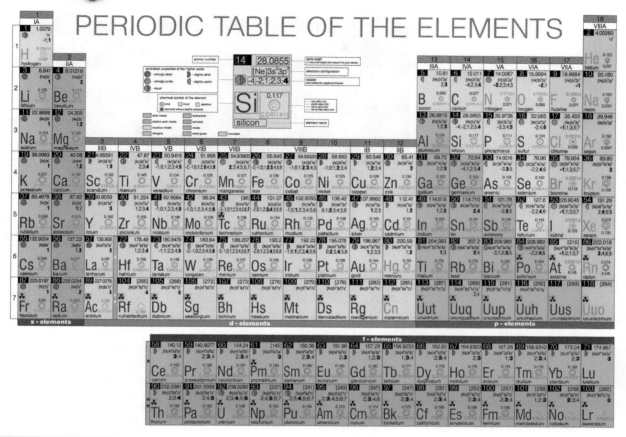

Source: Alexander Kaludov/Shutterstock

audience. Consider how clearly information is presented in the Periodic Table of Elements (see Key 7.10).

Photographs or Diagrams

Pictures put a face on your subject. They can provide vivid, colorful, emotional dimensions to your visual support. In addition, they are easy to prepare and edit with programs like Photoshop, convenient to transport, and can be projected for all to see. Diagrams allow you to simplify complex information by showing relationships visually. An electrical schematic, an exploded view of a firearm, or installation instructions for your on-demand hot water system all make use of diagrams. Notice too how photos and diagrams work together to emphasize a major difference between two hybrid automobiles when carlist.com presented the new Toyota (see Key 7.11).

The media for presenting these visuals can be equally diverse. They include flip charts and poster boards, slides, DVD's, computer-generated graphics, and handout materials.

Deciding on the type of visual and the choice of media for presentation is dependent upon several factors. First, what is the nature of your subject? Highly complex information, for example, might demand the use of slides

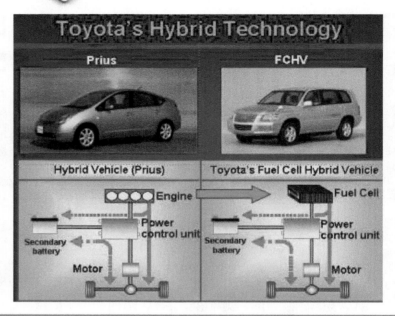

Four Factors Influence Your Selection of Visual Support

1. The nature of your subject

2. The audience's level of sophistication

3. The place your presentation will occur

4. The purpose the visual will serve

coupled with handout materials the audience can take with them at the conclusion of the presentation. Simpler, more straightforward information might be easily presented on a flip chart.

Second, what is the audience's level of sophistication? Audiences that are accustomed to hearing professional speakers may come to expect a PowerPoint presentation. Other audiences may be easily accommodated with the use of poster boards.

Third, where will the presentation take place? A large lecture hall might necessitate the use of computerized displays. A small meeting room might be suitable for objects and models that the audience can examine up close.

Finally, what purpose is the visual intended to serve? If the visual is intended to provide step-by-step instructions of some process workers need to follow, a DVD that can be viewed again at a later date might work well. If, on the other hand, the visual is intended to record information from an audience brainstorming session, a flip chart or white board may suffice.

Regardless of a speaker's choice of visual, however, certain guidelines must be followed in order to maximize the visual's effectiveness.

Guidelines for effective
visual supports

1. Make sure the visual is large enough for the entire audience to see.

2. Keep the visual simple by resisting the temptation to cram too much information onto a single visual.

3. Create "eye appeal" by using colors, fonts, and graphics in imaginative ways.

4. Have a definite purpose in mind for using the visual.

5. Introduce the visual, explain it, and then put it away.

6. Be certain you have the necessary equipment available and in working order before the presentation.

7. Practice the speech using the visuals.

Visual supports **and technology**

With software like PowerPoint, designing sophisticated visuals has never been faster or easier. No wonder students and working professionals make frequent use of this medium in their presentations.

In addition, modern college classrooms and workplace facilities often provide media carts that allow speakers to project images from DVDs, the Internet, or still photographs.

Although the use of technology to create and project visuals seems like the ideal combination, you might want to consider the suggestions that follow.

1. Avoid the use of visual technology as a substitute for meaningful content in your presentations. It can be tempting to take shortcuts in your outline while expecting the visuals to make up for missing information.

2. Use visual technology to provide additional clarity and interest to your presentation. Some beginning speakers attempt to put their entire speech onto PowerPoint slides and then simply read the text projected on the screen. A better approach involves using visual images that complement rather than repeat what you are saying.

3. More is not necessarily better. Resist the tendency to fill your presentation with one visual after another. Too many visuals can distract your audience from what you are saying and lessen the effectiveness of those visuals as well.

4. Make sure the equipment you are using is working. Nothing can ruin a good presentation more quickly than technical problems that do not allow you to project your visuals.

5. Always have a back-up plan. Be certain you have alternative visuals in case you encounter technical problems. These alternatives might include printouts of your visuals that you can display on a flip chart or files saved in more than one location.

As you begin preparation for a presentation, whether in the classroom, at work, or in your community, keep in mind the suggestions for including well-developed verbal and visual supports. Along with providing interest, understanding, and credibility, you will discover that well-chosen supports increase your confidence as a speaker and make your information memorable for your audience.

Delivery is **important**

Juan was enrolled in a speech course at the local community college. Although outgoing with his friends and family, Juan had never liked speaking in front of groups. However, Speech 101 was required, and Juan had to complete it if he hoped to obtain his associate's degree.

His first assignment was a three-minute personal experience talk. He decided to tell his classmates about the summer he did volunteer work for the Hunger Task Force.

In anticipation of his presentation, Juan spent the next week outlining the information he wanted to share and practicing his delivery. He noticed, however, that every time he worked on his speech, he felt the symptoms of anxiety—the racing heart, faster breathing, discernable perspiration. Juan wondered how he was going to get through his speech when he was already feeling such nervousness.

Finally, the day arrived. Juan was third in his class to speak. As he approached the lectern, he felt the same uncomfortable symptoms he had experienced during his practice and preparation sessions. Afraid of embarrassing himself in front of his audience, Juan raced through his delivery, reading almost entirely from his note cards. When he finally sat down, Juan felt exhausted and discouraged, uncertain how he was going to make it through the rest of the semester and the other speeches that lay ahead.

If you find yourself recalling situations when you felt like Juan, you are not alone. Many celebrities and gifted artists have struggled with performance anxiety. Early in his career, singer Rod Stewart had such a severe case of nervousness that he sang an entire song while hiding behind a stack of speakers. Barbra Streisand forgot the lyrics to a song she was singing in public and stopped doing live performances for almost three decades (Enright, 2007). Recently, actress Catherine Heigl asked the audience at the Academy Awards where she was presenting to forgive her because she was so nervous.

Although fear of speaking or performing in public is often cited as the number one fear among people, you can successfully learn to manage your own apprehensions about addressing an audience. In fact, your ability to speak confidently before groups is certainly a skill well worth developing, especially in today's workplace.

"More than ever, public speaking—from presenting a status report to a small team to making a sales pitch before a packed room of potential investors—is a necessary skill. Across industries and in companies large and small, being able to convey crucial information credibly and convincingly before groups of all sizes has become as fundamental a job requirement as computer literacy. And being truly adept at it can propel you forward because public speaking gives you a visibility seldom achieved by sterling work alone" (Baskerville, 1994, p. 2).

In the upcoming sections of this chapter, you will discover ways to deliver a speech that captures audience interest, communicates self-confidence, and generates sincere applause. However, before you explore the strategies for an effective delivery, let's take a look at some of the reasons people fear public speaking and the techniques for coping with this fear.

Source: Cartoon by Nick Bland, www.panicfreepublicspeaking. com.au.

Coping with **speaker anxiety**

As you read in the opening to this chapter, public speaking is a common fear for many. In fact, some will go to great lengths in order to avoid delivering a speech. Rachel was one of those individuals. A recent graduate with an associate's degree in interior design, she took a position with a highly respected firm that specialized in customized home interiors. Rachel loved working with clients one-on-one where she was able to use her artistic flare and imagination to create warm and inviting living spaces.

Impressed by Rachel's talents, the owner of the firm thought Rachel's innate design abilities and pleasant personality would make her a perfect match for representing the firm at a local women's club meeting to speak about home decorating. When the owner approached Rachel about the idea, Rachel felt panic set in. Although she was perfectly at ease dealing with one or two clients at a time, the thought of addressing a group of 125 women was too much for her to consider. She requested more time to think about the opportunity, hoping she would be able to come up with some excuse for declining the owner's request.

The presentation at the women's club would have been a wonderful chance for Rachel to increase business for the design firm and enhance community relations. However, her fear prevented her from venturing out of her communication comfort zone.

For many, the physical sensations associated with speaker anxiety are the most difficult to bear. Actually, these sensations are very much like those you might experience in any stressful situation. Facing an upcoming exam, dealing with a difficult boss, having an argument with a spouse can all trigger a stress response, sometimes referred to as "fight or flight." Consider what happens to your body in such circumstances.

"The human body responds to stressors by activating the nervous system and specific hormones. The hypothalamus signals the adrenal glands to produce more of the hormones adrenaline and cortisol and release them into the bloodstream. These hormones speed up heart rate, breathing rate, blood pressure, and metabolism. Blood vessels open wider to let more blood flow to large muscle groups, putting our muscles on alert. Pupils dilate to improve vision. The liver releases some of its stored glucose to increase the body's energy. And sweat is produced to cool the body. All of these physical changes prepare a person to react quickly and effectively to handle the pressure of the moment" (Stress, 2008, p. 1).

In reality, when you experience sensations like these, your body and brain are responding normally to a perceived danger or challenge. For example, if you narrowly escape a car accident by quickly swerving your vehicle away from an oncoming motorist, you will be thankful for this stress response. It prepared your body to instinctively react in a way that may have saved your life.

However, speaking in public is not life threatening, and the symptoms of stress you experience are not the result of any true danger. The nervousness you feel before delivering a speech has more to do with how you think about the presentation. You will find it helpful to remember that you cannot have a feeling without first having had a thought. Consequently, one of the first ways to reduce speaker anxiety is to examine the unrealistic beliefs you may have about addressing an audience.

One unrealistic belief you may have is that the audience will be able to sense your nervousness and perceive you as incompetent. In truth, however, most audience members are not nearly as aware of your nervousness as you are. It is not uncommon for a speaker

"It was the classic fight or flight response. Next time, try flight."

Source: www.CartoonStock.com.

Delivery Improves with Practice

to confess feelings of anxiety after a presentation only to hear audience members comment they didn't even notice.

Another unrealistic fear can stem from the belief that somehow your delivery must be perfect. Be assured that if you have done your best to get ready for your speech, you can relax and just be yourself. You do not have to be perfect. Who you are is plenty good! Audiences respond to speakers who are genuine, as opposed to those who are stiff and artificial—fearful of making a mistake.

A third unrealistic belief is that you cannot deliver an effective speech because you are not a professional speaker. Remember that confidence in public speaking is built by practice. The more you speak before groups, the more comfortable you will become. Even those individuals who are not experienced speakers can deliver a memorable, heartfelt presentation by speaking with sincerity.

Along with confronting any unrealistic thoughts you might have about speaking in public, you will also find the additional guidelines helpful for coping with anxiety.

First, be well prepared. Some experts say that nervousness can be reduced by 75 percent with sufficient preparation and practice. Second, accept that some tension before a presentation is natural. In fact, it represents a heightened sense of awareness that can be used to add life and energy to your speech.

Third, consider doing some slow, deep breathing prior to speaking. Inhale through the nose for a count of two, counting one-one thousand, two-one thousand. Hold the breath for a second or two, and then exhale through the mouth for a count of four, counting one-one thousand, two-one thousand, three-one thousand, and so on. Repeat this cycle three to five times. This breathing exercise can slow your heart rate, reduce nervousness, and help you feel more relaxed.

Fourth, practice positive self-talk. What you say to yourself has a profound effect on how you feel. When you catch yourself engaged in negative self-talk such as, "I'm going to forget what I want to say and look like a fool," immediately replace that message with a positive one. "I'm well prepared; I have note cards with me, and if I forget some information, I'll just pause and take a look at my notes."

Fifth, have a strong introduction. Many speakers find that when they get off to a good start, much of their nervousness dissipates within the first few minutes of the presentation. Finally, remember that much, if not all, of your nervousness is not even visible to an audience. They are there to hear what you have to say and are not really interested in how you might feel at the moment.

In her website, *Facing the Fear,* Kathy Brady addresses several aspects of speech anxiety including "Why Speaking Makes You Sick," "Visualization and Desensitization," "Breathing," "Preparation," "Performance," and "Just How Nervous Are You?" You will find her personable, reassuring approach to speech anxiety helpful as you meet the challenges of your speaking assignments. Brady answers your most basic questions, such as, "What exactly does 'practicing' a speech mean? How many times should you practice your speech? What type of delivery method works best for students with speech anxiety?" She also addresses common concerns that involve volume and pacing, eye contact, and use of the body. Brady's comprehensive website should be your next stop for overcoming speech anxiety: http://www.uwm.edu/People/kabrady/visual.html.

Delivery styles

Before you begin practicing your speech delivery, you will want to be aware of the various types of delivery that exist. These deliveries include manuscript, memorized, extemporaneous, and impromptu.

Manuscript

As the name implies, manuscript deliveries are read word-for-word off the printed page. To avoid nervousness, some speakers think that if they write out their entire speech and then read it, they will be less likely to make a mistake. Although their perception may be true on the one hand, on the other hand, they run the risk of delivering a dull, lifeless presentation. Audiences easily become bored by speakers reading to them with little or no eye contact and spontaneity.

On occasion, you may need to read a quote or cite some important data exactly as it is written to ensure accuracy, but to read an entire speech should be avoided at all costs. In addition, with today's technology, speakers may become overly reliant on PowerPoint slides. The end result is a delivery that involves reading from the slides and losing a personal connection with the audience. Keep in mind that if you use PowerPoint, the slides should provide brief visuals to complement the spoken message.

Memorized

To reduce the tendency to read the speech, as with manuscript style, you might think it is a good idea to memorize the speech instead and avoid dependence upon notes. However, even without notes, speakers who memorize their speech still tend to sound stilted and artificial. In addition, you may actually increase your anxiety by worrying about the possibility of forgetting the information you memorized. Although you may choose to memorize a short quote or brief fact or two, committing the whole speech to memory is not the best choice of delivery styles.

Extemporaneous

This style is the most versatile of all the styles. It requires you to be thoroughly prepared and well rehearsed, but to deliver the speech in a conversational style with little reliance on notes. With this delivery, the audience feels as if you are speaking to them directly and personally. Obviously, to use this style, you must have a sound grasp of your subject matter and have practiced sufficiently so you can speak with ease. By far, extemporaneous speaking is the most effective delivery style.

Impromptu

As you probably already know, impromptu speaking involves speaking unexpectedly or off-the-cuff. Your manager may ask you to voice your opinion at a meeting; you may need to introduce yourself and to share some of your background with a group of new employees; at a company banquet, you may be asked to "say a few words." These are just some of the instances that require an impromptu delivery. Although it is never a good idea to use the impromptu style for a presentation that demands conscientious prior preparation, it can be a versatile style to cultivate in the situations just described. If you find yourself in an impromptu setting, consider doing the following: state your point briefly, offer any necessary information to clarify your point, and create a concise statement to indicate closure.

Practice delivery

As you read in the preceding section, the most versatile form of delivery is the extemporaneous style. This style of speaking is carefully prepared and well rehearsed but delivered conversationally. In other words, you know your material so well that you can share it without unnecessary reliance on your outline or speaker's notes. To ensure an extemporaneous presentation, you will find the following guidelines helpful.

Develop a speaking outline: Avoid speaking directly from the detailed outline you prepared. This type of outline is an excellent way to solidify your thoughts and to make sure you are expressing your ideas clearly and specifically. However, speaking from this outline can tempt you to read the information with little audience eye contact. Instead, consider constructing a speaker's outline, note cards, or map. A **speaker's outline** is an abbreviated form of the detailed outline you prepared. It may contain your central idea and main points, along with some key words and phrases to remind you of what you want to say. In other words, this outline serves mainly as a memory jogger and not as a complete transcript of your speech. Such an abbreviated outline will discourage you from becoming overly dependent upon your notes and force you to speak more directly to your listeners. Take a look at the sample speaker's outline shown in Key 7.12.

If you choose to prepare **note cards** instead (Key 7.13), remember some of these tips: number them sequentially; keep the information on each card as brief as possible; write legibly or type them; use boldfacing, underlining, or

SAMPLE SPEAKER'S OUTLINE

I. Introduction

   A. Story about Bonnie
   B. Citation from John Marcus
   C. Successful interviewing requires attention to many details.
   D. Dress, behavior, follow-up

II. Body

   A. Before the interview, dress for success.

      1. Explanation of proper dress
      2. Citation from Molloy
      3. Example of selections

   Transition Now that you are dressed, how should you behave?

   B. During the interview, behave confidently.

      1. Explain posture
      2. Citation from P. Eckman on eye contact
      3. Compare confident to less confident

   Transition When the interview ends, more work needs to be done.

   C. After the interview, follow up with additional contacts.

      1. Explain thank-you note
      2. Statistic on those who wrote
      3. Citation from *Excel* video

III. Conclusion

   A. Pay attention to details: dress before, behavior during, and follow-up after the interview.
   B. A successful interview depends on paying close attention to many details.
   C. Citation from *What Color Is Your Parachute?* by R. N. Bolles.

SAMPLE SPEAKING **NOTE CARDS**

I. INTRODUCTION   Note card #1

   A. **Story** about Bonnie
   B. In the months ahead, we will be conducting job searches, the most important part of which is the interview. **Citation** J. Marcus, *Complete Job Interview Handbook.*
   C. Successful interviewing requires attention to many details.
   D. I will be discussing the dress, behavior, and follow-up required for success.

II. BODY   Note card #2

   A. Before the interview, dress for success.

      1. **Explain** proper dress for. . . .
      2. **Citation** from Molloy's *Dress For Success*
      3. **Examples** of combinations that work. . . .

   Transition: Now that you are ready for the interview, how should you behave during the interview?

BODY   Note card #3

   B. During the interview, behave confidently.

      1. **Explain** appropriate posture
      2. **Cite** P. Eckman on eye contact
      3. **Compare** confident to less confident applicants

   Transition: You may think the interview is over when it ends, but there is more work to do.

BODY   Note card #4

   C. After the interview, follow up with additional contacts.

      1. **Explain** what to write in thank-you note
      2. Placement office **statistics** on those who write. . . .
      3. **Citation** on telephone contact from *Excel* video

---

III. CONCLUSION   Note card #5

   A. So you can see that you must pay close attention to details before, during, and after the interview.
   B. A successful interview depends on paying close attention to many details.
   C. **Citation** from *What Color Is Your Parachute?* by Richard N. Bolles.

---

colored highlighting to make key information stand out; practice your delivery with your note cards; use them as inconspicuously as possible.

    If you choose to prepare a **map** for your speaking notes, you will be designing a visual representation of your information. Maps can look like a solar system, with main points orbiting around a central idea, or they may resemble an organizational chart with boxed information arranged in a linear pattern. Inspiration Software is a user-friendly computer program for creating speakers' maps. Key 7.14 shows a speaking map prepared with Inspiration so you can see what one looks like. If you would like more information about this program, you can go to the website at www.inspiration.com/.

Practice out loud: Once you have prepared a speaker's outline, a set of note cards, or a map, you can actually practice delivering your speech. Effective practice involves going over your entire speech several times out loud. Some speakers make the mistake of simply reading their notes silently. Practicing out loud, however, gives you the opportunity to develop a conversational style and to incorporate effective use of eye contact, gestures, posture, and facial expressions.

Practice in front of an audience if you can: Friends, family, and co-workers are often willing to lend an ear and offer constructive feedback as you rehearse. Videotaping can be another excellent tool to help you review strengths and weaknesses in your delivery. In addition, if you are able, try to schedule at least one rehearsal in the room where you will be delivering your presentation.

SAMPLE SPEAKING **MAP**

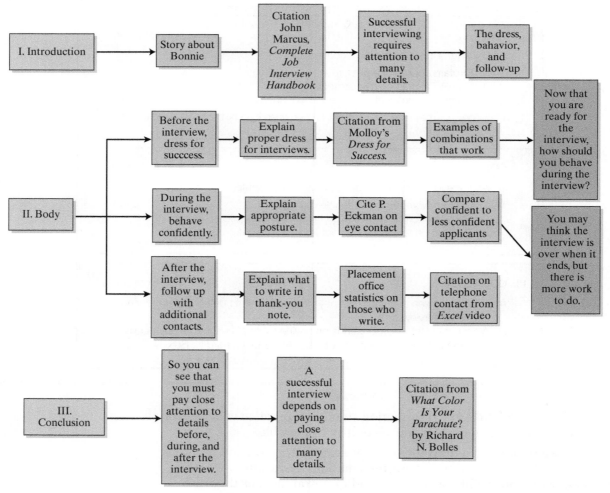

Practice with your visuals: It is always a good idea to rehearse your speech using your visual aids. Whether you have flip charts, models, or computer-generated graphics, practicing with them will enable you to create a smooth flow as you move from your text to the visuals. Also, as mentioned earlier, if you rehearse in the room you will use for the presentation, make certain any equipment you need is in good working order. Particularly if you are using computer-generated graphics, you will be wise to have a back-up plan in case you encounter computer problems on the day of your delivery. For instance, print out your slides so they can be used on a projection device if the computer fails.

Time your speech: Unless you actually time yourself during rehearsal, you may not know for certain if your speech is too long or too short. For a classroom assignment especially, your instructor might deduct points if the speech doesn't conform to the assignment requirements. By timing yourself during rehearsal, you can determine if you need to add or delete information, as well as slow or pick up your rate of speaking.

Use visualization: Another technique many speakers find helpful as part of their rehearsal involves the use of visualization. Here's how it works. Go to a spot where you won't be interrupted and lie down or sit in a comfortable chair. Close your eyes and take a few slow, deep breaths while releasing any muscle tension you may feel in your body. Then picture yourself delivering your speech in front of your audience. Be very specific and detailed as you visualize this scene in your mind's eye. Imagine what you will be wearing, what the room looks like, who will be present in the audience, and so on. Then see yourself approaching the front of the room, looking out at your listeners and feeling calm and confident. Talk through your entire speech, observing positive feedback from your listeners and experiencing a sense of accomplishment and self-assurance. Try this exercise several times before your actual presentation. The secret of using visualization is to make your mental picture as detailed as possible and to see yourself as being successful.

Vocal elements of delivery

Your voice is one of your most unique personal characteristics. Much like a fingerprint, each person's voice contains qualities that set it apart from other voices. In fact, for some time, individual speech patterns have played a part in criminal investigations. Since the tragedy of 9-11, these speech patterns have taken on even greater importance in the field of law enforcement.

"Voice prints are being used to verify the authenticity of terrorists' taped messages, and psychological stress evaluation of their speech provides information about general levels of anxiety and tension of speakers in airports and other ports of entry. Accent and dialect can be used in speaker profiling as one method of determining whether a suspect is traveling from a hostile country. Finally, speech patterns provide important screening information about intoxication, giving law enforcement officers probable cause for detainment and further investigation" (Amazon.com, 2008, p. 1).

In addition to law enforcement agencies using the voice as an indicator of criminal intent, the media also capitalizes on the human voice to sell products, promote causes, and provide entertainment. Think about the distinctive voice of your favorite radio D.J., for example, or the memorable voice of James Earl Jones as Darth Vader in the Star Wars movies (see Key 7.15). Who could forget the voice of Mel Blanc as he portrayed Porky Pig, Bugs Bunny, Barney Rubble, and Daffy Duck? Talented individuals like these were able to make a living as a result of their vocal qualities.

DARTH VADER,
VOICE OF JAMES EARL JONES

Although you may not be seeking celebrity status using your voice, you can certainly learn to make your voice work for you as an effective public speaker. Remember, 38 percent of the impression you create for an audience comes from your voice. So let's take a closer look at some tips you can follow to create a successful delivery.

Watch your pitch, rate, and volume: Pitch refers to how high or low you speak; rate describes the speed at which you speak; and volume is characterized by loudness or softness of the voice. Ideally, your natural speaking voice is the best voice to use when delivering a presentation. However, you can enhance your voice by varying pitch, rate, and volume. In other words, if your voice is typically low, incorporate a variety of inflections so that you occasionally raise your pitch. The reverse is true if your voice is on the high side; explore opportunities to lower your range from time to time.

Although an abnormally slow rate of speaking can put an audience to sleep, many speakers face the problem of speaking too rapidly, especially if they are a bit nervous. Consequently, it's often helpful to speak somewhat slower than your conversational rate. As for volume, make certain you speak loudly enough to be heard. You can also vary your volume in order to hold audience attention. When making a particularly important point, for example, either raise or lower your normal volume. These kinds of periodic changes keep the audience's attention from drifting off.

Pay attention to articulation and pronunciation: First let's look at the difference between these two. Articulation refers to the clarity with which you speak your words. Failing to speak clearly may result in your audience misunderstanding what you are trying to communicate. Careful articulation becomes more of an issue when you are addressing a large group of people. You want to make sure that those in the back of the room can understand you just as well as those in the front.

Pronunciation, on the other hand, involves placing correct emphasis on the various syllables of a word. If you look in a dictionary, you will discover that some words can be pronounced in more than one way. For example, the word *diverse* can be pronounced with a short "i" or a long "i." Usually the first pronunciation cited is the preferable one. However, most words have a standard pronunciation that you will want to use. In particular, speakers may find difficulty when they are using technical terms. If you need to use technical terms, make certain you are saying them correctly. Consult a good technical dictionary if you are in doubt.

Choose language carefully: Everyday conversation is generally informal. You use informal language when communicating with classmates, co-workers, family, and friends. This type of language also commonly incorporates slang. Here is an example of informal English:

Informal: *Man, I was really bummed by that last psych test. I mean like I didn't even know where the prof got some of those questions from; you know?*

Although informal English is perfectly appropriate in day-to-day interactions, public speaking demands more formal language choices. Take a look at the following same message expressed more formally.

Formal: *I felt discouraged after taking that last test in psychology. In fact, I wasn't certain of the source the professor used to design some of the questions.*

The difference between informal and formal language should be pretty evident from these two examples. It also should go without saying that sexist or racist terms, stereotypes, and profanity have no place in a public presentation.

Avoid nonfluencies: A final consideration to keep in mind is the avoidance of nonfluencies. These are words or vocalizations that serve no purpose. The most common are "you knows" and "ums" and "uhs." Most people use a few of these nonfluencies from time to time in speech, but repeated use of them is distracting and may reveal a lack of confidence. To determine if nonfluencies are a problem for you, tape record or videotape your speech and play it back. You can also have someone listen to your speech rehearsal, paying special attention to the inclusion of "ums," "uhs," and "you knows." If you lose your train of thought during your speech, you will be better off pausing momentarily rather than reverting to nonfluencies.

Nonverbal elements of delivery

Finally, your posture, gestures, and facial expressions are major nonverbal elements of your delivery that also require careful consideration.

In reality, your speech delivery begins the moment you leave your seat and approach the lectern. The audience is already paying attention to the way you carry yourself. Communicate assurance by standing tall and walking confidently to the speaker's platform.

Once you have arrived at the lectern, set your speaker's notes down and take a few seconds to establish eye contact with your listeners. You will also feel more comfortable if you balance your weight evenly on both feet rather than crossing one ankle in front of or behind the other or corkscrewing your legs around one another. Notice the posture of the two speakers pictured in Key 7.16. Which speaker looks most ready to deliver an effective presentation?

SPEAKER POSTURES: A) TOO RELAXED; B) READY TO GO

(A)

(B)

Your next challenge may involve knowing what to do with your hands and arms. Although you can rest your hands on the lectern, you don't want to lock them in that position for the entire speech. Instead, gesture naturally as you would in more casual conversation. For example, you might raise a hand when you want to emphasize a point. You can use descriptive gestures to illustrate the size or shape of something. Possibly extend your arms with open palms when you want to invite your listeners to consider a particular point of view.

When you practice your speech, make a deliberate attempt to incorporate gestures until you find several that seem comfortable to you. Then insert cues in your speaker's outline, note cards, or map as reminders of where you want to gesture. Although this suggestion might seem somewhat artificial, after several practice sessions, your movements will become more natural.

By all means, avoid any fidgeting, nervous, or distracting gestures that focus your audience's attention away from your message. In addition, keep your hands out of your pockets and free from distracting note cards.

Like posture and gestures, your facial expressions are also important. Perhaps your greatest ally in establishing rapport with an audience is your smile. Use your smile to communicate your friendly desire to share information with your audience.

Accompany your smile with eye contact that establishes and maintains a visual connection with your audience. The extended eye contact method is

Smiles Communicate Beyond Words

a helpful way to make this connection. Look at one or two members of your audience for four to five seconds. Then shift your gaze to another few members of the audience. Continue this rotation until you have created eye contact with your entire audience. In the case of a very large audience, you can use this technique with sections of the audience instead of with specific individuals.

Lastly, let the expressiveness of your face reveal your feelings about the message you are communicating. Think of the way in which your face becomes animated when you run into a good friend, hear a sad story, or receive some surprising news. In these instances, your facial expressions are certainly not static. They change moment by moment with each thought and feeling you experience. In a similar way, let your face tell the audience about your reactions to the information you are sharing. In so doing, you will maintain the interest of your listeners and give them the opportunity to empathize with your own thoughts and feelings.

By following the guidelines offered in this chapter, you will be pleased to experience not only an effective delivery but a feeling of self-confidence that will carry over into all of your interactions with others.

References

Amazon.com. (2008). *Forensic aspects of speech patterns: Voice prints, speaker profiling, lie and intoxication detection*. Retrieved March 20, 2008, from http:// www.amazon.com/Forensic-Aspects-Speech-Patterns-Intoxication/dp/1930056400/ref5tag_tdp_sv_edpp_i

Baskerville, D. M. (1994, May 1). Public speaking rule #1: Have no fear. *Black Enterprise*. Retrieved September 21, 2007, from http://www.encyclopedia.com/doc/1G1-15131799.html

CNN.com. (2001). Credit cards on campus get bad marks by some. Retrieved August 9, 2007, from http://www .cnn.com/US/9906/09/college.kids.debt/

Creditor Web. (2008, June 20). Bank of America issues credit card to boy, age 6. Retrieved October 31, 2008, from http://blog.creditorweb.com/index.php/2008/06/20/bank-of-america-issues-credit-card-to-boy-age-6/

DUI Multiple Offenders. (n.d.). *Department of Public Safety, Driver License Division*. Retrieved April 13, 2007, from http://deseretnews.com/photos/b0722dui.gif

Eggleston, S. (2005). *Fear of public speaking: Stories, myths and magic*. Retrieved March 7, 2008, from http://www.the-eggman.com/writings/fearspk1.html

Enright, P. (2007, September 12). Even stars get stage fright. Retrieved March 18, 2008, from http://www.msnbc.msn.com/id/20727420/

Hogan, D. (2005, August 8). *Not born with a gift of gab? There's help available: Tips for public speaking*. Retrieved July 19, 2007, from http://jobs.aol.com/article/?id=20050808184609990032

Holub, T. (2003–2004). Credit card usage and debt among college and university students. *ERIC Digest*. Retrieved August 9, 2007, from http://www.ericdigests.org/2003-2/credit.html

Laskowski, L. (1996). *Overcoming speaking anxiety in meetings & presentations*. Retrieved June 11, 2001, from http://www.ljlseminars.com/anxiety.htm

Model Heart (n.d.) Retrieved April 13, 2007, from http://www.3-dmodels.com/3d-model_files/371m765.htm

Slutsky, J. & Aun, M. (1997). *The Toastmasters International guide to successful speaking*. Chicago: Deaborn Financial.

Stress. (2008). TeensHealth. Retrieved March 18, 2008, from http://www.kidshealth.org/teen/your_mind/emotions/stress.html

Toyota's Hybrid Technology. (n.d.). Retrieved April 13, 2007, from http://www.carlist.com/autonews/2004/image/toyota_hybrid_diagram.jpg

part 2

Introduction to Business Concepts

chapter 8

Understanding the Canadian Business System

Opportunities and Challenges in the Mobile Phone Market

During the last decade, a Canadian company called Research In Motion (RIM) has emerged as a high-tech star in the mobile phone industry. The company was started in 1984 by two engineering students—Mike Lazaridis at the University of Waterloo and Douglas Fregin at the University of Windsor. Its first wireless handheld device—called the Inter@ctive Pager—was introduced in 1996. The now-famous BlackBerry hit the market in 1998. The BlackBerry 850, which combined email, a wireless data network, and a tiny QWERTY keyboard, was introduced in 1999. Other products have been developed since then, including the BlackBerry Pearl (2006), the BlackBerry 8300 (2008), the BlackBerry Storm 2 (2009), a 3G version of its Pearl flip phone (2010), and OS 6.0 (2010). The latter product is a touch-screen smart phone that is designed to browse the web faster than previous models. In the first quarter of 2010, RIM was one of the top five mobile phone companies in the world, and at the 2010 Wireless Enterprise Symposium trade show, Lazaridis announced RIM's plans to dominate the global smart phone market.

RIM raised $30 million from venture capital firms in the years before its initial public offering (IPO) in 1998 that raised $115 million. RIM was listed on NASDAQ in 1999 and raised another $250 million. In 2000, it raised another $950 million. As of mid-2009, RIM had 12,000 employees worldwide. In 2009, *Fortune* magazine named RIM as the fastest-growing company in the world. There are over 40 million corporate and consumer BlackBerry users, and RIM's goal is to have 100 million customers.

RIM is a remarkable Canadian success story, but industry analysts see potential challenges on the horizon for companies in the smart phone market. The market potential is huge, but competition is intense and new product introductions are occurring at a

---

After reading this chapter, you should be able to:

> Define the nature of Canadian *business* and identify its main goals. p. 223

> Describe different types of global *economic systems* according to the means by which they control the *factors of production* through *input and output markets*. p. 228

> Show how *demand* and *supply* affect resource distribution in Canada. p. 238

> Identify the elements of *private enterprise* and explain the various *degrees of competition* in the Canadian economic system. p. 241

ScanLife™ Barcode: At the beginning and end of each chapter in the book, you will find a unique 2D barcode like the one above. Please go to http://web.scanlife.com/us_en/downloadapplication to see how you can download the ScanLife app to your smartphone for free. Once the app is installed, your phone will scan the code and link to a website containing Pearson Canada's Study on the Go content, including the popular study tools Glossary Flashcards, Audio Summaries, and Quizzes, which can be accessed anytime.

All businesses are subject to the influences of economic forces. But these same economic forces also provide astute managers and entrepreneurs with opportunities for profits and growth. The ideas presented in this chapter will help you to better understand (1) how managers deal with the challenges and opportunities resulting from economic forces, and (2) how consumers deal with the challenges and opportunities of price fluctuations.

dizzying pace. For example, Nokia has introduced a smart phone—the Booklet 3G—that is designed to bridge the gap between a PC and a cellphone. The device (described as a mini-laptop) gives consumers the computing power of a PC with the mobility of a cellphone. Another new product is Motorola's Droid phone, which was launched by Verizon, the largest U.S. wireless carrier (and RIM's biggest customer). A third entry comes from Google, which has developed a touch-screen mobile phone that uses Google's own Android operating system (this product may also cause problems for Apple's iPhone). A fourth new product is Apple's iPhone, which will be a strong competitor to the BlackBerry as RIM shifts its emphasis from corporate clients to consumers.

There are also two industry trends that make it difficult to predict the future for any of the competitors in the smart phone industry. The first is the so-called "bring your own device" trend, which means that companies are shifting the responsibility for having a phone onto employees. The second trend is "sandboxing," which means separating work functions from the rest of the smart phone for security reasons, and allowing employees to use the phone at work without losing access to other applications like games or social networking. Both these trends may hurt RIM in the corporate market because employees may decide to buy something other than a BlackBerry. Some analysts are now fairly pessimistic about RIM's future; they think the company may continue to grow, but that shareholder returns will decline.

Another major area of concern is patent infringement lawsuits. During the past decade, RIM and other firms have sued and been sued for patent infringement. In 2006, RIM agreed to pay Virginia-based NTP $612.5 million for infringing on NTP's patent. RIM also sued Samsung after Samsung introduced a smart phone called the BlackJack. In 2009, Klausner Technologies filed suit against RIM for infringing one of its visual voicemail patents. These lawsuits have created great uncertainty in the smart phone industry.

Yet another problem is the negative publicity RIM received regarding stock options. In 2007, the company announced a $250 million restatement of earnings after it was learned that hundreds of stock options had been backdated (timed to a low share price to make them more lucrative for managers who received them). In 2009, Canadian regulators were seeking $80 million in penalties from co-CEOs Mike Lazaridis and Jim Balsillie, and several other executives agreed to pay penalties for backdating stock options.

All of these things have had a negative effect on RIM's stock price. In 2007, stock market analysts began saying that RIM's stock was overvalued (it was then selling for $84 per share). By August 2008, the stock had defied predictions and had increased to $123 per share, but by early 2010 it had dropped to $61 per share. RIM spent $1.2 billion to buy back some of its shares, which should have increased the share price because fewer shares were on the market, but RIM still has to demonstrate that it can compete with other companies that are bringing out new models of smart phones. In April 2010, RIM announced a series of initiatives to increase investor confidence in the company, but analysts were skeptical, and by the end of June 2010, the price of RIM's stock had declined to $54 per share.

RIM has taken several strategic actions in an attempt to improve its future prospects. Historically,

RIM's international footprint has not been large (about 80 percent of RIM's revenue comes from the U.S., Canada, and the U.K.). But in 2009, RIM signed a deal with Digital China to distribute BlackBerrys in China. The potential market in China is obviously large, but consumers in China may not be willing to pay the high price of a BlackBerry. As well, the production of unauthorized copycat phones (knock-offs) is a problem in China. For example, the "BlockBerry" is one of the competing phones sold in China.

RIM is also responding to competitive threats by positioning the BlackBerry as a general purpose smart phone for the average consumer, not just business users. More stylish models are being produced and are aimed at students, "soccer moms,"

and consumers in general. RIM also developed a new advertising campaign, sponsored a high-profile tour of Irish rock group U2, and provided better web browsers and applications for internet shopping. RIM's security standards mean it is safe for customers to do things like shop online from their smart phone.

According to the research firm IDC, there were 450 million mobile internet users in 2009, but that number should increase to 1 billion by 2013. Over 80 percent of RIM's new subscribers are individuals, not businesses. One positive trend for RIM is increasing consumer interest in smart phones. About 40 percent of the mobile phones purchased in 2010 were smart phones, and that proportion will increase over the next few years.

The idea of business and profit

The opening case illustrates the dynamic and rapidly changing nature of modern business activity, and the opportunities and challenges that are evident. It also shows how business managers must pay attention to many different things, including the actions of competitors, rapid technological change, new product development, corporate strategy, risk management, stock prices, and a host of other variables that you will read about in this book.

Let's begin by asking what you think of when you hear the word *business*. Do you think of large corporations like Shoppers Drug Mart and Walmart, or smaller companies like your local supermarket or favourite restaurant? Do you think about successful companies like CN and Research In Motion, or less successful companies like GM Canada? Actually, each of these firms is a **business**—an organization that produces or sells goods or services in an effort to make a profit. **Profit** is what remains after a business's expenses have been subtracted from its revenues. Profits reward the owners of businesses for taking the risks involved in investing their time and money. In 2008, the most profitable Canadian companies were Encana Corp. ($6.3 billion), the Canadian Wheat Board ($5.7 billion), and Canadian Natural Resources Ltd. ($4.9 billion).[1]

The prospect of earning profits is what encourages people to start and expand businesses. Today, businesses produce most of the goods and services that we consume, and they employ many of the working people in Canada. Profits from these businesses are paid to thousands upon thousands of owners and shareholders, and business taxes help support governments at all levels. In addition, businesses help support charitable causes and provide community leadership. A 2010 study by KPMG of the G7 industrialized countries revealed that Canada ranked as the most cost-effective place to do business.[2]

In addition to for-profit business firms, there are also many not-for-profit organizations in Canada. **Not-for-profit organizations** do not try to make a profit; rather, they use the funds they generate (from government grants or the sale of goods or services) to provide services to the public. Charities, educational institutions, hospitals, labour unions, and government agencies

BUSINESS
An organization that seeks to earn profits by providing goods and services.

PROFIT
What remains (if anything) after a business's expenses are subtracted from its sales revenues.

NOT-FOR-PROFIT ORGANIZATION
An organization that provides goods and services to customers, but does not seek to make a profit while doing so.

are examples of not-for-profit organizations. Business principles are helpful to these not-for-profit organizations as they try to achieve their service goals.

Business sectors

What is the difference between the public and private business sectors?

❶

Explain the difference between private and public business sectors.

Businesses are often categorized into specific groupings called sectors, which can be based on business activities, how profits are managed, or the industry in which the business operates.

The **public business sector** includes goods and services produced, delivered, and allocated by the government and public sector organizations (publicly controlled government business enterprises). The government sector includes all federal, provincial, municipal, and territorial government ministries and departments. It also includes public schools boards, public universities and colleges, and public health and social service institutions. Public sector organizations operate in the marketplace, often in competition with privately owned organizations. Government may have direct or indirect control over public sector organizations, which are also referred to as Crown corporations. The aim of the public sector is to provide services that benefit the public as a whole, either because it would be difficult to charge people for the goods and services concerned, or because people might not be able to afford to pay for them. The government can provide these goods and services at a lower price than if they were provided by a for-profit company. Examples include public utilities, such as water and sewage, electricity, and gas, and nationalized industries, such as coal and steel.

The **private business sector** includes goods and services produced and delivered by private individuals or groups as a means of enterprise for profit. The sector is not controlled by government. These businesses can be small firms owned by just one person, or large multinational businesses that operate globally. Large businesses may have many thousands of owners. A public (or publicly traded) company within the private business sector is not part of the public sector (government-provided services and government-owned organizations); it is a particular kind of private sector company that can offer its shares for sale to the general public (Microsoft, Apple, Procter & Gamble).

The **non-profit and voluntary sector** includes non-governmental, non-profit organizations that receive support from individual citizens, governments, and businesses. Non-profit organizations (NPOs) are also referred to as private voluntary organizations (PVOs); not-for-profit organizations (NFPOs); or non-profit making, non-governmental organizations (NGOs). In the global business world, there is inconsistency in how these terms are defined. A non-profit organization could be a not-for-profit corporation or an unincorporated association. A not-for-profit corporation is usually created with a specific purpose in mind and could be a foundation or charity or other type of non-profit organization. A private voluntary association is a group of volunteers who enter an agreement to form an organized body to accomplish a purpose. In this textbook, not-for-profit corporations, private voluntary organizations, and non-governmental organizations are classified in the non-profit and voluntary sector as non-profit organizations.

Non-profit organizations have the ability to respond to issues more quickly than government and are usually formed or expanded in reaction to a community need not being met by the government. The Canadian government recognizes the importance of the non-profit sector as a key partner in building a stronger Canada, and it supports the sector in a number of ways, such as partnering, streamlining funding practices and accountability, and developing knowledge on the non-profit sector.[3] The non-profit sector often relies heavily on the government for funding.[4]

PUBLIC BUSINESS SECTOR
The public business sector includes goods and services produced, delivered, and allocated by the government and public sector organizations (publicly controlled government business enterprises).

PRIVATE BUSINESS SECTOR
The private business sector includes goods and services produced and delivered by private individuals or groups as a means of enterprise for profit.

NON-PROFIT AND VOLUNTARY SECTOR
The non-profit and voluntary sector includes non-governmental, non-profit organizations that receive support from individual Canadians, governments, and businesses.

Non-profit organizations operate in a variety of areas, including sports, religion, arts, culture, fundraising, and housing. The various organizations include hospitals, universities and colleges, education and research organizations, business and professional associations, and unions—CARE, Save the Children, Habitat for Humanity, Greenpeace, and World Vision are all non-profit organizations. Non-profit organizations experience problems with planning for the future, recruiting the types of volunteers needed by the organization, and obtaining board members and funding.[5] People who work in non-profit organizations may be paid employees or unpaid volunteers, which is why the sector is called the "non-profit and voluntary sector."

Many people are confused as to which business sector certain organizations belong. Is a hospital in the public or private sector? Are all hospitals non-profit organizations? Is a private sector university a non-profit or for-profit organization? This confusion exists because some types of organizations typically thought of as belonging to the non-profit sector can cross sectors. For example, in Ontario there are four types of hospitals, including public, private, federal, and Cancer Care Ontario hospitals.[6] Public sector hospitals are owned by the government and receive government funding. Private sector hospitals are privately owned, often by a for-profit company or a non-profit organization, and are funded through patient payments, insurers, grants, donations, and foreign embassies. Private hospitals and health care clinics are classified as being in either the private, for-profit or private, non-profit sectors and are quite common in the United States and Australia. Canada's mix of public and private health care options leaves many people thinking that the hospitals in Canada belong to the public sector because hospital services are publicly delivered, funded, and governed, and hospitals are accountable to the public. In fact, hospital services in many provinces are delivered largely by private sector, non-profit organizations.[7]

Similarly, Canada has private sector, for-profit and private sector, non-profit colleges and universities in addition to its many public, non-profit universities and colleges. There are over 500 registered private career colleges in Ontario alone.[8] A private career college operating in Ontario must be registered and must have its programs approved by the Ministry of Training, Colleges, and Universities. Private universities and colleges are not operated by the government, although many receive public subsidies, and depending on the province in which they are located, private universities and colleges may be subject to government regulation. Some of the world's most renowned universities, such as Harvard University, Stanford University, and Massachusetts Institute of Technology (MIT), are private sector, non-profit universities.

In 2003, Statistics Canada conducted a national survey of non-profit and voluntary organizations. At that time, approximately 161 000 non-profit organizations were formally registered or incorporated in Canada, of which about 80 000 were registered charities. Charities registered with the federal government are exempt from a variety of taxes and enable donors to claim tax credits for the donations they make. Collectively, these charities reported annual revenues of $112 billion and employed more than two million people. With the exclusion of hospitals, universities, and colleges, the sector had $75 billion in revenues and 1.3 million employees.[9]

What are the different industries across the three business sectors?

Across these three sectors, businesses may be classified by industry, such as services-producing industries and goods-producing industries. The five economic sectors specified by the North American Industry Classification System (NAICS) as goods-producing industries are:[10]

▶ agriculture, forestry, fishing, and hunting
▶ mining, and oil and gas extraction

- utilities
- construction
- manufacturing

The fifteen economic sectors specified by NAICS as services-producing industries are:[11]

- wholesale trade
- retail trade
- transportation and warehousing
- information and cultural industries
- finance and insurance
- real estate, and rental and leasing
- professional, scientific, and technical services
- management of companies and enterprises
- administrative and support, waste management, and remediation services
- educational services
- health care and social assistance
- arts, entertainment, and recreation
- accommodation and food services
- other services, except public administration
- public administration

Do all businesses create a product?

Whether a business is for-profit or non-profit, one of its goals is to provide some sort of product to its customer base. A product can be either a good or a service. **Goods** are any physical products offered by a business. A roast beef sandwich at Arby's, a forty-two-inch LCD television at Best Buy, and a Honda Civic at your local car dealer are all considered goods because they are tangible items. Conveyer belts, pumps, and sundries sold to other businesses are also goods, even though they are not sold directly to consumers. **Services** refer to intangible products that are bought or sold. Unlike a polo shirt on the rack at Old Navy, services cannot be physically handled. Services include products such as haircuts, health care, car insurance, and theatrical productions.

Some companies offer products that are both goods and services. Take, for example, an establishment like Montana's franchise of restaurants. When you order a stuffed chicken breast meal at the restaurant, you are paying for the good (a stuffed chicken breast meal) as well as the service of preparing, cooking, and serving the meal.

Factors of production

What resources are needed to produce goods or services?

To understand fully how a business operates, you must consider the **factors of production**, which are the resources (inputs) used to produce goods and services (outputs). For years, businesses focused on four traditional factors: labour, natural resources, capital, and entrepreneurial talent. However, in the economy of the twenty-first century, an additional factor has become increasingly important: technology.

- **Labour.** Businesses need people to get things produced. **Labour** is the human resource that refers to any physical or intellectual work people contribute to business production.

GOODS

Goods are any physical products offered by a business.

SERVICES

Services refer to intangible products that are bought or sold.

FACTORS OF PRODUCTION

The factors of production are the resources used to produce goods and services.

❷
Describe the factors of production.

LABOUR

Labour is the human resource that refers to any physical or intellectual work people contribute to business production.

- **Natural resources.** Most workers who provide the labour to produce a good need something tangible to work with. Natural resources are the raw materials provided by nature and used to produce goods and services. Soil used in agricultural production; trees used for lumber to build houses; and coal, oil, and natural gas used to create energy are all examples of natural resources.

- **Capital.** There are two types of capital: real capital and financial capital. Real capital refers to the physical facilities used to produce goods and services. Financial capital is money used to facilitate a business enterprise. Financial capital can be acquired through business loans, from investors, or through other forms of fundraising, or even by tapping into personal savings.

- **Entrepreneurs.** An entrepreneur is someone who assumes the risk of creating, organizing, and operating a business and who directs all the business resources. Entrepreneurs are a human resource, just like labour, but what sets entrepreneurs apart from labour is their willingness to bear risks and their ability to manage an enterprise effectively. Successful entrepreneurs are rewarded with profits for bearing risks and for their managerial expertise.

- **Technology.** Technology includes human knowledge, work methods, physical equipment, electronics and telecommunications, and various processing systems used to perform business activities. Technology refers to items and services such as smartphones, computer software, and digital broadcasting that make businesses more efficient and productive. Successful companies are able to keep pace with technological progresses and harness new knowledge, information, and strategies. Unsuccessful organizations typically fail because they have not kept pace with the latest technology and techniques.

Why are entrepreneurs so important?

Entrepreneurs are the innovators who create business ideas and start businesses from those ideas. They attempt to make a profit by combining the factors of production (inputs) to create goods and services (outputs). The factors of production used to produce a pizza in a pizza restaurant would include:

- ▶ the land that the pizza restaurant is located on, the electricity used to run the store, and the wheat and other food products from which the pizza is made;

NATURAL RESOURCES
Natural resources are the raw materials provided by nature and used to produce goods and services.

REAL CAPITAL
Real capital refers to the physical facilities used to produce goods and services.

FINANCIAL CAPITAL
Financial capital is money used to facilitate a business enterprise.

ENTREPRENEUR
An entrepreneur is someone who assumes the risk of creating, organizing, and operating a business and who directs all the business resources.

TECHNOLOGY
Technology includes human knowledge, work methods, physical equipment, electronics and telecommunications, and various processing systems used to perform business activities.

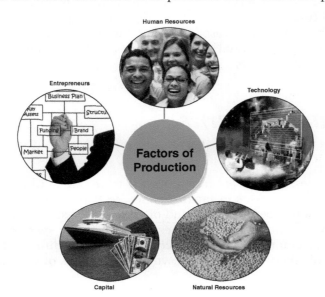

- the labourers who make the pizzas;
- the store and equipment used to make the pizza, and the money used to operate the business;
- the technology used to gather customer information, market to customers, deliver to customers, track inventory, and reorder supplies; and
- the entrepreneurship skills used to coordinate the other factors of production to initiate the production process.

Why is technology a key factor in production?

Companies do not require technology for the sake of technology alone. Rather, technology has become a critical factor for obtaining and managing **information and knowledge**, which are quickly becoming the key factors of production as the new competitive business environment places a premium on these factors. Not only do companies need technology to obtain and manage information, they need human resources (knowledge workers) with the skills to manipulate the information and turn it into knowledge that the company can use for competitive advantage. Knowledge is a tricky thing to manage, but companies can translate their information assets into real value for the business by learning from past successes or failures, identifying opportunities to improve profitability, or simply enabling teams to become more productive. With increased mobility of information and the global workforce, information and knowledge can be transported around the world.

Functional areas of business

What activities are needed to operate a business?

Functional areas in businesses are often separate departments where business activities are grouped by similar tasks or skills. Most large businesses consist of a number of different departments, each of which has a specific function. Smaller businesses must conduct the same business functions, but on a smaller scale. Therefore, they do not always have separate departments for each functional area. People are organized in different ways in different organizations, depending on factors such as the size of the organization, the culture of the organization, the nature of the industry, and the preferred structures of the managers. The main functional areas you will often see in businesses are sales and marketing; customer service; information technology and communications; accounting and finance; research and development; manufacturing, production, and distribution; human resources; and administration (shown in Key 8.1). Each of the functional areas of business will be discussed in more detail in subsequent chapters.

Economic systems **around the world**

A Canadian business is different in many ways from one in China, and both are different from businesses in Japan, France, or Peru. A major determinant of how organizations operate is the kind of economic system that characterizes the country in which they do business. An **economic system** allocates a nation's resources among its citizens. Economic systems differ in terms of who owns and controls these resources, known as the "factors of production" (see Key 8.2).

INFORMATION AND KNOWLEDGE
Information and knowledge are quickly becoming the key factors of production as the new competitive business environment places a premium on these factors.

FUNCTIONAL AREAS
Functional areas in businesses are often separate departments where business activities are grouped by similar tasks or skills.

❸
Identify the functional areas of most businesses.

ECONOMIC SYSTEM
The way in which a nation allocates its resources among its citizens.

Key 8.1

FUNCTIONAL AREAS OF BUSINESS

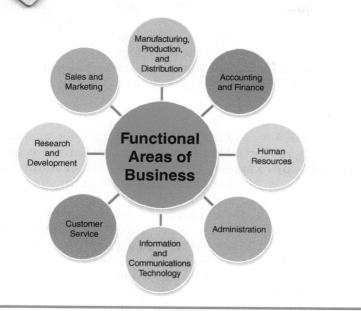

- Manufacturing, Production, and Distribution
- Sales and Marketing
- Accounting and Finance
- Research and Development
- **Functional Areas of Business**
- Human Resources
- Customer Service
- Administration
- Information and Communications Technology

Key 8.2

FACTORS OF PRODUCTION ARE **THE BASIC RESOURCES A BUSINESS USES** TO CREATE GOODS AND SERVICES. **THE FOUR FACTORS** ARE NATURAL RESOURCES, LABOUR, CAPITAL, AND ENTREPRENEURS

Natural resources

Labour (human resources)

Factors of production

Capital

Entrepreneurs

Types of economic systems

Different types of economic systems manage the factors of production in different ways. In some systems, ownership is private; in others, the factors of production are owned by the government. Economic systems also differ in the ways decisions are made about production and allocation. A **command economy**, for example, relies on a centralized government to control all or most factors of production and to make all or most production and allocation decisions. In **market economies** individuals—producers and consumers—control production and allocation decisions through supply and demand.

Command economies

The two most basic forms of command economies are communism and socialism. As originally proposed by nineteenth-century German economist Karl Marx, **communism** is a system in which the government owns and operates all sources of production. Marx envisioned a society in which individuals would ultimately contribute according to their abilities and receive economic benefits according to their needs. He also expected government ownership of production factors to be only temporary. Once society had matured, government would "wither away" and the workers would gain direct ownership.

But Marx's predictions were faulty. During the last 20 years, most countries have abandoned communism in favour of a more market-based economy. Even countries that still claim to be communist (for example, China, Vietnam, and Cuba) now contain elements of a market-based economy. Whether communism can be maintained alongside a market-based economy remains to be seen.

In a less extensive command economic system called **socialism**, the government owns and operates only selected major industries. Smaller businesses such as clothing stores and restaurants may be privately owned. Although workers in socialist countries are usually allowed to choose their occupations or professions, a large proportion generally work for the government. Many government-operated enterprises are inefficient, since management positions are frequently filled based on political considerations rather than ability. Extensive public welfare systems have also resulted in very high taxes. Because of these factors, socialism is generally declining in popularity.[12]

Market economies

A **market** is a mechanism for exchange between the buyers and sellers of a particular good or service. For example, the internet is a technologically sophisticated market that brings buyers and sellers together through e-commerce. People usually think of e-commerce as being business-to-consumer (B2C) transactions, such as buying books over the internet for personal use. But business-to-business (B2B) transactions are also a very important market. B2B involves businesses joining together to create e-commerce companies that make them more efficient when they purchase the goods and services they need. B2B transactions actually far exceed B2C transactions in dollar value.

In a market economy, B2C and B2B exchanges take place without much government involvement. To understand how a *market economy* works, consider what happens when a customer goes to a fruit stand to buy apples. Assume that one vendor is selling apples for $1 per kilogram, and another is charging $1.50. Both vendors are free to charge what they want, and customers are free to buy what they choose. If both vendors' apples are of the same quality, the customer will likely buy the cheaper ones. But if the $1.50 apples are fresher, the customer may buy them instead. Both buyers and sellers enjoy freedom of choice (but they also are subject to risks, as the financial meltdown of 2008 demonstrated).

COMMAND ECONOMY
An economic system in which government controls all or most factors of production and makes all or most production decisions.

MARKET ECONOMY
An economic system in which individuals control all or most factors of production and make all or most production decisions.

COMMUNISM
A type of command economy in which the government owns and operates all industries.

SOCIALISM
A kind of command economy in which the government owns and operates the main industries, while individuals own and operate less crucial industries.

MARKET
An exchange process between buyers and sellers of a particular good or service.

entrepreneurship and
New Ventures

A Shrine to Wine

Wine connoisseurs, also known as oenophiles, have a love of and devotion to wine, and they take just as much care in the procurement and storage of their vino as they do in the tasting. Robb Denomme and Lance Kingma own Winnipeg-based Genuwine Cellars, which sells custom-designed wine cellars, some of which have six-figure price tags. The company was started somewhat by accident in 1995 when someone asked Kingma if he thought he could build a wine cellar. He took on the challenge, and the first order led to another, and he eventually partnered with Denomme, who was just 17 at the time. As the saying goes, the rest is history. Today, the business is a multimillion-dollar operation selling to clients around the world, with the majority of sales being to the U.S.

Genuwine's international success probably wouldn't have happened, or at least not as easily, without the help of the Department of Foreign Affairs and International Trade (DFAIT). According to Robb, "Working with the TCS [Trade Commissioner Service] you get results, you get where you want to go. Trade commissioners are there to help and always get back to you with the answers you need." The TCS is a division of Foreign Affairs and its goal is to help companies succeed globally. Not only did TCS help Genuwine Cellars get connected with a business consultant, it also helped with financing. Other governmental agencies, including the Prairie Centre for Business Intelligence and the National Research Council, have also provided business support.

In addition to market development strategies, Genuwine Cellars is credited with some other good moves. "Genuwine is doing all the right things a growing company should do—lean manufacturing, continual investments in technology, importing contract manufactured goods from Asia, setting up a design office in Latin America to take advantage of a lower cost structure and access to skilled professionals, the list goes on," says Joanne MacKean, senior manager, Business Development Canada. Further, Genuwine Cellars is one of the largest wine cellar manufacturers in North America and the only company with a manufacturing facility in Canada. Very little competition, niche market, upscale consumer—so just what's "in store" for this business?

According to Denomme, the recent recession had some effect, but the company is still experiencing growth. Denomme's enthusiasm and drive are not quashed, however. He says, "You've got to keep a positive attitude." Sounds like this entrepreneur looks upon his wine glass as being half full rather than half empty.

Critical Thinking Questions

1. Discuss the factors of production as they apply to Genuwine Cellars.

2. What do you think about the company's decision to move some of its operations to Latin America because of a lower cost structure?

A GlobeScan poll of over 20 000 people in 20 countries asked people whether they agreed with the following statement: "The free market economy is the best system." Where do you think the highest support for the free market economy was found? Not in Canada, the United States, Germany, or Japan, but in *China*, where 74 percent of people polled agreed with the statement.[13] This is a surprising finding, given the Chinese government's strong support of the communist economic ideology. It seems hard to believe now, but before 1979, people who sold watches on street corners in China were sentenced to years of hard labour. After China's constitution was amended to legitimate private enterprise, the private sector has become incredibly productive. It is estimated that China produces 60 percent of all the toys in the world.[14] China's reputation for being a low-cost producer of goods is legendary. It is also a vast and rapidly growing market for many of the products that Canadian firms produce—chemicals, ores, cereals, and wood products.

Input and output markets

INPUT MARKET
Firms buy resources that they need in the production of goods and services.

OUTPUT MARKET
Firms supply goods and services in response to demand on the part of consumers.

A useful model for understanding how the factors of production work in a pure market economy is shown in Key 8.3.[15] In the **input market**, firms buy resources from households, which then supply those resources. In the **output market** firms supply goods and services in response to demand on the part of the households. The activities of these two markets create a circular flow. Ford Motor Co., for example, buys labour directly from households, which may also supply capital from accumulated savings in the form of stock purchases. Consumer buying patterns provide information that helps Ford decide which models to produce and which to discontinue. In turn, Ford uses these inputs in various ways and becomes a supplier to households when it designs and produces various kinds of automobiles, trucks, and sport-utility vehicles and offers them for sale to consumers.

Individuals are free to work for Ford or an alternative employer and to invest in Ford stock or alternative forms of saving or consumption. Similarly, Ford can create whatever vehicles it chooses and price them at whatever

Key 8.3

CIRCULAR FLOW
IN A MARKET ECONOMY

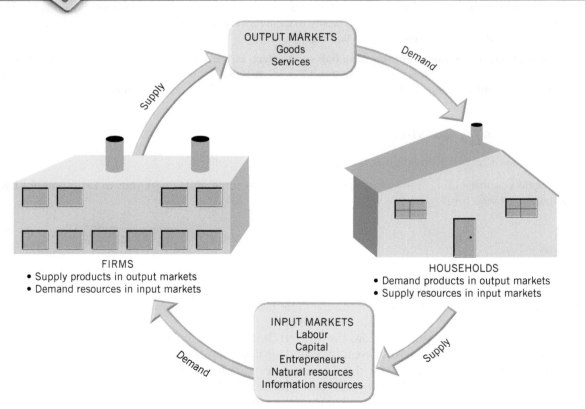

OUTPUT MARKETS
Goods
Services

Supply

Demand

FIRMS
• Supply products in output markets
• Demand resources in input markets

HOUSEHOLDS
• Demand products in output markets
• Supply resources in input markets

INPUT MARKETS
Labour
Capital
Entrepreneurs
Natural resources
Information resources

Demand

Supply

value it chooses. Consumers are free to buy their next car from Ford, Toyota, BMW, or any other manufacturer. The political basis for the free market economy is called **capitalism**, which allows private ownership of the factors of production and encourages entrepreneurship by offering profits as an incentive. This process contrasts markedly with that of a command economy, in which individuals may be told where they can and cannot work, companies may be told what they can and cannot manufacture, and consumers may have little or no choice as to what they purchase or how much they pay for items.

Mixed market economies

Command and market economies are two extremes, or opposites. In reality, most countries rely on some form of **mixed market economy** that features characteristics of both command and market economies. One trend in mixed market economies that began in the 1990s is **privatization**—converting government enterprises into privately owned companies. In Canada, for example, the air traffic control system was privatized, and the federal government sold several other corporations, including Canadian National Railway and Air Canada. The Netherlands privatized its TNT Post Group N.V., and India privatized 18 industries, including iron, steel, machinery, and telecommunications.[16] In 2010, the Organisation for Economic Co-operation and Development (OECD) said that Canada Post's monopoly should be ended and it should be privatized.[17] However, when a worldwide recession began in 2008, the trend slowed. Government bailouts of Chrysler and GM in both Canada and the U.S. meant that government was once again a part-owner of some business firms. A few countries are even pursuing a policy of **nationalization**—converting private firms into government-owned firms. Venezuela, for example, nationalized its telecommunications industry.

Deregulation means a reduction in the number of laws affecting business activity and in the powers of government enforcement agencies. This trend also developed during the 1990s, and deregulation occurred in many industries, including airlines, pipelines, banking, trucking, and communications. But this trend has also slowed (and even reversed in some cases) due to the 2008 recession. For example, there have been calls for a dramatic tightening up of the laws regulating business activity, particularly in the financial sector. The British Petroleum (BP) oil spill in the Gulf of Mexico in 2010 caused the U.S. government to put pressure on BP to reimburse individuals and businesses that were harmed by the spill. Incidents like these have created a dilemma for government policy makers; a 2009 study by the Conference Board of Canada showed that deregulation (in tandem with privatization and increased competition) caused a sharp increase in productivity in sectors like freight and airlines.[18]

As a result of the recession of 2008, mixed market economies are now characterized by more government involvement than was evident just a few years ago. Governments in mixed market economies have intervened in the economic system in an attempt to stabilize it, but this has led to higher deficits (see Chapter 9) and more control of business activity.

Interactions between business and government

In Canada's mixed market economy, there are many important interactions between business and government. The ways in which government influences business and the ways business influences government are described below.

CAPITALISM
An economic system in which markets decide what, when, and for whom to produce.

MIXED MARKET ECONOMY
An economic system with elements of both a command economy and a market economy; in practice, typical of most nations' economies.

PRIVATIZATION
The transfer of activities from the government to the private sector.

NATIONALIZATION
The transfer of activities from private firms to the government.

DEREGULATION
A reduction in the number of laws affecting business activity.

How government influences business

Government plays several key roles in the Canadian eco-nomy, and each of these roles influences business activity in some way. The roles government plays are as follows.

Government as a customer

Government buys thousands of different products and services from business firms, including office supplies, office buildings, computers, battleships, helicopters, highways, water treatment plants, and management and engineering consulting services. Many businesses depend on government purchasing, if not for their survival then at least for a certain level of prosperity. Total government expenditures in 2009 were $234 billion.[19]

Government as a competitor

Government also competes with business through Crown corporations, which are accountable to a minister of parliament for their conduct. Crown corporations like Hydro Quebec (revenues of $12.7 billion), Canada Post ($7.4 billion), and the Canadian Wheat Board ($8.4 billion) account for a significant amount of economic activity in Canada.[20] Crown corporations exist at both the provincial and federal levels.

Government as regulator

Federal, and provincial governments in Canada regulate many aspects of business activity through administrative boards, tribunals, and commissions. Illustrative examples include the **Canadian Radio-television and Telecommunications Commission (CRTC)** (which issues and renews broadcast licences) and the **Canadian Wheat Board** (which regulates the price of wheat). Provincial boards and commissions also regulate business activity, but different situations exist in different provinces. For example, the provinces of Quebec and B.C. allowed mixed martial arts events such as the UFC, but Ontario didn't (Ontario began allowing these events in 2011).[21] Reasons for regulating business activity include protecting competition, protecting consumers, achieving social goals, and protecting the environment.

Promoting Competition Competition is crucial to a market economy, so government regulates business activity to ensure that healthy competition exists among business firms. Without these restrictions, a large company with vast resources could cut its prices and drive smaller firms out of the market. The guidelines for Canada's competition policy are contained in the Competition Act, which prohibits a variety of practices (see Table 8.1). Section 61, for example, prohibits something called *resale price maintenance*. Labatt Brewing Co. recently pled guilty to resale price maintenance and was fined $250 000 after its sales representatives gave money to store operators who agreed to not lower prices on some brands of beer. This activity meant that customers had to pay higher prices for beer.[22]

The Act prohibits agreements among companies that are designed to reduce competition. Formerly, the government had to prove that such agreements actually reduced competition, but recent changes to the legislation mean that the mere existence of a conspiracy is assumed to be proof that competition has been reduced.[23] Another big change is the dramatically increased fines for

Despite becoming a territory of the communist People's Republic of China in 1997, Hong Kong remains one of the world's freest economies. In Hong Kong's Lan Kwai Fong district, for example, traditional Chinese businesses operate next door to well-known international chains.

CANADIAN RADIO-TELEVISION AND TELECOMMUNICATIONS COMMISSION (CRTC)
Regulates and supervises all aspects of the Canadian broadcasting system.

CANADIAN WHEAT BOARD
Regulates the price farmers receive for their wheat.

Table 8.1 The Competition Act

Section 45	Prohibits conspiracies and combinations formed for the purpose of unduly lessening competition in the production, transportation, or storage of goods. Persons convicted may be imprisoned for up to five years or fined up to $1 million or both.
Section 50	Prohibits illegal trade practices. A company may not, for example, cut prices in one region of Canada while selling at a higher price everywhere else if this substantially lessens competition. A company may not sell at "unreasonably low prices" if this substantially lessens competition. (This section does not prohibit credit unions from returning surpluses to their members.)
Section 51	Prohibits giving allowances and rebates to buyers to cover their advertising expenses, unless these allowances are made available proportionally to other purchasers who are in competition with the buyer given the rebate.
Section 52	Prohibits marketing (promotion) activities that are false or misleading. Includes telemarketing activities.
Section 53	Prohibits the deceptive notice that a person has won a prize if the recipient is asked to pay money as a condition of winning the prize.
Section 54	Prohibits charging the higher price when two prices are shown on a product.
Section 55.1	Prohibits pyramid selling (a participant in the plan receives compensation for recruiting other individuals into the plan).
Section 61	Prohibits resale price maintenance. No person who produces or supplies a product can attempt to influence upward, or discourage reduction of, the price of the good in question. It is also illegal for the producer to refuse to supply a product to a reseller simply because the producer believes the reseller will cut the price.
Section 74	Prohibits bait-and-switch selling. No person can advertise a product at a bargain price if there is no supply of the product available to the consumer. (This tactic baits prospects into the store, where salespeople switch them to higher-priced goods.) This section also controls the use of contests to sell goods, and prohibits the sale of goods at a price higher than the advertised one.

misleading marketing practices by corporations (formerly $100 000 for the first offence, but now $10 million).[24]

Businesses often complain that the Competition Bureau is too slow in approving or denying merger plans. For example, when Labatt Brewing wanted to take over Lakeport Brewing, it was told that the Competition Bureau would need up to six months to determine whether the takeover would lessen competition. Labatt therefore appealed to the Competition Tribunal to speed up the process. The Tribunal agreed with Labatt, and the merger went ahead sooner than it otherwise would have.[25] There was, however, some interesting fallout later. The federal industry minister began an investigation after a Federal Court judge accused the Competition Bureau of providing misleading information in order to get a court order for Labatt's records during its review of the proposed merger.[26]

Protecting Consumers The federal government has initiated many programs that protect consumers. Consumer and Corporate Affairs Canada administers many of these. Important legislation includes the **Hazardous Products Act** (which requires poisonous, flammable, explosive, or corrosive products to be appropriately labelled), the **Tobacco Act** (which prohibits cigarette advertising on billboards and in stores), the **Weights and Measures Act** (which sets standards of accuracy for weighing and measuring devices), the **Textile Labelling Act** (which regulates the labelling, sale, importation, and advertising of consumer textile articles), and the **Food and Drug Act** (which prohibits the sale of food that contains any poisonous or harmful substances). Consumers are also protected by municipal bylaws such as "no smoking" bylaws.

Achieving Social Goals Social goals, which promote the well-being of Canadian society, include things like universal access to health care, safe workplaces, employment insurance, and decent pensions. All of these goals require the interaction of business firms and the Canadian government. But the decisions of foreign governments—as they pursue their own social goals—can also affect Canadian businesses. For example, when the U.S. government introduced legislation making

HAZARDOUS PRODUCTS ACT
Regulates banned products and products that can be sold but must be labelled hazardous.

TOBACCO ACT
Prohibits cigarette advertising on billboards and in retail stores, and assigns financial penalties to violators.

WEIGHTS AND MEASURES ACT
Sets standards of accuracy for weighing and measuring devices.

TEXTILE LABELLING ACT
Regulates the labelling, sale, importation, and advertising of consumer textile articles.

FOOD AND DRUG ACT
Prohibits the sale of food unfit for human consumption and regulates food advertising.

The Hazardous Products Act requires poisonous, flammable, explosive, or corrosive products to have warning labels to protect consumers who use them.

CANADA WATER ACT
Controls water quality in fresh and marine waters of Canada.

FISHERIES ACT
Regulates the discharge of harmful substances into water.

ENVIRONMENTAL CONTAMINANTS ACT
Establishes regulations for airborne substances that are a danger to human health or to the environment.

REVENUE TAXES
Taxes whose main purpose is to fund government services and programs.

PROGRESSIVE REVENUE TAXES
Taxes levied at a higher rate on higher-income taxpayers and at a lower rate on lower-income taxpayers.

REGRESSIVE REVENUE TAXES
Taxes that cause poorer people to pay a higher percentage of income than richer people pay.

RESTRICTIVE TAXES
Taxes levied to control certain activities that legislators believe should be controlled.

it difficult for online gambling companies to operate in the U.S., the stock prices of Canadian firms like Cryptologic Inc. and Chartwell Technology dropped.[27]

Protecting the Environment Government legislation designed to protect the environment includes the **Canada Water Act** (which controls water quality in fresh and marine waters), the **Fisheries Act** (which controls the discharge of any harmful substance into water), and the **Environmental Contaminants Act** (which establishes regulations for airborne substances that are a danger to human health or the environment).

Government as a taxation agent

Taxes are imposed and collected by the federal, provincial, and local governments. **Revenue taxes** (e.g., income taxes) are levied by governments primarily to provide revenue to fund various services and programs. **Progressive revenue taxes** are levied at a higher rate on higher-income taxpayers and at a lower rate on lower-income taxpayers. **Regressive revenue taxes** (e.g., sales tax) are levied at the same rate regardless of a person's income. They cause poorer people to pay a higher percentage of their income for these taxes than rich people pay. **Restrictive taxes** (e.g., taxes on alcohol, tobacco, and gasoline) are levied partially for the revenue they provide, but also because legislative bodies believe that the products in question should be controlled.

Government as a provider of incentives and financial assistance

Federal, provincial, and municipal governments offer incentive programs that attempt to stimulate economic development. The Province of Quebec, for example, has attracted video game companies like Ubisoft by giving them multimillion-dollar subsidies if they locate in the province.[28] The Provinces of Ontario and B.C. have given hundreds of millions of dollars in subsidies to film companies to motivate them to make major films in those provinces. But the government of Alberta (which spends about $20 million each year on subsidies to filmmakers) has decided not to increase the amount of its subsidies.[29]

Governments also offer incentives through the many services they provide to business firms through government organizations. Examples include the Export Development Corporation (which assists Canadian exporters by offering export insurance against non-payment by foreign buyers and long-term loans to foreign buyers of Canadian products), Natural Resources Canada (which provides geological maps of Canada's potential mineral-producing areas), and Statistics Canada (which provides data and analysis on almost every aspect of Canadian society). Industry Canada offers many different programs designed to help small businesses. The Canada Business program, for example, provides information on government programs, services, and regulations in order to improve the start-up and survival rates of small and medium-sized businesses. It also encourages businesses to focus on sound business planning and the effective use of market research. DFAIT helps Canadian companies doing business internationally by promoting Canada as a good place to invest and to carry on business activities. It also assists in negotiating and administering trade agreements.

There are many other government incentive programs, including municipal tax rebates for companies that locate in certain areas, design assistance programs, and remission of tariffs on certain advanced technology production equipment. Government incentive programs may or may not have the desired effect of stimulating the economy. They may also cause difficulties with our trading partners, as we shall see in Chapter 12. Some critics also argue that business firms are too willing to accept government assistance—either in the form of incentives or bailouts—and that managers should put more emphasis on innovation and creativity so business firms can better cope with economic difficulties when they arise, as they did during the 2008–2009 recession.

Government as a provider of essential services

The various levels of government facilitate business activity through the services they supply. The federal government provides highways, the postal service, the minting of money, the armed forces, and statistical data on which to base business decisions. It also tries to maintain stability through fiscal and monetary policy (discussed in Chapter 9). Provincial and municipal governments provide streets, sewage and sanitation systems, police and fire departments, utilities, hospitals, and education. All of these activities create the kind of stability that encourages business activity.

How business influences government

Businesses also try to influence the government through the use of lobbyists, trade associations, and advertising. A lobbyist is a person hired by a company or industry to represent that company's interests with government officials. The Canadian Association of Consulting Engineers, for example, regularly lobbies the federal and provincial governments to make use of the skills possessed by private-sector consulting engineers on projects like city water systems. Some business lobbyists have training in the particular industry, public relations experience, or a legal background. A few have served as legislators or government regulators.

The federal Lobbying Act requires lobbyists to register with the Commissioner of Lobbying so it is clear which individuals are being paid for their lobbying activity. It also sets rules for accountability and transparency, and requires lobbyists to report detailed information about their communications with what are known as Designated Public Office Holders (DPOHs).[30] For many lobbying efforts, there are opposing points of view. For example,

LOBBYIST
A person hired by a company or an industry to represent its interests with government officials.

Glossary (margin)

TRADE ASSOCIATION
An organization dedicated to promoting the interests and assisting the members of a particular industry.

MARKET
An exchange process between buyers and sellers of a particular good or service

DEMAND
The willingness and ability of buyers to purchase a product or service.

SUPPLY
The willingness and ability of producers to offer a good or service for sale.

LAW OF DEMAND
The principle that buyers will purchase (demand) more of a product as price drops.

LAW OF SUPPLY
The principle that producers will offer (supply) more of a product as price rises.

DEMAND AND SUPPLY SCHEDULE
Assessment of the relationships between different levels of demand and supply at different price levels.

DEMAND CURVE
Graph showing how many units of a product will be demanded (bought) at different prices.

SUPPLY CURVE
Graph showing how many units of a product will be supplied (offered for sale) at different prices.

---

the Canadian Cancer Society and the Tobacco Institute present very different points of view on cigarette smoking and cigarette advertising.

Employees and owners of small businesses that cannot afford lobbyists often join **trade associations**, which may act as an industry lobby to influence legislation. They also conduct training programs relevant to the particular industry, and they arrange trade shows at which members display their products or services to potential customers. Most publish newsletters featuring articles on new products, new companies, changes in ownership, and changes in laws affecting the industry.

Corporations can influence legislation indirectly by influencing voters. A company can, for example, launch an advertising campaign designed to get people to write their MPs, MPPs, or MLAs demanding passage—or rejection—of a particular bill that is before parliament or the provincial legislature.

The canadian market economy

Understanding the complex nature of the Canadian economic system is essential to understanding Canadian business. In this section, we will examine the workings of our market economy, including markets, demand, supply, private enterprise, and degrees of competition.

Demand and supply in a market economy

In economic terms, a **market** is not a specific place, like a supermarket, but an exchange process between buyers and sellers. Decisions about production in a market economy are the result of millions of exchanges. How much of what product a company offers for sale and who buys it depends on the laws of demand and supply.

The laws of supply and demand

In a market economy, decisions about what to buy and what to sell are determined primarily by the forces of demand and supply. **Demand** is the willingness and ability of buyers to purchase a product or service. **Supply** is the willingness and ability of producers to offer a good or service for sale. The **law of demand** states that buyers will purchase (demand) more of a product as its price drops. Conversely, the **law of supply** states that producers will offer (supply) more for sale as the price rises.

Demand and supply schedule

To appreciate these laws in action, consider the market for pizza in your town. If everyone is willing to pay $25 for a pizza (a relatively high price), the local pizzeria will produce a large supply. If, however, everyone is willing to pay only $5 (a relatively low price), the restaurant will make fewer pizzas. Through careful analysis, we can determine how many pizzas will be sold at different prices. These results, called a **demand and supply schedule**, are obtained from marketing research and other systematic studies of the market. Properly applied, they help managers understand the relationships among different levels of demand and supply at different price levels.

Demand and supply curves

The demand and supply schedule can be used to construct demand and supply curves for pizza. A **demand curve** shows how many products—in this case, pizzas—will be *demanded* (bought) at different prices. A **supply curve** shows how many pizzas will be *supplied* (cooked) at different prices.

Media Solutions

Virtual Goods: An Emerging E-Market

Not too long ago, people doubted the commercial sales potential of bottled water because a perfectly good substitute was available for virtually no cost. At the time, many skeptics made comments like "What's next, are we going to sell air?" Today, consumers purchase approximately 200 billion litres of bottled water worldwide each year. The skeptics did not foresee an era dominated by the internet, smart phones, and social media.

At least bottled water is a physical product. But how much is an avatar worth? How much would you spend on a virtual good? If your answer is $0, you don't know what's going on in the virtual gaming world. Have you heard of Zynga? World of Warcraft? Mafia Wars? FarmVille? If you answered "no" to all these questions, you may be shocked to learn that, in 2010, virtual goods sales were expected to reach $1.6 billion in the U.S. alone, and are projected to grow to $3.6 billion by 2012.

As we've noted, a market is an exchange process between buyers and sellers of a particular good or service. This definition fits the evolving virtual goods world as well. Whether you are buying a potato to make French fries (to eat), or a virtual potato to plant in your own FarmVille virtual garden (for entertainment), you are involved in a market of buyers and sellers. Hard-core virtual gamers are willing to spend good money to ensure that they have the best gear available in games like World of Warcraft.

Facebook links people to the virtual world and has over 500 million users. The company is now trying to capitalize on its popularity by adding a new revenue stream. It plans to charge 30 percent on virtual game props (similar to Apple's approach to apps). It is also testing the extended use of its Facebook credits. If all goes as planned, Zynga (which has 120 million game users) may be forced to adopt this model. Facebook could collect as much as $500 million over the next three years from Zynga and other gaming companies, including Electronic Arts, CrowdStar, Slide, RockYou, and Digital Chocolate. One thing is certain, there is nothing virtual about the revenue potential.

Critical Thinking Question

1. Have you ever purchased a virtual good? If so, describe it. Were you satisfied? If not, what do you think of the prospects for this growing market?

2. What do you think of Facebook's new revenue stream model? Will it work?

Key 8.4 shows the hypothetical demand and supply curves for pizzas in our illustration. As you can see, demand increases as price decreases, and supply increases as price increases. When the demand and supply curves are plotted on the same graph, the point at which they intersect is the **market price**, or **equilibrium price**—the price at which the quantity of goods demanded and the quantity of goods supplied are equal. In Key 8.4, the equilibrium price for pizzas is $10. At this point, the quantity of pizzas demanded and the quantity of pizzas supplied are the same—1000 pizzas per week.

MARKET PRICE (EQUILIBRIUM PRICE) Profit-maximizing price at which the quantity of goods demanded and the quantity of goods supplied are equal.

Surpluses and shortages

What would happen if the owner tried to increase profits by making more pizzas to sell? Or, what if the owner wanted to reduce overhead, cut back on

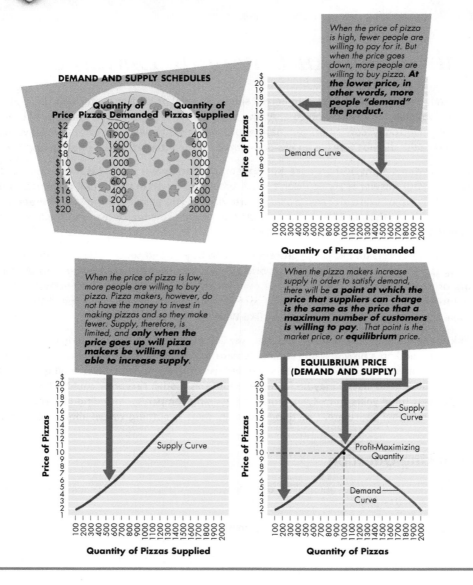

DEMAND AND SUPPLY SCHEDULES

Price	Quantity of Pizzas Demanded	Quantity of Pizzas Supplied
$2	2000	100
$4	1900	400
$6	1600	600
$8	1200	800
$10	1000	1000
$12	800	1200
$14	600	1300
$16	400	1600
$18	200	1800
$20	100	2000

When the price of pizza is high, fewer people are willing to pay for it. But when the price goes down, more people are willing to buy pizza. **At the lower price, in other words, more people "demand" the product.**

Quantity of Pizzas Demanded

When the price of pizza is low, more people are willing to buy pizza. Pizza makers, however, do not have the money to invest in making pizzas and so they make fewer. Supply, therefore, is limited, and **only when the price goes up will pizza makers be willing and able to increase supply.**

Quantity of Pizzas Supplied

When the pizza makers increase supply in order to satisfy demand, there will be **a point at which the price that suppliers can charge is the same as the price that a maximum number of customers is willing to pay.** *That point is the market price, or* **equilibrium** *price.*

EQUILIBRIUM PRICE (DEMAND AND SUPPLY)

Quantity of Pizzas

SURPLUS
Situation in which quantity supplied exceeds quantity demanded.

SHORTAGE
Situation in which quantity demanded exceeds quantity supplied.

store hours, and reduced the number of pizzas offered for sale? In either case, the result would be an inefficient use of resources. For example, if the restaurant supplies 1200 pizzas and tries to sell them for $10 each, 200 pizzas will not be purchased. The demand schedule clearly shows that only 1000 pizzas will be demanded at this price. The pizza maker will therefore have a **surplus**—a situation in which the quantity supplied exceeds the quantity demanded. The restaurant will thus lose the money that it spent making those extra 200 pizzas.

Conversely, if the pizzeria supplies only 800 pizzas, a **shortage** will result because the quantity demanded will be greater than the quantity supplied. The pizzeria will "lose" the extra money that it could have made by producing 200 more pizzas. Even though consumers may pay more for pizzas because of the shortage, the restaurant will still earn lower profits than it would have if it had made 1000 pizzas. In addition, it may risk angering customers who cannot buy pizzas. To optimize profits, therefore, all businesses must constantly seek the right combination of price charged and quantity supplied. This "right combination" is found at the equilibrium point.

Maple syrup is a quintessential Canadian commodity (we produce 80 percent of the total world's supply), but its price fluctuates because weather influences the supply. Unfavourable weather reduced the supply in 2008, but good weather in 2009 caused yields to increase by 85 percent over 2008.[31] Price fluctuations in several other commodities are described in the boxed insert entitled "The High Price of High Prices."[32]

Canada is the dominant supplier of maple syrup for the world market. But variable weather conditions can create conditions of either surplus or shortage.

Private enterprise and competition

Market economies rely on a **private enterprise** system—one that allows individuals to pursue their own interests with minimal government restriction. Private enterprise requires the presence of four elements: private property rights, freedom of choice, profits, and competition.

- **Private property.** Ownership of the resources used to create wealth is in the hands of individuals.[33]

- **Freedom of choice.** You can sell your labour to any employer you choose. You can also choose which products to buy, and producers can usually choose whom to hire and what to produce.

- **Profits.** The lure of profits (and freedom) leads some people to abandon the security of working for someone else and to assume the risks of entrepreneurship. Anticipated profits also influence individuals' choices of which goods or services to produce.

- **Competition.** Profits motivate individuals to start businesses, and competition motivates them to operate those businesses efficiently. **Competition** occurs when two or more businesses vie for the same resources or customers. To gain an advantage over competitors, a business must produce its goods or services efficiently and be able to sell at a reasonable profit. Competition forces all businesses to make products better or cheaper.

Degrees of competition

Economists have identified four basic degrees of competition within a private enterprise system: perfect competition, monopolistic competition, oligopoly, and monopoly.

Perfect competition

For **perfect competition** to exist, firms must be small in size (but large in number), the products of each firm are almost identical, both buyers and sellers know the price that others are paying and receiving in the marketplace, firms find it easy to enter or leave the market, prices are set by the forces of supply and demand, and no firm is powerful enough individually to influence the price of its product in the marketplace. Agriculture is usually considered to be a good example of pure competition in the Canadian economy. There are thousands of wheat farmers, the wheat produced on one farm is essentially the same as wheat produced on another farm, producers and buyers are well aware of prevailing market prices, and it is relatively easy to get started or to quit producing wheat.

PRIVATE ENTERPRISE
An economic system characterized by private property rights, freedom of choice, profits, and competition.

COMPETITION
The vying among businesses in a particular market or industry to best satisfy consumer demands and earn profits.

PERFECT COMPETITION
A market or industry characterized by a very large number of small firms producing an identical product so that none of the firms has any ability to influence price.

The High Price of High Prices

Economic theory tells us that when demand for a commodity increases, its price goes up, and people try to find substitutes that are cheaper. For example, when the price of oil is high, companies use corn to make ethanol to add to gasoline, and palm oil is used to make diesel fuel (called biodiesel). But, as more producers start using corn or palm oil, the demand for those commodities goes up and so does their price. During 2006, for example, the price of palm oil rose from less than US$400 per metric tonne to more than US$500 per metric tonne.

When prices of commodities rise rapidly, there are usually some unanticipated outcomes. One of these is increased criminal activity. As the price of stainless steel and aluminum rose during the last few years, thieves began stealing items such as beer kegs, railway baggage carts, railroad tracks, light poles, and highway guard-rails. These items were then sold to scrap yards for cash.

The impact of stealing is limited to lost revenue (it's only money), but sky-high prices for food can actually threaten people's lives. Global food prices increased 83 percent between 2005 and 2008, and that put a lot of stress on the world's poorest countries. In some countries, families are spending one-half their income just on food. One culprit, ironically, is the push to convert corn into biofuel. In countries like Haiti, Cameroon, Senegal, and Ethiopia, citizens have rioted over higher prices for important staple items such as beans and rice. In Pakistan and Thailand, army troops were deployed to prevent the theft of food from warehouses. The World Bank has identified 33 countries that are at risk for serious social upheaval because of high food prices. To cope with the problem, some countries are slashing import duties and imposing export duties. This is just the reverse of what countries normally do.

Critical Thinking Questions

1. It is obvious that negative outcomes can occur with high prices. Can high prices ever lead to positive outcomes? Explain.

2. Consider the following statement: *"The high price of commodities like copper is not a concern because we do not need copper to survive, but the high price of food is a concern because it threatens people's lives. The central governments of the world should therefore coordinate their efforts and put in place rules to ensure that food prices are kept low."* Do you agree or disagree with the statement? Explain your reasoning.

Monopolistic competition

MONOPOLISTIC
COMPETITION
A market or industry characterized by a large number of firms supplying products that are similar but distinctive enough from one another to give firms some ability to influence price.

In **monopolistic competition**, there are fewer sellers than in pure competition, but there are still many buyers. Sellers try to make their products appear to be at least slightly different from those of their competitors by tactics such as using brand names (Tide and Cheer), design or styling (Ralph Lauren and Izod clothes), and advertising (like that done by Coca-Cola and Pepsi). Monopolistically competitive businesses may be large or small, because it is relatively easy for a firm to enter or leave the market. For example, many small clothing manufacturers compete successfully with large apparel makers. Product differentiation also gives sellers some control over the price they charge. Thus, Ralph Lauren polo shirts can be priced with little regard for the price of shirts sold at the Bay, even though the Bay's shirts may have very similar styling.

Oligopoly

When an industry has only a handful of very large sellers, an (oligopoly) exists. Competition is fierce because the actions of any one firm in an oligopolistic market can significantly affect the sales of all other firms.[34] Most oligopolistic firms avoid price competition because it reduces profits. For example, the four major cereal makers (Kellogg, General Mills, General Foods, and Quaker Oats) charge roughly the same price for their cereals. Rather than compete on price, they emphasize advertising, which claims that their cereals are better tasting or more nutritious than the competition's. Entry into an oligopolistic market is difficult because large capital investment is usually necessary. Thus, oligopolistic industries (such as the automobile, rubber, and steel industries) tend to stay oligopolistic. As the trend toward globalization continues, it is likely that more global oligopolies will come into being.[35]

Monopoly

When an industry or market has only one producer, a (monopoly) exists. Being the only supplier gives a firm complete control over the price of its product. Its only constraint is how much consumer demand will fall as its price rises. For centuries, wine bottles were sealed using natural cork made from tree bark. But a new technology allows wine bottles to be sealed with plastic corks that are cheaper and work just as well. The natural wine cork industry has lost its monopoly.[36] In Canada, laws such as the Competition Act forbid most monopolies. **Natural monopolies**—such as provincial electric utilities—are closely watched by provincial utilities boards, and the assumption that there is such a thing as a natural monopoly is increasingly being challenged. For example, the Royal Mail Group's 350-year monopoly of the British postal service ended in 2006, and rival companies are now allowed to compete with Royal Mail.[37] In India, private couriers like FedEx and United Parcel Service now provide more than half the delivery business in that country after they were allowed to compete with India Post, which had a monopoly on mail delivery for several hundred years.[38]

OLIGOPOLY
A market or industry characterized by a small number of very large firms that have the power to influence the price of their product and/or resources.

MONOPOLY
A market or industry with only one producer, who can set the price of its product and/or resources.

NATURAL MONOPOLIES
A market or industry in which having only one producer is most efficient because it can meet all of consumers' demand for the product.

Consumers often buy products under conditions of monopolistic competition. For example, there are few differences between various brands of toothpaste, cold tablets, detergents, canned goods, and soft drinks.

Summary of Learning Objectives

1. **Define the nature of Canadian *business* and identify its main goals.** Businesses are organizations that produce or sell goods or services to make a profit. *Profits* are the difference between a business's revenues and expenses. The prospect of earning profits encourages individuals and organizations to open and expand businesses. The benefits of business activities also extend to wages paid to workers and to taxes that support government functions.

2. **Describe different types of global *economic systems* according to the means by which they control the *factors of production* through *input* and *output markets*.** An *economic system* is a nation's system for allocating its resources among its citizens. Economic systems differ in terms of who owns or controls the five basic factors of production: labour, capital, entrepreneurs, physical resources, and information resources. In *command economies*, the government controls all or most of these factors. In *market economies*, which are based on the principles of *capitalism*, individuals and businesses control the factors of production and exchange them through *input* and *output markets*. Most countries today have *mixed market economies* that are dominated by one of these systems but include elements of the other. The processes of *deregulation* and *privatization* are important means by which many of the world's planned economies are moving toward mixed market systems.

3. **Show how *demand and supply* affect resource distribution in Canada.** The Canadian economy is strongly influenced by markets, demand, and supply. *Demand* is the willingness and ability of buyers to purchase a good or service. *Supply* is the willingness and ability of producers to offer goods or services for sale. Demand and supply work together to set a *market* or *equilibrium price*—the price at which the quantity of goods demanded and the quantity of goods supplied are equal.

4. **Identify the elements of *private enterprise* and explain the *various degrees of competition* in the Canadian economic system.** The Canadian economy is founded on the principles of *private enterprise, private property rights, freedom of choice, profits*, and *competition*. Degrees of competition vary because not all industries are equally competitive. Under conditions of *pure competition*, numerous small firms compete in a market governed entirely by demand and supply. In *monopolistic competition*, there are a smaller number of sellers, and each one tries to make its product seem different from the products of competitors. An *oligopoly* involves only a handful of sellers who fiercely compete with each other. A *monopoly* involves only one seller.

Questions and Exercises

Questions for Analysis

1. On various occasions, government provides financial incentives to business firms. For example, the Canadian government provided export assistance to Bombardier Inc. with its Technology Transfer Program. Is this consistent with a basically free market system? Explain how this might distort the system.

2. In recent years, many countries have moved from planned economies to market economies. Why do you think this has occurred? Can you envision a situation that would cause a resurgence of planned economies?

3. In your opinion, what industries in Canada should be regulated by the government? Defend your arguments.

4. Familiarize yourself with a product or service that is sold under conditions of pure competition. Explain why it is an example of pure competition and identify the factors that make it so. Then do the same for a product in each of the other three competitive situations described in the chapter (monopolistic competition, oligopoly, and monopoly).

5. Analyze how the factors of production (labour, capital, entrepreneurs, natural resources, and information) work together for a product or service of your choice.

6. Government plays a variety of roles in the Canadian mixed economy (customer, regulator, taxation agent, provider of services, etc.). Consider each of the roles discussed in the text and state your view as to whether government involvement in each role is excessive, insufficient, or about right. What criteria did you use to make your assessments?

Application Exercises

7. For a product that is not discussed in Chapter 8, find an example where a surplus led to decreased prices. Then find an example where a shortage led to increased prices. What eventually happened in each case? Why? Is what happened consistent with what economic theory predicts?

8. Choose a locally owned business. Interview the owner to find out (1) how demand and supply affect the business, and (2) how each factor of production is used in the business.

9. Visit a local shopping mall or shopping area. List each store that you see and determine what degree of competition it faces in its immediate environment. For example, if there is only one store in the mall that sells shoes, that store represents a monopoly. Note those businesses with direct competitors (e.g., two jewellery stores) and show how they compete with one another.

10. Go to the library or log on to the internet and research 10 industries. Classify each according to degree of competition.

Team Exercises

Building Your Business Skills

ANALYZING THE PRICE OF DOING E-BUSINESS

Goal

To encourage students to understand how the competitive environment affects a product's price.

Situation

Assume that you own a local business that provides internet access to individuals and businesses in your community. Yours is one of four such businesses in the local market. Each of the four companies charges the same price: $20 per month for unlimited DSL service. Your business also provides users with email service; two of your competitors also offer email service. One of these same two competitors, plus the third, also provides the individual user with a free, basic personal webpage. One competitor just dropped its price to $15 per month, and the other two have announced their intentions to follow suit. Your break-even price is $10 per customer. You are concerned about getting into a price war that may destroy your business.

Method

Divide into groups of four or five people. Each group is to develop a general strategy for handling competitors' price changes. In your discussion, take the following factors into account:

- how the demand for your product is affected by price changes
- the number of competitors selling the same or a similar product
- the methods—other than price—you can use to attract new customers and/or retain current customers

Analysis

Develop specific pricing strategies based on each of the following situations:

- Within a month after dropping the price to $15, one of your competitors raises its price back to $20.
- Two of your competitors drop their prices further—to $12 per month. As a result, your business falls off by 25 percent.
- One of your competitors that has provided customers with a free webpage has indicated that it will start charging an extra $2 per month for this optional service.
- Two of your competitors have announced that they will charge individual users $12 per month, but will charge businesses a higher price (not yet announced).
- All four providers (including you) are charging $12 per month. One goes out of business, and you know that another is in poor financial health.

Follow-up questions

1. Discuss the role that various inducements other than price might play in affecting demand and supply in the market for internet service.
2. Is it always in a company's best interest to feature the lowest prices?
3. Eventually, what form of competition is likely to characterize the market for internet service?

Exercising Your Ethics

Making the Right Decision

THE SITUATION

Hotel S is a large hotel in a Maritime city. The hotel is a franchise operation run by an international hotel chain. The primary source of revenue for the hotel is convention business. A major tropical storm is working its way up the east coast and is about to hit the city. When that happens, heavy flooding is likely.

THE DILEMMA

Because Hotel S is a licensed operation, it must maintain numerous quality standards in order to keep its licence. This licence is important because the international management company handles advertising, reservations, and so on. If it were to lose its licence, it is almost certain that the hotel would have to reduce its staff.

For the past few years, members of the Hotel S team have been lobbying the investors who own the hotel to undertake a major renovation. They fear that without such a renovation, the hotel will lose its licence when it comes up for renewal in a few months. The owners, however, have balked at investing more of their funds in the hotel itself but have indicated that hotel management can use revenues earned above a specified level for upgrades.

The approaching storm has cut off most major transportation avenues and telephone service is also down. The Hotel S staff are unable to reach the general manager, who has been travelling on business. Because the city is full of conventioneers, hotel rooms are in high demand. Unfortunately, because of the disrepair at the hotel, it only has about 50 percent occupancy. Hotel S staff have been discussing what to do and have identified three options:

1. The hotel can reduce room rates in order to help both local citizens and out-of-town visitors. The hotel can also provide meals at reduced rates. A few other hotels are also doing this.
2. The hotel can maintain its present pricing policies. Most of the city's hotels are adopting this course of action.
3. The hotel can raise its rates by approximately 15 percent without attracting too much attention. It can also start charging for certain things it has been providing for free, such as local telephone calls, parking, and morning coffee. The staff members see this option as one way to generate extra profits for the renovation and to protect jobs.

TEAM ACTIVITY

Assemble a group of four students and assign each group member to one of the following roles:

- A member of the hotel staff
- The Hotel S manager
- A customer at the hotel
- A Hotel S investor

ACTION STEPS

1. Before discussing the situation with your group, and from the perspective of your assigned role, which of the three options do you think is the best choice? Write down the reasons for your position.
2. Before discussing the situation with your group, and from the perspective of your assigned role, what are the underlying ethical issues, if any, in this situation? Write down the issues.
3. Gather your group together and reveal, in turn, each member's comments on the best choice of the three options. Next, reveal the ethical issues listed by each member.
4. Appoint someone to record the main points of agreement and disagreement within the group. How do you explain the results? What accounts for any disagreement?
5. From an ethical standpoint, what does your group conclude is the most appropriate action that should have been taken by the hotel in this situation?
6. Develop a group response to the following question: Can your team identify other solutions that might help satisfy both extreme views?

Business Case 1

Are We Running Out of Oil?

Oil is a product that is much in the news these days (remember the huge oil spill in the Gulf of Mexico in 2010). Beyond the environmental issues of oil, several important questions have been raised about this important commodity: Are we running out of oil? If so, when will it happen? Is oil production going to peak and then rapidly decline? Answers to these questions are hotly debated. Much of the debate is focused on an idea called "peak oil theory," which says that oil production will soon peak and will then decline rapidly, causing a major oil crisis in the world. Opponents of the peak oil theory reject the argument and point to several predictions of peak oil theorists that have been wrong in the past. Illustrative claims of each group are summarized below.

THE ARGUMENTS OF PEAK OIL SUPPORTERS

Those who support the idea of peak oil make the following arguments:

- Output from oil fields around the world is declining (in some fields the decline is about 18 percent a year). Declines are particularly evident in the Middle East, Europe, and the U.S. That means that 3–4 million barrels a day of new oil will have to be found for global oil production just to remain steady.
- Many big oil-producing countries are very secretive about their year-to-year production rates, so it is difficult to know just how fast their output is really declining. Their oil fields may be in worse shape than they will admit.
- Several top-level executives in the oil industry say that there is a limit to how much oil can be produced each year (about 100 million barrels per day), and that ceiling may be reached as early as 2012. The International Energy Agency (IEA) also predicts that oil production of more than 100 million barrels of oil per day will be difficult to achieve.
- Oil production will peak because of factors such as restricted access to oil fields, shortages of oil field workers, rapidly increasing costs, political crises, and complex oil field geology.
- The IEA has questioned the 174 billion barrel reserves figure commonly cited for the Alberta oil sands, saying that uncertain project economics make it unlikely that that much oil could be extracted. It says that a number closer to 15 billion barrels is more accurate.

- New oil discoveries have declined sharply. For example, new discoveries in the Middle East during 1963–1972 totalled 187 billion barrels, but new discoveries during 1993–2002 totalled only 16 billion barrels.
- In 1956, M.K. Hubbert predicted that U.S. oil production would peak in the early 1970s, and he was right. The same thing will happen with world oil production.

THE ARGUMENTS OF PEAK OIL OPPONENTS

Those who reject the peak oil theory make the following arguments:

- World oil production has been steadily increasing, and in 2006 was the highest in history, averaging over 85 million barrels per day (over 31 billion barrels per year). Oil output will eventually *plateau*, but it will not peak and then fall rapidly.
- A widely used measure of oil reserves is "ultimate recoverable reserves" (URR). TrendLines, a Canadian research company, notes that the world's URR is *increasing* at an increasing rate. For example, during the period 1957–2006, URR grew at an annual rate of 2.4 percent, but during 2000–2007, it grew at an annual rate of 6 percent.
- The U.S. Geological Survey (USGS) predicts that URR will grow by about 2.4 percent annually for the next few years. The URR was 1.6 trillion barrels in 1995 and was predicted to rise to 3.3 trillion barrels in 2025, but it had already reached 3.2 trillion barrels in 2006, years ahead of schedule.
- In 1979, the "life index" of oil was estimated to be about 35 years (at 1979 consumption rates). That meant that we would experience an oil crisis early in the twenty-first century. But by 2003, the life index had actually risen to 40 years, and by 2007 it had risen to 45 years. These increases have occurred even though oil consumption rates now far exceed those of 1979.
- There have been several major new discoveries in the last couple of years (for example, off the coast of Brazil and in the Gulf of Mexico). The new Gulf of Mexico oil field may contain up to 15 billion barrels of oil. If it does, that single new field would increase U.S. oil reserves by 50 percent. The new oil field off the coast of Brazil may contain 33 billion barrels of oil.
- M.K. Hubbert's prediction for *U.S.* oil production was correct, but his prediction for *world* production was far off the mark. He predicted that global oil production would peak at 12 billion barrels per year by early in the twenty-first century, but actual production in 2006 was 31 billion barrels.

Critics of peak oil also use several general arguments from economics to support their claims that the peak oil idea is not correct. First, they note that the higher the price of oil, the greater the amount that can be extracted in an economically viable way. Second, higher oil prices will also discourage consumption, and that will make the existing supply of oil last longer. Third, higher oil prices will motivate the development of alternate sources of fuel, and that will also make the existing oil supply last longer. Fourth, new technologies for extracting oil are constantly being developed and old technologies are being refined. This means that more oil can be extracted than was originally thought. For example, Canadian and Japanese researchers have succeeded in extracting natural gas from structures called gas hydrates. The energy locked in gas hydrates may exceed the total world supply of energy available from coal, oil, and natural gas combined. If this new technology becomes commercially viable, it will have a dramatic effect on the total supply of fossil fuels.

Irrespective of what the supporters and opponents of peak oil say, there is another factor that bears on this argument: the business cycle. Most of the arguments presented above were generated before the worldwide recession began in 2008. The recession substantially reduced demand for oil and caused its price to drop from $147 a barrel to less than $40 in 2008 (in 2010 the price rose again to $75). In an attempt to prop up the price, the Organization of the Petroleum Exporting Countries (OPEC) countries cut output by 4 million barrels per day. This reduced output will extend the supply of oil even further into the future. Some experts are now predicting that weak economic growth around the world will mean that the demand for oil will be low for many years to come. So, these developments support the opponents of peak oil. But peak oil supporters point out that that low demand for oil will cause less exploration for oil, and that means we will be facing an oil shortage in the future.

It is difficult to know what is going to happen, isn't it?

QUESTIONS FOR DISCUSSION

1. Which group—peak oil supporters or their opponents—do you think makes more persuasive arguments about the future of oil production and the demand for oil? Explain your reasoning.
2. After considering the arguments in support of peak oil theory and the arguments against it, draw a graph that shows your predictions of world oil production from now until the year 2100. Show your prediction of annual world oil production—in billions of barrels—on the vertical axis and time on the horizontal axis. Defend your predictions.
3. Consider the following statement: *"There are so many uncertainties that must be taken into account when trying to predict world oil production that it is impossible to have any confidence in anyone's predictions."* Do you agree or disagree with the statement? Explain your reasoning.

Notes

1. "Canada's 500 Largest Corporations," *The Financial Post*, June 2009, 42–43.
2. Richard Blackwell, "Canada Ranks High in Low Business Costs," *The Globe and Mail*, March 31, 2010, B5.
3. Human Resources and Skills Development Canada, "Support for the Not-for-Profit Sector," http://www.hrsdc.gc.ca/eng/community_partnerships/voluntary_sector/index.shtml, Accessed June 18, 2011.
4. Statistics Canada, "Summary of the Findings of the National Survey of Nonprofit and Voluntary Organizations," http://www.statcan.gc.ca/pub/61-533-s/61-533-s2005001-eng.htm, Accessed February 6, 2011.
5. Ibid.
6. Ontario Ministry of Health and Long-Term Care, "Health Services in Your Community," http://www.health.gov.on.ca/english/public/contact/hosp/hospfaq_dt.html, Accessed June 19, 2011.
7. Parliament of Canada, "Private Health Care Funding and Delivery Under the *Canada Health Act*," http://www.parl.gc.ca/Content/LOP/researchpublications/prb0552-e.htm, Accessed June 19, 2011.
8. Ontario Ministry of Training, Colleges and Universities, "Private Career Colleges (PCC)," http://www.tcu.gov.on.ca/pepg/audiences/pcc/private.html, Accessed June 19, 2011.
9. Community Sector Council Newfoundland and Labrador, "Voluntary Sector in Canada," *Envision.ca*, http://www.envision.ca/templates/profile.asp?ID=54, Accessed June 18, 2011.
10. Industry Canada, "Goods-Producing Industries," http://www.ic.gc.ca/eic/site/cis-sic.nsf/eng/h_00007.html, Accessed February 6, 2011.
11. Industry Canada, "Services-Producing Industries," http://www.ic.gc.ca/eic/site/cis-sic.nsf/eng/h_00008.html, Accessed February 6, 2011.
12. Richard I. Kirkland Jr., "The Death of Socialism," *Fortune*, January 4, 1988, 64–72.
13. Andres Oppenheimer, "Latin America Is Skeptical," *The Orlando Sentinel*, February 20, 2006, A19.
14. James Kynge, "Private Firms' Growth in China Striking: Report," *National Post*, May 11, 2000, C14.
15. See Karl E. Case and Ray C. Fair, *Principles of Economics*, 5th ed. (Upper Saddle River, NJ: Prentice Hall, 1999), 69–74; Robert A. Collinge and Ronald M. Ayers, *Economics by Design: Principles and Issues*, 2nd ed. (Upper Saddle River, NJ: Prentice Hall, 2000), 51–52.
16. Andres Oppenheimer, "While Latin America Nationalizes, India Opens Up," *Orlando Sentinel*, January 22, 2007, A11.
17. Barry Critchley, "Canada Post Should Be Privatized: OECD; Productivity Issue," *National Post*, March 11, 2010, FP2.
18. John Greenwood, "Study Cites Privatization in Productivity Gains," *National Post*, June 26, 2009, FP1.
19. *Bank of Canada Banking and Financial Statistics*, Series G1, Government of Canada Fiscal Position, April 2010, S84.
20. *The Financial Post*, June 2009, 82.
21. "UFC May Have Long Wait to Crack Ontario Market," thestar.com, May 23, 2010, www.thestar.com/printarticle/783892.
22. Andy Hoffman, "Labatt Convicted in Quebec Discount Beer Case," *The Globe and Mail*, November 24, 2005, B10.
23. Jim Middlemiss, "Don't Get Caught Offside in Rules Changes; Wrong Advice on Competition Act Could Be Costly," *National Post*, March 23, 2009, FP6. For an analysis of the current situation in the U.S. regarding resale price maintenance, see Joseph Pereira, "Price-Fixing Makes

Comeback after Supreme Court Hearing," *The Wall Street Journal*, August 18, 2008, A1, A12.

24. Hollie Shaw, "Bogus Ads: If You Mislead the Consumer, Be Ready to Suffer the Financial Fallout," *National Post*, May 22, 2009, FP12.

25. Shirley Won and Jacquie McNish, "Antitrust Watchdog Loses Beer Battle," *The Globe and Mail*, March 29, 2007, B1, B6.

26. Steven Chase and Jacquie McNish, "Prentice Probes Watchdog's Court Conduct," *The Globe and Mail*, January 30, 2008, B1–B2.

27. John Gray, "Texas Fold 'Em," *Canadian Business*, October 9–22, 2006, 44–46.

28. "Video Gaming: The Next Level," *Venture*, March 20, 2005.

29. "Alberta Film, TV Production Faces Decline," May 19, 2010, CBC News, www.cbc.ca/arts/film/story/2010/05/18/alberta-film-production-decline.html.

30. Jennifer Allen, "New Lobby Rules Mean More Work for Lawyers," *The Globe and Mail*, August 13, 2008, B5.

31. "Canada's Maple Syrup Output Rises in '09," *National Post*, March 11, 2010, FP6.

32. For a detailed analysis of the rise in food prices, see Sinclair Stewart and Paul Waldie, "The Byzantine World of Food Pricing: How Big Money Is Wreaking Havoc," *The Globe and Mail*, May 31, 2008, B4–B7.

33. See Paul Heyne, Peter J. Boettke, and David L. Prychitko, *The Economic Way of Thinking*, 10th ed. (Upper Saddle River, NJ: Prentice Hall, 2003), 190, 358–359.

34. Karl E. Case and Ray C. Fair, *Principles of Economics*, 6th ed., updated (Upper Saddle River, NJ: Prentice Hall, 2003), 300–309.

35. *Hoover's Handbook of World Business 2002* (Austin: Hoover's Business Press, 2002), 74–75.

36. Timothy Aeppel, "Show Stopper: How Plastic Popped the Cork Monopoly," *The Wall Street Journal*, May 1, 2010, A1.

37. "Royal Mail's Reign Comes to an End," *The Globe and Mail*, January 2, 2006, B7.

38. Eric Bellman, "As Economy Zooms, India's Postmen Struggle to Adapt," *The Wall Street Journal*, October 3, 2006, A1, A12.

chapter 9

The Environment of Business

Air Canada's Challenging Environment: Competition, Economic Crisis, Fuel Prices, Volcanoes, and More

The name Air Canada does not always conjure up warm images for Canadian travellers. But it is the fifteenth largest airline in the world and it wins international awards. In 2010, it was named the "best airline in North America" by independent research firm Skytrax (which surveyed over 17 million worldwide travellers). There have been many ups and downs for Air Canada, but the company continues to control the majority of the domestic market, with WestJet as its main competitor. Back in 2004, Air Canada used bankruptcy protection to deal with major financial problems. It may be tempting to blame that dark period on general turmoil in the travel industry, following the 9/11 terrorist attacks, but placing all the blame on that significant event would be overly simplistic. The airline business is always extremely complicated; it's a difficult business environment that is shaped by relationships with many stakeholders.

Airlines must efficiently plan their capacity. They don't buy a fleet of planes overnight; airlines make projections and try to maximize the use of planes and other resources. Some of this planning is done two to five or even seven years into the future and this sort of lengthy timeline is complicated. Air Canada must contend with *competitor actions* (e.g., WestJet, Porter) at home, and on international routes (e.g., Air France, British Airways, JAL); it must deal with government regulations (e.g., tax laws, flight restrictions, and international agreements), economic conditions (e.g., recessions, fuel/food prices), and natural weather conditions

After reading this chapter, you should be able to:

> Explain the concepts of *organizational boundaries* and *multiple organizational environments*. p. 255

> Explain the importance of the *economic environment* to business and identify the factors used to evaluate the performance of an economic system. p. 257

> Describe the *technological environment* and its role in business. p. 264

> Describe the *political–legal environment* and its role in business. p. 267

> Describe the *socio-cultural environment* and its role in business. p. 268

> Identify emerging challenges and opportunities in the *business environment*. p. 276

> Understand recent trends in the *redrawing of corporate boundaries*. p. 278

(e.g., snowstorms and even volcanic ash). Let's take a closer look at these challenges.

In recent years, a major spike in fuel costs hurt air travel and caused ticket prices to skyrocket at times. The global recession, which started in 2008, decreased tourist and business travel. In fact, in 2009 the global airline business saw its most steep decline in air traffic since the Second World War. According to the International Air Transport Association (IATA), the global industry lost

ScanLife

How Will This *Help Me?*

By understanding the material in this chapter, you'll be better able to assess (1) the impact that events outside a business can have on its *owners* and *managers,* (2) how environmental change impacts you as a *consumer,* and (3) the challenges and opportunities that environmental change provides to you as an employee or an *investor.*

$10 billion that year, with additional losses expected in the $3 billion range in 2010. Air Canada worked hard to get its finances under control by creating new agreements with suppliers and major credit providers. However, in the first quarter of 2010, the airline still had an operating loss of $138 million (Air Canada pointed out that this was an improvement from the $188 million loss a year earlier indicated in the first quarter).

At home, Air Canada competes with WestJet and a host of smaller players. The rivalry has pushed it to launch its lower priced Tango fares to compete in the low-frill, budget travel segment. In addition, the company created a regional partner called Jazz mainly for short-haul flights. In order to effectively compete on the global stage Air Canada has forged alliances to cut costs. It is a founding member of the leading airline network called Star Alliance. These 26 members permit passengers on partner airlines to connect with over 1100 airports in 175 countries. The airlines code-share flights (e.g., booking Air Canada seats on a Lufthansa flight) and share airline lounges in airports around the world. In 2009, Air Canada also extended its partnerships with Continental, United, and Lufthansa to create Atlantic-Plus-Plus, which further enables it to integrate routes and compete in the transatlantic segment.

Governments are strongly linked to airline success or failure. Here are some key facts to consider. The government recently negotiated an agreement

between Canada and the EU that created new opportunities by reducing restrictions for Air Canada and EU airlines. So in 2010, Air Canada launched new direct services to five popular European gateway cities: Geneva, Barcelona, Brussels, Copenhagen, and Athens. A similar deal with the United States government back in 1995 was an important step in Air Canada's extensive expansion (Air Canada is the largest airline in the U.S.–Canada trans-border market, serving 60 destinations in the U.S.). Of course, the relationship with the government is not all rosy. Air Canada has stated that the government is making it impossible for the airline to be profitable with higher security charges, airport improvement fees, and federal and provincial fuel excise taxes. For example, the federal government collects over $300 million in rent from airports each year. This makes it much more expensive to land a plane in Canada than in the U.S. Air Canada pays $3400 to land an Airbus 320 in Canada's largest airports but less than half that amount ($1650) in the U.S. Total federal tax collected in Halifax alone amounted to $3.2 million in rent charges in 2009 and is expected to top $5 million by 2014. Since the airline is based in Canada, it has a tax cost disadvantage.

Weather can play a tricky role in airline operations. If you travel on a regular basis you are very familiar with airline delays. Snowstorms, severe thunder showers, icy weather, and severe winds can disrupt travel and cause delays. This creates frustrated passengers and forces airline employees and travel agents to scramble. In April 2010, a new issue hit the headlines when a volcano in Iceland halted all air travel to and from Europe for five long days, cancelling over 100 000 flights. The name of the volcano is Eyjafjallajokull (pronounced ay-yah-FYAH-lah-yer-kuhl), and customers were heard muttering similar sounds as they tried to get home. It cost the airline industry huge sums of money through no fault of its own. Air Canada lost $20 million per day; Air Transat lost approximately $750 000 per day;

Air France-KLM lost an estimated $35 million per day. Airlines demanded compensation from the EU for more than $1 billion in losses. It remains to be seen what the ultimate response will be.

As you can see, airlines must create efficient strategies and plan for the unexpected. But there are so many elements far outside their control that impact success or failure. In addition to the issues mentioned above, there are the massive new security challenges, flu pandemics, and political conflict (e.g., civil war) that can erupt anywhere in the world. This is why it is so hard to find an airline that is profitable on a consistent basis. This is truly a challenging industry.

Organizational boundaries and environments

As discussed in the opening case on Air Canada, all businesses, regardless of their size, location, or mission, operate within a larger external environment that plays a major role in determining their success or failure. The **external environment** consists of everything outside an organization that might affect it. Managers must understand the key features of the external environment, and then strive to operate and compete within it. No single firm can control the environment, but managers should not simply react to changes in the external environment; rather, they should be proactive and at least try to influence their environment.

To better explain the environment of business, we begin by discussing *organizational boundaries* and *multiple organizational environments*.

EXTERNAL ENVIRONMENT Everything outside an organization's boundaries that might affect it.

Organizational boundaries

An **organizational boundary** separates the organization from its environment. Consider the simple case of a small neighbourhood grocery store that includes a retail customer area, a storage room, and the owner/manager's office. In many ways, the store's boundary coincides with its physical structure: When you walk through the door, you're crossing the boundary into the business, and when you go back onto the sidewalk, you cross the boundary back into the environment. But this is an oversimplification. During the business day, distributors of soft drinks, snack foods, ice, and bread products may enter the store, inventory their products, and refill coolers and shelves just as if they were employees. These distributors are normally considered part of the environment rather than the organization, but during the time they're inside the store, they are essentially part of the business. Customers may even assume that these distributors are store employees and ask them questions as they restock shelves.

For larger firms, the situation is even more complex. McDonald's, for example, has a contract with Coca-Cola to sell only Coke soft-drink products. McDonald's also has partnerships with Walmart and Disney that allow it to open stores inside their facilities. So when you buy a Coca-Cola soft drink from a McDonald's restaurant located inside a Walmart store or Disney theme park, you are essentially affecting, and being affected by, multiple businesses.

ORGANIZATIONAL BOUNDARY That which separates the organization from its environment.

Multiple organizational environments

Organizations have multiple environments. Some, like prevailing economic conditions, affect the performance of almost every business. But other dimensions of the environment are much more specific. The neighbourhood grocery store, for example, will be influenced not only by an increase in unemployment

DIMENSIONS OF
THE EXTERNAL ENVIRONMENT

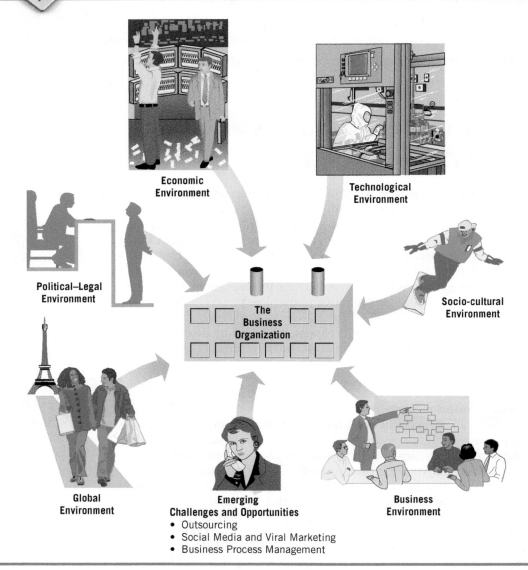

Economic
Environment

Technological
Environment

Political–Legal
Environment

Socio-cultural
Environment

The
Business
Organization

Global
Environment

Emerging
Challenges and Opportunities
• Outsourcing
• Social Media and Viral Marketing
• Business Process Management

Business
Environment

in its area but also by the pricing and other marketing activities of its nearest competitors. As we saw in the opening case, Air Canada will be affected by competitive pressures from WestJet, from the general economic conditions (like unemployment levels and business confidence), and even from major global events like the volcanic ash that caused 100 000 flight cancellations in Europe.[1]

Key 9.1 shows the major elements of the external environment: economic conditions, technology, political–legal considerations, social issues, the global environment, issues of ethical and social responsibility, the business environment itself, and emerging challenges and opportunities. We will cover global issue in detail in Chapter 12, so we discuss them here only as they relate directly to the other areas in this chapter.

Table 9.1 Pest Model for Analysis

POLITICAL-LEGAL	ECONOMIC	SOCIO-CULTURAL	TECHNOLOGICAL
Government type and stability	Levels of disposable income (after paying taxes) and income distribution	Cultural aspects, health consciousness, population growth rate, age, distribution	Maturity of technology, rate of obsolescence, and competing technologies
World trade agreements, regulations and restrictions	Interest rates, taxes, and inflation	Migration flows—labour mobility	Research and technological break-throughs and improvements
Environmental regulations and protection	Overseas economic growth and emerging markets	Consumer demand for environ-mentally safe business practices	Government spending on research and development
Freedom of press, rule of law, and levels of bureau-cracy and corruption	Current and projected economic growth	Lifestyle changes and trends	Industry focus on technology
Tax policies, and trade and tariff controls	Stage in the business cycle	Demographics: gender, age, family size, etc.	Energy use and costs
Consumer protection laws, employment laws, health and safety laws and regulations	Impact of technological changes on the economy	Living conditions, level of education, and earning capacity	Information technology, Internet, and mobile technology
Political stability	Government spending	Work–life balance attitudes	Global and local communications
Competition laws and regulations	Unemployment and supply of labour	Ethical and moral standards gov-erning the practices of business—customer values, market values, stakeholder values	Technology access, licensing, intellectual property issues, and advances in manufacturing
Government organization and attitude	Labour costs and supply		Waste removal and recycling

The economic environment

The economic environment refers to the conditions of the economic sys-tem in which an organization operates.[2] For example, McDonald's Canadian operations are (as of this writing) functioning in an economic environment characterized by moderate growth, moderate unemployment, and low infla-tion. Moderate unemployment means that most people can afford to eat out, and low inflation means that McDonald's pays relatively constant prices for its supplies. But it also means that McDonald's can't easily increase the prices it charges because of competitive pressures from Burger King and Wendy's.

> ECONOMIC ENVIRONMENT
> Conditions of the economic system in which an organization operates.

Economic growth

At one time, about half the Canadian population was involved in producing the food that we eat. Today, less than 2.5 percent of the population works in agriculture because agricultural efficiency has improved so much that far fewer people are needed to produce the food we need. We can therefore say that agri-cultural production has *grown* because the total output of the agricultural sec-tor has increased. We can apply the same idea to a nation's economic system, but the computations are much more complex, as we shall see.

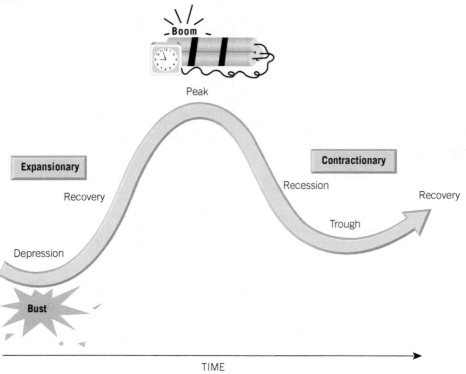

Aggregate output and the standard of living

AGGREGATE OUTPUT
Total quantity of goods
and services produced by
an economic system
during a given period.

How do we know whether or not an economic system is growing? The main measure of *growth* is **aggregate output:** the total quantity of goods and services produced by an economic system during a given period.[3] To put it simply, an increase in aggregate output is economic growth.[4] When output grows more quickly than the population, two things usually follow: output per capita (the quantity of goods and services per person) goes up and the system provides relatively more of the goods and services that people want.[5] And when these two things occur, people living in an economic system benefit from a higher **standard of living**—the total quantity and quality of goods and services that they can purchase with the currency used in their economic system.

STANDARD OF LIVING
Total quantity and quality of
goods and services that a
country's citizens can
purchase with the currency
used in their economic system.

The business cycle

BUSINESS CYCLE
Pattern of short-term ups
and downs (expansions and
contractions) in an
economy.

The growth (and contraction) pattern of short-term ups and downs in an economy is called the **business cycle.** It has four recognizable phases: peak, recession, trough, and recovery (see Key 9.2). A **recession** is usually defined as two consecutive quarters when the economy shrinks, but it is probably more helpful to say that a recession starts just after the peak of the business cycle is reached and ends when the trough is reached.[6] A **depression** occurs when the trough of the business cycle extends two or more years. Periods of expansion and contraction can vary from several months to several years. During the latter half of the 1990s, the Canadian economy was continuously expanding, leading some people to believe that the business cycle was a thing of the past. That belief was shattered twice in the last 10 years: in 2000, when the high-tech bubble burst, and in 2008, when a major financial crisis and worldwide recession occurred. Many economists predicted that the most recent recession would be long, and some compared it to the Great Depression of the 1930s.

Gross domestic product and gross national product

The term **gross domestic product (GDP)** refers to the total value of all goods and services produced within a given period by a national economy through domestic factors of production. If GDP is going up, the nation is experiencing economic growth. Canada's GDP in 2009 was $1.56 trillion.[7]

GDP measures all business activity within a nation's borders and it has widely replaced **gross national product (GNP)**, which refers to the total value of all goods and services produced by a national economy within a given period regardless of where the factors of production are located. For example, the profits from a Canadian-owned manufacturing plant in Brazil are included in Canadian GNP—but not in GDP—because its output is not produced in Canada. Conversely, those profits are included in Brazil's GDP—but not GNP—because they are produced domestically (that is, in Brazil) but not by a Brazilian company.

Today, GDP is the key measure of economic growth because it tracks an economy's performance over time. However, some argue that such measures are flawed. A commission created by French president Nicolas Sarkozy and chaired by famous economist Joseph Stiglitz declared that our obsession with GDP helped contribute to the strength of the most recent recession. According to the findings, if a bit more attention had been paid to other indicators, like rising debt, governments may have reacted more cautiously. An article in The *Economist* magazine even referred to GDP as "grossly deceptive product."[8] An organization called Redefining Progress has proposed a more realistic measure to assess economic activity—the Genuine Progress Indicator (GPI). GPI treats activities that harm the environment or our quality of life as costs and gives them negative values. For example, in 2010, activities required to clean the mess from the BP Gulf of Mexico oil drilling disaster were included in measurements of economic growth. But the oil spill was not a good thing. The GPI measure shows that while GDP has been increasing for many years, GPI has been falling for over 30 years.[9]

Real growth rates

GDP is the preferred method of calculating national income and output. The *real growth rate of GDP*—the growth rate of GDP *adjusted for inflation and changes in the value of the country's currency*—is what counts. Remember that *growth depends on output increasing at a faster rate than population*. If the growth rate of GDP exceeds the rate of population growth, then our standard of living should be improving.

GDP per capita

GDP per capita means GDP per person. We get this figure by dividing total GDP by the total population of a country. As a measure of economic well-being of the average person, GDP per capita is a better measure than GDP. Norway has the highest GDP per capita of any country ($40 807), followed by the United States ($38 808), Ireland ($35 306), and Switzerland ($34 440). Canada ranked eighth at ($31 369).[10]

GROSS DOMESTIC PRODUCT (GDP) Total value of all goods and services produced within a given period by a national economy through domestic factors of production.

GROSS NATIONAL PRODUCT (GNP) Total value of all goods and services produced by a national economy within a given period regardless of where the factors of production are located.

GDP PER CAPITA Gross domestic product per person.

Real GDP

REAL GDP
GDP calculated to account for changes in currency values and price changes.

Real GDP means that GDP has been adjusted. To understand why adjustments are necessary, assume that pizza is the only product in an economy. Assume that in 2010, a pizza cost $10 and in 2011 it cost $11.

In both years, exactly 1000 pizzas were produced. In 2010, the GDP was $10 000 ($10 × 1000); in 2011, the GDP was $11 000 ($11 × 1000). Has the economy grown? No. Since 1000 pizzas were produced in both years, aggregate output remained the same. If GDP is not adjusted for 2011, it is called **nominal GDP,** that is, GDP measured in current dollars.[11]

NOMINAL GDP
GDP measured in current dollars or with all components valued at current prices.

Purchasing power parity

In our example, *current prices* would be 2011 prices. On the other hand, we calculate real GDP when we account for *changes in currency values and price changes.* When we make this adjustment, we account for both GDP and **purchasing power parity**—the principle that exchange rates are set so that the prices of similar products in different countries are about the same. Purchasing power parity gives us a much better idea of what people can actually buy. In other words, it gives us a better sense of standards of living across the globe.

PURCHASING POWER PARITY
Principle that exchange rates are set so that the prices of similar products in different countries are about the same.

Productivity

A major factor in the growth of an economic system is **productivity,** which is a measure of economic growth that compares how much a system produces with the resources needed to produce it. Let's say, for instance, that it takes one Canadian worker and one Canadian dollar to make 10 soccer balls in an eight-hour workday. Let's also say that it takes 1.2 Saudi workers and the equivalent of $1.2 (in riyals, the currency of Saudi Arabia) to make 10 soccer balls in the same eight-hour workday. We can say, then, that the Canadian soccer-ball industry is more *productive* than the Saudi soccer-ball industry.

PRODUCTIVITY
Measure of economic growth that compares how much a system produces with the resources needed to produce it.

The two factors of production in this extremely simple case are labour and capital. According to the Organisation for Economic Co-operation and Development (OECD) rankings, Canada stood in sixteenth place with a productivity ratio of 78.2 percent compared to the United States. Luxembourg was the most productive nation at 140.4 percent. Norway (136 percent) and the Netherlands (100.4 percent) were also classified above the benchmark U.S. statistics.[12]

If more products are being produced with fewer factors of production, what happens to the prices of these pro-ducts? They go down. As a consumer, therefore, you would need less of your currency to purchase the same quantity of these products. Thus, your standard of living—at least with regard to these products—has improved. If your entire economic system increases its productivity, then your overall standard of living improves. In fact, the standard of living improves only through increases in productivity.[13]

The balance of trade and the national debt

There are several factors that can help or hinder the growth of an economic system, but here we focus on just two of them: *balance of trade* and the national debt.

Balance of trade

BALANCE OF TRADE
The total of a country's exports (sales to other countries) minus its imports (purchases from other countries).

The balance of trade is the economic value of all the products that a country exports minus the economic value of its *imported* products. A negative balance of trade is commonly called a *trade deficit,* and a positive balance of trade is called a *trade surplus.* Canada traditionally has had a positive balance of trade. It is usually a *creditor nation* rather than a debtor nation. For example, Canada received $47 billion more from exports than it spent on imports in 2008, but in 2009 a long trend was reversed when Canada had a trade deficit of $4.8 billion.[14] The United States usually has a negative balance of trade; it spends more on imports than it receives for exports.[15] It is therefore a consistent debtor nation. A trade deficit negatively affects economic growth because the money that flows out of a country can't be used to invest in productive enterprises, either at home or overseas.

National debt

A country's **national debt** is the amount of money that the government owes its creditors. Like a business, the government takes in revenues (e.g., taxes) and has expenses (e.g., military spending, social programs). For many years, the government of Canada incurred annual **budget deficits,** that is, it spent more money *each year* than it took in. These accumulated annual deficits have created a huge national debt (estimated above $600 billion by the end of 2010). A typical recession causes an 86 percent increase in the national debt.[16]

From Confederation (1867) to 1981, the *total* accumulated debt was only $85.7 billion, but in the period 1981–1994, *annual deficits* were in the $20- to $40-billion range. But from 1997 to 2008, Canada was the only highly industrialized country in the world that had annual budget surpluses. That all changed in 2009 when the government announced a deficit of $46.9 billion. The good news, if you can call it that, was that this figure was actually 12 percent lower than initially expected.[17] The bad news was that another $49 billion deficit was projected in 2010 as well as $27.6 billion in 2011 and $17.5 billion in 2012.[18] Big increases in annual deficits are also predicted for the United States because of the multibillion-dollar bailouts that were given to companies in the financial sector. In spite of this, the United States is still able to borrow large amounts of money from countries like China because the United States is seen as a strong economy and a safe haven in troubled economic times.[19]

How does the national debt affect economic growth? When the government of Canada sells bonds to individuals and organizations (both at home and overseas), this affects economic growth because the Canadian government competes with every other potential borrower—individuals, households, businesses, and other organizations—for the available supply of loanable money. The more money the government borrows, the less money is available for the private borrowing and investment that increases productivity.

Economic stability

A key goal of an economic system is **stability:** a condition in which the amount of money available in an economic system and the quantity of goods and services produced in it are growing at about the same rate. Several factors threaten stability—namely, *inflation, deflation,* and *unemployment.*

Inflation

Inflation is evident when the amount of money injected into an economic system outstrips the increase in actual output. When inflation occurs, people have more money to spend, but there will still be the same quantity of products available for them to buy. As they compete with one another to buy available products, prices go up. Before long, high prices will erase the increase in the amount of money injected into the economy. Purchasing power, therefore, declines. Key 2.3 shows how inflation has varied over the last 30 years in Canada.

Inflation varies widely across countries. One dramatic example occurred in Zimbabwe in 2008, when inflation reached an astonishing annual rate above 40 million percent (most countries have rates between 2 and 15 percent). One

NATIONAL DEBT
The total amount of money that a country owes its creditors.

BUDGET DEFICITS
The result of the government spending more in one year than it takes in during that year.

STABILITY
Condition in an economic system in which the amount of money available and the quantity of goods and services produced are growing at about the same rate.

INFLATION
Occurrence of widespread price increases throughout an economic system.

DURING THE PAST FIFTEEN YEARS, THE RATE OF PRICE INCREASES IN CANADA HAS BEEN LOW AND QUITE STABLE

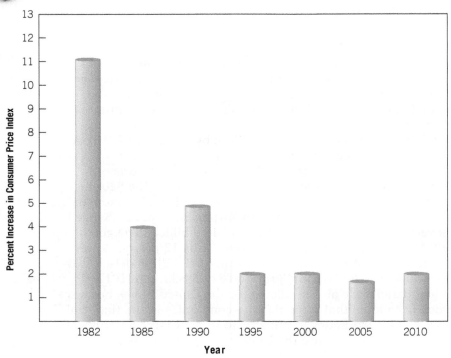

Zimbabwean dollar from 2005 would have been worth one trillion Zimbabwean dollars in 2008. Many workers simply stopped going to their jobs because their pay was not enough to cover their bus fare.[20] The problem was finally solved in 2009 when the government began allowing people to pay their bills using other currencies, like the U.S. dollar or the South African rand.[21]

Measuring inflation: the CPI

The **consumer price index (CPI)** measures changes in the cost of a "basket" of goods and services that a typical family buys. What is included in the basket has changed over the years. For example, the first CPI in 1913 included items like coal, spirit vinegar, and fruit, while today the index includes bottom-freezer fridges, flat-screen TVs, energy-saving light bulbs, and laser eye surgery.[22] These changes in the CPI reflect changes that have occurred in the pattern of consumer purchases. For example, in 1961, about 53 percent of consumer spending went to necessities like food, housing, and clothing. By the turn of the century, only 40 percent of consumer spending went to necessities.[23]

CONSUMER PRICE INDEX (CPI)
Measure of the prices of typical products purchased by consumers living in urban areas.

Deflation

Deflation (falling prices) is evident when the amount of money injected into an economic system lags behind increases in actual output. Prices may fall because industrial productivity is increasing and cost savings are being passed on to consumers (this is good), or because consumers have high levels of debt and are therefore unwilling to buy very much (this is bad).

DEFLATION
A period of generally falling prices.

Unemployment

In 2009, there were 7.7 million men and 6.9 million women (over age 25) working in Canada's labour force.[24] But there were many additional people who wanted a job but could not get one. **Unemployment** is the level of joblessness among people actively seeking work. There are various types of unemployment: *frictional unemployment* (people are out of work temporarily while looking for a new job); *seasonal unemployment* (people are out of work because of the seasonal nature of their jobs); *cyclical unemployment* (people are out of work because of a downturn in the business cycle); and *structural unemployment* (people are unemployed because they lack the skills needed to perform available jobs). Unemployment rates have varied greatly over the years, as Key 2.4 shows, with the rates for men generally being higher than the rates for women. In June 2010, the Canadian unemployment rate stood at 8.1 percent, which was higher than the 6 to 7 percent average range for the previous decade, before the recession, but was better than the rate in the Unites States, which stood at 9.7 percent and the depressing 20.1 percent rate found in Spain at the time.[25]

When unemployment is low there is a shortage of labour available for businesses. As businesses compete with one another for the available supply of labour, they raise the wages they are willing to pay. Then, because higher labour costs eat into profit margins, businesses raise the prices of their products. If prices get too high, consumers will respond by buying less. Businesses will then reduce their workforces because they don't need to produce as much. But this causes unemployment to go up and the cycle starts all over again.

> UNEMPLOYMENT
> The level of joblessness among people actively seeking work in an economic system.

During the depression of the 1930s, unemployment was very high, with nearly one-quarter of the population unable to find work. Lines of unemployed workers outside soup kitchens were an unfortunate reality during those difficult economic times.

Managing the Canadian economy

The federal government manages the Canadian economic system through two sets of policies: fiscal and monetary. **Fiscal policies** involve the collection and spending of government revenues. For example, when the growth rate of the economy is decreasing, tax cuts will normally stimulate renewed economic growth. **Monetary policies** focus on controlling the size of the nation's money supply. Working primarily through the Bank of Canada, the government can influence the ability and willingness of banks throughout the country to lend money. The power of the Bank of Canada to make changes in the supply of money is the centrepiece of the Canadian government's monetary policy. The principle is fairly simple:

> FISCAL POLICIES
> Policies whereby governments collect and spend revenues.

> MONETARY POLICIES
> Policies whereby the government controls the size of the nation's money supply.

- Higher interest rates make money more expensive to borrow and thereby reduce spending by companies that produce goods and services and consumers who buy them. When the Bank of Canada restricts the money supply, we say that it is practising a *tight monetary policy*.

- Lower interest rates make money less expensive to borrow and thereby increase spending by both companies that produce goods and services and consumers who buy them. When the Bank of Canada loosens the money supply, we say that it is practising an *easy monetary policy*. When the financial crisis hit in the fall of 2008, the central banks around the world cut their interest rates in an attempt to stimulate their countries' economies.

HISTORICAL UNEMPLOYMENT RATE. FROM 1970 TO 1996, THERE WAS A STEADY UPWARD TREND IN UNEMPLOYMENT RATES, BUT THE RATE BEGAN TO DECLINE IN THE LATE 1990S. THE RECESSION, WHICH BEGAN IN 2008, CAUSED A CLEAR INCREASE IN UNEMPLOYMENT, AS SEEN IN THE CHART

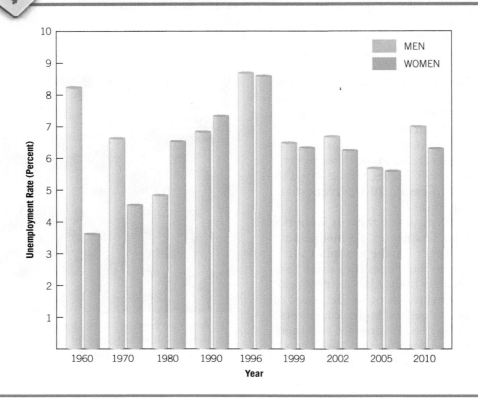

The technological **environment**

TECHNOLOGY
All the ways firms create value for their constituents.

As applied to the environment of business, **technology** generally includes all the ways by which firms create value for their constituents. Technology includes human knowledge, work methods, physical equipment, electronics and telecommunications, and various processing systems that are used to perform business activities. Although technology is applied within organizations, the forms and availability of that technology come from the general environment. Boeing, for example, uses computer-assisted manufacturing and design techniques developed by external vendors to simulate the four miles of hydraulic tubing that run through its new 777 aircraft.

RESEARCH AND DEVELOPMENT (R&D)
Those activities that are necessary to provide new products, services, and proesses.

Research and development (R&D)

Technological improvements and innovation in general are important contributors to the economic development of a country. The innovation process includes **research and development (R&D)**, which provides new ideas for products, services, and processes. There are two types of R&D.

Basic (or pure) R&D involves improving knowledge in an area without a primary focus on whether any discoveries that might occur are immediately marketable. For example, chemists in a laboratory might examine how certain chemical compounds behave. The knowledge gained from this activity might or might not result in a marketable product. **Applied R&D** on the other hand, means focusing specifically on how a technological innovation can be put to use in the making of a product or service that can be sold in the marketplace. For example, H.J. Heinz developed a tomato that is sweeter than the variety it previously used to make its ketchup. This reduced the need for corn syrup, which had been rapidly increasing in price.[26]

R&D spending in Canada in 2009 totalled about $16.1 billion.[27] The Canadian private sector accounts for about 55 percent of R&D, the government 10 percent, and universities 34 percent.[28] In the private sector, just 100 businesses account for over half of all R&D money that is spent.[29] The largest expenditures on R&D in Canada are concentrated in industries like computer system design, information, communications equipment, and scientific research.[30]

Canada's level of R&D investment lags behind that of other countries; it typically spends less than 1 percent of GDP on R&D, while Japan, Germany, and the U.S., for example, spend from 1.5 to 2 percent of GDP. This lag exists partly because many Canadian businesses are subsidiaries of large U.S. companies that carry out their R&D in the United States. When we take into account that the GDP of these three countries is much larger than the GDP of Canada, it means that R&D spending in Canada (in absolute dollars) is a tiny fraction of what is spent by these nations.

The boxed insert entitled "The Hydrogen Fuel Cell" describes how complex and time-consuming research and development work can be.

Product and service technologies

Product and service technologies are employed for creating products—both physical goods and services—for customers. Although many people associate technology with manufacturing, it is also a significant factor in the service sector. Just as an automobile is built as it follows a predetermined pathway along an assembly line, a hamburger at McDonald's is cooked, assembled, and wrapped as it moves along a predefined path. The rapid advancement of the internet into all areas of business is also a reflection of the technological environment. Indeed, new technologies continue to revolutionize nearly every aspect of business, ranging from the ways that customers and companies interact to where, when, and how employees perform their work.

Companies must constantly be on the lookout for technological breakthroughs that might make their products or services obsolete and thereby threaten their survival. Many of these breakthroughs do not come from direct competitors or even from the industry the company is part of. Technology is the basis of competition for some companies, especially when their goal is to be the technology leader in their industry. A company, for example, might focus its efforts on having the most technologically advanced products on the market. Intel exemplifies the challenge and the risks of adopting a strategic dependence on technological leadership. Before co-founding Intel with Bob Noyce in 1968, Gordon Moore made a prediction about microprocessors (the processing components of microcomputers) that eventually became known as Moore's Law: The number of transistors in a microprocessor would double every 18 months. In effect, this rate would entail a twofold increase in processing power every 18 months—a seemingly impossible pace. Intel, however, adopted Moore's Law as a performance requirement for each new generation of processor and has kept up this pace for over 40 years.[31]

BASIC (OR PURE) R&D Improving knowledge in an area without a primary focus on whether any discoveries that might occur are immediately marketable.

APPLIED R&D Focusing specifically on how a technological innovation can be put to use in the making of a product or service that can be sold in the marketplace.

TECHNOLOGY
TRANSFER
The process of getting a
new technology out of
the lab and into the
marketplace.

Because of the rapid pace of new developments, keeping a leadership position based on technology is increasingly difficult. **Technology transfer** refers to the process of getting a new technology out of the lab and into the marketplace where it can generate profits for the company. Efficient technology transfer means an increased likelihood of business success. A related challenge is meeting the constant demand to decrease *cycle time*—the time from beginning to end that it takes a firm to accomplish some recurring activity or function. Since businesses are more competitive if they can decrease cycle times, many companies now focus on decreasing cycle times in areas ranging from developing products to making deliveries and collecting credit payments. Twenty years ago, it took automakers about five years from the decision to launch a new product until it was available in dealer showrooms. Now most companies can complete the cycle in less than two years.

the Greening of
Business

The Hydrogen Fuel Cell

The hydrogen fuel cell combines hydrogen (one of earth's most common elements) with oxygen to produce electricity. The electricity generated by the fuel cell can be used to power anything that runs on electricity, including cars, and the only exhaust is warm water. When Vancouver-based Ballard Power Systems announced in the 1990s that it was developing the hydrogen fuel cell, excitement was high because automakers had tried for years to develop a new engine to replace the internal combustion engine that has powered automobiles for over a century. DaimlerChrysler and Ford Motor Co. invested hundreds of millions of dollars to pursue the development of fuel cells. Ballard sold prototypes to several public transportation companies in the U.S. and Canada, but more than 15 years have now passed, and the hydrogen fuel cell is still not ready for the mass market.

What happened? Why is the fuel cell—which looks like a fantastic product—still not widely available? Consider the daunting list of problems facing the fuel cell:

▶ Hydrogen must first be extracted from substances that contain it (e.g., natural gas), but stripping the hydrogen from natural gas creates carbon dioxide, which is precisely what the standard internal combustion car engines emit.

▶ Safety is an issue (when the word "hydrogen" is mentioned, many people immediately think of the spectacular explosion and fire that destroyed the hydrogen-powered Hindenburg airship in 1937).

▶ If insufficient numbers of hydrogen-dispensing gas stations are built, consumer demand will never be high enough to encourage mass production of cars that are powered by fuel cells.

▶ Hybrid cars like the Toyota Prius and the Honda Civic have been very successful and are providing strong competition for the hydrogen fuel cell.

The fuel cell may be commercially viable in 20 or 30 years, but there are still many developmental problems to be overcome and progress is slow. In 2008, Honda began producing the FCX Clarity, a zero-emission, fuel cell–powered car, but mass market sales are not likely until 2018. The company says that the biggest impediments to sales are the high price of the car and the lack of availability of hydrogen fuelling stations.

Maybe the hydrogen fuel cell will eventually become popular. Keep in mind what critics said when internal combustion–powered automobiles were introduced early in the twentieth century: "They'll never become popular because there would have to be gas stations all over the place." Well, now we have gas stations all over the place.

Critical Thinking Questions

1. Review the section on new product development. At what stage of the new product development process is the hydrogen fuel cell?

2. Consider the following statement: "If the fuel cell had any value, it would have been fully developed by now and there would already be many cars on the road that are powered by the fuel cell." Do you agree or disagree with the statement? Explain your reasoning.

The political–legal environment

The **political–legal environment** reflects the relationship between business and government, including government regulation of business. The legal system defines what an organization can and can't do. Although Canada is a free market economy, there is still significant regulation of business activity, as we saw in Chapter 8. At times government policy can be tremendously advantageous to businesses. The home renovation tax credit, which expired in 2010, brought a 30 percent sales increase for Winnipeg-based Acrylon Plastics (maker of window frames) and had hardware retailers smiling from coast to coast.[32] On the other hand, Shoppers Drug Mart was very vocal about its opposition to a new Ontario government regulation that would see generic drugs priced at as low as 25 percent of the original brand name product's cost, down from 50 percent. This regulation would have a tremendous impact on pharmacy profits.[33]

Society's general view of business (pro or anti) is also important. During periods of anti-business sentiment, companies may find their competitive activities restricted.

Political stability is also an important consideration, especially for international firms. No business wants to set up shop in another country unless trade relationships with that country are relatively well defined and stable. Thus, Canadian firms are more likely to do business in England rather than in Haiti. For example, in 2010, mining companies were concerned about rumours that members of the South African ruling government were considering nationalization (government takeover of resources, forcing private companies to sell at a price deemed fair by the government) of up to 60 percent of the country's mining sector. This was a dangerous prospect for Vancouver-based Great Basin Gold Ltd., which was developing a $230 million gold mining operation at the time.[34]

Relations between sovereign governments can also affect business activity. When Canada refused to send troops to support the U.S. invasion of Iraq, relations between the two nations were very cool for a time. Similar issues also pertain to assessments of local and provincial governments. A new mayor or provincial leader can affect many organizations, especially small firms that do business in a single location and are susceptible to zoning restrictions, property and school taxes, and the like.

Another aspect of the political–legal environment is described in the boxed insert entitled "Nova Scotia's Golden Nectar."

POLITICAL–LEGAL ENVIRONMENT Conditions reflecting the relationship between business and government, usually in the form of government regulation.

The socio-cultural environment

The **socio-cultural environment** includes the customs, values, attitudes, and demographic characteristics of the society in which a company operates. The socio-cultural environment influences the customer preferences for goods and services, as well as the standards of business conduct that are seen as acceptable.

Customer preferences and tastes

Customer preferences and tastes vary both across and within national boundaries. In some countries, consumers are willing and able to pay premium prices for designer clothes with labels such as Armani. But the same clothes have virtually no market in other countries. Product usage also varies between nations. In China, bicycles are primarily seen as a mode of transportation, but in Canada, they are marketed primarily for recreational purposes.

Consumer preferences can also vary widely within the same country. Customs and product preferences in Quebec, for example, differ from those in other parts of Canada. In the United States, pre-packaged chilli is more popular in the southwest than in the northeast. McDonald's is just one company that is affected by socio-cultural factors. In response to concerns about nutrition and health, McDonald's has added salads to its menus and experimented with other low-fat foods. It was the first fast-food chain to provide customers with information about the ingredients in its products, and it attracted media attention when it announced that it would reduce the fat content in its popular French fries.

Consumer preferences and tastes also change over time. Preferences for colour, style, taste, and so forth change from season to season. In some years, brightly coloured clothes sell best, while in other years, people want more subdued colours. Some of these changes are driven by consumers, and some are driven by companies trying to convince consumers to adopt new styles. These and many other related issues regarding businesses and their customers are explored more fully in Part IV of this book, which deals with the marketing of goods and services.

Socio-cultural factors also influence the way workers in a society feel about their jobs and organizations. In some cultures, work carries meaningful social significance, with certain employers and job titles being highly desired by workers. But in other cultures, because work is simply a means to an end, people are concerned only with pay and job security. McDonald's has occasionally struggled with its operations in the Middle East because many people there are not interested in working in food-service operations.

Ethical compliance and responsible business behaviour

An especially critical element of the socio-cultural environment is the practice of ethical conduct and social responsibility. But they are sufficiently important that we describe a couple of points briefly here: the reporting of a company's financial position and a company's social responsibility toward citizens.

Keeping up with today's increasingly fast-paced business activities is putting a strain on the accounting profession's traditional methods for auditing, financial reporting, and time-honoured standards for professional ethics. The

Nova Scotia's Golden Nectar: Glen Breton Rare

Cape Breton, Nova Scotia–based Glenora Distilleries battled fiercely to keep its Glen Breton Rare Single Malt Whisky on store shelves. It's not like the product lacked demand; Glenora distils the only single-malt whisky produced in Canada. The court battle dragged on from 2000 until mid-2009. The Scotch Whisky Association, a group representing over 50 whisky distillers in Scotland, claimed the company's use of "Glen" in its brand is confusing consumers and leading them to believe that the product is distilled in Scotland.

Lauchie MacLean, Glenora's president, strongly disagreed. He argued the name referred to Glenora Distillery's home community: Glenville, Cape Breton. Fortunately, a Canadian Federal Court of Appeal's ruling, in January 2009, allowed the company to continue to use the name. This ruling was supported, in June 2009, when the Supreme Court of Canada refused to hear the case and put an end to the legal battle. This move cleared the way for Glen Breton to get a legal trademark in Canada.

The latest clash hasn't been the only form of legal restriction imposed on Glenora Distillery and other whisky producers around the globe. Distillers based in Scotland have set out to protect the use of the label "scotch." One such move was an agreement signed by Canada and the European Union in 2003 that prevented Canadian whisky distillers from using the word "scotch" in their label. This term is reserved for Scotland-based distillers only. Glenora has always complied with this ruling but wasn't ready to lie down when the association's latest assault threatened its "Glen Breton" brand. But now, the future looks bright for a company that has had its fair share of challenges. Not only has it secured its most valuable possession, its brand name, it is also excited about the growing whisky market.

Because of increased demand in Europe and Asia, some single-malt whisky distillers have found their products in short supply. As a result, many distillers are pulling out of some markets and entering others. It's simple economics according to MacLean: "They [distillers] have an asset, and they're looking at selling that asset for the most money that they can get out of it." Glenora is a relatively small producer, but the company hopes to increase production at a later date to better match demand. Currently, Glenora is not "heavily into the Asian market," but expect that to change over the next few years.

Glenora's successes have partly been due to its entrepreneurial flexibility. The company experienced serious cash flow problems not long after its launch in 1991 because distilling doesn't happen overnight—it can take 10 to 12 years before a distillery will see revenues. However, some innovative approaches, which involved selling whisky futures and adding rum bottling and complementary tourism operations to the business, brought the company through the tough times. The business environment hasn't always been kind to Glenora, but in true entrepreneurial fashion, it has persevered. *Sláinte!*

Critical Thinking Question

1. Which of the external environments have had the most effect on Glenora Distilleries?

stakeholders of business firms—employees, stockholders, consumers, labour unions, creditors, and the government—are entitled to a fair accounting so they can make enlightened personal and business decisions, but they often get a blurred picture of a firm's competitive health. Nortel went from being the pride and joy of Canada to a historical warning. Nortel suffered at the turn of the century because the internet bubble burst. This was an external factor that had an impact on all technology companies but was not why Nortel failed; a major reason for the bankruptcy was the failure to get its financial house in order. The company made accounting restatement after restatement of its financials throughout the last decade of its existence. Restatement is a clever way of saying that the figures that the company presented to its stakeholders were inaccurate. When that happens one time it can be seen as an error. When it is repeated over time it is a clear attempt to deceive the market.

In 2010, British Petroleum (BP) was in the news for all the wrong reasons and faced the consequences of the massive Gulf of Mexico oil spill. For years, BP and other oil companies said that high-tech offshore drilling was extremely safe. But in 2010, when disaster struck, it became clear that the deep-sea environment was difficult and that BP did not have an adequate solution for the problem. For months the oil spewed into the Gulf, devastating coastlines, endangering wildlife, and battering the local fishing and tourism businesses. This failure had consequences and the various stakeholders were lining up to make BP pay. Within a few days, a Facebook page promoting a BP boycott had 360 000 supporters. Advocacy groups like Public Citizen held rallies against BP. The U.S. government was publicly pushing the company for a quick solution while demanding BP halt a $10.5 billion dividend payment to shareholders. The U.S. government was also planning a legal response to make BP pay for its mistake in the court system. The future of BP was at stake (something that was unimaginable before the crisis).[35]

The business environment

Business today is faster paced, more complex, and more demanding than ever before. As businesses aggressively try to differentiate themselves, there has been a trend toward higher-quality products, planned obsolescence, and product life cycles measured in weeks or months rather than years. This, in turn, has created customer expectations for instant gratification. Ultimate consumers and business customers want high-quality goods and services—often customized—with lower prices and immediate delivery. Sales offices, service providers, and production facilities are shifting geographically as new markets and resources emerge in other countries. Employees want flexible working hours and opportunities to work at home. Stockholder expectations also add pressure for productivity increases, growth in market share, and larger profits. At the same time, however, a more vocal public demands more honesty, fair competition, and respect for the environment.

A C-Suite survey found that the three most important issues facing Canadian businesses are (1) the value of the Canadian dollar, (2) a skilled labour shortage, and (3) the environment. These three issues are all important elements of the business environment.[36]

The industry environment

Each business firm operates in a specific industry, and each industry has different characteristics. The intensity of the competition in an industry has a big influence on how a company operates. To be effective, managers must understand the competitive situation, and then develop a competitive stra-tegy to exploit opportunities in the industry.

One of the most popular tools to analyze competitive situations in an industry is Michael Porter's five forces model.[37] The model (see Key 9.5) helps mana-gers analyze five important sources of competitive pressure and then decide what their competitive strategy should be. We briefly discuss each of the elements of the model in the following paragraphs.

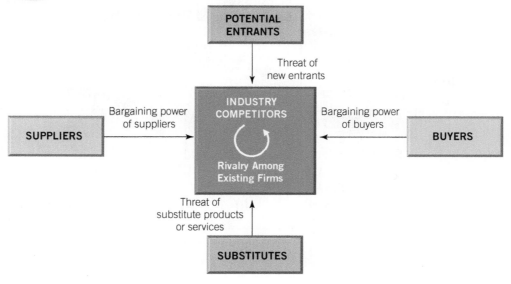

Porter's five forces model

One of the earliest models used to examine industry economics and industry attractiveness is Michael Porter's Five Forces Model (Key 9.6).[38] Rooted in economic theory, Porter suggests that there are five competitive forces at play in any industry that will determine that industry's profitability: competitive rivalry, threat of new entrants, supplier power, buyer power, and threat of substitute products. The weaker these forces, which describe the key structural features of the industry, the greater the opportunity for superior performance by firms within the industry; the stronger these forces, the more difficult it will be. Understanding industry structure is therefore the starting point for strategic analysis and strategy formulation. As well, examining the five forces helps organizations understand how value that is created by companies, is actually captured by the industry players.

Threat of entry

The rationale behind new entrants as a major competitive force relates to basic economic models suggesting that the greater the number of competitors, the closer the industry is to perfect competition. In contrast, where there is only one competitor a monopoly exists. The fewer the competitors, the greater the likelihood of higher profits. In addition, new entrants who are diversifying from outside an industry may be able to leverage capabilities or offset costs, such that they alter the economics of how firms compete in an industry, as Apple did when it entered the music industry.[39] Porter suggests there are six major barriers to entry: economies of scale, product differentiation, capital requirements, cost disadvantages independent of size, access to distribution channels, and government policy. The key with each is to consider the impact on costs, price, and thus profitability.

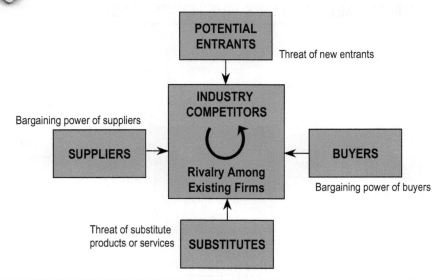

Economies of scale

There are supply-side economies of scale whereby, as the absolute volume of production increases, unit costs per product tend to decrease, resulting in economies of scale. As such, existing firms that have already made significant investments in manufacturing (or marketing, distribution, purchasing, sales force utilization, etc.) will likely hold an absolute cost advantage over potential new entrants. Furthermore, multi-business firms may also be able to create scale economies by sharing operational or functional costs with other business units in the company or by exploiting existing vertically integrated production and distribution systems. There are also demand-side economies of scale called network effects when the likelihood of customers purchasing a product or service increases with volume. For example, eBay has demand-side economics in its favour in the on-line auction industry.[40] Economies of scale, therefore, pose a barrier to entry by either forcing new entrants to come into the industry at a larger scale with great risk, or at a smaller scale with cost disadvantages.

Product differentiation

Established firms may also enjoy the benefits of brand recognition and customer loyalty that have been built on past marketing, advertising, and sales efforts. New entrants, on the other hand, may be forced to spend heavily to win customers and capture market share. Establishing a market presence in an industry with strong product differentiation can be both risky and expensive, thereby creating a strong barrier to entry.

Capital requirements

The capital investments required to compete in some industries can be prohibitive. For example, oil and gas, automotive, and airline industries necessitate larger upfront capital than most online service industries. Capital requirements, therefore, will serve as a barrier to entry to those firms that either cannot secure the funds or cannot bear the risk premiums charged. However, it is important to note that capital markets have become very efficient and effective at financing large-scale investments. Whereas at one time the sheer magnitude of an investment posed a barrier to entry, that is no longer the case.

Cost disadvantages

Potential entrants may face other cost disadvantages that serve as barriers to entry that are irrespective of scale. For example, established firms may benefit from longer learning curves, which reduce unit costs and allow for a cost advantage. Existing firms may also possess proprietary product technology, have secured favourable access to limited raw materials, or already captured the most favorable geographic locations in a market space. In multi-national settings especially, incumbents may also benefit from preferential government subsidies. These cost disadvantages may be sufficiently large to prevent potential new players from entering the industry.

Access to distribution channels

In some industries, established distribution channels can also leave little room for new players to enter given the nature of the channel itself or due to established channel relationships. Barriers to entry are strong if new entrants face fierce competition for limited space or cannot break through long-standing partnerships. For example, a new producer of breakfast cereal will first have to pay large fees to have its product listed in a national supermarket chain, as well as convince the retailer that it will provide extensive support through advertising and promotion to ensure that the cereal generates sufficient sales for the channel. Difficulties and costs associated with securing the required distribution channels are therefore also a barrier to entry.

Government policy

Lastly, many industries such as liquor and tobacco retailing, mineral extraction, and air transportation are by nature highly regulated. Government policies can be impediments on their own, creating strong barriers to entry through legislation, the imposition of standards, lengthy approvals, monitoring or control processes, and licensing issues.

In summary, Porter argues that where there are high economies of scale, incumbents with a differentiated product or service, large capital requirements to enter, incumbents who have advantages other than size such as location or patents, difficult-to-access distribution channels, and prohibitive government policies, new entrants will be deterred from the industry by these very high barriers to entry. New players may also be deterred by the potential for retaliation by existing competitors should they decide to enter regardless of the barriers. Incumbents with substantial resources, entrenched commitments to the industry, and/or a history of retaliatory actions are more likely to respond forcefully to the threat of new entrants in order to protect their established profit margins.

Suppliers

The second force affecting industry structure is the bargaining power of suppliers. Porter suggests that suppliers' power can impact industry profitability as they have the potential to place firms at the mercy of rising input costs or reduced quality of necessary products or services. For example, in the fall of 2007, a worldwide shortage of hops raised the cost of a key ingredient in the production of beer, placing many microbreweries dangerously close to extinction. What characteristics render suppliers particularly powerful? As in the case of hops growers, suppliers are more powerful if their industry is dominated by a few companies and are more concentrated than the industry to which they sell, if there are no other substitute products to be sold into the industry, or if the supplier's product is an important input to the buyer's business. Suppliers can also wield bargaining power if they sell to a number of different industries and their product is differentiated. Furthermore, if there are large switching costs in changing suppliers, then suppliers will have more bargaining power. Many of these elements explain why Microsoft has been a very powerful supplier to many industries.[41] Labour is another example of a particularly powerful supplier force, as the need for highly skilled labour and/or the presence of highly unionized employees can significantly influence an entire industry's profit structure.

Buyers

The bargaining power of an industry's most important buyer groups—be they intermediaries or customers—can also alter the profitability of an entire industry. For example, companies that want to sell their products to major retailers, such as Wal-Mart (the buyer), are at the mercy of such large distributors. With similar attributes as supplier power, there are several circumstances that can affect a buyer group's overall bargaining power: Buyers are more powerful if they are concentrated or purchase in large volumes, if they have full information, if they face few switching costs (i.e., not locked in to a single supplier) and if they earn low profits. Furthermore, if the products being purchased represent a significant portion of the buyer's costs, they are more likely to shop around for the best deal, especially if the products themselves are standard or undifferentiated or are not important to the overall quality of the buyer's product or service. Lastly, if buyers pose a credible threat to backward integration they can also yield significant bargaining power. Where there are several downstream buyers, it is important to examine where the power lies. For example, "DuPont has created enormous clout by advertising its Stainmaster brand of carpet fibers not only to the carpet manufacturers that actually buy them but also to downstream consumers. Many consumers request Stainmaster carpet even though DuPont is not a carpet manufacturer".[42] Generally, individual consumers have little or no power as a buyer. Yes, individuals can buy from one firm over another, or not at all, but individual consumers are not usually organized to purchase in large volumes. As an airline passenger (a buyer of a flight), an individual consumer is relatively powerless to affect price or quality of service.

Substitute products

Substitute products are products from outside the industry that can provide a similar package of benefits or otherwise perform the same function as the main product or service in the industry. Substitute products can reduce profitability in the industry as they place a new ceiling on the price that can be charged for the original product or service. Often, the assessment of threat by substitute products can be difficult and quite dynamic as there are a variety of forces that shape product features that can be 'replaced' by substitutes with superior cost competitiveness. For example, water is a substitute for cola, although in its traditional form, it did not provide the same package of benefits. However, branded bottled water was introduced with a different package of benefits and began to steal market share from the cola products. Similarly, video conferencing can be a substitute for business air travel, just as VoIP can be a substitute for more traditional telecommunications. Substitute products have the potential to alter significantly the structural dynamics of an industry.

Intensity of competitive rivalry

Competitive rivalry is affected by the other forces, but also has a dynamic of its own that can be witnessed by advertising and price wars, escalating promotional tactics, and new product extensions or introductions. Some industries can be characterized by relatively moderate competitive rivalry, while others are described as very intense, where brands "battle it out for market share" in public confrontations. However, even in cases of very intense and public rivalry it is important to understand the basis for the rivalry and its impact on profitability. Rivalry is affected by the interaction of other structural forces as well as through the sheer number and nature of competitors in an industry. Where there are only a few large players, the balance of power can be easily observed and the extent to which these firms direct the competition on price, brand, or distribution, for example, is relatively transparent. Where there are many small firms, however, rogue behavior is more likely. Diverse competitors, especially foreign entrants, add complexity and create instability in the competitive landscape of the industry. Where strategic stakes are high, the nature of competitive activity can also be unpredictable.

The intensity of competitive rivalry is also affected by the rate of growth in the industry. The greater the rate of growth, the less the competitive rivalry since all "boats rise with the tide." However, slow or no-growth industries and especially industries in decline can turn into bitter market share battles for the remaining pieces of the pie. In some cases, even despite negative returns, management may become unwilling to let go emotionally from the business or be prevented from disengaging by some other social or governmental restriction. Rather, stuck with specialized asset configurations, long-term fixed costs, and strategic partnerships which now act as barriers to *exit* from the industry, firms engage in desperate competitive tactics to stay afloat. Porter warns that it is competitive rivalry on the basis of price which may be the most dangerous since it transfers profitability from firms directly to customers in the form of increased value. As well, it is important to pay attention to the various dimensions on which firms compete since, if competitors are undifferentiated, it results in zero sum competition, whereas if they compete on different dimensions targeted to different customer segments then rivalry can actually increase industry profitability.[43]

How do you define your industry? Porter suggests using the five forces to determine whether the product market scope is similar for the various products, services, and geographic markets. The more they differ, the greater the likelihood that a firm may be operating in multiple industries and therefore it would be important to examine each industry using a five forces analysis. He offers the following common pitfalls:

▶ Defining the industry too broadly or too narrowly;

▶ Making lists instead of engaging in rigorous analysis;

▶ Paying equal attention to all of the forces rather than digging deeply into the most important ones;

▶ Confusing effect (price sensitivity) with cause (buyer economics);

▶ Using static analysis that ignores industry trends;

▶ Confusing cyclical or transient changes with true structural changes;

▶ Using the framework to declare an industry attractive or unattractive rather than using it to guide strategic choices.[44]

In summary, Porter views industries with low supplier power, low threat of entry, low buyer power, low threat of substitute products, and low competitive rivalry as five-star industries with a high level of expected profitability for firms within the industry. Once the strengths and weaknesses of the forces affecting the industry as a whole have been identified, the firm can then determine the strengths and weaknesses of its position relative to the industry to formulate its competitive strategy. Porter also cautions that industries are dynamic and while the structure of the industry shapes strategy, firms can also shape industry structure.

Emerging challenges and opportunities in the business environment

CORE COMPETENCIES
Skills and resources with which an organization competes best and creates the most value for owners.

The most successful firms are dealing with challenges and opportunities in today's business environment by focusing on their **core competencies**—the skills and resources with which they compete best and create the most value for owners. They outsource non-core business processes and pay suppliers and distributors to perform them, thereby increasing their reliance on suppliers. These new business models call for unprecedented coordination—not only among internal activities but also among customers, suppliers, and strategic partners—and they often involve globally dispersed processes and supply chains.

In this section, we discuss some of the most popular steps that companies have taken to respond to challenges and opportunities in the business environment. These include *outsourcing, social media and viral marketing,* and *business process management.*

Outsourcing

OUTSOURCING
Strategy of paying suppliers and distributors to perform certain business processes or to provide needed materials or services.

Outsourcing is the strategy of paying suppliers and distributors to perform certain business processes or to provide needed materials or services. For example, the cafeteria in a museum may be important to employees and customers, but the museum's primary focus is on exhibits that will interest the general public, not on food-service operations. That's why museums usually outsource cafeteria operations to food-service management companies. The result is more attention to museum exhibits and better food service for customers. Firms today outsource numerous activities, including payroll, employee training, and research and development.

Social media and viral marketing

Social media sites such as Facebook are now an important part of everyday life for consumers (especially the youth market). Companies are addressing this new reality by providing content and creating links for consumers. Most organizations are being careful about their online presence because they don't want it to be seen as an imposition but rather a natural extension to their real-world relationship with clients. As we discuss throughout this book, in the E-Business and Social Media Solutions boxes, some companies are making strong inroads as this new model evolves and companies learn to deal with an empowered consumer base.

VIRAL MARKETING
Strategy of using the internet and word-of-mouth marketing to spread product information.

Viral marketing predates the social media craze and first gained prominence through basic email transfer; it describes word of mouth that spreads information like a virus from customer to customer, and relies on the internet to replace face-to-face communications. Messages about new cars, sports events, and numerous other goods and services travel on the internet among potential customers, who pass the information on. Using various formats—games, contests, chat rooms, and bulletin boards—marketers encourage potential customers to try out products and tell other people about them.[45] This approach has even more potential today with the likes of Twitter providing even quicker means to move messages.

Viral marketing works because people increasingly rely on the internet for information that they used to get from other media such as radio and newspapers, and because the customer becomes a participant in the process of spreading the word by forwarding information to other internet users. Take a look at the E-Business and Social Media Solutions box entitled "Corus Entertainment Looking for Listeners and Revenues in New Places."

Business process management

A process is any activity that adds value to some input, transforming it into an output for a customer (whether external or internal).[46] For example, human resource departments perform interviewing and hiring processes; payroll departments perform the employee-payment process; the purchasing department performs the process of ordering materials; accounting performs the financial reporting process; and marketing performs the process of taking orders from customers.

Business Process Management means moving away from organizing around departments and moving toward organizing around process-oriented team structures that cut across old departmental boundaries. Often, companies begin by asking, "What must we do well to stay in business and win new orders?" Next, they identify the major processes that must be performed well to achieve these goals. Then they organize resources and skills around those essential processes. By organizing according to processes rather than functional departments, decision making is faster and more customer-oriented, materials and operations are coordinated, and products get to customers more rapidly.[47]

> **PROCESS**
> Any activity that adds value to some input, transforming it into an output for a customer (whether external or internal).

> **BUSINESS PROCESS MANAGEMENT**
> Approach by which firms move away from department-oriented organization and toward process-oriented team structures that cut across old departmental boundaries.

Much concern has been expressed by government officials and labour unions that the outsourcing of jobs will hurt the Canadian economy. Here, women work in one of many call centres in New Delhi, India, work that has been outsourced by Canadian and U.S. companies.

ACQUISITION
The purchase of a company by another, larger firm, which absorbs the smaller company into its operations.

MERGER
The union of two companies to form a single new business.

HORIZONTAL MERGER
A merger of two firms that have previously been direct competitors in the same industry.

VERTICAL MERGER
A merger of two firms that have previously had a buyer–seller relationship.

CONGLOMERATE MERGER
A merger of two firms in completely unrelated businesses.

FRIENDLY TAKEOVER
An acquisition in which the management of the acquired company welcomes the firm's buyout by another company.

HOSTILE TAKEOVER
An acquisition in which the management of the acquired company fights the firm's buyout by another company.

POISON PILL
A defence that management adopts to make a firm less attractive to an actual or potential hostile suitor in a takeover attempt.

DIVESTITURE
Occurs when a company sells part of its existing business operations to another company.

SPINOFF
Strategy of setting up one or more corporate units as new, independent corporations.

Redrawing corporate boundaries

Successful companies are responding to challenges in the external environment by redrawing traditional organizational boundaries, and by joining together with other companies to develop new goods and services. Several trends have become evident in recent years: *acquisitions and mergers, divestitures and spinoffs, employee-owned corporations, strategic alliances,* and *subsidiary/parent corporations.*

Acquisitions and mergers

In an **acquisition,** one firm simply buys another firm. For example, Kraft Foods Inc. recently bought British candy giant Cadbury for US$19 billion.[48] The transaction is similar to buying a car that becomes your property. In contrast, a **merger** is a consolidation of two firms, and the arrangement is more collaborative. In the first quarter of 2010, there were 246 mergers and acquisitions in Canada, with a value of $19.7 billion, but this figure was much lower than the previous quarter, which had 285 deals worth $34.4 billion.[49]

When the companies are in the same industry, as when Molson Inc. merged with Adolph Coors Co., it is called a **horizontal merger.** When one of the companies in the merger is a supplier or customer to the other, it is called a **vertical merger.** When the companies are in unrelated businesses, it is called a **conglomerate merger.** A merger or acquisition can take place in one of several ways. In a **friendly takeover,** the acquired company welcomes the acquisition, perhaps because it needs cash or sees other benefits in joining the acquiring firm. But in a **hostile takeover,** the acquiring company buys enough of the other company's stock to take control even though the other company is opposed to the takeover. Montreal-based Couche-Tard has plenty of experience in the merger and takeover game (in the past 15 years it has acquired Mac's, Dairy Mart, Circle K, and Winks); it is one of the biggest convenience store operators in North America with over 5800 stores. In 2010, it made a US$1.9 billion hostile takeover bid for Iowa-based Casey's after failing to come to a friendly agreement for the 1500-store chain.[50]

A **poison pill** is a defence that management adopts to make a firm less attractive to an actual or potential hostile suitor in a takeover attempt. The objective is to make the "pill" so distasteful that a potential acquirer will not want to swallow it. BCE Inc., for example, adopted a poison pill that allowed its shareholders to buy BCE stock at a 50 percent discount if another company announced its intention to acquire 20 percent or more of BCE's shares.[51]

Divestitures and spinoffs

A **divestiture** occurs when a company decides to sell part of its existing business operations to another corporation. For example, Unilever—the maker of Close-Up toothpaste, Dove soap, Vaseline lotion, and Q-tips—at one time owned several specialty chemical businesses that made ingredients for its consumer products. The company decided that it had to focus more on the consumer products themselves, so it sold the chemical businesses to ICI, a European chemical company.

In other cases, a company might set up one or more corporate units as new, independent businesses because a business unit might be more valuable as a separate company. This is known as a **spinoff.** For example, PepsiCo spun off Pizza Hut, KFC, and Taco Bell into a new, separate corporation now known

e-business and social Media Solutions

Corus Entertainment Looking for Listeners and Revenues in New Places

Do you remember when cameras were used to create photos, phones were used to make phone calls, and TVs were used to watch TV programs? Today things are different. You can watch TV on your phone, laptop, or even the LCD on your wall. Your smart phone or regular cell is a great tool for photos and your camera has an ever-increasing level of mega-pixels. As for music, it can come from your iPod, smart phone, a satellite station, or streamed from a website from your favourite station in Surrey, Saskatoon, St. John's, or even South Africa. Options are limitless. Faced with this new reality, the companies that own your favourite stations are looking for new ways to attract listeners like you.

Corus Entertainment is extending its relationship with listeners and finding ways to profit from it as well. In the early days of the internet, stations were simply excited about the chance to share music and shows with anyone who would listen online. However, this also meant that their listeners could migrate to stations from anywhere—a scary prospect. Corus Entertainment has come a long way in the last decade. Visiting one of its radio websites (e.g., Vancouver's 99.3 The Fox, Toronto's Edge 102.1, Calgary Country 105, Edmonton's 92.5 Joe FM, Winnipeg's Power 97, and Hamilton's Y108) makes it clear that even if the call letters are the same, these stations are no longer simply your father's radio station (unless Dad is especially media savvy). There are links

An example of a Corus Entertainment radio station web site (Vancouver's 99.3 The Fox).

to Facebook, Flickr, MySpace, Twitter, Viigo (for BlackBerry), YouTube, and more. There are blogs and podcasts and the tools to connect, join contests, and create virtual bonds. Corus also takes it a step further; it was the first to offer an iPhone streaming app and the first to form direct links with iTunes. You can purchase, via a special version of the Apple iTunes music store linked to your station, the song that you're currently listening to. In the process, Corus stands to add a few pennies to its bottom line.

Here is the new math that Corus and its advertising partners are studying. In 2009, Corus achieved over 7 million online listening hours per month; one out of every 20 listeners was accessing their stations through mobile devices or online, and this figure was expected to grow rapidly. However, with all of these positive signs, Corus sold its 12 Quebec-based stations to Cogeco Cable Inc. for $81 million in 2010. Corus stated that it wanted to focus on its other key markets. Was this a sign that all was not well or was Corus simply focusing on selected stations and reinvesting its new business model in key spots? This was not clear at the time. In the e-business age one thing is certain: companies must be ready to adjust and evolve in order to be successful.

Critical Thinking Question

1. How do you listen to music? Have you joined or visited a social media group linked to your favourite stations? Why? Why not?

as Yum! Brands Inc., and Canadian Pacific spun off Canadian Pacific Railway, CP Ships, Pan Canadian Petroleum, and Fording Coal.

Employee-owned corporations

Corporations are sometimes owned by the employees who work for them. The current pattern is for this ownership to take the form of **employee stock ownership plans**, or ESOPs. A corporation might decide to set up an ESOP to increase employee motivation or to fight a hostile takeover attempt. The company first secures a loan, which it then uses to buy shares of its stock on the open market. Some of the future profits made by the corporation are used to pay off the loan. The stock, meanwhile, is controlled by a bank or other trustee. Employees gradually gain ownership of the stock, usually on the basis of seniority. But even though they might not have physical possession of the stock for a while, they control its voting rights immediately.

A survey of 471 Canadian and U.S. companies conducted by Western Compensation & Benefits Consultants of Vancouver found that three-quarters of the companies that have adopted ESOPs have experienced improvement in both sales and profits. Charlie Spiring, the CEO of Wellington West Holdings Inc., says that one of the fundamental principles of his business is employee ownership. People really have to be entrepreneurs to work well in the company.[52]

Strategic alliances

A **strategic alliance**, or joint venture, involves two or more enterprises cooperating in the research, development, manufacture, or marketing of a product. For example, GM and Suzuki formed a strategic alliance at the Ingersoll, Ontario, plant where the Equinox and Grand Vitaras are made. Companies form strategic alliances for two main reasons: (1) to help spread the risk of a project, and (2) to get something of value (like technological expertise) from their strategic partner.

Subsidiary and parent corporations

A **subsidiary corporation** is one that is owned by another corporation. The corporation that owns the subsidiary is called the **parent corporation.** For example, the Hudson's Bay Company (HBC) is the parent corporation of Zellers and Home Outfitters.

Summary of Learning Objectives

1. **Explain the concepts of *organizational boundaries and multiple organizational environments*.** All businesses operate within a larger *external environment* consisting of everything outside an organization's boundaries that might affect it. An *organizational boundary* is that which separates the organization from its environment. Organizations have multiple environments: economic conditions, technology, political–legal considerations, social issues, the global environment, issues of ethical and social responsibility, the business environment itself, and numerous other emerging challenges and opportunities.

2. **Explain the importance of the *economic environment* to business and identify the factors used to evaluate the performance of an economic system.** The *economic environment* is the economic system in which business firms operate. The health of this environment affects business firms. The key goals of the Canadian system are economic growth, economic stability, and full employment. *Gross domestic product (GDP)* is the total value of all goods and services produced within a given period by a national economy domestically. The government manages the economy through *fiscal* and *monetary policies*.

3. **Describe the *technological environment* and its role in business.** *Technology* refers to all the ways firms create value for their constituents, including human knowledge, work methods, physical equipment, electronics and telecommunications, and various processing systems. There are two general categories of business-related technologies: *product and service technologies and business process technologies*.

4. **Describe the *political–legal environment* and its role in business.** The *political–legal environment* reflects the relationship between business and government. The legal system defines what an organization can and can't do. Various government agencies regulate important areas such as advertising practices, safety and health considerations, and acceptable standards of business conduct. Pro- or anti-business sentiment in government can further influence business activity.

5. **Describe the *socio-cultural environment* and its role in business.** The *socio-cultural environment* includes the customs, values, and demographic characteristics of society. Socio-cultural processes determine the goods and services as well as the standards of business conduct that a society values and accepts. Appropriate standards of conduct also vary across cultures. The shape of the market, the ethics of political influence, and the attitudes of its workforce are only a few of the many ways in which culture can affect an organization.

6. **Identify emerging challenges and opportunities in the *business environment*.** Successful companies are focusing on their core competencies. The innovative ways in which companies respond to emerging challenges and opportunities include *outsourcing, social media* and *viral marketing*, and *business process management*.

7. **Understand recent trends in the *redrawing of corporate boundaries*.** An *acquisition* occurs when one firm buys another. A *merger* occurs when two firms combine to create a new company. A *divestiture* occurs when a corporation sells a part of its existing business operations or sets it up as a new and independent corporation. When a firm sells part of itself to raise capital, the strategy is known as a *spin-off*. The *ESOP plan* allows employees to own a significant share of the corporation through trusts established on their behalf. In a *strategic alliance,* two or more organizations collaborate on a project for mutual gain.

Questions and Exercises

Questions for Analysis

1. It has been argued that inflation is both good and bad. Explain. Are government efforts to control inflation well-advised? Explain.
2. What are the benefits and risks of outsourcing? What, if anything, should be done about the problem of Canadian companies outsourcing jobs to foreign countries? Defend your answer.
3. Why is it important for managers to understand the environment in which their businesses operate?
4. Explain how current economic indicators such as inflation and unemployment affect you personally. Explain how they affect managers.
5. At first glance, it might seem as though the goals of economic growth and stability are inconsistent with one another. How can this apparent inconsistency be reconciled?
6. What is the current climate in Canada regarding the regulation of business? How might it affect you if you were a manager today?

Application Exercises

1. Select two businesses you are familiar with. Identify the major elements of their external environments that are most likely to affect them in important and meaningful ways.
2. Assume that you are the owner of an internet pharmacy that sells prescription drugs to U.S. citizens. Analyze the factors in the external environment (economic, technological, political–legal, and socio-cultural) that might facilitate your company's activities. Analyze the factors in the external environment that might threaten your company's activities.
3. Select a technology product, such as Amazon's Kindle e-reader, and research how the various environments of business (economic, technological, socio-cultural, global, political–legal, and general business) are currently impacting the sales possibilities of the product or service.
4. Interview two business owners or managers. Ask them to answer the following questions: (a) What business functions, if any, do they outsource? (b) Are they focusing more attention on business process management now than in the past? (c) How have internet applications and the growth of social media changed the way they conduct business?

Team Exercises

Building Your Business Skills

THE LETDOWN FROM ENVIRONMENTAL UPHEAVAL

Goal

To encourage students to understand how local events can affect other businesses.

Situation

The collapse of Enron affected literally hundreds of other businesses. While attention has been directed primarily at the demise of Arthur Andersen, many other businesses suffered as well. For example, Enron's headquarters were located in a large office building on the edge of Houston's downtown business district. Because of both Enron's rapid growth and the prosperity of its employees, numerous other service providers had set up shop nearby—a shoeshine stand, a coffee shop, a dry cleaner, and two restaurants. When Enron collapsed, the demand for services provided by these small businesses dropped sharply.

Larger businesses were also caught up in the ripple effect. Enron, for example, had bought the rights to name the new home of Houston's baseball team, the Astros, Enron Field. The Astros were forced to remove all Enron signage and seek a new sponsor. Continental Airlines dominates the air traffic market out of Houston, and Enron was one of Continental's largest corporate clients; the end of business travel by Enron managers cost the airline considerable revenue.

Method

Divide into groups of four or five students; each group should begin by doing the following:

Step 1 Identify five kinds of small businesses likely to have been affected by Enron's collapse. You can include some of those identified above, but identify at least two others.

Step 2 Identify five kinds of large businesses likely to have been affected by Enron's collapse. Again, you can use some of those identified above, but identify at least two others.

Step 3 As a group, develop answers to each of the following:

1. For each company that you identify, both small and large, describe the specific effects of the Enron collapse on its business.
2. Describe the most logical organizational response of each company to these effects.
3. What kinds of plans, if any, should each organization develop in the event of similar future events?
4. Identify businesses that might have benefited economically from the collapse of Enron.

Alternative Assignment

Select a different high-profile environmental upheaval, such as the economic crisis that nearly caused the collapse of the major North American automakers. Then proceed with Steps 1–3 above.

Follow-Up Questions

1. What does this exercise demonstrate about the pitfalls of relying too heavily on one business?
2. Could any of these businesses have been better prepared for the Enron collapse?
3. Managers must be on the alert for environmental changes that might negatively affect their business. Is it possible for a manager to spend too much time trying to anticipate future events? Why or why not?.

Exercising Your Ethics

Finding the Balance

THE SITUATION

Managers often find it necessary to find the right balance among the interests of different stakeholders. For instance, paying employees the lowest possible wages can enhance profits, but paying a living wage might better serve the interests of workers. As more businesses outsource production to other countries, these trade-offs become more complicated.

THE DILEMMA

The Canadian Delta Company currently uses three suppliers in Southeast Asia for most of its outsourced production. Due to increased demand for its products, it needs to double the amount of business it currently subcontracts to one of these suppliers. (For purposes of this exercise, assume that the company must award the new supplier contract to a single firm, and that it must be one of these three. You can also assume that the quality provided is about the same for all three companies.)

Subcontractor A provides a plain but clean work environment for its workers. Even though the local weather conditions are usually hot and humid, the plant is not air conditioned. Canadian Delta safety experts have verified that the conditions are not dangerous but are definitely uncomfortable. The firm pays its workers the same prevailing wage rate that is paid by its local competitors. While it has never had a legal issue with its workforce, Subcontractor A does push its employees to meet production quotas and it has a very tough disciplinary policy regarding tardiness. An employee who is late gets probation; a second infraction within three months results in termination. This subcontractor provides production to Canadian Delta at a level such that it can attach a 25 percent mark-up.

Subcontractor B also provides a plain work environment. It pays its workers about 5 percent above local wage levels and hence is an attractive employer. Because of its higher pay, this firm is actually quite ruthless in some of its policies. For instance, any employee who reports to work more than 15 minutes late without a medical excuse is automatically terminated. This supplier's costs are such that Delta Company can achieve a 20 percent mark-up.

Subcontractor C runs a much nicer factory than either A or B, and the plant is air-conditioned. It pays its workers about 10 percent above local wage levels. The company also operates an on-site school for the children of its employees, and provides additional training for its workers so they can improve their skills. Due to its higher costs, Canadian Delta's mark-up on this firm's products is only around 15 percent.

TEAM ACTIVITY

Assemble a group of four students and assign each group member to one of the following roles:

- Canadian Delta executive
- Canadian Delta employee
- Canadian Delta customer
- Canadian Delta investor

ACTION STEPS

1. Before discussing the situation with your group, and from the perspective of your assigned role, decide which firm should get the additional business. Which firm is your second choice? Write down the reasons for your position.
2. Before discussing the situation with your group, and from the perspective of your assigned role, identify the underlying ethical issues in this situation. Write down the issues.
3. Gather your group together and reveal, in turn, each member's comments on their choices. Next, reveal the ethical issues listed by each member.
4. Appoint someone to record main points of agreement and disagreement within the group. How do you explain the results? What accounts for any disagreement?
5. From an ethical standpoint, what does your group conclude is the most appropriate choice for the company in this situation? Why?

Business Case 2

Inflation, Deflation, and the Validity of the CPI

Between 2008 and 2010, there was great fear and confusion in financial markets. The stock market saw a major decline and a major recovery and the roller coaster ride seemed far from over. It wasn't just because of the credit crisis, the housing crisis, the sovereign debt crisis, and the worldwide recession.

There was also uncertainty about whether *inflation* or *deflation* was going to add to the problems that already existed. On one hand, it seemed logical to predict that inflation was going to get worse because central governments around the world cut interest rates and were injecting billions of dollars into their financial systems to get their economies moving again. On the other hand, the recession became so bad that the demand for goods and services was declining, commodity prices (including oil) were falling fast, banks were not loaning money (because they feared that borrowers wouldn't be able to repay their loans), consumers were reluctant to spend money, and everyone was hoarding cash. All of those factors suggested that deflation was going to occur.

To see how this complicated situation developed, we have to look back. In the first half of 2008, prices increased for many different products and services, including food, metals, energy, air transportation, gasoline, cable services, and mortgages. The Bank of Canada became concerned that inflation was becoming a real threat. The weakening of the Canadian dollar against the U.S. dollar also increased the threat since imported goods would be more expensive for Canadians. The International Monetary Fund (IMF) expressed concern that the strong demand for food and other resources in rapidly growing countries like India and China was going to cause increased inflation elsewhere in the world. The IMF's deputy managing director noted that there were about 50 countries in the world with inflation rates above 10 percent, mostly developing nations.

The interconnectedness of the global economy was also a problem. The U.S. Federal Reserve cut interest rates in an attempt to get the U.S. economy moving, but that caused the value of the U.S. dollar to decline relative to other currencies (at least for a while). That, in turn, meant that U.S. consumers would have to pay more for imported products. The rate cut also created problems for Middle Eastern and Asian countries that had pegged their dollar to the U.S. dollar in an attempt to stabilize their economies. When the United States reduced interest rates, those countries really had to follow suit; if they didn't, people would move more money into their country (because they could earn a higher rate of return than they could in the United States). That, in turn, would create upward pressure on the currency of those Middle Eastern and Asian countries. It would also cause increased inflation because when interest rates decline, it is easier for people to borrow money.

All of these factors suggested that inflation was going to be a problem. But economic circumstances can change very quickly. Just a few months after the Bank of Canada expressed concerns about inflation, it decided to *cut* interest rates, even though doing so typically increases the chance of inflation. The Bank of Canada did this because commodity prices had suddenly declined and a worldwide recession had started. In spite of the rate cut, prices soon started dropping for meat, automobiles, computers, fresh fruit, furniture, appliances, tools, hardware, and a wide range of commodities, including oil. In China, overproduction of everything from laptop computers to building materials raised fears that many products would soon be dumped on world markets at cut-rate prices. That increased the chance of deflation (negative inflation). Support for deflation fears could be found in the fact that the rate of inflation in the U.S. economy between March 2008 and March 2009 was −0.1 percent. That was the first year of negative inflation since 1955.

Fears about deflation were not without foundation. Japan experienced deflation for 15 years after its housing bubble burst in the early 1990s. Then, just when it looked like Japan would escape from that problem, the U.S. Federal Reserve cut interest rates to almost 0 percent to get the U.S. economy moving. Japan's central bank followed suit; it didn't want the yen to rise in value because that would depress Japan's exports. But in 2010, matters were further complicated when the Bank of Canada announced it was raising rates and signalling that future rate hikes may be significant in the near term (partially because of fears of a potential housing bubble).

It is difficult to predict whether inflation or deflation is more likely partly because both situations are influenced by self-fulfilling prophecies. For example, if people think inflation is going to be a problem, they are motivated to buy things now in order to avoid paying the higher prices that they assume are soon to come. But buying things now creates more demand, and that causes prices to rise. Conversely, if people think deflation is going to occur, they are motivated to delay purchases to the time when the price will be lower. But putting off purchases lowers demand, and that causes prices to fall.

There is yet another angle to consider in this debate. According to statistician Phil Green, our measurement tool (CPI) is inaccurate and inflation is actually much higher than typically reported in the past 20 years. The way CPI is measured has changed, and some believe that governments are fudging the numbers. Green claims that the inflation rate in the U.S. was actually closer to 10 percent in 2010 if measured using traditional methods. The U.S. is not alone in this. Governments have changed the CPI equation many times in major industrialized nations. This is no secret. But informed individuals were questioning the very integrity of this key leading indicator.

Given all this complexity, we should not be surprised if economists have trouble accurately predicting whether inflation or deflation will be the next problem we face. Inflation definitely lurks in the background. If the crisis in confidence can be overcome, people will start spending again, and with all that money that governments dished out still in the system, demand could soar and inflation could become a big problem. On the other hand, if the recession is long and deep, deflation is a distinct possibility because there will be very little demand for goods and services, and that will cause prices to fall.

QUESTIONS FOR DISCUSSION

1. Based on your own observations in the marketplace, do you believe we are in an inflationary or deflationary period?
2. Go to the Bank of Canada website and find the latest inflation figures. Based on the latest statistics, is inflation or deflation a bigger problem today?
3. What do you think of Phil Green's contention that the CPI has become a deceptive tool? Do you believe that governments are purposefully massaging the numbers? If so, explain why.

SCANLIFE

Notes

1. Eric Reguly, "As Ash Spreads, So Does Damage," *The Globe and Mail*, April 19, 2010, B1.
2. See Jay B. Barney and William G. Ouchi, eds., *Organizational Economics* (San Francisco: Jossey-Bass, 1986), for a detailed analysis of linkages between economics and organizations.
3. Karl E. Case and Ray C. Fair, *Principles of Economics*, 6th ed., updated (Upper Saddle River, NJ: Prentice Hall, 2003), 432–433.
4. Karl E. Case and Ray C. Fair, *Principles of Economics*, 6th ed., updated (Upper Saddle River, NJ: Prentice Hall, 2003), 15.
5. Karl E. Case and Ray C. Fair, *Principles of Economics*, 6th ed., updated (Upper Saddle River, NJ: Prentice Hall, 2003), 15.
6. Richard Blackwell, "The 'R' Word," *The Globe and Mail*, October 16, 2008, B5.
7. Bank of Canada Banking and Financial Statistics, Table H1 (May 2010): S96.
8. Matthew McLearn, "Our Dangerous Addiction to GDP," *Canadian Business*, October 12, 2009, 23.
9. Green Economics website, www.greeneconomics.ca/gpi, accessed June 9, 2010; Barry Marquardson, "GDP Fails as a Measurement," *The Globe and Mail*, July 16, 1998, B2.
10. Conference Board of Canada website, www.conferenceboard.ca/hcp/details/economy/income-per-capita.aspx, accessed June 7, 2010.

11. Olivier Blanchard, *Macroeconomics*, 3rd ed. (Upper Saddle River, NJ: Prentice Hall, 2003), 24–26.

12. OECD website, http://stats.oecd.org/Index. aspx?DatasetCode=LEVEL, accessed June 9, 2010; Kevin Lynch, "Canada's Productivity Trap," *The Globe and Mail*, January 29, 2010, B1.

13. Jay Heizer and Barry Render, *Operations Management*, 6th ed. (Upper Saddle River, NJ: Prentice Hall, 2001), 15–16.

14. Statistics Canada website, www40.statcan. gc.ca/l01/cst01/gblec02a-eng.htm, accessed June 9, 2010.

15. Greg Hitt and Murray Hiebert, "U.S. Trade Deficit Ballooned to a Record in 2005," *The Wall Street Journal*, February 11–12, 2006, A1, A10.

16. Neil Reynolds, "Stimulating Our Way into a Crisis," *The Globe and Mail*, February 18, 2009, B2.

17. Paul Viera, "Federal Deficit for 2009 Smaller than Expected, Finance Department Says," *The Financial Post*, May 29, 2010.

18. Canadian Federal Budget website, www.budget.gc.ca/2010/pdf/budget-planbudgetaire-eng.pdf, accessed June 9, 2010.

19. Neil Reynolds, "U.S. Debt: Don't Worry, Be Happy (till 2017)," *The Globe and Mail*, April 3, 2009, B2.

20. Celia Dugger, "Life in Zimbabwe: Wait for Useless Money, Then Scour for Food," *The New York Times*, October 2, 2008, A1, A14.

21. Geoffrey York, "How Zimbabwe Slew the Dragon of Hyperinflation," *The Globe and Mail*, March 23, 2009, B1.

22. Tavia Grant, "A Snapshot of How We Spend," *The Globe and Mail*, April 20, 2010, B2; Tavia Grant, "Lard in 1913, Plasma TV Now: CPI Tracks Changes," *The Globe and Mail*, April 21, 2005, B1, B15.

23. Bruce Little, "There's Been a Huge Shift in How Consumers Spend," *The Globe and Mail*, July 5, 2004, B4. Figure 2.3 shows how inflation has varied over the last 20 years in Canada.

24. Statistics Canada website, www.statcan. gc.ca/subjects-sujets/labour-travail/lfs-epa/t100604a1-eng.htm, accessed June 10, 2010.

25. Jeremy Torobin and Tavia Grant, "Slow Jobs Growth, Growing Debt Fears: U.S., European Recoveries Show Signs of Strain," *The Globe and Mail*, June 5, 2010, B1, B5.

26. Julie Jargon, "Seeking Sweet Savings," *The Wall Street Journal*, October 2, 2007, B1–B2.

27. Statistics Canada, *Industrial Research and Development: Intentions*, Catalogue no. 88-202-X, Table 4, Concentration of Total Intramural Research and Development Expenditures by Companies Size (Ottawa: Minister of Industry, 2010), www.statcan.gc.ca/pub/88-202-x/2009000/tablesectlist-listetableauxsect-eng.htm.

28. Statistics Canada, *Industrial Research and Development: Intentions* (Ottawa: Minister of Industry, 2009). www.statcan.gc.ca/pub/88-202-x/2009000/t003-eng.htm.

29. Statistics Canada, 2008, *Industrial Research and Development: Intentions*, Catalogue no. 88-202-X, Table 4, Concentration of Total Intramural Research and Development Expenditures by Companies Size, www.statcan.gc.ca/pub/88-202-x/2009000/t050-eng.htm.

30. Invest in Ontario, "Canadian Industrial Intramural R&D Expenditures, Selected Industries," www.investinontario.com/siteselector/bcrd_508.asp.

31. Intel website, Moore's Law, www.intel.com/technology/mooreslaw/, accessed June 11, 2010.

32. Tavia Grant, "Wishful Thinking, a Tax Credit That Doesn't End," *The Globe and Mail*, January 20, 2010, B5.

33. Michael Babad, "How Ontario's Drug Reforms Could Hit Shoppers Drug Mart," *The Globe and Mail*, April 8, 2010, B1; Marina Strauss, "Cost-Lowering Drug Reform Expected to Hit Shoppers," *The Globe and Mail*, July 23, 2009, B5.

34. Geoffrey York, "Nationalization Talks Put Miners on Edge," *The Globe and Mail*, February 2, 2010, B3.

35. David Ebner, "BP Spill Causes Transatlantic Tensions," *The Globe and Mail*, June 11, 2010, B5; Eric Reguly, "Now Come the Lawyers," *The Globe and Mail*, June 5, 2010, B1, B4; Peter Coy and Stanley Reed, "Lessons of the Spill," *Bloomberg BusinessWeek*, May 10–16, 2010.

36. Richard Blackwell, "The Greening of the Corner Office," *The Globe and Mail*, March 26, 2007, B1, B4.

37. Michael Porter, *Competitive Strategy: Techniques for Analyzing Industries and Competitors* (New York: The Free Press, 1980).

38. Porter, Michael E. "How Competitive Forces Shape Strategy." *Harvard Business Review* 57 (March–April 1979): 137. Print.

39. Porter, Michael E. "The Five Competitive Forces That Shape Strategy." *Harvard Business Review* 86.1 (2008): 78–93. Business Source Complete, EBSCO. Web. 16 Aug. 2011.

40. Porter, Michael E. "The Five Competitive Forces That Shape Strategy." *Harvard Business Review* 86.1 (2008): 78–93. Business Source Complete, EBSCO. Web. 16 Aug. 2011.

41. Porter, Michael E. "The Five Competitive Forces That Shape Strategy." *Harvard Business Review* 86.1 (2008): 78–93. Business Source Complete, EBSCO. Web. 16 Aug. 2011.

42. Porter, Michael E. "The Five Competitive Forces That Shape Strategy." *Harvard Business Review* 86.1 (2008): 78–93. Business Source Complete, EBSCO. Web. 16 Aug. 2011.

43. Porter, Michael E. "The Five Competitive Forces That Shape Strategy." *Harvard Business Review* 86.1 (2008): 78–93. Business Source Complete, EBSCO. Web. 16 Aug. 2011.

44. Porter, Michael E. "The Five Competitive Forces That Shape Strategy." *Harvard Business Review* 86.1 (2008): 78–93. Business Source Complete, EBSCO. Web. 16 Aug. 2011.

45. Judy Strauss and Raymond Frost, *E-Marketing* (Upper Saddle River, NJ: Prentice Hall, 2001), 245–246.

46. Lee J. Krajewski and Larry P. Ritzman, *Operations Management: Strategy and Analysis*, 6th ed. (Upper Saddle River, NJ: Prentice Hall, 2002), 3–4.

47. Lee J. Krajewski and Larry P. Ritzman, *Operations Management: Strategy and Analysis*, 6th ed. (Upper Saddle River, NJ: Prentice Hall, 2002), Chapter 3.

48. Gordon Pitts, "Kraft CEO Still Digesting Cadbury Takeover," *The Globe and Mail*, June 7, 2010, B8.

49. Tim Kiladze, "Takeover Activity Eases Off," *The Globe and Mail*, June 11, 2010, B6.

50. Andrew Willis, "Couche-Tard Shows No Stomach for Casey's Fight," *The Globe and Mail*, June 9, 2010, B16.

51. Lawrence Surtees, "Takeover Concern Prompts BCE Poison Pill Plan," *The Globe and Mail*, February 25, 2000, B5.

52. "Culture of Fun Benefits Clients, Staff," *National Post*, October 27, 2008, FP12.

chapter 10

Entrepreneurship, Small Business, and New Venture Creation

Parasuco Jeans:
The Story of a Born
Entrepreneur

Salvatore Parasuco's company recently celebrated its thirty-fifth year of operation, so his successful denim business is definitely not a new venture, but it is a great tale of entrepreneurship. Words like *drive*, *determination*, *self-starter*, and *vision* are commonly used to describe entrepreneurs. All of these terms fit the founder of Parasuco Jeans to a T. The story begins with a budding entrepreneur whose ambition is announced at a very young age when he begins selling jeans out of his high school locker in Montreal. As legend has it, he managed to convince his principal to let him sell the jeans by telling him he needed to make money to help support his family and avoid going down the wrong path. Today, Parasuco Jeans are sold in locations around the world with distribution in Canada, the United States, Europe, and Asia. The company has a particularly good presence in Italy, Hong Kong, Russia, Japan, and Korea. Celebrities such as Jessica Alba, Kate Hudson, Chris Daughtry, and many more have been photographed wearing a pair of Parasuco's trendy jeans. Yet despite the success and the longevity of the brand it does not have as much visibility across Canada as the owner thinks it deserves. He openly wonders why we Canadians (and the local media in particular) aren't as patriotic toward our homegrown brands as Americans are.

Salvatore is a Canadian whose family came here from Italy when he was just a young boy. From his humble beginnings, he learned the value of a dollar and credits his father for teaching him the art of negotiation at an early age. The rise of Parasuco Jeans is not a modern-day instant success story with a major internet IPO launch. It is a story about blood, sweat, and some tears. Before getting into the denim design business, Salvatore opened a clothing store, where he learned a lot about the business that would become his life's work. Mr. Parasuco launched Santana Jeans in 1975 and changed the name to Parasuco due to legal issues in 1988. From the early days it was clear that innovation and design would be at the foundation of the company.

After reading this chapter, you should be able to:

> Explain the meaning and interrelationship of the terms *small business, new venture creation, and entrepreneurship.* p. 293

> Describe the role of small and new businesses in the Canadian economy. p. 296

> Explain the *entrepreneurial process* and describe its three key elements. p. 300

> Describe three alternative strategies for becoming a business owner—*starting from scratch, buying an existing business, and buying a franchise.* p. 310

> Describe four forms of *legal organization* for a business and discuss the advantages and disadvantages of each. p. 313

> Identify four key reasons for success in small businesses and four key reasons for failure. p. 319

*With contributions from Dr. Monica Diochon, St. Francis Xavier University.

Parasuco Jeans has been successful because its entrepreneurial founder has adhered to sound business practices and made effective decisions. By understanding the material discussed in this chapter, you'll be better prepared to (1) understand the challenges and opportunities provided in new venture start-ups, (2) assess the risks and benefits of working in a new business, and (3) evaluate the investment potential inherent in a new business.

Parasuco was the first to launch pre-washed jeans in Canada. The company was also the first brand to introduce stretch denim to the market; a product feature that is central to the company image to this day. In a recent interview, the owner talked about how customers tend to instinctively start to stretch and pull his famous jeans. Success in business requires good vision to compete. This is even more complicated in this industry because staying ahead of the fashion trends is no easy task. The guiding mission of the company is based on eight pillars of strength: (1) respect, (2) people, (3) passion, (4) promotion of innovation, (5) performance, (6) pride, (7) pursuit of excellence, and (8) professionalism. Based on a track record that spans over 35 years, it is obvious that this company has done something right in meeting customer needs. But there are significant existing domestic and emerging international competitors; there are even other major brands based in Montreal, such as Buffalo by David Bitton (which has its own niche).

Parasuco Jeans is a brand known for its provocative ads. It has shocked and pushed boundaries for years with sexy billboards, magazine spreads, and bus shelter ads. In order to gain more attention, the company placed 25 ads in giant ice blocks around the city of Toronto to coincide with Fashion Week in 2009, with a tag line to match: "Styles so hot they will melt the ice." Like most fashion companies, Parasuco uses Twitter and Facebook to build buzz and spread the word. There is also a great deal of content on YouTube, which is a testament to the brand's cult-like following.

Even the most successful businesses have their share of disappointments and failures, but true entrepreneurs know how to overcome them, reduce their losses, and to capitalize on the best available opportunity. In 2010, when Parasuco decided to close his flagship New York store, he quickly found a tenant (drugstore chain Duane Reade) that agreed to pay $1 million in rent per year, to Parasuco, who had bought the retail condominium four years earlier for about $9 million dollars. At the same time he announced intentions to build a high-end boutique hotel in Toronto. At 57 years of age, Salvatore Parasuco does not seem to be slowing down one bit; he is visibly promoting his brand and searching for new opportunities. What do you expect? Salvatore Parasuco has the DNA of a pure entrepreneur.

Small business, new venture creation, and entrepreneurship

In this chapter we examine old companies with an enduring entrepreneurial spirit (Parasuco); we look at exciting growth-oriented newcomers (Twitter); and we examine major family organizations that have stood the test of time (McCain) and a host of small organizations with dreams and aspirations. Each of these examples gives us a glimpse of an important element of the Canadian business landscape. We begin by examining the lifeblood of an economy: small business, entrepreneurship, and new ventures.

One positive result of the recent recession was a new wave of entrepreneurial efforts. In 2009, the number of self-employed Canadians increased by 115 000.[1] Every day, approximately 380 businesses are started in Canada.[2] New firms create the most jobs, are noted for their entrepreneurship, and are typically small.[3] But does this mean that most small businesses are entrepreneurial? Not necessarily.

The terms *small business, new venture,* and *entrepreneurship* are closely linked terms, but each idea is distinct. In the following paragraphs we will explain these terms to help you understand these topics and how they are interrelated.

Small business

Defining a "small" business can be a bit tricky. Various measures might be used, including the number of people the business employs, the company's sales revenue, the size of the investment required, or the type of ownership structure the business has. Some of the difficulties in defining a small business can be understood by considering the way the Canadian government collects and reports information on small businesses.

Industry Canada is the main federal government agency responsible for small business. In reporting Canadian small business statistics, the government relies on two distinct sources of information, both provided by Statistics Canada: the *Business Register* (which tracks businesses) and the *Labour Force Survey* (which tracks individuals). To be included in the Register, a business must have at least one paid employee, annual sales revenues of $30 000 or more, or be incorporated (we describe incorporation later in the chapter). A goods-producing business in the Register is considered small if it has fewer than 100 employees, while a service-producing business is considered small if it has fewer than 50 employees. The Labour Force Survey uses information from *individuals* to make estimates of employment and unemployment levels. Individuals are classified as self-employed if they are working owners of a business that is either incorporated or unincorporated, if they work for themselves but do not have a business (some musicians, for example, would fall into this category), or if they work without pay in a family business.[4] In its publication *Key Small Business Statistics* (www.strategis.gc.ca/sbstatistics), Industry Canada reports that there are 2.3 million "business establishments" in Canada and about 2.6 million people who are "self-employed."[5] There is no way of identifying how much overlap there is in these two categories, but we do know that an unincorporated business operated by a self-employed person (with no employees) would not be counted among the 2.3 million *businesses* in the Register. This is an important point because the majority of businesses in Canada have no employees (just the owner), nor are they incorporated.

A study by the Panel Study of Entrepreneurial Dynamics (PSED), conducted by members of the Entrepreneurship Research Consortium (ERC), tracked a sample of Canadian nascent entrepreneurs—people who were trying to start a business—over four years. Only 15 percent of those who reported establishing an operating business had incorporated their firm.[6]

For our purposes, we define a small business as an owner-managed business with less than 100 employees. We do so because it enables us to make better use of existing information, and because you are now aware of how definitions can affect our understanding of small businesses. Industry Canada estimates the percentage of small business's contribution to Canada's GDP over the past decade at 26 percent annually.[7]

Each year, the Queen's Centre for Business Venturing develops a ranking of the top 50 small- and medium-sized employers to work for. The top 10 firms

> NASCENT ENTREPRENEURS
> People who are trying to start a business from scratch.

> SMALL BUSINESS
> An independently owned and managed business that does not dominate its market.

Table 10.1 Top Small and Medium-Sized Employers in Canada, 2010

	COMPANY	LOCATION
1.	Booty Camp Fitness Inc.	Toronto, Ontario
2.	ISL Engineering and Land Services Ltd.	Edmonton, Alberta
3.	Hood Group	Sherwood Park, Alberta
4.	RL Solutions	Toronto, Ontario
5.	Radiology Consultants Associated	Calgary, Alberta
6.	Concept Electric Ltd.	Calgary, Alberta
7.	Gibraltar Solutions Inc.	Mississauga, Ontario
8.	PEOPLEsource Staffing Solutions	Toronto, Ontario
9.	EPIC Information Solutions Inc.	Winnipeg, Manitoba
10.	Vista Projects Ltd.	Calgary, Alberta

NEW VENTURE
A recently formed commercial organization that provides goods and/or services for sale.

ENTREPRENEURSHIP
The process of identifying an opportunity in the marketplace and accessing the resources needed to capitalize on it.

ENTREPRENEUR
A business person who accepts both the risks and the opportunities involved in creating and operating a new business venture.

in the 2010 study are shown in Table 10.1. Each of these companies exhibited superiority in employee recognition, managing performance, career opportunities, and organizational reputation.[8]

The new venture/firm

Various criteria can also be used to determine when a new firm comes into existence. Three of the most common are when it was formed, whether it was incorporated, and if it sold goods and/or services.[9] A business is considered to be new if it has become operational within the previous 12 months, if it adopts any of the main organizational forms (proprietorship, partnership, corporation, or co-operative), and if it sells goods or services. Thus, we define a **new venture** as a recently formed commercial organization that provides goods and/or services for sale.

Entrepreneurship

Entrepreneurship is the process of identifying an opportunity in the marketplace and accessing the resources needed to capitalize on that opportunity.[10] People start new businesses because they want to control their own destiny and prefer to take a chance rather than looking for a secure job. **Entrepreneurs** are people who recognize and seize these opportunities. For example, Mark Zuckerberg created Facebook, and in 2010 it had 500 million active users. He is one of the richest people in the world under the age of 30. However, it takes more than a good idea to be successful. Zuckerberg worked long hours, and he is constantly tailoring the website to suit its expanding audience.[11]

Each year, the Heritage Foundation publishes an index of economic freedom, which assesses the extent to which entrepreneurs have freedom to pursue new business opportunities. In 2010, the top three countries were Hong Kong, Singapore,

A common type of small business in Canada is the convenience store. It attracts customers from its immediate area through its long hours of operation and the product lines it carries.

and Australia, with freedom scores of 89.7, 86.1, and 82.6 respectively. Canada ranked seventh with a score of 80.4 and North Korea ranked last with a score of 1.0. Canada now ranks higher than the U.S. partly due to the U.S. government's stimulus spending, which the foundation believes will hurt the U.S. economy's long-term prospects.[12]

Small businesses often provide an environment to use personal attributes— such as creativity—that have come to be associated with entrepreneurs.[13] Because starting a business involves dealing with a great deal of uncertainty, ambiguity, and unpredictability, every new venture founder needs to exercise some of the personal attributes that entrepreneurs are noted for. But do not assume that only small business owners exhibit entrepreneurial characteristics.[14] Many successful managers in large organizations in both the public and private sectors also exhibit similar characteristics. Entrepreneurship therefore occurs in a wide range of contexts: not just in small or new commercial firms, but also in old firms, in large firms, in firms that grow slowly, in firms that grow rapidly, in non-profit organizations, and in the public sector.[15]

People who exhibit entrepreneurial characteristics and create something new within an existing firm or organization are called **intrapreneurs**. One large firm renowned for encouraging intrapreneurship is Proctor & Gamble. It has earned this reputation by having divisions that focus on creating new products for specific markets.[16] The Swiffer product line is one example. Once the basic Swiffer mop was launched successfully, a whole range of products was added, such as the Swiffer WetJet and Swiffer Dusters. A key difference between intrapreneurs and entrepreneurs is that intrapreneurs typically don't have to concern themselves with getting the resources needed to bring the new product to market, since big companies tend to have the necessary resources already available.

INTRAPRENEURS People who create something new within an existing large firm or organization.

As we explore the entrepreneurial process later in the chapter, we will do so within a new-venture context. We begin by outlining the role of small and new businesses in the Canadian economy.

Mark Zuckerberg is the new-age entrepreneur who created Facebook, the hugely successful social networking site.

The role of small and new businesses in the canadian economy

As we will see in this section, small and new businesses play a key role in the Canadian economy. However, the recognition of this role has really only been acknowledged in the last two decades. Previously, large businesses were the focus of attention in terms of economic impact within industrialized nations.

Small businesses

It may surprise you to learn that 97.8 percent of all businesses in Canada are small (they have fewer than 100 employees), and more than half of them have fewer than 5 employees. Medium-sized businesses (100–499 employees) comprise 1.9 percent of employer businesses, and large businesses (those with 500 or more employees) represent just 0.3 percent (see Key 10.1).[17] This pattern is consistent across all provinces. While one large business has many more employees than one small business, as a group, small businesses provide more jobs than large businesses. Small businesses also lead the way when it comes to innovation and new technology.

Ontario and Quebec together account for the largest proportion of business establishments in Canada (about 57 percent), followed by the western provinces (37 percent) and the Atlantic provinces (6 percent). Northwest Territories, Yukon, and Nunavut represent just 0.3 percent of Canada's businesses.[18]

While the previous figures profile the number of businesses in Canada by size, we now look at how many people work in small- versus medium- and large-sized businesses. According to Statistics Canada, there were 10 901 100 **private sector** (companies and organizations not owned or controlled by government) employees in 2010.[19]

The distribution of employment by size of firm varies considerably across industries. Small businesses account for over two-thirds of employment in four industries: non-institutional health care (90 percent), the construction industry (77 percent), other services (73 percent), and accommodation and food (69 percent).[20] In another five industries, at least half of the workforce is employed by small businesses.

PRIVATE SECTOR
The part of the economy that is made up of companies and organizations that are not owned or controlled by the government.

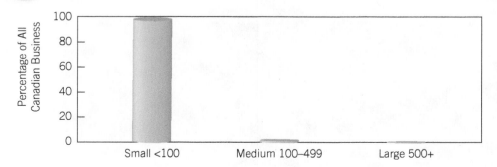

SMALL, MEDIUM, AND LARGE BUSINESSES
AS A PERCENTAGE OF TOTAL BUSINESSES

Key 10.1

Businesses by Size (Number of Employees) Category

- Small <100
- Medium 100–499
- Large 500+

Percentage of All Canadian Business

One increasingly important area is the field of green technologies and green applications for businesses of all sizes. The box entitled "Small Businesses Go Green" provides information on the growing interest around environmental concerns for small business owners.

New ventures

New firms are not only the main source of job creation, they are also responsible for the vast majority of new products and services.[21] In 2007, small business created 100 000 jobs in Canada; this represented 40 percent of all jobs that were created that year. Between 2002 and 2006, approximately 130 000 new small businesses were started each year in Canada. During that same period, an equal number of small businesses ceased operations each year.[22]

More and more women are starting their own small businesses; women now account for half of all new businesses that are formed. According to a recent Statistics Canada report, there are about 877 000 women entrepreneurs in Canada, and 47 percent of small- and medium-sized enterprises have some degree of female ownership.[23] For example, Kyla Eaglesham, the owner of Madeleines Cherry Pie and Ice Cream Parlour, left her job as a flight attendant and opened her dessert café in Toronto's trendy Annex neighbourhood. The store attracts customers who want "a little bit of cottage country in the city."[24] However, women lead only 12 percent of the small- and medium-sized businesses that export goods and services.[25]

Female entrepreneurs are honoured each year at the Canadian Woman Entrepreneur Awards. Previous winners included Cora Tsouflidou (Montreal-based Cora Franchise Group), Teresa Coady (Vancouver-based Bunting Coady Architects), and Yvonne Tollens (Okotoks, Alberta–based ComputerAid Professional Services).[26]

Women who run businesses from their homes are sometimes called "mompreneurs."[27] The Mompreneur Networking Group organizes seminars and publishes *Mompreneur*, a free magazine that helps women who want to start a business. More information on mompreneurs is provided in Video Case I-1 and the Entrepreneurship and New Ventures box below.

Many young entrepreneurs are also involved in creating new ventures in Canada. Consider the following examples:

- Daisy and Adam Orser were among the winners of the BDC Young Entrepreneurs Award in 2009 for their Victoria, B.C.–based company called The Root Cellar Village Green Grocer. They are capitalizing on the movement for fresh local produce and healthier lifestyles. The company already employees 50 people and the future looks bright.[28]

- The Ben Barry Agency is an Ottawa-based modelling businesses that promotes models who are considered unorthodox—various sizes and ages, different racial backgrounds, and those who have physical disabilities. The models have appeared in government advertising campaigns and on fashion runways in shopping malls. Barry works with company management to define their clientele and then chooses models who will best reflect the store's typical shoppers.[29]

- Tell Us About Us (TUAU) is a Winnipeg-based company specializing in market research and customer satisfaction programs. Owners Tyler Gompf and Scott Griffith recently signed a seven-figure deal to provide mystery shopper service to Dunkin' Donuts, Baskin-Robbins, and Togo's in the United States and Canada. The mystery shoppers will note any problems at a retail site and TUAU will then measure how quickly the problems are fixed.[30]

the Greening of Business

Small Businesses Go Green

Small business owners have plenty of operational problems that demand their attention, so they often don't spend enough time thinking about how their company could become more eco-friendly. Even if they did find the time, they might think that they couldn't afford to go green. But there are a lot of inexpensive ways that small business owners can show concern for the environment.

Simple things like changing to energy-efficient lighting and turning off photocopiers and computers overnight is a good start. The energy departments of most provinces have websites that provide information on how companies can save money by using water and energy more efficiently. For more aggressive or longer-term projects, small business owners can access the federal government's ecoACTION program website, which contains information about programs that help organizations reduce energy costs. The ecoENERGY retrofit program, for example, provides financial incentives of up to 25 percent of project costs to help small and medium-sized companies implement energy-saving projects.

Saving energy is just one possible area for improvement. There are also many other ideas that small business owners can implement, such as using recycled paper, eco-friendly cleaning supplies, and pens made of compostable material instead of plastic. And employees can be encouraged to organize car pools, bicycle to work, or use public transit.

Green Enterprise Ontario (GEO) is a group of eco-minded businesses that pay $199 each year to belong to a network where they can trade business, advice, and referrals. All of the businesses in the group are committed to activities such as sustainable purchasing, manufacturing, and recycling of products. GEO runs regular workshops on topics of importance to small businesses—for example, finance and marketing—but it also offers information on environment and social responsibility initiatives. Chris Lowry, the coordinator of the Toronto affiliate, says that many small business owners have become interested in going green after being asked "uncomfortable" questions by their children and staff members about why they aren't doing more for the environment. Small business owners are also starting to respond to social pressure from customers.

Critical Thinking Questions

1. Find a small business in your local area that is committed to being eco-friendly. Why did the owner decide to commit to having an eco-friendly business?

2. Consider the following statement: *"It is unrealistic to expect small business owners to spend much time thinking about or implementing green practices. The failure rate of small businesses is high, so small business owners have to focus all their energies on trying to ensure the survival of their businesses. They simply don't have the time (or money) to 'go green.'"* Do you agree or disagree with the statement? Explain your reasoning.

entrepreneurship and
New Ventures

Spotlight on Mompreneurs

An increasing number of Canadian women have decided to be stay-at-home entrepreneurs (called mompreneurs). Most of them aren't trying to be supermoms that can do everything; rather, they want to use their skills to run a business and at the same time achieve a better work-life balance. Here are some of their interesting success stories.

Laughing Belly Productions

Shirley Broback won the SavvyMom Entrepreneur of the Year Award in 2009. She earned the acknowledgement for her work in organizing the Vancouver Island Baby Fair. Shirley has put her event planning background to good use. She designs these events to provide an enjoyable family experience while providing marketing opportunities for companies that cater to the needs of pregnant women and children from birth to pre-school age.

More and more women, like Shirley Broback, are starting and successfully operating their own small businesses. They now account for half of all new businesses that are formed.

Sweetpea Baby Food

Erin Green and Tamar Wagman started their frozen baby food company from scratch and now their organic products are distributed in over 350 stores nationally with revenues that exceed $500 000. Part of their strategy focuses on an ambassador program for women from across Canada enlisted to make Sweatpea Baby Food a success. This grassroots approach makes a lot of sense. Moms love to talk about how they deal with their little ones; in return, Sweetpea provides organic products to moms as they spread the word in their yoga classes and baby groups.

Spoon Fed Soup

Carmie Nearing of Calgary had a career as a chef, but found the hours she needed to work didn't fit with raising children. She quit and got a 9-to-5 job. But that didn't satisfy her, so she decided to start her own company—called Spoon Fed Soup—to provide gourmet soups to customers. Nearing found that as her business grew, she had to hire employees and spend more and more time dealing with customers. She now realizes that she has a passion for entrepreneurship that goes beyond the simple desire to stay at home with her children.

Green Please! Inc.

Melanie Derwin of Winnipeg became interested in green living when her 20-month-old son's repeated ear and throat infections were not helped by standard antibiotics. She eventually founded Green Please! Inc., a company that provides customers with suggestions for "greening up" their lifestyle. Her company is an e-boutique offering products like bamboo crib sheets, organic cotton rattles, non-toxic toys, and organic soaps. Melanie operates on the principle that it is better to be proactive than reactive about health problems.

Some observers of the mompreneur trend have noted that things are not always as positive as they seem. Barbara Orser, a management professor at the University of Ottawa's School of Management, says that most mompreneurs work long hours, run low-growth businesses, don't make much money, and don't get benefits. She cites a Statistics Canada report showing that only 17 percent of self-employed women earn more than $30 000 per year. In spite of this, increasing numbers of women are becoming mompreneurs.

Critical Thinking Questions

1. What is the difference between small business and entrepreneurship? Are mompreneurs entrepreneurs? Explain.

2. Interview a mompreneur and ask the following questions: (a) Why did you start your business? (b) What are the advantages and disadvantages of being a mompreneur?

The entrepreneurial process

The entrepreneurial process is like a journey (see Key 10.2). It is influenced by the social, economic, political, and technological factors in the broader environment, but we will focus our attention on understanding the three key elements in the entrepreneurial process—the entrepreneur, the opportunity, and resources—and how they interact. As these key elements interact, they may be mismatched or well matched. For example, if an entrepreneur identifies an opportunity for a new health service but does not have the relevant background and skills to deliver the service, the business may never get off the ground. Conversely, if all three process elements are well matched, the new business will likely become operational at some point.

Since the entrepreneur is at the heart of the entrepreneurial process, considerable attention has been paid to identifying the personal characteristics of entrepreneurs. Research shows that these characteristics are wide-ranging. Some are behavioural (e.g., taking initiative), others are personality traits (e.g., independence), and still others are skills (e.g., problem-solving).[31] Some people think that entrepreneurs are rare; however, entrepreneurial characteristics have been found to be widely distributed in the population.[32] We also know that personal characteristics often have less impact on a person's action than the situation a person is in.[33] What is really important is not who the person *is* but what the person *does*.[34] Entrepreneurs must (1) identify an opportunity and (2) access resources.

Identifying opportunities

Identifying opportunities involves generating ideas for new (or improved) products, processes, or services, screening those ideas, and developing the best ones.

THE ENTREPRENEURIAL PROCESS
IN A NEW VENTURE CONTEXT

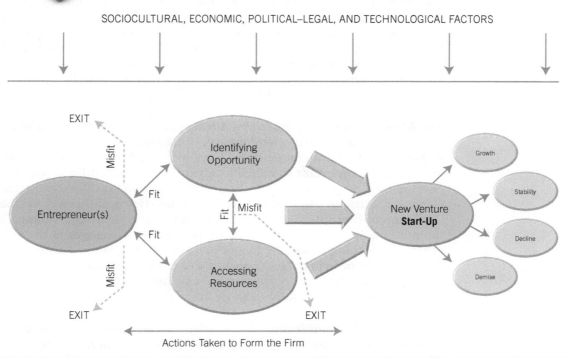

SOCIOCULTURAL, ECONOMIC, POLITICAL–LEGAL, AND TECHNOLOGICAL FACTORS

EXIT

Misfit

Entrepreneur(s)

Fit

Fit

Identifying Opportunity

Fit   Misfit

Misfit

Accessing Resources

New Venture **Start-Up**

Growth

Stability

Decline

Demise

EXIT

EXIT

Actions Taken to Form the Firm

Idea generation

Typically, generating ideas involves abandoning traditional assumptions about how things work and how they ought to be, and seeing what others do not. If the prospective new (or improved) product, process, or service can be profitably produced and is attractive relative to other potential venture ideas, it might present an opportunity.

Where do ideas come from? Most new ventures do not emerge from a deliberate search for viable business ideas. Rather, the majority originate from events relating to work or everyday life.[35] In fact, work experience is the most common source of ideas, accounting for 45 to 85 percent of those generated. This happens because as employees of a company, prospective entrepreneurs are familiar with the product or service, the customers, the suppliers, and the competitors. They are also aware of marketplace needs, can relate those needs to personal capabilities, and can determine whether they are capable of producing products or services that can fill the void.

Other frequent sources of new venture ideas include a personal interest/hobby (16 percent) or a chance happening (11 percent).[36] A chance happening refers to a situation in which a venture idea comes about unexpectedly. For example, while on vacation in another country you might try a new snack food that you feel would be in demand if introduced to the Canadian market.

Screening

Entrepreneurs often generate many ideas, and screening them is a key part of the entrepreneurial process. The faster you can weed out the "dead-end" venture ideas, the more time and effort you can devote to the ones that remain.

The more of the following characteristics that an idea has, the greater the opportunity it presents.

The Idea Creates or Adds Value for the Customer A product or service that creates or adds value for the customer is one that solves a significant problem, or meets a significant need in new or different ways. Consider Sally Fox's idea for eliminating the dyeing process in textile operations.[37] By cross-breeding long-fibre white cotton and short-fibre coloured cotton she developed FoxFibre, an environmentally friendly new cotton fibre that is naturally grown in several colours and is long enough to be spun commercially.

The Idea Provides a Competitive Advantage That Can Be Sustained A competitive advantage exists when potential customers see the product or service as better than that of competitors. Toronto-based Sentinelle Medical is counting on a very important sustainable advantage. Cameron Piron spent 10 years developing a better cancer detection technology and another two years to get General Electric to use it in its MRI machines. He recently received the Ontario Government Innovation Award.[38] Sustaining a competitive advantage involves maintaining it in the face of competitors' actions or changes in the industry. All other things being equal, the longer markets are in a state of flux, the greater the likelihood of being able to sustain a competitive advantage. The absence of a competitive advantage or developing a competitive advantage that is not sustainable constitute two fatal flaws of many new ventures.[39]

The Idea Is Marketable and Financially Viable While it is important to determine whether there are enough customers who are willing to buy the product or service, it is also important to determine whether sales will lead to profits.[40] Estimating the market demand requires an initial understanding of who the customers are, what their needs are, and how the product or service will satisfy their needs better than competitors' products will. It also requires a thorough understanding of the key competitors who can provide similar products, services, or benefits to the target customer. For example, 10 years ago few people thought that manufacturers of cellphones would be competitors of camera manufacturers in providing real-time photos through digital imaging. Customers define the competition in terms of who can best satisfy their needs.

After learning about the competition and customers, the entrepreneur must prepare a **sales forecast** which is an estimate of how much of a product or service will be purchased by the prospective customers for a specific period of time—typically one year. Total sales revenue is estimated by multiplying the units expected to be sold by the selling price. The sales forecast forms the foundation for determining the financial viability of the venture and the resources needed to start it.

Determining financial viability involves preparing financial forecasts, which are two- to three-year projections of a venture's future financial position and performance. They typically consist of an estimate of *start-up costs, a cash budget, an income statement*, and a balance sheet. These projections serve as the basis for decisions regarding whether to proceed with the venture, and, if so, the amount and type of financing to be used in financing the new business.

The Idea Has Low Exit Costs The final consideration is the venture's exit costs. Exit costs are low if a venture can be shut down without a significant loss of time, money, or reputation.[41] If a venture is not expected to make a profit for a number of years, its exit costs are high, since the project cannot be reasonably abandoned in the short term. For example, Toronto-based zero-emission car manufacturer Zenn Motors has very-long-term projections. On the

SALES FORECAST
An estimate of how much of a product or service will be purchased by prospective customers over a specific period.

other hand, if the venture is expected to make a profit quickly, its exit costs will be lower, making the idea more attractive.

Developing the opportunity

As the "dead-end" venture ideas are weeded out, a clear notion of the business concept and an entry strategy for pursuing it must be developed. The business concept often changes from what was originally envisioned. Some new ventures develop entirely new markets, products, and sources of competitive advantage once the needs of the marketplace and the economies of the business are better understood. So, while a vision of what is to be achieved is important, it is equally important to be responsive to new information and to be on the lookout for unanticipated opportunities. For example, if customers are not placing orders it is important to find out why and make adjustments.

New ventures use one or more of three main entry strategies: they introduce a totally new product or service; they introduce a product or service that will compete directly with existing competitive offerings but adds a new twist (customization of the standard product); or they franchise.[42] A franchise is an arrangement in which a buyer (franchisee) purchases the right to sell the product or service of the seller (franchiser). We discuss franchising in more detail later in the chapter.

> FRANCHISE
> An arrangement that gives franchisees (buyers) the right to sell the product of the franchiser (the seller).

When capital requirements are high, such as when a manufacturing operation is being proposed, there is a need for considerable research and planning. Similarly, if product development or operations are fairly complex, research and analysis will be needed to ensure that the costs associated with effectively coordinating tasks will be minimized. In these circumstances, or when the aim is to attract potential investors, a comprehensive written business plan is required. A business plan is a document that describes the entrepreneur's proposed business venture; explains why it is an opportunity; and outlines its marketing plan, its operational and financial details, and its managers' skills and abilities.[43] The contents of a business plan are shown in Table 10.2.

> BUSINESS PLAN
> Document in which the entrepreneur summarizes her or his business strategy for the proposed new venture and how that strategy will be implemented.

If market conditions are changing rapidly, the benefits gained from extensive research and planning diminish quickly. By the time the entrepreneur is ready to start, new competitors may have entered the market, prices may have changed, a location may no longer be available, and so on. Similarly, if the product is highly innovative, market research is of less value, since the development of entirely new products involves *creating* needs and wants rather than simply responding to existing needs. Consequently, measuring the capacity of the product or service to fill existing customer needs or wants is less critical.

Contrary to what many people think, planning does not have to be completed before action is taken. For example, if an electrical contracting business is being proposed in an area where there is a shortage of tradespeople, it would be important to seek out qualified employees prior to conducting other analyses that are needed to complete the business plan. Such early action also helps to build relationships that can be drawn on later. Obviously, some ventures do not lend themselves to early action, particularly those that are capital intensive. Since most entrepreneurs have limited resources, it is important to concentrate on the issues that can be dealt with, *and* that will help determine whether to proceed and how to proceed.[44]

Accessing resources

Typically, entrepreneurs acquire the various resources needed to make the venture a reality by bootstrapping, which means "doing more with less." Usually the term refers to financing techniques whereby entrepreneurs make do with as few resources as possible and use other peoples' resources wherever they

> BOOTSTRAPPING
> Doing more with less.

Table 10.2 A Business Plan

A well-written business plan is formally structured, easy to read, and avoids confusion. Organizing the information into sections makes it more manageable. The amount of detail and the order of presentation may vary from one venture to another and according to the intended audience (if the plan is intended for potential investors it will require more detail than if it is intended for internal use by the entrepreneur). An outline for a standard business plan is provided below.

I.	**Cover Page:** Name of venture and owners, date prepared, contact person, his/her address, telephone and fax numbers, email address, Facebook link, and the name of the organization the plan is being presented to. The easier it is for the reader to contact the entrepreneur, the more likely the contact will occur.
II.	**Executive Summary:** A one- to three-page overview of the total business plan. Written after the other sections are completed, it highlights their significant points, and aims to create enough excitement to motivate the reader to continue.
III.	**Table of Contents:** This element lists major sections with page numbers for both the body and the appendices of the plan.
IV.	**Company Description:** Identifies the type of company: manufacturing, retail, etc. It also describes the proposed form of organization: sole proprietorship, partnership, corporation, or co-operative. A typical organization of this section is as follows: name and location; company objectives; nature and primary product or service of the business; current status (start-up, buyout, or expansion) and history, if applicable; and legal form of organization.
V.	**Product or Service Description:** Describes the product or service and indicates what is unique about it. This section explains the value that is added for customers—why people will buy the product or service; features of the product or service providing a competitive advantage; legal protection (patents, copyrights, trademarks, if relevant); and dangers of technical or style obsolescence.
VI.	**Marketing:** This section has two key parts, the market analysis and the marketing plan. The market analysis convinces the reader that the entrepreneur understands the market for the product or service and can deal effectively with the competition to achieve sales projections. The marketing plan explains the strategy for achieving sales projections.
VII.	**Operating Plan:** Explains the type of manufacturing or operating system to be used. Describes the facilities, labour, raw materials, and processing requirements.
VIII.	**Management:** Identifies the key players—the management team, active investors, and directors—and cites the experience and competence they possess. This section includes a description of the management team, outside investors and directors and their qualifications, outside resource people, and plans for recruiting and training employees.
IX.	**Financial Plan:** Specifies financial needs and expected financing sources. Presents projected financial statements, including cash budget, balance sheet, and income statement.
X.	**Supporting Details/Appendix:** Provides supplementary materials to the plan such as resumés and other supporting data.

can. However, bootstrapping can also refer to the acquisition of other types of resources, such as people, space, equipment, or materials that are loaned or provided free by customers or suppliers.

Financial resources

There are two main types of financing—*debt* and *equity*. Since a business is at its riskiest point during the start-up phase, equity is usually more appropriate and accessible than debt. However, most new venture founders prefer debt because they are reluctant to give up any control to outsiders. To obtain debt financing, the entrepreneur must have an adequate equity investment in the business—typically 20 percent of the business's value—and collateral (or security).

Collateral refers to items (assets) owned by the business (such as a building and equipment) or by the individual (such as a house or car) that the borrower uses to secure a loan or other credit. These items can be seized by the lender if the loan isn't repaid according to the specified terms. To lenders,

COLLATERAL
Assets that a borrower uses to secure a loan or other credit, and that are subject to seizure by the lender if the loan isn't repaid according to the specified repayment terms.

Entrepreneurs who want to obtain financing for a start-up business must have collateral such as a house or car in order to get a loan. Would you be willing to give your house or car as collateral, knowing that if you couldn't repay the loan the bank would take your house or car?

equity investment demonstrates the commitment of the entrepreneur, as individuals tend to be more committed to a venture if they have a substantial portion of what they own invested in it.

The most common sources of *equity* financing include:

1. *Personal savings.* New venture founders draw heavily on their own finances to start their businesses. Most save as much as they can in preparation for start-up.

2. *Love money.* This type of financing includes investments from friends, relatives, and business associates. It is called "love money" because it is often given more on the basis of the relationship than on the merit of the business concept.

3. *Private investors.* One popular source of equity capital is informal capital from private investors called *angels*. Usually, these investors are financially well off individuals; many are successful entrepreneurs who wish to recycle their wealth by investing in new businesses. For example, Saxx & Co. makes high-performance men's underwear. The company was started by Trent Kitsch, who developed the idea as part of a project requirement in his MBA program. He put $18 000 of his own money into the company, but he needed a major cash injection to compete with the bigger companies in the industry. Eventually, he received $50 000 from a private investor in return for a 5 percent ownership stake in the business. Kitsch wants to get an additional $500 000, and he is willing to give an investor 15 percent of the business. He also wants a mentor who has experience in the business.[45]

4. *Venture capitalists.* Investments by venture capitalists come from professionally managed pools of investor money (venture capital). Since the risk of receiving little or no return on investment is high, only deals that present an attractive, high-growth business opportunity with a return between 35 and 50 percent are considered. Very few new ventures meet this criterion. Venture capital investment in Canada dropped to $1 billion in 2009—the lowest level in about 15 years—so angels are becoming more important in providing start-up money to entrepreneurs.[46] In a move to improve the environment and increase financing options, the Canadian government reduced red-tape hurdles for foreign venture capital firms to invest in Canada. Among other things, it eliminated a punitive 25 percent tax on capital gains aimed at foreign investors. This is good news for firms looking at the venture capital route.[47]

The most common sources of *debt* financing include:

1. *Financial institutions.* While commercial banks are the main providers of debt financing for established small businesses, it is usually difficult for a new business to borrow from a bank. Banks are risk averse, and loans to new businesses are considered very risky, largely because the business has yet to establish its ability to repay the loan. Typically, entrepreneurs have more luck obtaining financing for a new venture with a personal loan (as opposed to a business loan). The most common way to obtain a personal loan is to mortgage a house or borrow against the cash value of a life insurance policy. In addition to commercial banks, other sources of debt financing include trust companies, co-operatives, finance companies, equipment companies, credit unions, and government agencies. Since finance companies lend in high-risk situations, their interestrates tend to be high.

2. *Suppliers.* Another source of financing is suppliers who provide goods (e.g., inventory) or services to the entrepreneur with an agreement to bill them later. This is referred to as *trade credit*. Trade credit can be helpful in getting started, because inventory can be acquired without paying cash, freeing up money to pay other start-up costs. This type of financing is short term; 30 days is the usual payback period. The amount of trade credit available to a new firm depends on the type of business and the supplier's confidence in the firm. Frequently, though, a new business has trouble getting trade credit since its capacity to repay has not been demonstrated.

Besides these conventional sources of financing, the possibilities for bootstrap financing are endless. For example, an entrepreneur might require an advance payment from customers. Equipment can be leased rather than purchased (which reduces the risk of obsolete equipment). Office furniture can be rented, premises can be shared, and manufacturing can be subcontracted, thereby avoiding the expense of procuring material, equipment, and facilities. All of these activities free up cash that can then be used for other purposes.

Other resources

Businesses have other resources to help them with financing, legal, marketing, or operational advice or support. The federal and provincial governments have a wide range of financial assistance programs for small businesses. Among the various forms of assistance are low-interest loans, loan guarantees, interest-free loans, and wage subsidies. We examine three sources of information and assistance below: Business Development Bank of Canada, business incubators, and the internet.

Business Development Bank of Canada The Business Development Bank of Canada (BDC) has a mandate to help develop Canadian businesses, with a particular focus on small- and medium-sized companies. It provides financing, venture capital, and consulting strategies. The BDC provides services to over 28 000 businesses from coast to coast and serves them through over 100 branch offices. The BDC is a financial institution wholly owned by the Government of Canada. Information can be found at www.bdc.ca or by calling 1-877-BDC-Banx.[48]

Incubators Business incubators provide new businesses (newborns) with support to help nurture them into a successful future. The type of support varies but some key forms of assistance include consulting services, legal advice, accounting services, business contacts, clerical services, and office space. According to the Canadian Association of Business Incubation (CABI), business survival rates are greatly improved by getting involved with an incubator. Survival rates after five years stand at about 80 percent, which is far above the average rates for businesses that don't use incubators. You can learn more by visiting www.cabi.ca. Take a look at Table 10.3 for examples of incubators across the country.

> INCUBATORS
> Facilities that support small businesses during their early growth phase by providing basic services, office space, legal advice and more.

The Internet There are countless resources available online that can help budding entrepreneurs gather research information, write a business plan, and access government grants. The banks all have major sites dedicated to small business and entrepreneurship resources. For example, Royal Bank of Canada (RBC) has a great site that provides checklists, business plan formats and samples, and advice on selecting business structures and more (www.rbcroyalbank.com/sme/index.html). There are also government sites such as the Canada Business Services for Entrepreneurs dedicated to providing information and advice on every aspect of starting a business, including accessing government grants (www.canadabusiness.ca/eng/).

Building the right team

A business may be owned by one person, but entrepreneurship is not a solo process. As we have just seen, there are various stakeholders who can provide resources to the venture. When ownership is shared, decisions must be made regarding who to share it with, how much each stakeholder will own, at what cost, and under what conditions. The form of legal organization chosen affects whether ownership can be shared and whether resources can be accessed.

Table 10.3 Business Incubators Across Canada

NAME	LOCATION
NRC Institute for Fuel Cell Innovation	Victoria, British Columbia
Duncan McNeill Centre for Innovation	Edmonton, Alberta
Smart Virtual Incubation Winnipeg	Winnipeg, Manitoba
AgriTech Park	Truro, Nova Scotia
The Venture Centre	Pasadena, Newfoundland
NRC Institute for Information Technology	Fredericton, New Brunswick
Mississauga Technology Business Accelerator	Mississauga, Ontario
Saskatchewan Ideas Inc.	Saskatoon, Saskatchewan
J.-Armand-Bombardier Incubator	Montreal, Quebec
LaunchPad Incubator Facility in the Atlantic Technology Centre	Charlottetown, Prince Edward Island

Deciding whether to share ownership by forming a *venture team* involves consideration of two main issues:

- ■ ***The size and scope of the venture***—How many people does the venture require? Is it a one-person operation or does it need contributions from others? Can people be hired to fill the key roles as they are required?

- ■ ***Personal competencies***—What are the talents, know-how, skills, track record, contacts, and resources that the entrepreneur brings to the venture? How do these match with what the venture needs to succeed?

The nature of the team depends upon the match between the lead entrepreneur and the opportunity and how fast and aggressively he or she plans to proceed. Most teams tend to be formed in one of two ways: (1) one person has an idea (or wants to start a business), and then several associates join the team in the first few years of operation, or (2) an entire team is formed at the outset based on such factors as a shared idea, a friendship, or an experience.

The ideal team consists of people with complementary skills covering the key success areas for the business (i.e., marketing, finance, production). Small founding teams tend to work better than big ones. It is quite common for the initial team to consist of just two people—a craftsperson and a salesperson.

If the entrepreneur does not intend to establish a high-growth venture, going solo may be a realistic option. Some new venture founders bring on additional team members only as the business can afford them. Most successful solo businesses are simple types of ventures, such as small retail stores or services.[49] The odds for survival, growth, profitability, and attracting capital are increased by a team approach.[50] Read the E-Business and Social Media Solutions case "New Age Entrepreneurs" to learn about the team and the challenges behind the popular site.

Assessing the "fit" between elements in the entrepreneurial process

Assessing the "fit" between the various elements in the entrepreneurial process is an ongoing task, since the shape of the opportunity, and consequently the resources and people needed to capitalize on it, typically changes as it is developed. It is the entrepreneur who stands to gain the most by attending to these "fits" and any changes they may require, although other stakeholders, such as investors, will be considering them as well.

The entrepreneur–opportunity fit

The first assessment of fit is between the entrepreneur and the opportunity. The entrepreneur needs to decide whether the opportunity is something he or she *can do* and *wants to do*. A realistic self-assessment is important. Prospective ventures that are of limited personal interest and require skills and abilities that do not fit well with those of the entrepreneur should be quickly eliminated. For example, it does little good to identify an opportunity for an ecotourism business in a wilderness area if the entrepreneur loves city life and hates spending time outdoors.

Once the entrepreneur has chosen the opportunity he or she wants to pursue, the success of the venture depends heavily upon the individual or individuals involved. No matter how good the product or service concept is, as the opportunity changes shape it may demand skills a single entrepreneur lacks. This may prompt a decision either to acquire the needed skills by forming a team or by getting further training.

New Age Entrepreneurs: The Rise of Twitter

Entrepreneurs have effective new promotion tools thanks to social media sites. But what about the entrepreneurs who created these new information highways? Biz Stone, Jack Dorsey, and Evan Williams created and launched Twitter, the micro-blogging site, in 2006. Before Twitter, Biz Stone helped launch Blogger, Odeo, Obvious, and Xanga. He is a blogging expert who has written two books on the subject. Jack Dorsey is the inventor on the software side of the business and Evan Williams is an entrepreneur who also built internet start-ups like Pyra Labs. A good team, a good idea, and a lot of entrepreneurial spirit, and the next thing you know "tweet" and "re-tweet" are part of our everyday lexicon.

So why is Twitter so popular? It is an instantaneous source of information (not all of it useful) deli-vered 140 characters at a time. As the website states, it allows you to stay informed on the issues that matter most to you. Today, Twitter is heavily promoting business applications complete with cases in a section called Twitter 101 for Businesses. You can read all about some of the showcase companies. For example, Best Buy has set up "real-time twelp" for instantaneous customer feedback from their "twelp force"; customers send queries to Best Buy's famous technical "geek squad" and receive quick answers to problems. There are YouTube video demonstrations to provide insight on how to maximize Twitter for small business applications. Of course, Twitter can also be used to spread negative word of mouth about organizations, so Best Buy's proactive engaging approach is quite intelligent.

Popularity does not necessarily translate into profitability. Biz Stone has faced tough questions from reporters, analysts, and even comedians. While appearing on the Stephen Colbert show, the host mocked him by joking that Biz is obviously not short for "business model." The crowd laughed and he smiled, but the issue behind the joke was very real. Popularity is great, but popularity does not pay the bills. You need a business model that can generate profits. In 2010, Twitter executives announced the creation of "promoted tweets," which enable companies to pay for their messages to be displayed in a more prominent manner on the site while providing Twitter with a new revenue stream. Starbucks and Red Bull were among the first companies to sign up. Even before this decision, companies were using Twitter's social power. Molson used Twitter to help launch Molson 67 and create pre-launch buzz. Authors and musicians use the site to generate buzz. Now Twitter appears ready to cash in on its success. Is this the beginning of sustainable revenues for Twitter? Will the tweeting masses object? It will be interesting to see how this business model evolves.

Critical Thinking Question

1. Are you in favour of promoted tweets? Debate Twitter's decision to implement this model.

The opportunity–resources fit

Assessing the opportunity–resources fit involves determining whether the resources needed to capitalize on the opportunity can be acquired. As the opportunity changes shape, so will the resource requirements. When challenges or risks arise, the aim is to determine whether they can be resolved and to deal with them quickly. For example, if the venture requires a greater financial investment than originally anticipated, this does not necessarily mean that the venture should be abandoned. Other options such as taking on partners or leasing rather than building a facility may be viable. Of course, some ventures may not be viable regardless of the alternatives considered.

The entrepreneur–resources fit

Once the resource requirements of the venture have been determined, the entrepreneur needs to assess whether he or she has the capacity to meet those requirements. For example, an entrepreneur with a stellar reputation for software development will have an easier time attracting employees for a venture specializing in software than someone with no track record. If that same entrepreneur is well connected with people in the industry, he or she will be more likely to gain commitments from customers, and in turn, investors.

Start-up and beyond

Entrepreneurs must make the right start-up decisions, but they must also pay attention to how the business will be run once it is started. In this section, we examine three important topics that are relevant to these issues. First, we describe the three main ways that entrepreneurs start up a small business. Next, we look at the four main organizing options that are available to entrepreneurs. We conclude the chapter with a look at the reasons for success and failure in small business.

Starting up a small business

Most entrepreneurs start up a small business in one of three ways: they start from scratch, they buy an existing business, or they buy a franchise. We have already examined the "starting from scratch" alternative in detail in the preceding section, so we turn now to the latter two alternatives.

Buying an existing business

About one-third of all new businesses that were started in the past decade were bought from someone else. Many experts recommend buying an existing business because it increases the likelihood of success; it has already proven its ability to attract customers and has established relationships with lenders, suppliers, and other stakeholders. The track record also gives potential buyers a clearer picture of what to expect than any estimate of a new business's prospects.

But an entrepreneur who buys someone else's business may not be able to avoid certain problems. For example, there may be uncertainty about the exact financial shape the business is in, the business may have a poor reputation, the location may be poor, or it may be difficult to determine an appropriate purchase price.

Taking Over a Family Business A special case of buying an existing business involves family businesses. Taking over a family business poses both opportunities and challenges. On the positive side, a family business can provide otherwise unobtainable financial and management resources; it often has a valuable reputation that can result in important community and business relationships; employee loyalty is often high; and an interested, unified family management and shareholders group may emerge. Toronto-based hosiery manufacturer Phantom Industries Inc. is an example of a family-owned business that has been successful through three generations of family members.[51]

On the other hand, major problems can arise in family businesses. There may be disagreements over which family members assume control. If the parent sells his or her interest in the business, the price to be paid may be an issue. The expectation of other family members may also be problematic. Some family members may feel that they have a right to a job, promotion, and impressive title simply because they are part of the family.[52] Choosing an appropriate successor is a key issue for continuity and it is vital to carefully groom successors over time. Finally, handling disagreements among family members about the future of the business can be a challenge. How do you fire a loved one if things are not working out?[53]

Buying a franchise

If you drive around any canadian town or city, you will notice retail outlets with names like McDonald's, Pizza Pizza, Re/Max, Canadian Tire, Chez Cora, Comfort Inn, Second Cup, and Tim Hortons. These diverse businesses all have one thing in common: they are all franchises, operating under licences issued by parent companies to local entrepreneurs who own and manage them.

A **franchising agreement** outlines the duties and responsibilities of each party. It stipulates the amount and type of payment that franchisees must make to the franchiser. These franchise agreements have become increasingly complicated; they are often 60 or even 100 pages long. Tim Hortons avoids this trend with a streamlined contract of about 26 pages.[54] Franchisees usually make an initial payment for the right to operate an outlet. They also make royalty payment to the franchiser ranging from 2 to 30 percent of the franchisee's annual revenues or profits. The franchisee may also pay an advertising fee to the franchiser. Franchise fees vary widely, from $23 500 for a Mad Science franchise, to over $1 million for a Burger King franchise, to hundreds of millions for a professional sports franchise.

Franchising is very popular in Canada. It offers individuals who want to run their own business an opportunity to establish themselves quickly in a local market.

FRANCHISING AGREEMENT Stipulates the duties and responsibilities of the franchisee and the franchiser.

The Advantages of Franchising Both franchisers and franchisees benefit from the franchising way of doing business (see Table 10.4).

Table 10.4   The Benefits of Franchising

FOR THE FRANCHISER	FOR THE FRANCHISEE
• The franchiser can attain rapid growth for the chain by signing up many franchisees in many different locations.	• Franchisees own a small business that has access to big business management skills.
• Franchisees share in the cost of advertising.	• The franchisee does not have to build up a business from scratch.
• The franchiser benefits from the investment money provided by franchisees.	• Franchisee failure rates are lower than when starting one's own business.
• Advertising money is spent more efficiently.	• A well-advertised brand name comes with the franchise and the franchisee's outlet is instantly recognizable.
• Franchisees are motivated to work hard for themselves, which creates profit for the franchiser.	• The franchiser may send the franchisee to a training program run by the franchiser (e.g., the Canadian Institute of Hamburgerology run by McDonald's).
• The franchiser is freed from all details of a local operation, which are handled by the franchisee.	• The franchiser may visit the franchisee and provide expert advice on how to run the business.
	• Economies in buying allow franchisees to get lower prices for the raw materials they must purchase.
	• Financial assistance is provided by the franchiser in the form of loans; the franchiser may also help the franchisee obtain loans from local sources.
	• Franchisees are their own bosses and get to keep most of the profit they make.

The Disadvantages of Franchising There are always two sides to any story. Table 10.4 clearly outlines the obvious advantages. However, many experienced people will tell you that buying a franchise is like buying a job. The agreements are long because franchisers want to protect their image and recipes, and they want franchisees to abide by their rules. If they don't, they may be sued. If you have a great new breakfast menu idea for your store and have creative promotional ideas, then franchising may not be for you. If things go well it can be lucrative, but it is important to do your homework because there are many disappointed franchise owners out there. For example, you should carefully read the agreement and ensure that your territory is protected and that you have the right of first refusal on new potential stores within a certain distance (e.g., 10–15 kilometres or exclusivity of your particular town). Some franchisees have been shocked to see their franchiser place a new franchisee a few blocks away or even across the street. Franchisees can benefit from support and advertising, but that does not come for free. For example, a Harvey's franchisee pays a 5 percent royalty fee and a 4 percent advertising fee (based on gross sales), and these fees are payable each week in addition to regular operating costs and rent.[55] There are plenty of franchisees who belong to popular chains that are barely surviving and are wondering whatever happened to that promised success.

Is Franchising for You? Do you think you would be happy being a franchisee? The answer depends on a number of factors, including your willingness to work hard, your ability to find a good franchise to buy, and the financial resources you possess. If you are thinking seriously of going into franchising, you should consider several areas of costs that you will incur:

- ▶ the franchise sales price
- ▶ expenses that will be incurred before the business opens
- ▶ training expenses
- ▶ operational expenses for the first six months
- ▶ personal financial needs for the first six months
- ▶ emergency needs

Table 10.5 lists some helpful websites for potential franchisees.

Table 10.5 Helpful Websites for Potential Franchisees

www.betheboss.ca	BeTheBoss.ca is an information and resource directory for buying a franchise in Canada.
www.cfa.ca	The Canadian Franchise Association (CFA) educates Canadians about franchising, specific franchise opportunities, and proper due diligence.
www.canadabusiness.ca/eng	Canada Business offers government services for entrepreneurs, information about grants and loans, and links to many other resources.
www.entrepreneur.com/franchises/index.html	Entrepreneur.com's Franchise Zone allows users to search a directory of franchising opportunities and provides tips on buying a franchise. This site also ranks the top franchises in terms of growth, cost, global appeal, and other aspects.
www.franchise.org	The International Franchise Association provides answers to frequently asked questions about franchising and resources for potential and current franchisees. This site also hosts a directory of franchising opportunities in various industries.
www.franchiseinfo.ca	*Canadian Business Franchise Magazine* (online edition) offers a unique, behind-the-scenes look at those entrepreneurs who have embraced the franchise lifestyle.

Forms of business ownership

Whether they intend to run small farms, large factories, or online e-tailers, entrepreneurs must decide which form of legal ownership best suits their goals: *sole proprietorship, partnership, corporation,* or *co-operative.*

The sole proprietorship

The **sole proprietorship** is a business owned and operated by one person. Legally, if you set up a business as a sole proprietorship, your business is considered to be an extension of yourself (and not a separate legal entity). Though usually small, a sole proprietorship may be as large as a steel mill or as small as a lemonade stand. While the majority of businesses in Canada are sole proprietorships, they account for only a small proportion of total business revenues.

Advantages of a Sole Proprietorship Freedom may be the most important benefit of a sole proprietorship. Sole proprietors answer to no one but themselves, since they don't share ownership. A sole proprietorship is also easy to form. If you operate the business under your own name, with no additions, you don't even need to register your business name to start operating as a sole proprietor—you can go into business simply by putting a sign on the door. The simplicity of legal setup procedures makes this form appealing to self-starters and independent spirits, as do the low start-up costs.

Another attractive feature is the tax benefits. Most businesses suffer losses in their early stages. Since the business and the proprietor are legally one and the same, these losses can be deducted from income the proprietor earns from personal sources other than the business.

Disadvantages of a Sole Proprietorship A major drawback is **unlimited liability** which means that a sole proprietor is personally liable (responsible) for all debts incurred by the business. If the business fails to generate enough cash, bills must be paid out of the owner's pocket. Another disadvantage is lack of continuity: a sole proprietorship legally dissolves when the owner dies. Finally, a sole proprietorship depends on the resources of one person whose managerial and financial limitations may constrain the business. Sole proprietors often find it hard to borrow money to start up or expand. Many bankers fear that they won't be able to recover loans if the owner becomes disabled.

The partnership

A **partnership** is established when two or more individuals (partners) agree to combine their financial, managerial, and technical abilities for the purpose of operating a business for profit. This form of ownership is often used by professionals such as accountants, lawyers, and engineers. Partnerships are often an extension of a business that began as a sole proprietorship. The original owner may want to expand, or the business may have grown too big for a single person to handle.

There are two basic types of partners in a partnership. **General partners** are actively involved in managing the firm and have unlimited liability. **Limited partners** don't participate actively in the business, and their liability is limited to the amount they invested in the partnership. A **general partnership** is the most common type and is similar to the sole proprietorship in that all the (general) partners are jointly liable for the obligations of the business. The other type of partnership—the **limited partnership**—consists of at least one general partner (who has unlimited liability) and one or more limited partners.

SOLE PROPRIETORSHIP Business owned and usually operated by one person who is responsible for all of its debts.

UNLIMITED LIABILITY A person who invests in a business is liable for all debts incurred by the business; personal possessions can be taken to pay debts.

PARTNERSHIP A business with two or more owners who share in the operation of the firm and in financial responsibility for the firm's debts.

GENERAL PARTNER A partner who is actively involved in managing the firm and has unlimited liability.

LIMITED PARTNER A partner who generally does not participate actively in the business, and whose liability is limited to the amount invested in the partnership.

GENERAL PARTNERSHIP A type of partnership in which all partners are jointly liable for the obligations of the business.

LIMITED PARTNERSHIP A type of partnership with at least one general partner (who has unlimited liability) and one or more limited partners. The limited partners can not participate in the day-to-day management of the business or they risk the loss of their limited liability status.

The limited partners cannot participate in the day-to-day management of the business or they risk the loss of their limited liability status.

Advantages of a Partnership The most striking advantage of a general partnership is the ability to grow by adding talent and money. Partnerships also have an easier time borrowing funds than sole proprietorships. Banks and other lending institutions prefer to make loans to enterprises that are not dependent on a single individual. Partnerships can also invite new partners to join by investing money.

Like a sole proprietorship, a partnership is simple to organize, with few legal requirements. Even so, all partnerships must begin with an agreement of some kind. It may be written, oral, or even unspoken. Wise partners, however, insist on a written agreement to avoid trouble later. This agreement should answer such questions as:

- ▶ Who invested what sums of money in the partnership?
- ▶ Who will receive what share of the partnership's profits?
- ▶ Who does what and who reports to whom?
- ▶ How may the partnership be dissolved?
- ▶ How will leftover assets be distributed among the partners?
- ▶ How would surviving partners be protected from claims by surviving heirs if a partner dies?
- ▶ How will disagreements be resolved?

The partnership agreement is strictly a private document. No laws require partners to file an agreement with some government agency. Nor are partnerships regarded as legal entities. In the eyes of the law, a partnership is nothing more than two or more people working together. The partnership's lack of legal standing means that the partners are taxed as individuals.

Disadvantages of a Partnership As with sole proprietorships, unlimited liability is the greatest drawback of a general partnership. By law, each partner may be held personally liable for all debts incurred in the name of the partnership. And if any partner incurs a debt, even if the other partners know nothing about it, they are all liable if the offending partner cannot pay up. Another problem with partnerships is lack of continuity. When one partner dies or pulls out, a partnership dissolves legally, even if the other partners agree to stay to continue the business.

A related drawback is the difficulty of transferring ownership. No partner may sell out without the other partners' consent. Thus, the life of a partnership may depend on the ability of retiring partners to find someone compatible with the other partners to buy them out. Finally, a partnership provides little or no guidance in resolving conflicts between the partners. For example, suppose one partner wants to expand the business rapidly and the other wants it to grow slowly. If under the partnership agreement the two are equal, it may be difficult for them to decide what to do.

A practical illustration of the kinds of problems that can arise in partnerships is described in the Exercising Your Ethics assignment found at the end of the chapter.

The corporation

When you think of corporations you probably think of giant businesses such as Air Canada, Imperial Oil, or RIM. The very word "corporation" suggests bigness and power. Yet, the tiny corner newsstand has as much right to incorporate as does a giant oil refiner. And the newsstand and oil refiner have the same basic characteristics that all corporations share: legal status as a separate entity, property rights and obligations, and an indefinite lifespan. (See Table 10.6 for a list of the top 10 corporations in Canada.)

A corporation has been defined as "an artificial being, invisible, intangible, and existing only in contemplation of the law." As such, corporations may sue and be sued; buy, hold, and sell property; make and sell products to consumers; and commit crimes and be tried and punished for them. Simply defined, a **corporation** is a business that is a separate legal entity, that is liable for its own debts, and whose owners' liability is limited to their investment.

Stockholders—investors who buy shares of ownership in the form of stock—are the real owners of a corporation. Profits may be distributed to stockholders in the form of dividends, although corporations are not required to pay dividends. Instead, they often reinvest any profits in the business. Common stockholders have the last claim to any assets if the company folds. Dividends on **common stock** are paid on a per share basis (if a dividend is declared). Thus, a shareholder with 10 shares receives 10 times the dividend paid a shareholder with one share. *Class A* common shares always have voting rights, but *Class B* common shares usually do not. Shareholder rights advocates argue that Class B common shares prevent democracy from working in companies because controlling shareholders hold most of the Class A stock and sell non-voting Class B stock to the general public. When investors cannot attend a shareholders' meeting, they can grant voting authority to someone who will attend. This procedure, called voting by *proxy*, is the way almost all individual investors vote.

The **board of directors** is the governing body of a corporation. Its main responsibility is to ensure that the corporation is run in the best interests of the stockholders. The directors choose the president and other officers of the business and delegate the power to run the day-to-day activities of the business to those officers. The directors set policy on paying dividends, on financing major spending, and on executive salaries and benefits. Large corporations tend to have large boards with as many as 20 or 30 directors. Smaller corporations,

CORPORATION A business considered by law to be a legal entity separate from its owners with many of the legal rights and privileges of a person; a form of business organization in which the liability of the owners is limited to their investment in the firm.

STOCKHOLDERS Investors who buy shares of ownership in the form of stock.

COMMON STOCK Shares whose owners usually have last claim on the corporation's assets (after creditors and owners of preferred stock) but who have voting rights in the firm.

BOARD OF DIRECTORS A group of individuals elected by a firm's shareholders and charged with overseeing, and taking legal responsibility for, the firm's actions.

Table 10.6   Top 10 Corporations in Canada, 2009[56]

	COMPANY	SALES REVENUES (IN BILLIONS OF $)
1.	Manulife Financial Corp.	40.1
2.	Royal Bank of Canada	38.1
3.	Power Corp. of Canada	33.1
4.	George Weston Ltd.	31.8
5.	Petro-Canada	27.6
6.	Sun Life Financial Inc.	27.5
7.	Toronto-Dominion Bank	25.4
8.	Bank of Nova Scotia	25.1
9.	Suncor Energy Inc.	25.0
10.	Onex Corp.	24.8

INSIDE DIRECTORS ←
Members of a corporation's board of directors who are also full-time employees of the corporation.

OUTSIDE DIRECTORS ←
Members of a corporation's board of directors who are not also employees of the corporation on a day-to-day basis.

CHIEF EXECUTIVE OFFICER (CEO)
The highest ranking executive in a company or organization.

PUBLIC CORPORATION ←
A business whose stock is widely held and available for sale to the general public.

PRIVATE CORPORATION ←
A business whose stock is held by a small group of individuals and is not usually available for sale to the general public.

INITIAL PUBLIC OFFERING (IPO) ←
Selling shares of stock in a company for the first time to a general investing public.

PRIVATE EQUITY FIRMS
Companies that buy publicly traded companies and then make them private.

INCOME TRUST ←
A structure allowing companies to avoid paying corporate income tax if they distribute all or most of their earnings to investors.

on the other hand, tend to have no more than five directors. Usually, these are people with personal or professional ties to the corporation, such as family members, lawyers, and accountants. Each year, *The Globe and Mail* analyzes the governance practices of Canadian companies in four areas: board composition, compensation, shareholder rights, and disclosure. The top-ranked companies in 2010 were Loblaw Corp., George Weston Corp., and IamGold Corp. The lowest-ranked companies were Shaw Communications and Biovail.[57] **Inside directors** are employees of the company and have primary responsibility for the corporation. That is, they are also top managers, such as the president and executive vice-president. **Outside directors** are not employees of the corporation in the normal course of its business. Attorneys, accountants, university officials, and executives from other firms are commonly used as outside directors.

Corporate officers are the top managers hired by the board to run the corporation on a day-to-day basis. The **chief executive officer (CEO)** is responsible for the firm's overall performance. Other corporate officers typically include the president, who is responsible for internal management, and various vice-presidents, who oversee functional areas such as marketing or operations.

Types of Corporations A **public corporation** is one whose shares of stock are widely held and available for sale to the general public. Anyone who has the funds to pay for them can buy shares of companies such as Petro-Canada, Bombardier, or Air Canada. The stock of a **private corporation** on the other hand, is held by only a few people and is not generally available for sale. The controlling group may be a family, employees, or the management group. Pattison and Cirque du Soleil are two well-known Canadian private corporations.

Most new corporations start out as private corporations, because few investors will buy an unknown stock. As the corporation grows and develops a record of success, it may issue shares to the public as a way of raising additional money. This is called an **initial public offering** (IPO). IPOs are not very attractive to investors during stock market declines, but they become more popular when stock markets recover. This is one of the reasons why Porter Aviation withdrew plans for an IPO in mid-2010 because of the turbulent markets at the time.[58] However, others moved forward despite turbulent markets. Capital Power Corp. raised $500 million from its IPO and retailer Dollarama raised $300 million.[59]

A public corporation can also "go private," which is the reverse of going public. In 2008, Clearwater Seafoods announced that it would be taken private by a consortium led by Clearwater Fine Foods.[60] **Private equity firms** buy publicly traded companies and then take them private. They often make major changes to company operations in order to increase its value.

During the period from 2000 to 2005, many corporations converted to an **income trust** structure, which allowed them to avoid paying corporate income tax if they distributed all or most of their earnings to investors. For example, Bell Canada Enterprises could have avoided an $800 million tax bill in one year by becoming an income trust. The federal government estimated that it was going to lose billions of dollars of tax revenue because so many corporations were becoming income trusts. In a surprise move in 2006, the Canadian government announced that it would begin taxing income trusts more like corporations by 2011. This announcement caused a significant decline in the market value of income trusts and it also put an end to the rush to convert.[61] In 2010, income trusts were widely being ignored in the markets, however, according to Alex Sasso, of Hesperian Capital Management, there were many hidden gems in the market, such as Black Diamond Group, a provider of temporary workforce accommodation to the energy, mining, and other sectors.[62]

Formation of the Corporation The two most widely used methods to form a corporation are federal incorporation under the Canada Business Corporations Act and provincial incorporation under any of the provincial corporations acts. The former is used if the company is going to operate in more than one province; the latter is used if the founders intend to carry on business in only one province. Except for banks and certain insurance and loan companies, any company can be federally incorporated under the Canada Business Corporations Act. To do so, articles of incorporation must be drawn up. These articles include such information as the name of the corporation, the type and number of shares to be issued, the number of directors the corporation will have, and the location of the company's operations. The specific procedures and information required for provincial incorporation vary from province to province.

All corporations must attach the word "Limited" (Ltd./Ltée), "Incorporated" (Inc.), or "Corporation" (Corp.) to the company name to indicate clearly to customers and suppliers that the owners have limited liability for corporate debts. The same sorts of rules apply in other countries. British firms, for example, use PLC for "public limited company" and German companies use AG for "Aktiengesellschaft" (corporation).

Advantages of Incorporation The biggest advantage of the corporate structure is **limited liability**, which means that the liability of investors is limited to their personal investment in the corporation. In the event of failure, the courts may seize a corporation's assets and sell them to pay debts, but the courts cannot touch the investors' personal possessions. If, for example, you invest $25 000 in a corporation that goes bankrupt, you may lose your $25 000, but no more. In other words, $25 000 is the extent of your liability.

Another advantage of a corporation is continuity. Because it has a legal life independent of its founders and owners, a corporation can, in theory, continue forever. Shares of stock may be sold or passed on to heirs, and most corporations also benefit from the continuity provided by professional management. Finally, corporations have advantages in raising money. By selling **stock**, they expand the number of investors and available funds. The term "stock" refers to a share of ownership in a corporation. Continuity and legal status tend to make lenders more willing to grant loans to corporations.

Disadvantages of Incorporation One of the disadvantages for a new firm in forming a corporation is the cost (approximately $2500). In addition, corporations also need legal help in meeting government regulations because they are far more heavily regulated than are proprietorships or general partnerships. Some people say that **double taxation** is another problem with the corporate form of ownership. By this they mean that a corporation must pay income taxes on its profits, and then shareholders must also pay personal income taxes on the **dividends** they receive from the corporation. The dividend a corporation pays is the amount of money, normally a portion of the profits, that is distributed to the shareholders. Since dividends paid by the corporation are paid with after-tax dollars, this amounts to double taxation. Others point out that shareholders get a dividend tax credit, which largely offsets double taxation.

The co-operative

A **co-operative** is an incorporated form of business that is organized, owned, and democratically controlled by the people who use its products and services, and whose earnings are distributed on the basis of use of the co-operative rather than level of investment. As such, it is formed to benefit its owners in the form of reduced prices and/or the distribution of surpluses at year-end. The process works like this: Suppose some farmers believe they can get cheaper fertilizer prices if they form their own company and purchase in large volumes.

> **LIMITED LIABILITY**
> Investor liability is limited to their personal investments in the corporation; courts cannot touch the personal assets of investors in the event that the corporation goes bankrupt.

> **STOCK**
> A share of ownership in a corporation.

> **DOUBLE TAXATION**
> A corporation must pay income taxes on its profits, and then shareholders must also pay personal income taxes on the dividends they receive from the corporation.

> **DIVIDENDS**
> The amount of money, normally a portion of the profits, that is distributed to the shareholders.

> **CO-OPERATIVE**
> An organization that is formed to benefit its owners in the form of reduced prices and/or the distribution of surpluses at year-end.

They might then form a co-operative, which can be either federally or provincially chartered. Prices are generally lower to buyers and, at the end of the fiscal year, any surpluses are distributed to members on the basis of how much they purchased. If Farmer Jones bought 5 percent of all co-op sales, he would receive 5 percent of the surplus.

The co-operative's start-up capital usually comes from shares purchased by the co-operative's members. Sometimes all it takes to qualify for membership in a co-operative is the purchase of one share with a fixed (and often nominal) value. Federal co-operatives, however, can raise capital by issuing investment shares to members or non-members. Co-operatives, like investor-owned corporations, have directors and appointed officers.

Types of Co-operatives There are hundreds of different co-operatives, but they generally function in one of six main areas of business:

- ***Consumer co-operatives.*** These organizations sell goods to both members and the general public (e.g., Mountain Equipment Co-op).

- ***Financial co-operatives.*** These organizations operate much like banks, accepting deposits from members, giving loans, and providing chequing services (e.g., Vancouver City Savings Credit Union).

- ***Insurance co-operatives.*** These organizations provide many types of insurance coverage, such as life, fire, and liability (e.g., Co-operative Hail Insurance Company of Manitoba).

- ***Marketing co-operatives.*** These organizations sell the produce of their farm members and purchase inputs for the production process (e.g., seed and fertilizer). Some, like Federated Co-operatives, also purchase and market finished products.

- ***Service co-operatives.*** These organizations provide members with services, such as recreation.

- ***Housing co-operatives*** These organizations provide housing for members, who purchase a share in the co-operative, which holds the title to the housing complex.

In terms of numbers, co-operatives are the least important form of ownership. However, they are of significance to society and to their members; they may provide services that are not readily available or that cost more than the members would otherwise be willing to pay. Table 10.7 compares the various forms of business ownership using different characteristics.

Advantages of a Co-operative Co-operatives have many of the same advantages as investor-owned corporations, such as limited liability of owners and continuity. A key benefit of a co-operative relates to its structure. Each member has only one vote in the affairs of the co-operative, regardless of how many shares he or she owns. This system prevents voting and financial control of the business by a few wealthy individuals. This is particularly attractive to the less-wealthy members of the co-operative.

Unlike corporations, which are not allowed a tax deduction on dividend payments made to shareholders, co-operatives are allowed to deduct patronage refunds to members out of before-tax income. Thus, income may be taxed only at the individual member level rather than at both the co-operative and member level.[63]

Disadvantages of a Co-operative One of the main disadvantages of co-operatives relates to attracting equity investment. Since the benefits from being a member of a co-operative arise through the level of use of the co-operative rather than the level of equity invested, members do not have an incentive to invest in equity capital of the co-operative. Another drawback is that democratic voting arrangements and dividends based purely on patronage discourage some entrepreneurs from forming or joining a co-operative.

Success and failure
in small business

Of every 100 small businesses that begin operation, 96 will still be operating after one year, 85 after three years, and 67 after five years.[64] A study conducted by CIBC World Markets found that small businesses with above-average revenue growth were run by owners who had more education, used professional advisers, adopted the corporate form of ownership, did outsourcing work for other companies, had a high level of internet connectivity, and used the internet to sell outside Canada.[65]

Reasons for success

Beyond the specific findings like the CIBC study, four general factors typically are cited to explain the success of small business owners:

1. *Hard work, drive, and dedication.* Small business owners must be committed to succeeding and be willing to put in the time and effort to make it happen. Long hours and few vacations generally characterize the first few years of new business ownership.

2. *Market demand for the product or service.* Careful analysis of market conditions can help small business people assess the probable reception of their products. If the area around a college has only one pizza parlour, a new pizzeria is more likely to succeed than if there are already 10 in operation.

3. *Managerial competence.* Successful small business people have a solid understanding of how to manage a business. They may acquire competence through training (taking courses), experience, or by using the expertise of others. Few, however, succeed alone or straight out of school. Most spend time in successful companies or partner with others to bring expertise to a new business.

Table 10.7 A Comparison of Four Forms of Business Ownership

CHARACTERISTIC	SOLE PROPRIETORSHIP	PARTNERSHIP	CORPORATION	CO-OPERATIVE
Protection against liability for bad debts	low	low	high	high
Ease of formation	high	high	medium	medium
Permanence	low	low	high	high
Ease of ownership transfer	low	low	high	high
Ease of raising money	low	medium	high	high
Freedom from regulation	high	high	low	medium
Tax advantages	high	high	low	high

4. *Luck.* Luck also plays a role in the success of some firms. For example, after one entrepreneur started an environmental clean-up firm, he struggled to keep his business afloat. Then the government committed a large sum of money for toxic waste clean-up. He was able to get several large contracts, and his business is now thriving.

Reasons for failure

Small businesses fail for many *specific* reasons (see Table 10.7). Entrepreneurs may have no control over some of these factors (for example, weather, fraud,

Table 10.8   Causes of Small Business Failure

POOR MANAGEMENT SKILLS	PERSONAL REASONS
• poor delegation and organizational ability • lack of depth in management team • entrepreneurial incompetence, such as a poor understanding of finances and business markets • lack of experience	• loss of interest in business • accident, illness • death • family problems
INADEQUATE MARKETING CAPABILITIES	**DISASTERS**
• difficulty in marketing product • market too small, non-existent, or declining • too much competition • problems with distribution systems	• fire • weather • strikes • fraud by entrepreneur or others
INADEQUATE FINANCIAL CAPABILITIES	**OTHER**
• weak skills in accounting and finance • lack of budgetary control • inadequate costing systems • incorrect valuation of assets • unable to obtain financial backing	• mishandling of large project • excessive standard of living • lack of time to devote to business • difficulties with associates or partners • government policies change
INADEQUATE FINANCIAL CAPABILITIES	
• poorly designed production systems • old and inefficient production facilities and equipment • inadequate control over quality • problems with inventory control	

accidents), but they can influence most items on the list. Although no set pattern has been established, four *general* factors contribute to failure:

1. *Managerial incompetence or inexperience.* Some entrepreneurs put their faith in common sense, overestimate their own managerial skills, or believe that hard work alone ensures success. If managers don't know how to make basic business decisions or don't understand basic management principles, they aren't likely to succeed in the long run.

2. *Neglect.* Some entrepreneurs try to launch ventures in their spare time, and others devote only limited time to new businesses. But starting a small business demands an overwhelming time commitment. If an entrepreneur isn't willing to put in the time and effort that a business requires, it isn't likely to survive.

3. *Weak control systems.* Effective control systems keep a business on track and alert managers to potential trouble. If the control systems don't signal impending problems, the business may be in serious trouble before obvious difficulties are spotted.

4. *Insufficient capital.* Some entrepreneurs are overly optimistic about how soon they'll start earning profits. In most cases, it takes months or even years. Amazon.com didn't earn a profit for 10 years, but obviously still required capital to pay employees and cover expenses. Experts say you need enough capital to operate six months to a year without earning a profit.[66]

On a positive note, business failures were lower than expected in the most recent recession. According to Laurie Campbell, director of the credit counselling organization Credit Canada, this was due to the fact that the recession hit the U.S. first before having an impact in Canada. Many businesses took necessary precautions to cut expenses before it hit.[67]

PEARSON mybusinesslab

To improve your grade, visit the MyBusinessLab website at **www.pearsoned.ca/ mybusinesslab.** This online homework and tutorial system allows you to test your understanding and generates a personalized study plan just for you. It provides you with study and practice tools directly related to this chapter's content. MyBusinessLab puts you in control of your own learning! Test yourself on the material for this chapter at **www.pearsoned.ca/mybusinesslab.**

Summary of Learning Objectives

1. **Explain the meaning and interrelationship of the terms** *small business*, *new venture creation*, **and** *entrepreneurship*. A small business has less than 100 employees. A new firm is one that has become operational within the previous 12 months, has adopted any of four main organizational forms—*proprietorship, partnership, corporation,* or *co-operative*—and sells goods or services. Entrepreneurship is the *process* of identifying an opportunity in the marketplace and accessing the resources needed to capitalize on it. In relation to small and/or new businesses, entrepreneurship is the process by which a small business or a new business is created.

2. **Describe the role of small and new businesses in the Canadian economy.** While 98 percent of employer businesses in Canada are small (less than 100 employees), about half of the total private sector labour force work for small businesses. The distribution of employment by size of firm varies across industries. The small business sector's capacity for entrepreneurship and innovation accounts for much of the job creation; this sector contributes to the economy, with start-ups accounting for most of the growth. Women are playing a major role in the growth of small businesses.

3. **Explain the** *entrepreneurial process* **and describe its three key elements.** The entrepreneurial process occurs within a social, political, and economic context and consists of three key elements: the *entrepreneur,* the *opportunity,* and *resources.* Entrepreneurs typically access the various resources needed by bootstrapping—doing more with less. These resources are both financial and non-financial. Two types of financing—*debt* and *equity*—can be accessed from a range of sources.

4. **Describe three alternative strategies for becoming a business owner—**starting from scratch, *buying an existing business*, **and** *buying a franchise.* It is necessary to work through the entrepreneurial process in order to *start a business from scratch.* Whether start-up efforts will result in a new business often depends upon how well matched the entrepreneur's skills and abilities are with the opportunity and the resources required, as well as how well matched the opportunity and resources are. Some new ventures will grow; others will decline, die, or remain stable. Generally, when someone buys an *existing business,* the odds of success are better because it has existing customers; established relationships (e.g., lenders, suppliers), and an existing track record. Potential buyers have a clearer picture of what to expect. However, the business may have a poor reputation, poor location, and it may be difficult to determine an appropriate purchase price. A special case of buying an existing business involves family businesses, which pose both opportunities and challenges. In buying a *franchise* the buyer (franchisee) purchases the right to sell the product or service of the seller (franchiser) according to the terms of the franchising agreement. In return the franchiser provides assistance with the business's start-up as well as with ongoing operations once the business opens its doors.

5. **Describe four forms of *legal organization* for a business and discuss the advantages and disadvantages of each.** *Sole proprietorships* are owned and operated by one person, are easy to set up, have low start-up costs, enjoy tax benefits, and their owners enjoy freedom. However, sole proprietorships have unlimited liability, a lack of continuity, and limited resources.

Under a *general partnership* all partners have unlimited liability. Partnerships may lack continuity, and transferring ownership may be difficult. On the positive side, partnerships can grow by adding new talent and money, partners are taxed as individuals, and banks prefer to make loans to enterprises that are not dependent on one individual. All partnerships should have a partnership agreement.

Corporations are separate legal entities, they have property rights and obligations, and they have indefinite life spans. They may sue and be sued; buy, hold, and sell property; make and sell products; commit crimes and be tried and punished for them. The biggest advantage of incorporation is limited liability. Other advantages include continuity, professional management, and improved ability to raise money by selling stock. Disadvantages of the corporation include high start-up costs, complexity, and *double taxation*. The vast majority of corporations are privately held. In forming a corporation, a business will incorporate federally if it is going to operate in more than one province and provincially if it is going to operate in only one province.

A *co-operative* is an organization that is formed to benefit its owners in the form of reduced prices and/or the distribution of surpluses at year-end. On the positive side, co-operatives are democratically controlled, enjoy limited liability, continuity, and are not subject to double taxation. The main disadvantages include difficulty in raising equity. Co-operatives usually function in one of six areas of business: consumer co-operatives, financial co-operatives, insurance co-operatives, marketing co-operatives, service co-operatives, or housing co-operatives.

6. **Identify four key reasons for success in small businesses and four key reasons for failure.** Four basic factors explain most small-business success: (1) hard work, drive, and dedication; (2) market demand for the products or services being provided; (3) managerial competence; and (4) luck. Four factors contribute to small-business failure: (1) managerial incompetence or inexperience; (2) neglect; (3) weak control systems; and (4) insufficient capital.

Questions and Exercises

Questions for Analysis

1. What are some of the problems that are encountered when we try to define the term "small business"?
2. Why are new ventures the main source of job creation and new product/service ideas?
3. Do you think that you would be a successful entrepreneur? Why or why not?
4. Consider a new product or service that has recently become available for purchase by consumers. To what extent did this product or service possess the "screening" characteristics that are described in the chapter (adding value, providing competitive advantage, etc.)?
5. Using the product or service you described in Question 4, analyze the extent to which there is a good "fit" between the various elements in the entrepreneurial process.
6. Why might a private corporation choose to remain private? Why might it choose to "go public"?

Application Exercises

7. Identify three trends—whether in fashion, lifestyle, or something else—and describe at least five ideas for capitalizing on one of them.
8. Find a newspaper or magazine article that describes someone who is an entrepreneur. Use the information provided to explain what makes this person an entrepreneur.

9. Spend some time watching what people do and how they do it, and then (a) identify two ways to make what they do easier, and (b) describe two problems you observed and identify strategies for resolving those problems.

10. Interview the owners of several small businesses in your local area. Ask them what they have done to make their businesses more environmentally friendly. If they have not done anything, ask them what has prevented them from taking the initiative to be more environmentally friendly.

Team Exercises

Building Your Business Skills

WORKING THE INTERNET

Goal

To encourage students to define opportunities and problems for small companies doing business on the internet.

Situation

Suppose you and two partners own a gift basket store, specializing in special-occasion baskets for individual and corporate clients. Your business is doing well in your community, but you believe there may be opportunity for growth through a virtual storefront on the internet.

Method

Step 1 Join with two other students and assume the role of business partners. Start by researching internet businesses. Look at books and articles at the library and search the following websites for help:

- Canada Business Service Centres: www.canadabusiness.ca/eng/
- Small Business Administration (United States): www.sba.gov
- IBM Small Business Center: www.businesscenter.ibm.com
- Apple Small Business Home Page: www.apple.com/business/
- These sites may lead you to other sites, so keep an open mind.

Step 2 Based on your research, determine the importance of the following small business issues:

- An analysis of changing company finances as a result of internet applications
- An analysis of your new competitive marketplace (the world) and how it affects your current marketing approach, which focuses on your local community
- Identification of sources of management advice as the expansion proceeds
- The role of technology consultants in launching and maintaining the website
- Customer service policies in your virtual environment

Follow-Up Questions

1. Do you think your business would be successful on the internet? Why or why not?
2. Based on your analysis, how will extended internet applications affect your current business practices? What specific changes are you likely to make?
3. Do you think that operating a virtual storefront will be harder or easier than doing business in your local community? Explain your answer.

Exercising Your Ethics

Public or Private? That Is the Question

THE SITUATION

The Thomas Corporation is a very well-financed private corporation with a solid and growing product line, little debt, and a stable workforce. However, in the past few months, there has been a growing rift among the board of directors that has created considerable differences of opinion as to the future direction of the firm.

THE DILEMMA

Some board members believe the firm should "go public" with a stock offering. Since each board member owns a large block of corporate stock, each would make a considerable amount of money if the company went public. Other board members want to maintain the status quo as a private corporation. The biggest advantage of this approach is that the firm maintains its current ability to remain autonomous in its operations. The third faction of the board also wants to remain private but clearly has a different agenda. Those board members have identified a small public corporation that is currently one of the company's key suppliers. Their idea is to buy the supplying company, shift its assets to the parent firm, sell all of its remaining operations, terminate employees, and then outsource the production of the parts it currently buys from the firm. Their logic is that the firm would gain significant assets and lower its costs.

TEAM ACTIVITY

Assemble a group of four students and assign each group member to one of the following roles:

- An employee at the Thomas Corporation
- A customer of the Thomas Corporation
- An investor in the Thomas Corporation
- A board member who has not yet decided which option is best

ACTION STEPS

1. Before discussing the situation with your group, and from the perspective of your assigned role, decide which option you think is best. Write down the reasons for your position.
2. Before discussing the situation with your group, and from the perspective of your assigned role, identify the underlying ethical issues, if any, in this situation. Write down the issues.
3. Gather your group together and reveal each member's comments on the situation. Next, reveal the ethical issues listed by each member.
4. Appoint someone to record the main points of agreement and disagreement. How do you explain the results? What accounts for any disagreement?
5. From an ethical standpoint, what is the most appropriate action that should be taken by the Thomas Corporation in this situation?
6. Develop a group response to the following question: What do you think most people would do in this situation?

Business Case 4

Family Business

Family businesses are a prominent feature in many countries of the world. Most family businesses are small, but some are very large. In addition to the usual challenges facing business firms, family businesses often are threatened by disagreements between family members about how the business should be run. Here are some classic examples.

THE IRVING FAMILY

The Irving family of New Brunswick is one of the great success stories of Canadian business. The company owns scores of businesses in oil refining, forestry, shipbuilding, food processing, publishing, transportation, and home improvement. The business was started in the nineteenth century by J.D. Irving and was expanded by his son K.C. The empire is now run by K.C.'s three sons, Arthur, J.K., and Jack, who are all in their seventies. Recently, it became clear that J.K.'s son Jim and Arthur's son Kenneth were competing for a chance to shape the company's fortunes, and they disagreed over the strategic direction the company should take. That disagreement drove a wedge between J.K. and his brothers.

This is a new situation for the Irving family, which has always presented a remarkably united front. The three brothers have a great deal of respect for each other, so when these succession tensions developed, they decided they would try to amicably divide the businesses. The energy business will go to Arthur's family, and the forestry business to J.K.'s family. Their approach contrasts sharply with what happened to the McCain family, another New Brunswick business dynasty.

THE McCAIN FAMILY

For many years, brothers Wallace and Harrison McCain were the key players at McCain Foods Ltd., the world's largest French fry producer. But in the mid-1990s, the two brothers had a falling out over the question of who would succeed Harrison as the CEO. Wallace wanted his son Michael to get the job, but Harrison wanted someone from outside the family to take over. After a nasty battle, Wallace was removed from the firm. He then took over Maple Leaf Foods and his son Michael eventually became CEO of that company.

THE MITCHELL FAMILY

Mitchell's Gourmet Foods Inc. was a Saskatchewan-based family business. A family feud developed when Fred Mitchell claimed that his mother and his brother Charles were trying to take control of the business from him. Both sides in the dispute then sued each other. An accommodation of sorts was reached when the disputing parties agreed to divide up the assets of the company. Fred (and his wife, LuAn) kept Mitchell's, and Charles (and his wife, Camille) kept a beef plant the company owned.

THE ANTINORI FAMILY

Some family businesses manage to avoid feuds. The Antinori family business in Florence, Italy, has been making wine since 1385, and for 26 generations the family has somehow managed to pass on management of the company to the next generation without getting in a big fight. How do they do it? By going against conventional wisdom—which says that you should clearly separate the family's interest from the interest of the business—and instead blurring the two interests as much as possible. For example, the current CEO and his wife live on the top two floors of their fifteenth-century mansion, and the business operates on the bottom two floors. Perhaps more importantly, the company plans far into the future for a company the grandchildren can run.

Maybe there is something about the wine business that makes family feuds less likely. For example, Catherine and Anne Monna and their father, Bernard, run Cassis Monna & Filles near Quebec City. The sisters are the fifth generation of the family to be involved in the wine business.

QUESTIONS FOR DISCUSSION

1. How is running a family business different from creating a business from scratch? What are the advantages? What are the disadvantages?
2. It seems as though the Antinori family has found a way to ensure that the entrepreneurial spirit is transferred from generation to generation in a positive manner. But this contrasts heavily with the experiences of many family businesses, even some of the biggest success stories. Are entrepreneurs born to be entrepreneurs or can they be created?
3. How does financing a family business differ from financing a franchise or a new start-up? Outline the unique challenges in each of these situations.

Notes

1. Tavia Grant, "Call It the Entrepreneurial Era," *The Globe and Mail*, March 30, 2010, B.

2. Statistics Canada, *Business Dynamics in Canada*, Catalogue no. 61–534-XIE (Ottawa: Minister of Industry, 2006).

3. P.D. Reynolds, S.M. Camp, W.D. Bygrave, E. Autio, and M. Hay, *Global Entrepreneurship Monitor: 2001 Executive Report* (Kansas City, MO: Kauffman Center for Entrepreneurial Leadership, 2001); P.D. Reynolds, M. Hay, W.D. Bygrave, S.M. Camp, and E. Autio, *Global Entrepreneurship Monitor: 2000 Executive Report* (Kansas City, MO: Kauffman Center for Entrepreneurial Leadership, 2000).

4. Industry Canada, *Key Small Business Statistics* (Ottawa: Public Works and Government Services Canada, 2006), 24.

5. Industry Canada, *Key Small Business Statistics*, 2010, http://dsp-psd.pwgsc.gc.ca/collection_2010/ic/Iu186-1-2010-1-eng.pdf (2009), 5, accessed June 23, 2010.

6. Monica Diochon, Teresa Menzies, and Yvon Gasse, "Exploring the Relationship between Start-Up Activities and New Venture Emergence: A Longitudinal Study of Canadian Nascent Entrepreneurs," *International Journal of Management and Enterprise Development*, Vol. 2, Issue 3/4 (2005): 408–426.

7. Industry Canada, *Key Small Business Statistics* (Ottawa: Small Business and Tourism Branch Canada, 2009), 23.

8. Queen's University business website, www.business.queensu.ca/news/2009/01-14-09-BSME.php.

9. Nancy M. Carter, William B. Gartner, and Paul D. Reynolds, "Firm Founding," in W.B. Gartner, K.G. Shaver, N.M. Carter, and P.D. Reynolds, eds., *Handbook of Entrepreneurial Dynamics:*

The *Process of Business Creation* (Thousand Oaks, CA: Sage, 2004), 311–323.

10. William D. Bygrave and C.W. Hofer, "Theorizing about Entrepreneurship," *Entrepreneurship Theory and Practice,* Vol. 16, Issue 2 (Winter 1991): 14; Donald Sexton and Nancy Bowman-Upton, *Entrepreneurship: Creativity and Growth* (New York: Macmillan, 1991), 7.

11. Fred Vogelstein, "How Mark Zuckerberg Turned Facebook into the Web's Hottest Platform," *Wired*, September 6, 2007, www.wired.com/techbiz/startups/news/2007/09/ff_facebook?currentPage=3; Ellen McGirt, "Hacker, Dropout, CEO," *Fast Company*, May 2007, www.fastcompany.com/magazine/115/open_features-hacker-dropout-ceo.html.

12. Heritage Foundation Index of Economic Freedom website, www.heritage.org/index/ranking.aspx, accessed June 23, 2010.

13. Angela Dale, "Self-Employment and Entrepreneurship: Notes on Two Problematic Concepts," in Roger Burrows, ed., *Deciphering the Enterprise Culture* (London: Routledge, 1991), 45, 48; Holt 1992, 11.

14. Donald Sexton and Nancy Bowman-Upton, *Entrepreneurship: Creativity and Growth* (New York: Macmillan, 1991), 11; Kao, 1991, 21.

15. Allan A. Gibb, "The Enterprise Culture and Education: Understanding Enterprise Education and Its Links with Small Business, Entrepreneurship and Wider Educational Goals," *International Small Business Journal,* Vol. 11, Issue 3 (1993): 13–34; Donald Sexton and Nancy Bowman-Upton, *Entrepreneurship: Creativity and Growth* (New York: Macmillan, 1991).

16. Terrence Belford, "Intrapreneurs Combine Big-Biz Clout with Entrepreneurial Style," *CanWest News* (March 23, 2005). Retrieved June 25, 2006, from CBCA Current Events database. (Document ID: 1009719591.)

17. Industry Canada, Small Business Research and Policy, Key Small Business Statistics, Table 3 (Ottawa: Public Works and Government Services Canada, 2008), www.ic.gc.ca/eic/site/sbrp-rppe.nsf/eng/rd02300.html.

18. Industry Canada, Small Business Research and Policy, Key Small Business Statistics (Ottawa: Public Works and Government Services Canada, 2010), http://dsp-psd.pwgsc.gc.ca/collection_2010/ic/Iu186-1-2010-1-eng.pdf.

19. Statistics Canada website, Employment by Class of Worker and Industry, www.statcan.gc.ca/daily-quotidien/100507/t100507a2-eng.htm, accessed June 23, 2010.

20. Industry Canada, Small Business Research and Policy, Key Small Business Statistics (Ottawa: Public Works and Government Services Canada, 2006), 10.

21. William B. Gartner, Kelly G. Shaver, Nancy M. Carter, and Paul D. Reynolds, *Handbook of Entrepreneurial Dynamics* (Thousand Oaks, CA: Sage, 2004), ix.

22. Industry Canada, Small Business Research and Policy, Key Small Business Statistics (Ottawa: Public Works and Government Services Canada, 2006), 10.

23. Industry Canada, Key Small Business Statistics (Ottawa: Public Works and Government Services Canada, 2009), 3.

24. Richard Bloom, "Building a Future on Sweet Dreams," *The Globe and Mail*, October 21, 2004, B9.

25. Lauren McKeon, "Tied to Home," *Canadian Business*, April 14, 2008, 33.

26. RBC website, Female Entrepreneur Awards, www.theawards.ca/cwea/past-winners.cfm, accessed June 24, 2010.

27. Roma Luciw, "Stay-at-Home Moms Stay the Business Course," *The Globe and Mail*, March 3, 2007, B10.

28. BDC website, Young Entrepreneurs Award, www.bdc.ca, accessed June 24, 2010.

29. Ben Barry website, www.benbarry.com, accessed June 24, 2010; Sarah Kennedy, "Self-Styled Pioneer Aims to Alter Face of Fashion," *The Globe and Mail*, July 1, 2002, B12.

30. Tell Us About Us website, www.tellusaboutus.com, accessed June 24, 2010; Geoff Kirbyson, "Market-Research Firm Lands Major Contract," *The Winnipeg Free Press*, July 19, 2004, D7.

31. Donald F. Kuratko and Richard M. Hodgetts, *Entrepreneurship: Theory, Process, Practice*, 7th ed. (Mason, OH: Thomson South-Western, 2007), 118–125; John A. Hornday, "Research about Living Entrepreneurs," in *Encyclopedia of Entrepreneurship*, Calvin Kent, Donald Sexton, and Karl Vesper, eds. (Englewood Cliffs, NJ: Prentice Hall, 1982), 26–27; Jeffry A. Timmons and Stephen Spinelli, *New Venture Creation: Entrepreneurship for the 21st Century* (Boston: McGraw-Hill Irwin, 2007), 9.

32. J.D. Kyle, R. Blais, R. Blatt, and A.J. Szonyi, "The Culture of the Entrepreneur: Fact or Fiction," *Journal of Small Business and Entrepreneurship*, 1991: 3–14.

33. R.H. Brockhaus and Pam S. Horwitz, "The Psychology of the Entrepreneur," in *The Art and Science of Entrepreneurship*, D.L. Sexton and Raymond W. Smilor, eds. (Cambridge, MA: Ballinger, 1986); William B. Gartner, "What Are We Talking about When We Talk about Entrepreneurship?" *Journal of Business Venturing,* Vol. 5, Issue 1 (1990): 15–29; Allan A. Gibb, "The Enterprise Culture and Education: Understanding Enterprise

Education and Its Links with Small Business, Entrepreneurship and Wider Educational Goals," *International Small Business Journal,* Vol. 11, Issue 3 (1993): 13–34; J.C. Mitchell, "Case and Situation Analysis," *Sociological Review,* Vol. 31, Issue 2 (1983): 187–211.

34. Donald Sexton and Nancy Bowman-Upton, *Entrepreneurship: Creativity and Growth* (New York: Macmillan, 1991); Karl H. Vesper, *New Venture Strategies* (Englewood Cliffs, NJ: Prentice Hall, 1990); W.D. Bygrave and C.W. Hofer, "Theorizing about Entrepreneurship," *Entrepreneurship Theory and Practice,* Vol. 16, Issue 2 (Winter 1991): 14.

35. Walter Good, *Building a Dream* (Toronto: McGraw-Hill Ryerson, 1998), 40.

36. Wayne A. Long and W. Ed McMullan, *Developing New Ventures* (San Diego: Harcourt Brace Jovanovich, 1990), 374–375.

37. "Sally Fox: Innovation in the Field," www.vreseis.com/sally_fox_story.htm, accessed June 27, 2006.

38. Rasha Mourtada, "Tested to the Limit," *The Globe and Mail,* April 14, 2009, B4.

39. Michael E. Porter, "Know Your Place," *Inc.,* Vol. 13, Issue 9 (September 1992): 90–93.

40. Howard H. Stevenson, H. Irving Grousbeck, Michael J. Roberts, and Amarnath Bhide, *New Business Ventures and the Entrepreneur* (Boston: Irwin McGraw-Hill, 1999), 19.

41. Howard H. Stevenson, H. Irving Grousbeck, Michael J. Roberts, and Amarnath Bhide, *New Business Ventures and the Entrepreneur* (Boston: Irwin McGraw-Hill, 1999), 21.

42. Marc J. Dollinger, *Entrepreneurship: Strategies and Resources* (Upper Saddle River, NJ: Prentice Hall, 1999), 94–101.

43. Thomas W. Zimmerer and Norman M. Scarborough, *Essentials of Entrepreneurship and Small Business Management,* 4th ed. (Upper Saddle River, NJ: Pearson Prentice Hall), 359.

44. Michael E. Porter, "Know Your Place," *Inc.,* Vol. 13, Issue 9 (September 1992): 90–93.

45. Saxx Apparel website, www.saxxapparel.com, accessed June 18, 2010; Rasha Mourtada, "Help Me Get an Angel in My Underwear," *The Globe and Mail,* January 28, 2008, B13.

46. Canada's Venture Capital and Private Equity website, www.cvca.ca/files/Downloads/Final_English_Q4_2009_VC_Data_Deck.pdf, accessed June 24, 2010.

47. Steve Ladurantaye, "New Rules Set Stage for Wave of Foreign Capital," *The Globe and Mail,* March 6, 2010, B1.

48. Business Development Bank of Canada website, www.bdc.ca, accessed June 24, 2010.

49. Karl H. Vesper, *New Venture Mechanics* (Englewood Cliffs, NJ: Prentice Hall, 1993), 105.

50. Jeffry A. Timmons, *New Venture Creation* (Boston: Irwin McGraw-Hill, 1999), 277.

51. Lisa Stephens, "With Some Shape Shifting, This Company Has Legs," *The Globe and Mail,* October 5, 2005, B10.

52. George Anders, Carol Hymowitz, Joann Lublin, and Don Clark, "All in the Family," *The Wall Street Journal,* August 1, 2005, B1, B4.

53. Harvey Schacter, "Honey, You're Fired," *The Globe and Mail,* October 18, 2010, E5.

54. Tony Wilson, "Legal Advice on Starting a Franchise," *The Globe and Mail,* March 16, 2010.

55. Harvey's website, http://harveysfranchising.ca/eng/franchising_2.php, accessed June 24, 2010.

56. "Top 10 Corporations in Canada, 2010," *The Financial Post,* Special Edition, June 2010, 40.

57. "Rankings for Corporate Governance Practices," *The Globe and Mail,* June 18, 2010, B7.

58. Brent Jang, "Porter's IPO: Figuring the Flight Plan," *The Globe and Mail,* April 19, 2010, B9; Scott Deveau, "Porter's Aviation Grounds IPO," *The Financial Post,* June 2, 2010.

59. Andrew Willis, "Market Survey Indicates Eager Demand for IPO's," *The Globe and Mail,* January 6, 2010, B9.

60. "Clearwater Foods Going Private," *National Post,* August 15, 2008, www.nationalpost.com/story-printer.html?id=725985.

61. Terry Pedwell, "Income Trusts Face Tough Rules," *Winnipeg Free Press,* November 1, 2006, B7.

62. Shirley Won, "Looking for Gems in 'Underloved' Trust Sector," *The Globe and Mail,* June 18, 2010, B13.

63. "An Overview of Available Business Structures," www.umanitoba.ca/afs/agric_economics/MRAC/structures.html#Cooperatives.

64. Industry Canada, *Key Small Business Statistics* (Ottawa: Public Works and Government Services Canada, 2009), 12.

65. Kevin Marron, "Want to Succeed? Read This," *The Globe and Mail,* October 19, 2005, E1, E5. Several excellent articles on starting and operating a small business are found in Section E, "Report on Small Business" in *The Globe and Mail,* October 19, 2005.

66. See Norman M. Scarborough and Thomas W. Zimmerer, *Effective Small Business Management: An Entrepreneurial Approach,* 7th ed. (Upper Saddle River, NJ: Prentice Hall, 2003).

67. Virginia Galt, "Business Bankruptcies Fall in Canada," *The Globe and Mail,* May 13, 2009, B4.

chapter 11

SUNC

ENERGY

Managing the Business Enterprise

Corporate **Culture**

The term "corporate culture" refers to the shared experiences, values, norms, and ethical stance that characterize an organization. It is important for managers to understand the concept of corporate culture because culture influences the behaviour of employees, and that, in turn, influences corporate performance. Consider these examples of corporate culture:

► At WestJet, employees have a big stake in the company's success because of profit-sharing, and they contribute ideas about how to best run the airline. For example, a group has formed that calls itself the WestJesters. They do things like develop the cornball jokes that WestJet flight attendants tell during flights.

The culture of the Toronto Blue Jays Baseball Club is making employees feel like they are part of a family. To facilitate the culture, former CEO Paul Godfrey invited small groups of employees to have "snacks with the president" so they could talk about how the operation of the organization. Godfrey encouraged questions from employees on virtually any topic.

The culture of Suncor is open and non-bureaucratic, and the company has a clear strategy that employees can relate to. The company hires many new people, so it must take steps to ensure that the new employees understand the "soul" of Suncor.

► At Wellington West Holdings Inc., the culture is simple, personal, and fun.

Companies that focus largely on one type of product (for example, Starbucks) may have a fairly homogeneous culture throughout the organization. But large companies with many different divisions and many different types of customers (for example, the Royal Bank of Canada) are likely to have several different subcultures because the various divisions pursue different goals, and because different types of people are found in the different divisions.

Culture Surveys

Waterstone Human Capital is a Toronto-based executive search firm that publishes a 10 Most Admired

---

After reading this chapter, you should be able to:

> Describe the four activities that constitute the *management process*. p. 333

> Identify *types of managers* by level and area. p. 338

> Describe the five basic *management skills*. p. 341

> Explain the importance of goal *setting and strategic management* in organizational success. p. 347

> Discuss *contingency planning and crisis management* in today's business world. p. 354

> Explain the idea of *corporate culture* and why it is important. p. 356

How Will This *Help Me?*

After reading this chapter, you will have a clearer understanding of how to effectively carry out various management responsibilities. From the perspective of a consumer or investor, you'll be better able to assess and appreciate the quality of management in various companies.

Corporate Cultures list each year. Companies on the list in 2009 included Ceridian Canada, Acklands-Grainger Inc., Corus Entertainment, Starbucks Canada, and Walmart Canada. The 10 companies on the list had compound annual growth rates for the period 2005–2008 that were triple those of the TSX/S&P index.

Many companies do not systematically monitor their corporate culture, but Starbucks does. Once every 18 months, employees fill out a Partner View survey, which contains questions that are designed to help the company determine whether it is making progress toward one of its key values—providing a work environment where people treat one another with respect and dignity. The survey is voluntary, but about 90 percent of employees fill it out (on company time). One reason the participation rate is so high is that the company actually pays attention to what employees say in the survey. For example, when one survey showed that employees were not clear about career progression possibilities in the company, Starbucks held career fairs in several Canadian cities where company managers spoke with employees about management opportunities at Starbucks.

Some culture surveys assess the business culture of countries rather than individual businesses. In summarizing the perceptions of 4875 people from 22 countries, the 2010 Edelman Trust Barometer ranked Canada and Sweden as the most trusted business cultures, and Russia and China as the least trusted cultures. Survey respondents said that trust—being able to count on business to do the right thing—was even more important than the quality of goods that companies produce.

Cultural Change

Companies sometimes decide that they need to change their culture. A realization of the need for change usually comes after top management sees that changes in the company's external environment are going to require some sort of response from the company. But just because someone recognizes the need for change does not mean that the change will actually be implemented; changing an organization's culture can be very difficult.

In 2007, several RCMP officers alleged that senior management was covering up mismanagement of the RCMP's pension and insurance plans. As a result of these charges, lawyer David Brown was appointed by the government to look into the matter. His report concluded that Commissioner Giuliano Zaccardelli had exercised absolute power, that no one questioned his management style, and that there was a "tone" at the top of the organization that resulted in little respect for employees and put pressure on them to not challenge authority. The report also said that whistleblowers within the RCMP were punished when they pointed out that there were problems. The report concluded that the culture and management structure at the RCMP was "horribly broken." These developments are discouraging, since a few years earlier the RCMP had completed a "visioning" process that resulted in a new mission statement, a new set of core values, and a commitment to the communities where it worked. At that time, it was reported that the culture of the RCMP was quite different from what it was in the days when military tradition dominated the organization, but subsequent events suggested that the culture had not actually changed.

Who are **managers?**

All businesses depend on effective management. Regardless of the type of business they work in, managers perform many of the same basic functions, are responsible for many of the same tasks, and have many of the same responsibilities. All managers must make plans, organize their work, direct the work of subordinates, and control operations.

Although our focus is on managers in *business* settings, the principles of management apply to all kinds of organizations. Managers work in charities, churches, community organizations, educational institutions, and government agencies. The prime minister of Canada, the president of the University of Toronto, the executive director of the United Way, the dean of your business school, and the chief administrator of your local hospital are all managers. Remember, too, that managers bring to small organizations many of the skills that they bring to large ones. Regardless of the nature and size of an organization, managers are among its most important resources.

The management **process**

Management is the process of planning, organizing, leading, and controlling an enterprise's financial, physical, human, and information resources to achieve the organization's goals. There are two important overall points to keep in mind when thinking about the management process. First, the planning, organizing, leading, and controlling aspects of a manager's job are interrelated. This means that a manager is likely to be engaged in all these activities during the course of any given business day.

Second, there is a difference between management effectiveness and management efficiency. **Efficiency** means achieving the greatest level of output with a given amount of input. **Effectiveness**, on the other hand, means achieving organizational goals that have been set. Thus, efficiency means doing things right, while effectiveness means doing the right things. A manager who focuses on being effective will likely also be efficient, but a manager who

> MANAGEMENT
> The process of planning, organizing, leading, and controlling a business's financial, physical, human, and information resources in order to achieve its goals.

> EFFICIENCY
> Achieving the greatest level of output with a given amount of input.

> EFFECTIVENESS
> Achieving set organizational goals.

As top managers (a) Marjorie Scardino (CEO of Pearson PLC), (b) Calin Rovinescu (president and CEO of Air Canada), and (c) James Sinegal (co-founder and CEO of Costco) are important resources for their companies. They set the strategic direction for their companies and provide leadership to other managers. They are also accountable to shareholders, employees, customers, and other key constituents for the performance and effectiveness of their businesses.

THE **FOUR FUNCTIONS** OF MANAGEMENT

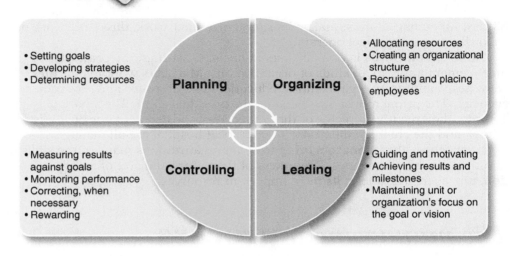

Planning
- Setting goals
- Developing strategies
- Determining resources

Organizing
- Allocating resources
- Creating an organizational structure
- Recruiting and placing employees

Controlling
- Measuring results against goals
- Monitoring performance
- Correcting, when necessary
- Rewarding

Leading
- Guiding and motivating
- Achieving results and milestones
- Maintaining unit or organization's focus on the goal or vision

focuses on being efficient may or may not be effective. The box entitled "What Do Managers Actually Do?" explains the nature of managerial jobs.

Planning

PLANNING
That portion of a manager's job concerned with determining what the business needs to do and the best way to achieve it.

Planning is the process of determining the firm's goals and developing a strategy for achieving those goals. The planning process involves five steps:

▶ In *step 1*, goals are established for the organization. A commercial airline, for example, may set a goal to fill 90 percent of the seats on each flight.

▶ In *step 2*, managers identify whether a gap exists between the company's desired and actual position. For example, the airline may analyze load data and find that only 73 percent of the seats on the average flight are filled.

▶ In *step 3*, managers develop plans to achieve the desired objectives. For example, the airline may reduce fares on heavily travelled routes in order to increase the percentage of the seats that are filled.

▶ In *step 4*, the plans that have been decided upon are implemented. For example, the fare from Toronto to Montreal may be reduced by 10 percent.

▶ In *step 5*, the effectiveness of the plan is assessed. The airline would measure the percentage of seats that were filled after the change was implemented to determine whether the goal was reached.

McDonald's experience in Canada over the past decade demonstrates the importance of planning. Until 2002, McDonald's was the largest fast-food chain in Canada. But then it was overtaken by Tim Hortons. In response to this development, McDonald's set a goal to reinvent itself and begin to grow again (*step 1*). The gap between where McDonald's was and where it wanted to be (*step 2*) was obvious, so McDonald's top managers developed a strategic plan (called "Plan to Win") in order to achieve the new objective (*step 3*). This involved developing many new menu items (like the Angus Burger, new salads, and snack wraps), renovating restaurants to look more like contemporary cafés or bistros (with polished stone tabletops and fireplaces), letting franchisees target local tastes with their menus (like the

McLobster sandwich in the Maritimes), and staying open longer (60 percent of McDonald's restaurants are now open 24 hours a day). These plans were implemented beginning in 2003 and 2004 (*step 4*). The effectiveness of the plan has now been assessed (*step 5*). Sales were $2.9 billion in 2008 (a record) and $3 billion in 2009 (another record). These sales levels were achieved in spite of the recession of 2008–2009. McDonald's was one of only two companies in the Dow Jones Industrial Average whose stock price rose during 2008 (the other was Walmart).[1]

Because it may be difficult to predict which plans will be successful, some managers use *prediction markets* to help assess future possibilities. This approach involves creating a market where people can buy "shares" in various answers to important questions that need to be answered. At Cisco Systems, for example, 20 employees in a chip-design unit bought shares based on how many defects they thought they would find in a new product (each share represented a range of possible number of defects). The winner of the game received an iPod. The actual number of defects found in the new chip was in the range that was predicted by the group. Other companies that use prediction markets include Microsoft, Best Buy, and Hewlett-Packard.[2]

A hierarchy of plans

Plans can be made on three general levels, with each level reflecting plans for which managers at that level are responsible. These levels constitute a hierarchy because implementing plans is practical only when there is a logical flow from one level to the next. **Strategic plans** reflect decisions about resource allocations, company priorities, and the steps needed to meet strategic goals, and are usually set by top management. Procter & Gamble's strategy to have its products rank first or second in their category is an example of a strategic plan. We look at strategic planning later in this chapter. **Tactical plans** are shorter-range plans concerned with implementing specific aspects of the company's strategic plans. They typically involve upper and middle management. Coca-Cola's decision to increase sales in Europe by building European bottling facilities is an example of tactical planning. **Operational plans**, which are developed by middle and lower-level managers, set short-term targets for daily, weekly, or monthly performance. McDonald's, for example, establishes operational plans when it explains precisely how Big Macs are to be cooked, warmed, and served.

Organizing

Organizing is the process of deciding which jobs must be performed, and how these jobs should be coordinated so that the company's goals are reached. Most businesses prepare organization charts that diagram the various jobs within the company and how those jobs relate to one another. These charts help everyone understand their job and to whom they report. In many larger businesses, roles and reporting relationships may be too complex to draw as a simple box-and-line diagram.

To help you appreciate the importance of the organizing function, consider the example of Hewlett-Packard (HP). The company was once one of the leading-edge, high-tech firms in the world, but it lost its lustre a few years ago. HP had long prided itself on being a corporate confederation of individual businesses, and sometimes these businesses ended up competing with each other. This approach had been beneficial for much of the firm's history. It was easier for each business to make its own decisions quickly and efficiently, and the competition kept each unit on its toes. By the late 1990s, however, problems had become apparent, and no one could quite figure out what was going on.

> **STRATEGIC PLANS** Plans that reflect decisions about resource allocations, company priorities, and steps needed to meet strategic goals.

> **TACTICAL PLANS** Generally, short-range plans concerned with implementing specific aspects of a company's strategic plans.

> **OPERATIONAL PLANS** Plans setting short-term targets for daily, weekly, or monthly performance.

> **ORGANIZING** That portion of a manager's job concerned with mobilizing the necessary resources to complete a particular task.

What Do Managers Actually Do?

Henry Mintzberg of McGill University conducted a detailed study of the work of five chief executive officers and found that managers work at an unrelenting pace; their activities are characterized by brevity, variety, and fragmentation; they have a preference for "live" action; they emphasize work activities that are current, specific, and well-defined; and they are attracted to verbal media.

Mintzberg says that a manager's formal authority and status give rise to three *interpersonal roles*: (1) *figurehead* (duties of a ceremonial nature, such as attending a subordinate's wedding); (2) *leader* (being responsible for the work of the unit); and (3) *liaison* (making contact outside the vertical chain of command). These interpersonal roles give rise to three *informational roles*: (1) *monitor* (scanning the environment for relevant information); (2) *disseminator* (passing information to subordinates); and (3) *spokesperson* (sending information to people outside the unit). The interpersonal and informational roles allow the manager to carry out four *decision-making roles*: (1) *entrepreneur* (improving the performance of the unit); (2) *disturbance handler* (responding to high-pressure disturbances, such as a strike at a supplier); (3) *resource allocator* (deciding who will get what in the unit); and (4) *negotiator* (working out agreements on a wide variety of issues, such as the amount of authority an individual will be given).

Managers in a study conducted by Pace Productivity felt that they should have spent about half their time on activities such as managing staff, providing direction, and coaching, but that they actually were able to spend less than 20 percent of their time on "people management." Managers also thought that they should have spent about 6 percent of their time on administrative tasks, but they actually spent 25 percent of their time on those activities. The amount of time managers thought they should spend on planning was about the same as what they actually spent. Consistent with Mintzberg's original findings, the Pace data also showed that managers' lives are very hectic, and their focus shifts rapidly from activity to activity. For example, Pace identified 43 different activities that lasted an average of just 16 minutes each.

Critical Thinking Questions

1. Why is the work of managers important?

2. Why do you think managers spend less time on "people management" than they think they should, and more time on administrative tasks than they think they should?

Ann Livermore, then head of the firm's software and services business, realized that the structure that had worked so well in the past was now holding the company back. To regain its competitive edge, HP needed an integrated, organization-wide strategy. Livermore led the charge to create one organization united behind one strategic plan. Eventually, a new team of top managers was handed control of the company, and every major component of the firm's structure was reorganized. The firm is now back on solid footing and has regained its place as one of the world's top technology businesses.[3]

Leading

When leading, managers guide and motivate workers to meet the company's objectives. Legendary leaders like Sam Walton (Walmart) and Clive Beddoe (West-Jet) were able to unite their employees in a clear and targeted manner, and motivate them to work in the best interests of their employer. While managers do have the power to give orders and demand results, leading goes beyond merely giving orders. Leaders must also have the ability to motivate their employees to set challenging goals and to work hard to achieve them. This is likely to lead to organizational success, which in turn means that employees will respect their leaders, trust them, and believe that by working together, both the firm and its employees will benefit.

> **LEADING**
> That portion of a manager's job concerned with guiding and motivating employees to meet the firm's objectives.

Controlling

Controlling is the process of monitoring a firm's performance to make sure that it is meeting its goals. Managers at WestJet and Air Canada, for example, focus relentlessly on numerous indicators of performance that they can measure and adjust. Everything from on-time arrivals to baggage-handling errors to the number of empty seats on an airplane to surveys of employee and customer satisfaction are regularly and routinely monitored. If on-time arrivals start to slip, managers focus on the problem and get it fixed. No single element of the firm's performance can slip too far before it's noticed and fixed.

> **CONTROLLING**
> That portion of a manager's job concerned with monitoring the firm's performance and, if necessary, acting to bring it in line with the firm's goals.

Key 11.2 illustrates the control process, which begins when management establishes standards (often for financial performance). If, for example, a company sets a goal of increasing its sales by 20 percent over the next five years, an appropriate standard to assess pro-gress toward the 20 percent goal might be an increase of about 4 percent a year. Managers then measure actual performance each year against standards. If the two amounts agree, the organization continues along its pre-sent course. If they vary significantly, however, one or the other needs adjustment. If sales have increased 3.9 per-cent by the end of the first year, things are probably fine. But if sales have dropped 1 percent, some revision in plans is needed.

Controlling applies to many activities, including the college or university courses that you are now taking. The instructor first indicates the knowledge areas where you must show competence, and the level of competence you must show. Next, the instructor measures your performance, usually through assignments and exams. The instructor then determines whether your performance meets the standard. If your performance is satisfactory (or unsatisfactory), you receive feedback in the form of a passing (or failing) grade in the course.

Control can also show where performance is better (or worse) than expected, and can serve as a basis for providing rewards or reducing costs. For example, when the distributor of the surprise hit movie *The March of the Penguins* saw how popular the movie was becoming, the firm was able to increase advertising and distribution, making the niche movie into a major commercial success. In contrast, when the sales of the Chevrolet Super Sport Roadster (a classic, late-1940s pickup-style vehicle with a two-seat roadster design) were much lower than expected, production of the vehicle was suspended.

Japanese organizations don't usually like radical restructuring, but when Senichi Hoshino took over the hapless Hanshin Tigers, he axed 24 of the team's 70 players and replaced them with free agents. He required everyone on the roster to compete for a position, tracked performance daily, and made individual coaches directly responsible for seeing that players executed certain skills. Soon after that, the Tigers won the pennant.

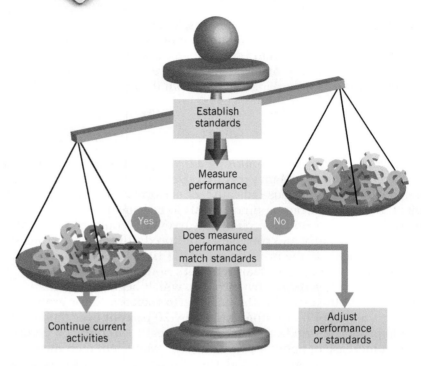

Types of **managers**

Although all managers plan, organize, lead, and control, not all managers have the same degree of responsibility for each activity. Moreover, managers differ in the specific application of these activities. Thus we can differentiate between managers based on their *level* of responsibility and their *area* of responsibility.

Levels of Management

The three basic levels of management are top, middle, and first-line management. As Key 11.3 shows, in most firms there are more middle managers than top managers and more first-line managers than middle managers. Moreover, as the categories imply, the authority of managers and the complexity of their duties increase as we move up the pyramid.

TOP MANAGERS
Those managers responsible
for a firm's overall
performance and
effectiveness and for
developing long-range plans
for the company.

Top managers

The managers who guide the fortunes of companies are **top managers.** Top managers set policies, formulate strategies, oversee significant decisions, and represent the company in its dealings with other businesses and government.[4] Top managers are responsible to the board of directors and stockholders for the firm's overall performance and effectiveness. Common titles for top managers include president, vice-president, chief executive officer (CEO), chief operating officer (COO), and chief financial officer (CFO). CEOs are the link between the organization and its markets and customers.[5]

MOST ORGANIZATIONS HAVE **THREE** **BASIC LEVELS** OF MANAGEMENT

Each year, *Canadian Business* develops an All-Star Execs list by examining financial data of Canadian companies, and by consulting with a panel of business leaders to determine which executives performed unusually well. In 2009, the top managers were Mayo Schmidt (CEO of Viterra), Colleen Johnston (CFO of TD Bank Financial Group), and Larry Conlee (COO of Research In Motion).[6]

Middle managers

Although below the ranks of the top executives, **middle managers** still occupy positions of considerable autonomy and importance. Titles such as plant manager, operations manager, and division manager are typical of middle-management positions. The producer of a Lion's Gate film like *Precious* is a middle manager. In general, middle managers are responsible for implementing the strategies, policies, and decisions made by top managers. For example, if top management decides to bring out a new product in 12 months or to cut costs by 5 percent, middle management will have to decide to increase the pace of new product development or to reduce the plant's workforce.

> MIDDLE MANAGERS
> Those managers responsible for implementing the decisions made by top managers.

First-line managers

Individuals with titles such as *supervisor*, *office manager*, and *group leader* are **first-line managers**. Although they spend most of their time working with and supervising the employees who report to them, first-line managers' activities are not limited to those activities. At a building site, for example, the project manager not only ensures that workers are carrying out construction as specified by the architect but also interacts extensively with materials suppliers, community officials, and middle and top managers at the home office. The manager of a Canadian Tire store and the flight-services manager for a specific Air Canada

> FIRST-LINE MANAGERS
> Those managers responsible for supervising the work of employees.

Table 11.1 The Three Levels of Management

LEVEL	EXAMPLES	RESPONSIBILITIES
Top managers	President, vice president, treasurer, chief executive officer (CEO), chief financial officer (CFO)	• Responsible for the overall performance and effectiveness of the firm • Set general policies, formulate strategies, and approve all significant decisions • Represent the company in dealings with other firms and with government bodies
Middle managers	Plant manager, operations manager, division manager, regional sales manager	• Responsible for implementing the strategies and working toward the goals set by top managers
First-line managers	Supervisor, office manager, project manager, group leader, sales manager	• Responsible for supervising the work of employees who report to them • Ensure employees understand and are properly trained in company policies and procedures

flight are first-line managers. Table 11.1 summarizes the duties of the three basic levels of management.

Areas of management

Within any large company, the top, middle, and first-line managers work in a variety of areas, including human resources, operations, information, marketing, and finance.

Human resource managers

HUMAN RESOURCE MANAGERS
Those managers responsible for hiring, training, evaluating, and compensating employees.

Human resource managers can be found in most companies; they hire employees, train them, evaluate their performance, decide how they should be compensated, and deal with labour unions (if the workforce is unionized). Large firms may have several human resource departments, each dealing with specialized activities. Imperial Oil, for example, has separate departments to deal with recruiting and hiring, wage and salary levels, and labour relations. Smaller firms may have a single department, while very small organizations may have a single person responsible for all human resource activities.

Operations managers

OPERATIONS MANAGERS
Those managers responsible for controlling production, inventory, and quality of a firm's products.

Operations managers are responsible for a company's system for creating goods and services. This includes production control, inventory control, and quality control, among other duties. Manufacturing companies like Steelcase, Bristol Aerospace, and Sony need operations managers at many levels. Such firms typically have a vice-president for operations (top), plant managers (middle), and supervisors (first-line). In recent years, sound operations management practices have also become increasingly important to service-producing organizations like hospitals, the government, and colleges and universities.

Information managers

INFORMATION MANAGERS
Those managers responsible for the design and implementation of systems to gather, process, and disseminate information.

Dramatic increases in both the amount of information available to managers and the ability to manage it have led to the emergence of **information managers**. These managers are responsible for designing and implementing various systems to gather, process, and disseminate information. Federal Express, for example, has a chief information officer. Middle managers engaged in information management help design information systems for divisions or plants. Computer systems managers within smaller businesses or operations are first-line managers. Information management is discussed in Appendix B.

Marketing managers

Marketing includes the development, pricing, promotion, and distribution of products and services. **Marketing managers** are responsible for getting these products and services to buyers. Marketing is especially important for firms producing consumer products, such as Procter & Gamble, Coca-Cola, and Sun Ice. These firms may have large numbers of marketing managers at various levels. For example, a large firm will probably have a vice-president for marketing (top manager), regional marketing managers (middle managers), and several district sales managers (first-line managers).

Financial managers

Management of a firm's finances is extremely important to its survival. Nearly every company has **financial managers** to plan and oversee its financial resources. Levels of financial management may include a vice-president for finance (top), division controller (middle), and accounting supervisor (first-line). For large financial institutions, effective financial management is the company's reason for being.

Other managers

Some firms have more specialized managers. Chemical companies like CIL have research and development managers, for example, whereas companies like Petro-Canada and Apple have public relations managers. The range of possibilities is almost endless, and the areas of management are limited only by the needs and imagination of the company.

Basic management skills

The degree of success that people achieve in management positions is determined by the skills and abilities they possess. Effective managers must have several skills: *technical, human relations, conceptual, time management,* and *decision-making skills*.

Technical skills

Technical skills help people to perform specialized tasks. A secretary's ability to type, an animator's ability to draw a cartoon, and an accountant's ability to audit a company's records are all technical skills. People develop their technical skills through education and experience. The secretary, for example, probably took an office systems technology course and has had many hours of practice both on and off the job. The animator may have had training in an art school and probably learned a great deal from experienced animators on the job. The accountant earned a university degree and a professional certification.

As Key 11.4 shows, technical skills are especially important for first-line managers. Most first-line managers spend considerable time helping employees solve work-related problems, monitoring their performance, and training them

DIFFERENT **LEVELS IN AN ORGANIZATION** REQUIRE DIFFERENT COMBINATION OF MANAGERIAL SKILLS

TOP MANAGEMENT	MIDDLE MANAGEMENT	FIRST-LINE MANAGEMENT
Technical	Technical	Technical
Human Relations	Human Relations	Human Relations
Conceptual	Conceptual	Conceptual

in more efficient work procedures. Such managers need a basic understanding of the jobs they supervise. As a manager moves up the corporate ladder, however, technical skills become less and less important. Top managers, for example, often need only a general familiarity with the mechanics of basic tasks performed within the company. A top manager at Disney, for example, probably can't draw Mickey Mouse or build a ride for Disney World.

Human relations skills

HUMAN RELATIONS
SKILLS
Skills in understanding and
getting along with people.

Human relations skills help managers to lead, motivate, communicate with, and get along with their subordinates. Managers with poor human relations skills will likely have conflicts with subordinates, cause valuable employees to quit or transfer, and contribute to poor morale. Key 11.4 shows that human relations skills are important at all levels of management. This is true because all managers in the hierarchy act as "bridges" between their bosses, their subordinates, and other managers at the same level in the hierarchy. A study by DDI Canada found that the top reason for managerial failure was poor people skills.[7]

To improve their insights into employee needs and company operations, some managers have decided to work alongside entry-level employees on a temporary basis. When the CEO of 7-Eleven (Joseph De Pinto) worked undercover at a 7-Eleven outlet, he discovered how hard the people worked, and why the location was selling so much coffee. Larry O'Donnell, the CEO of Waste Management, did jobs like sorting trash, picking up paper at a landfill, and cleaning portable toilets. The experience taught him the pressure for production that employees had to cope with, and he introduced changes based on what he had learned on the job.[8]

Conceptual skills

CONCEPTUAL SKILLS
Abilities to think in the
abstract, diagnose and
analyze various situations,
and see beyond the present
situation.

Conceptual skills refer to a person's ability to think in the abstract, to diagnose and analyze various situations, and to see beyond the present situation. Conceptual skills help managers recognize new market opportunities and threats. For example, in e-commerce businesses, conceptual skills help managers foresee how a particular business application will be affected by, or can be translated to, the internet. Key 11.4 shows that top managers depend most on conceptual skills, and first-line managers least, but at least some conceptual skills are needed in almost any management job.

Time management skills

(Time management skills) refer to the productive use that managers make of their time. In 2009, for example, the CEO of Thomson Reuters Corp., Thomas Glocer, was paid $36.6 million.[9] Assuming that he worked 50 hours a week and took two weeks' vacation, Glocer earned about $14 640 per hour, or about $244 per minute. Any time that he wastes represents a large cost to Thomson Reuters and its stockholders.

To manage time effectively, managers must address four leading causes of wasted time:

> *Paperwork.* Some managers spend too much time deciding what to do with letters and reports. Most documents of this sort are routine and can be handled quickly. Managers must learn to recognize those documents that require more attention.

> *The telephone.* Experts estimate that managers are interrupted by the telephone every five minutes. To manage time more effectively, they suggest having a secretary screen all calls and setting aside a certain block of time each day to return the important ones.

> *Meetings.* Many managers spend as much as four hours per day in meetings. To help keep this time productive, the person handling the meeting should specify a clear agenda, start on time, keep everyone focused on the agenda, and end on time.

> *Email.* With the introduction of devices like the BlackBerry, managers are relying more heavily on email and other forms of electronic communication. But many email messages are not important, and some are downright trivial. As the number of electronic messages grows, the potential time wasted also increases.

Decision-making skills

(Decision-making skills) help managers define problems and select the best course of action. It is a critical management skill because decision making affects all the functions of management. The Alternative Board (TAB) is devoted to improving management decision making and has 1000 peer groups around North America. These peer groups—which are attended by managers who are looking for solutions to problems that they are experiencing—provide a forum for discussions among managers who have had similar problems.[10]

The rational decision-making process

Key 11.5 shows the steps in the rational decision-making process. The key elements of each step are described below.

Recognizing and Defining the Decision Situation The first step in rational decision making is recognizing that a decision is necessary. There must be some stimulus or spark to initiate this process. For example, when equipment

TIME MANAGEMENT SKILLS
Skills associated with the productive use of time.

DECISION-MAKING SKILLS
Skills in defining problems and selecting the best courses of action.

The Pittsburgh Steelers are one of the most successful franchises in the history of professional football. They have won more Super Bowls (six) than any other team. The Rooney family has owned and managed the team since 1933. They have demonstrated technical and decision-making skills in selecting and retaining the best players for the team. In 2009, the Steelers won another Super Bowl.

THE **THREE LEVELS** OF MANAGEMENT

Key 11.5

Step	Detail	Example
1. Recognizing and defining the decision situation	Some stimulus indicates that a decision must be made. The stimulus may be positive or negative.	The plant manager sees that employee turnover has increased by 5 percent.
2. Identifying alternatives	Both obvious and creative alternatives are desired. In general, the more important the decision, the more alternatives should be generated.	The plant manager can increase wages, increase benefits, or change hiring standards.
3. Evaluating alternatives	Each alternative is evaluated to determine its feasibility, its satisfactoriness, and its consequences.	Increasing benefits may not be feasible. Increasing wages and changing hiring standards may satisfy all conditions.
4. Selecting the best alternative	Consider all situational factors and choose the alternative that best fits the manager's situation.	Changing hiring standards will take an extended period of time to cut turnover, so increase wages.
5. Implementing the chosen alternative	The chosen alternative is implemented into the organizational system.	The plant manager may need permission from corporate headquarters. The human resource department establishes a new wage structure.
6. Following up and evaluating the results	At some time in the future, the manager should ascertain the extent to which the alternative chosen in step 4 and implemented in step 5 has worked.	The plant manager notes that six months later, turnover dropped to its previous level.

malfunctions, managers must decide whether to repair it or to replace it. The stimulus for a decision may be either a problem or an opportunity. A manager facing cost overruns on a project is faced with a problem decision, while a manager who is trying to decide how to invest surplus funds is faced with an opportunity decision.

Understanding precisely what the problem or opportunity is comes from careful analysis and thoughtful consideration of the situation. Consider the international air travel industry. Because of the growth of international travel related to business, education, and tourism, global carriers like Singapore Airlines, KLM, JAL, British Airways, and American Airlines need to increase their capacity for international travel. Because most major international airports are already operating at or near capacity, adding a significant number of new flights to existing schedules is not feasible. As a result, the most logical alternative is to increase capacity on existing flights. Thus, Boeing and Airbus, the world's only manufacturers of large commercial aircraft, recognized an important opportunity and defined their decision situation as how best to respond to the need for increased global travel capacity.[11]

Identifying Alternatives Once the need for a decision has been recognized and defined, the second step is to identify possible alternative courses of effective action. In general, the more important the decision, the more attention is directed to developing alternatives. If the decision involves a multimillion-dollar relocation, a great deal of time and expertise should be devoted to identifying alternatives, but if the decision involves choosing a name for the company softball team, much less resources should be devoted to the task (although there may be a lot of arguing about what the name should be!).

Managers must accept that factors such as legal restrictions, moral and ethical norms, and available technology can limit their alternatives. For example, after assessing the question of how to increase international airline capacity, Boeing and Airbus identified three alternatives: They could independently develop new large planes, they could collaborate in a joint venture to create a single new large plane, or they could modify their largest existing planes to increase their capacity.

Evaluating Alternatives Once alternatives have been identified, they must be thoroughly evaluated to increase the chance that the alternative finally chosen will be successful. During its analysis of alternatives, Airbus concluded that it would be at a disadvantage if it tried to simply enlarge its existing planes, because the competitive Boeing 747 is already the largest aircraft being made and could readily be expanded. Boeing, meanwhile, was seriously concerned about the risk inherent in building a new and even larger plane, even if it shared the risk with Airbus as a joint venture.

Selecting the Best Alternative Choosing the best available alternative is a key activity in decision making. Even though many situations do not lend themselves to objective mathematical analysis, managers and leaders can often develop subjective estimates for choosing an alternative. Decision makers should also remember that finding multiple acceptable alternatives may be possible, so selecting just one alternative and rejecting all the others might not be necessary. For example, Airbus proposed a joint venture with Boeing, but Boeing decided that its best course of action was to modify its existing 747 to increase its capacity. Airbus then decided to proceed on its own to develop and manufacture a new jumbo jet called the A380. Meanwhile, Boeing decided that in addition to modifying its 747, it would also develop a new plane (the 787).

After a long decision-making process, Airbus decided to design its own new jumbo jet. Boeing, meanwhile, went through a similar decision-making process but concluded that the risks were too great to gamble on such an enormous project. Instead, the company decided to modify its existing 747 design and develop a new fuel-efficient aircraft called the 787.

Implementing the Chosen Alternative After an alternative has been selected, managers must implement it. In the case of an acquisition, for example, managers must decide how to integrate the activities of the new business into the firm's existing organizational framework. One of the key considerations during implementation is employee resistance to change. The reasons for such resistance include insecurity, inconvenience, and fear of the unknown. Managers must also recognize that even when all alternatives have been evaluated as precisely as possible and the consequences of each alternative have been weighed, unanticipated consequences are still likely. For example, both Boeing and Airbus have experienced unexpected delays in bringing their new planes to market.

Following up and Evaluating the Results The final step in the decision-making process requires managers to evaluate the effectiveness of their decision—that is, they should make sure that the chosen alternative has served its original purpose. If an implemented alternative appears not to be working, they can respond in several ways. One possibility is to adopt an alternative that had previously been discarded. Or they might recognize that the situation was not correctly defined to begin with and start the process all over again. In the Boeing/Airbus case, both companies are getting some feedback about whether or not they made a good decision. For example, increasing fuel prices may mean that the 787 was the best decision because it is so fuel efficient.

Behavioural aspects of decision making

Most managers try to be logical when they make decisions. But even when they try, they may not succeed. When Starbucks opened its first coffee shops in New York, it relied on scientific marketing research, taste tests, and rational deliberation in making a decision to emphasize drip over espresso coffee. However, that decision proved wrong when it became clear that New Yorkers strongly preferred the same espresso-style coffees that were Starbucks' mainstays in the west. Hence, the firm had to reconfigure its stores hastily to meet customer preferences.

To complicate matters, non-logical and emotional factors often influence managerial decision making. These factors include *organizational politics*, *intuition*, *escalation of commitment*, and *risk propensity*.

ORGANIZATIONAL POLITICS
The actions that people take as they try to get what they want.

Organizational Politics The term organizational politics refers to the actions that people take as they try to get what they want. These actions may or may not be beneficial to the organization, but they do influence decision making, particularly if the person taking the action is a powerful manager.

INTUITION
An innate belief about something, often without conscious consideration.

Intuition Managers sometimes decide to do something because it "feels right" or they have a "hunch." Intuition is usually based on years of experience and practice in making decisions in similar situations. Such an inner sense may actually help managers make an occasional decision without going through a rational sequence of steps. For example, the New York Yankees once contacted three major sneaker manufacturers—Nike, Reebok, and Adidas—and informed them that they were interested in signing a sponsorship deal. While Nike and Reebok were carefully and rationally assessing the possibilities, managers at Adidas quickly responded to the idea and ended up hammering out a contract while the competitors were still analyzing details.[12] These occasional successes can be very dramatic, but they should not cause managers to rely too heavily on intuition.

ESCALATION OF COMMITMENT
Condition in which a decision maker becomes so committed to a course of action that he or she stays with it even when there is evidence that the decision was wrong.

Escalation of Commitment When a manager makes a decision and then remains committed to its implementation in spite of clear evidence that it was a bad decision, escalation of commitment has occurred.[13] A good example of this is Expo '86, the world's fair that was held in British Columbia. When the project was first conceived, the deficit was projected at about $56 million. Over the next few years, the projected deficit kept rising until it was over $300 million. In spite of that, the project went forward. Managers can avoid overcommitment by setting specific goals ahead of time that deal with how much time and money they are willing to spend on a given project. These goals make it harder for managers to interpret unfavourable news in a positive light.

Risk Propensity Risk propensity refers to how much a manager is willing to gamble when making decisions. Managers who are very cautious when making decisions are more likely to avoid mistakes, and they are unlikely to make decisions that lead to big losses (or big gains). Other managers are extremely aggressive in making decisions and are willing to take risks.[14] They rely heavily on intuition, reach decisions quickly, and often risk big money on their decisions. These managers are more likely than their conservative counterparts to achieve big successes, but they are also more likely to incur greater losses.[15] The organization's culture is a prime ingredient in fostering different levels of risk propensity.

RISK PROPENSITY
→ *Extent to which a decision maker is willing to gamble when making a decision.*

Strategic management: setting goals and formulating strategy

Strategic management is the process of effectively aligning the organization with its external environment. The starting point in strategic management is setting goals that a business wants to achieve. Every business needs goals. Remember, however, that deciding what it intends to do is only the first step for an organization. Managers must also make decisions about what actions will and will not achieve company goals. Decisions cannot be made on a problem-by-problem basis or merely to meet needs as they arise. In most companies, a broad program underlies those decisions. That program is called a strategy—the broad set of organizational plans for implementing the decisions made for achieving organizational goals.

STRATEGIC MANAGEMENT
→ *The process of helping an organization maintain an effective alignment with its environment.*

STRATEGY
The broad set of organizational plans for implementing the decisions made for achieving organizational goals.

Setting business goals

Goals are performance targets, the means by which organizations and their managers measure success or failure at every level. Managers must understand the purposes of goal setting and the kinds of goals that need to be set.

The purposes of goal setting

There are four main purposes in organizational goal setting:

1. *Goal setting provides direction, guidance, and motivation for all managers.* For example, each manager at Kanke Seafood Restaurants Ltd. is required to work through a goal-setting exercise each year. Setting and achieving goals is the most effective form of self-motivation.

2. *Goal setting helps firms allocate resources.* Areas that are expected to grow, for example, will get first priority. Thus, 3M allocates more resources to new projects with large sales potential than to projects with low growth potential.

3. *Goal setting helps to define corporate culture.* General Electric's goal, for instance, is to push each of its divisions to number one or number two in its industry. The result is a competitive (and often stressful) environment, and a culture that rewards success and has little tolerance for failure.

4. *Goal setting helps managers assess performance.* If a unit sets a goal of increasing sales by 10 percent in a given year, managers in that unit who attain or exceed the goal can be rewarded. Units failing to reach the goal will also be compensated accordingly.

Kinds of Goals Goals differ from company to company, depending on the firm's vision and mission. Every organization has a **vision (or purpose)** that indicates *why* it exists and what kind of organization it wants to be. For example, businesses seek profit, universities discover and transmit new knowledge, and government agencies provide services to the public. Most organizations also have a **mission statement**—a statement of *how* they will achieve their purpose. DaimlerChrysler's mission statement emphasizes "delighted customers," while Atco Ltd.'s mission is to provide products and services to the energy and resource industries, and to invest in energy-related assets in North America. Mission statements often include some statement about the company's core values and its commitment to ethical behaviour.

Two business firms can have the same vision—for example, to sell watches at a profit—yet have very different missions. Timex sells low-cost, reliable watches in outlets ranging from department stores to corner drugstores. Rolex, on the other hand, sells high-quality, high-priced fashion watches through selected jewellery stores. Regardless of a company's purpose and mission, it must set long-term, intermediate, and short-term goals.

> ▶ **Long-term goals** relate to extended periods of time —typically five years or more into the future. American Express, for example, might set a long-term goal of doubling the number of participating merchants during the next 10 years.

> ▶ **Intermediate goals** are set for a period of one to five years into the future. Companies usually have intermediate goals in several areas. For example, the marketing department's goal might be to increase sales by 3 percent in two years. The production department might want to decrease expenses by 6 percent in four years. Human resources might seek to cut turnover by 10 percent in two years. Finance might aim for a 3 percent increase in return on investment in three years.

> ▶ Like intermediate goals, **short-term goals**—which are set for perhaps one year—are developed for several different areas. Increasing sales by 2 percent this year, cutting costs by 1 percent next quarter, and reducing turnover by 4 percent over the next six months are all short-term goals.

Whatever the time frame of the goals that are set, research shows that managers who set **SMART goals** (goals that are *S*pecific, *M*easurable, *A*chievable, *R*ealistic, and *T*ime-framed) have higher performance than managers who don't. The boxed insert entitled "Setting Green Goals" describes the importance of setting goals that take the environment into account.

Formulating strategy

After a firm has set its goals, it must develop a strategy for achieving them. In contrast to planning, strategy is wider in scope, and is a broad program that describes how a business intends to meet its goals, how it will respond to new challenges, and how it will meet new needs. Developing a strategy may not be easy (see the boxed insert entitled "Print Media").

VISION (OR PURPOSE) A statement indicating why an organization exists and what kind of organization it wants to be.

MISSION STATEMENT An organization's statement of how it will achieve its purpose in the environment in which it conducts its business.

LONG-TERM GOALS Goals set for extended periods of time, typically five years or more into the future.

INTERMEDIATE GOALS Goals set for a period of one to five years.

SHORT-TERM GOALS Goals set for the very near future, typically less than one year.

SMART GOALS Goals that are Specific, Measurable, Achievable, Realistic, and Time-framed.

the greening of Business

Setting Green Goals

The logic of goal setting is being applied to make businesses greener. Consider the following:

- **Walmart set a goal to reduce the amount of packaging used by 5 percent throughout its huge supply chain; it wants to achieve that goal by 2013.**

- **The province of Ontario has set a goal to reduce plastic bag usage by 50 percent by 2012.**

- **Scotiabank has set a goal to be in the top 10 percent of the companies listed on the Dow Jones Sustainability World Index.**

- **Employees on different floors of the Air Miles building in Toronto compete to see who can reduce energy usage the most in a specific month.**

For some organizations, the setting of green goals is closely tied to their success. For example, the CEO of Honda, Takeo Fukui, recognized that Toyota's popular Prius hybrid automobile outsold Honda's hybrid car by a wide margin during the last decade, so he set a goal to make Honda the greenest company in the automobile industry. Honda has set a goal to sell 500 000 hybrid automobiles each year (Toyota's goal is one million). In 2008, Honda introduced its Clarity FCX, which is the most advanced green vehicle ever made. It is powered by a hydrogen fuel cell that generates no pollution at all. Honda also launched a new gas–electric hybrid in 2009, and plans to launch several other hybrids by 2015.

Rona Inc., the home renovation chain, has set a goal of doing business only with suppliers who address environmental sustainability, and who do not contribute to deforestation. The goal for 2009 was to have all the plywood panels Rona sells made only from lumber that comes from forests that have been certified as sustainable. In 2010, the same goal was applied to spruce, pine, and fir. By 2012, Rona's goal is to have 25 percent of its total wood sales come from forests that are certified by the Forest Stewardship Council.

Green goals may be imposed on companies by external groups. In 2007, for example, the federal government notified Canada's biggest industrial polluters that they had six months to provide emissions data that the government would use in setting new emission reduction targets. Discussions also continue at the international level about what the goal for emissions should be, but to date there has been no agreement. A spokesman for 77 developing nations says that unless there is a goal, there can be no progress.

Critical Thinking Questions

1. What are the advantages associated with setting green goals? Are there disadvantages? Explain.

2. What difficulties might Rona encounter as it tries to reach the goal of having 25 percent of its total wood sales come from forests that are certified by the Forest Stewardship Council?

3. What are the advantages of the government setting emission reduction targets? What are the disadvantages?

e-business and social Media Solutions

Print Media: Are E-Readers the Solution or a New Problem?

The publishing business is dealing with significant changes that will require serious strategic thinking. Consider these facts:

- According to the Audit Bureau of Circulations, which measures statistics for 57 Canadian and 472 American magazines, the industry is suffering. Newsstand sales were down and ad page revenues were down 21 percent in Canada in 2009.

- According to the Newspaper Association of America, readership has fallen by more than 700 000 per year since 2000. Classified ad revenue is down 40 percent in the last decade because of online competitors like craigslist, Monster, and AutoTrader. Rupert Murdoch recently declared that news aggregator sites like Google and Digg.com are kleptomaniacs that steal content. As the owner of NewsCorp, a major media giant, his intention is to erect pay walls around his media sites.

- Book publishers and bookstore owners are also under pressure. According to Heather Reisman of Indigo Books, the e-reader threat may cause a 15 percent decline in book sales over the next five years. Others predict digital sales will comprise 25 percent of the market in three years and as high as 80 percent in 10 years.

There are several new electronic devices that are having a big impact on the publishing industry, including Kindle (with a grey and black screen can be read in direct sunlight), the iPad (which provides a colour touch screen and serves as a web surfer, video console, and iPod), Kobo (a Kindle-like competitor that undercut the competition in 2010 with a price of $150), the Sony Reader, Nook (Barnes and Noble), Eee Pad (AsusTek), and the Skiff. The EnTourage eDGe is an interesting dual screen reader that looks like a book. Imagine reading the newspaper on the bus without elbowing the person next to you each time you flip a page. Imagine packing one e-reader rather than three or four books on your next trip. Actually, you don't have to imagine it.

The online world has been having a negative impact on print media for some time, but the introduction of e-readers was a new tipping point. How will the print media providers and the technology device creators develop a strategic, sustainable model? The model must satisfy the needs of consumers, columnists, authors, and technology companies alike. Developing such a strategy is not easy. Major publishers like Macmillan used the iPad launch to negotiate higher prices on e-books than had previously been dictated by Amazon (because of its virtual monopoly). Five top publishers—including Penguin and HarperCollins—were on board for the launch of the iPad. Newspapers and magazine companies were even keener to form partnerships, since the iPad was seen as a way to display content in a new, exciting, and accessible fashion.

Critical Thinking Questions

1. How do you think e-readers will impact the print industry? In the short term? In the long term?

2. Which print media source (newspapers, magazines, or books) is more likely to benefit from the widespread adoption of e-readers? Why?

STRATEGY FORMULATION

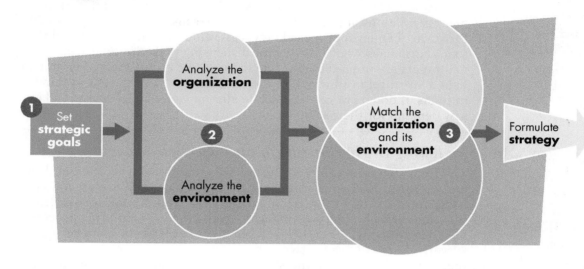

Strategy formulation involves three basic steps: (1) setting strategic goals, (2) analyzing the organization and its environment, and (3) matching the organization and its environment (see Key 11.6).

Setting Strategic Goals **Strategic goals** are long-term goals derived directly from the firm's mission statement. General Electric, for example, is pursuing four strategic goals to ensure continued success for the company: an emphasis on quality control, an emphasis on selling services and not just products, concentrating on niche acquisitions, and global expansion.

Analyzing the organization and its environment

After strategic goals have been set, managers assess both their organization and its environment using a **SWOT analysis.** This involves identifying organizational *S*trengths and *W*eaknesses, and identifying environmental *O*pportunities and *T*hreats. Strengths and weaknesses are factors *internal* to the firm, and are assessed using **organizational analysis.** Strengths might include surplus cash, a dedicated workforce, an ample supply of managerial talent, technical expertise, or weak competitors. For example, Pepsi's strength in beverage distribution through its network of soft-drink distributors was successfully extended to distribution of its Aquafina brand of bottled water. Weaknesses might include a cash shortage, aging factories, and a poor public image. Garden.com's reliance on the internet-based e-tailing model became its downfall when the dot-com bubble burst.

Opportunities and threats are factors *external* to the firm, and are assessed using **environmental analysis.** *O*pportunities include things like market demand for new products, favourable government legislation, or shortages

> **STRATEGY FORMULATION**
> Creation of a broad program for defining and meeting an organization's goals.

> **STRATEGIC GOALS**
> Long-term goals derived directly from the firm's mission statement.

> **SWOT ANALYSIS**
> Identification and analysis of organizational strengths and weaknesses and environmental opportunities and threats as part of strategy formulation.

> **ORGANIZATIONAL ANALYSIS**
> The process of analyzing a firm's strengths and weaknesses.

> **ENVIRONMENTAL ANALYSIS**
> The process of scanning the environment for threats and opportunities.

of raw materials that the company is good at producing. For example, when Pepsi managers recognized a market opportunity for bottled water, they moved quickly to launch their Aquafina brand and to position it for rapid growth. *Threats* include new products developed by competitors, unfavourable government regulations, and changes in consumer tastes. For example, in 2010, the Province of Ontario proposed new legislation that sharply reduced the revenue that pharmacies would receive for dispensing prescription drugs. Some external threats are unpredictable, like the volcanic eruption in Iceland in 2010 that halted air travel in Europe for a week. Commercial airlines lost hundreds of millions of dollars of revenue, while alternative service providers like trains saw demand for their services soar.

Matching the organization and its environment

The final step in strategy formulation is matching environmental threats and opportunities with corporate strengths and weaknesses. Matching companies with their environments lays the foundation for successfully planning and conducting business. Over the long term, this process may also determine whether a firm typically takes risks or behaves more conservatively. Just because two companies are in the same industry does not mean that they will use the same strategies. The Toronto-Dominion Bank, for example, aggressively expanded into the U.S. retail banking industry by acquiring U.S. banks, but the Royal Bank of Canada has been much less aggressive in this area.[16]

Levels of strategy

There are three levels of strategy in a business firm (see Key 6.7). A **corporate-level strategy** identifies the various businesses that a company will be in, and how these businesses will relate to each other. A **business-level (competitive) strategy** identifies the ways a business will compete in its chosen line of products or services. **Functional strategies** identify the basic courses of action that each department in the firm will pursue so that it contributes to the attainment of the business's overall goals.

Corporate-level strategies

There are several different corporate-level strategies that a company might pursue, including *concentration*, *growth*, *integration*, *diversification*, and *investment reduction*.

Concentration A **concentration strategy** involves focusing the company on one product or product line that it knows very well. Organizations that have successfully pursued a concentration strategy include McDonald's and Canadian National Railway.

Growth Companies have several growth strategies available to them, including **market penetration** (boosting sales of present products by more aggressive selling in the firm's current markets), **geographic expansion** (expanding operations in new geographic areas), and **product development** (developing improved products for current markets). These three strategies focus on internal activities that will result in growth.

Integration There are two basic integration strategies. **Horizontal integration** means acquiring control of competitors in the same or similar markets with the same or similar products. For example, Hudson's Bay Company owns Zellers

---

A CORPORATE-LEVEL STRATEGY Identifies the various businesses that a company will be in, and how these businesses will relate to each other.

BUSINESS-LEVEL (COMPETITIVE) STRATEGY Identifies the ways a business will compete in its chosen line of products or services.

FUNCTIONAL STRATEGIES Identify the basic courses of action that each department in the firm will pursue so that it contributes to the attainment of the business's overall goals.

CONCENTRATION STRATEGY Involves focusing the company on one product or product line.

MARKET PENETRATION Boosting sales of present products by more aggressive selling in the firm's current markets.

GEOGRAPHIC EXPANSION Expanding operations in new geographic areas or countries.

PRODUCT DEVELOPMENT Developing improved products for current markets.

HORIZONTAL INTEGRATION Acquiring control of competitors in the same or similar markets with the same or similar products.

HIERARCHY OF STRATEGY

Functional Strategy

Business or Competitive Strategy

Corporate Strategy

and Home Outfitters (Déco Découverte in Quebec). **Vertical integration** means owning or controlling the inputs to the firm's processes and/or the channels through which the products or services are distributed. Oil companies like Shell not only drill and produce their own oil but also sell it through company-controlled outlets across Canada. These two strategies focus on external activities that will result in growth.

Diversification **Diversification** helps the firm avoid the problem of having all of its eggs in one basket by spreading risk among several products or markets. *Related diversification* means adding new, but related, products or services to an existing business. For example, Maple Leaf Gardens Ltd., which already owned the Toronto Maple Leafs, acquired the Toronto Raptors basketball team. *Conglomerate diversification* means diversifying into products or markets that are not related to the firm's present businesses.

Investment Reduction **Investment reduction** means reducing the company's investment in one or more of its lines of business. One investment-reduction strategy is *retrenchment*, which means the reduction of activity or operations. For example, Federal Industries formerly was a conglomerate with interests in trucking, railways, metals, and other product lines, but it has now retrenched and focuses on a more limited set of products and customers. *Divestment* involves selling or liquidating one or more of a firm's businesses. For example, BCE sold its Yellow Pages and White Pages for $4 billion.

Business-level (competitive) strategies

Whatever corporate-level strategy a firm decides on, it must also have a competitive strategy. A *competitive strategy* is a plan to establish a profitable and sustainable competitive position.[17] Michael Porter identifies three competitive

VERTICAL INTEGRATION
Owning or controlling the inputs to the firm's processes and/or the channels through which the products or services are distributed.

DIVERSIFICATION
Expanding into related or unrelated products or market segments.

INVESTMENT REDUCTION
Reducing the company's investment in one or more of its lines of business.

strategies. **Cost leadership** means becoming *the* low-cost leader in an industry. Walmart is the best-known industry cost leader. Montreal-based Gildan Activewear is dedicated to achieving the lowest possible costs in producing its T-shirts. The company has captured 29 percent of the U.S. imprinted T-shirt market with this strategy.[18] A firm using a **differentiation strategy** tries to be unique in its industry along some dimension that is valued by buyers. For example, Caterpillar emphasizes durability, Volvo stresses safety, Apple stresses user-friendly products, and Mercedes-Benz emphasizes quality. A **focus strategy** means selecting a market segment and serving the customers in that market niche better than competitors. Before it was acquired by Nexfor, Fraser Inc. focused on producing high-quality, durable, lightweight paper that is used in bibles.

Functional strategies

Each business's choice of a competitive strategy (cost leadership, differentiation, or focus) is translated into supporting functional strategies for each of its departments to pursue. A *functional strategy* is the basic course of action that each department follows so that the business accomplishes its overall goals. To implement its cost-leadership strategy, for example, Walmart's distribution department pursued a functional strategy of satellite-based warehousing that ultimately drove distribution costs down below those of its competitors.

The strategy of one small business is described in the boxed insert entitled "From a Missouri Garage to Hollywood."

Contingency planning and crisis management

Most managers recognize that even the best-laid plans sometimes simply do not work out. When Walt Disney announced plans to launch a cruise line using Disney characters and themes, managers began aggressively developing and marketing packages linking three- and four-day cruises with visits to Disney World in Florida. The inaugural sailing was sold out more than a year in advance. But three months before the first sailing, the shipyard constructing Disney's first ship (the *Disney Magic*) notified the company that it was behind schedule and that delivery would be several weeks late. Because Disney had no other ship, it had no choice but to refund the money it had collected as pre-booking deposits for its first 15 cruises. The 20 000 displaced customers were offered big discounts if they rebooked on a later cruise, but many of them blamed Disney's poor planning for the problem. Fortunately for Disney, the *Disney Magic* was eventually launched and has now become very popular and very profitable.[19]

Two common methods of dealing with the unknown and unforeseen are *contingency planning* and *crisis management*.

Contingency planning

Contingency planning tries to identify in advance the important aspects of a business or its markets that might change, and how the company will respond if such changes actually occur. Suppose, for example, that a company develops a plan to create a new division, and it expects sales of this new division to reach a level of $1 million in sales revenue by the end of the first year. But suppose that sales revenues are only $500 000 by the end of the first year. Does the company abandon the business, invest more in advertising, or wait to see what happens in the second year? Any of these alternatives is possible. However, things will go more smoothly if managers have decided *in advance* what to do in the event of lower-than-expected sales. Contingency planning can help them do exactly that.

In the summer of 2008, a strike at the Potash Corp. of Saskatchewan created a shortage of potassium acetate, which is the key ingredient in runway de-icer that airports use to prevent airplanes from sliding off runways in sub-freezing weather. The strike ended in November 2008, but by then airports were having trouble obtaining potassium acetate. The U.S. Federal Aviation Administration informed all airports that they should develop contingency plans to get their potassium acetate from alternate sources. Cryotech Technologies, the biggest supplier of potassium acetate to airports, responded by getting supplies of a corn-based de-icer instead.[20]

Commercial airlines have contingency plans to deal with problems like major snowstorms. These contingency plans involve making sure that planes are not stranded at airports that are experiencing snow delays.

entrepreneurship and
New Ventures

From a Missouri Garage to Hollywood

The feature films *The Red Canvas* and *Way of the Guardian* were not developed by your typical Hollywood production team. For starters, one of the films' co-creators lives and works in Missouri. Adam Boster and his partner, Ken Chamitoff, started Photo-Kicks—a marketing company specializing in action photography—in their garages in 2002. From their beginnings as photographing students at local martial arts schools, Boster and Chamitoff built Photo-Kicks into a multimillion-dollar business employing photo-graphers, graphic designers, and marketers throughout the United States and Canada. In 2007, Photo-Kicks came in at number 592 on *Inc.* magazine's list of the 5000 fastest-growing private companies in America.

Just a quick glance at the many photographs on display at the Photo-Kicks website (www.photo-kicks.com) provides an eye-opening introduction to action photography. Athletes young and old punch, kick, and leap their way across the frames. But it's the countless other services that Photo-Kicks provides its customers that have allowed it to grow so rapidly. Photo-Kicks bills itself as "a fully equipped graphic design and marketing organization," creating such products as customized logos, brochures, websites, posters, and trading cards.

Then, of course, there are the movies. *Way of the Guardian* began as a card game and animated series also developed by Boster and Chamitoff. *The Red Canvas* is more personal. It tells the story of a struggling immigrant who finds success and redemption in the sport of mixed martial arts. Chamitoff acknow-ledges that the film could not have happened without the years he and Boster spent travelling the country photographing martial arts students. "I learned the stories of every person I encountered," said Chamitoff. "Those stories shaped not only *The Red Canvas* but Photo-Kicks as well."

Critical Thinking Question

1. What are the key differences between the various types of corporate and business-level strategies? Which strategies is Photo-Kicks pursuing?

Crisis management

CRISIS MANAGEMENT
An organization's methods for dealing with emergencies.

Crisis management involves an organization's plan for dealing with emergencies that require an immediate response. The listeria contamination problem at Maple Leaf Foods in 2008 is an example of a crisis that needed to be effectively managed. CEO Michael McCain acted quickly to handle the crisis and did not hide behind lawyers or let financial implications get in the way of his decisions. The company recalled 686 000 kilograms of tainted meat (which cost the company $19 million). McCain publicly apologized at news conferences and in television commercials, and assured consumers that the company would solve the problem.[21] By January 1, 2009, a survey revealed that 78 percent of respondents had recently purchased a Maple Leaf product. That was up from only 20 percent in September 2008.[22]

In 2010, Toyota faced a crisis when consumers began reporting that some models of its cars were accelerating out of control Also in 2010, BP faced a crisis when an explosion and fire at a drilling rig in the Gulf of Mexico resulted in the death of 11 workers and a huge oil spill. The intense news coverage of the oil spill, as well as some poorly chosen remarks by BP's CEO, created significant public relations problems for BP. The company is likely facing many lawsuits with huge financial implications.

To prepare for emergencies better, many organizations maintain crisis plans. These plans—which are designed to help employees cope when disaster strikes—typically outline who will be in charge in different kinds of circumstances, how the organization will respond, and the plans that exist for assembling and deploying crisis-management teams.

Crisis management involves an organization's methods for dealing with emergencies. Here, Red Cross volunteers organize and file paperwork submitted by Hurrican Katrina victims in Texas.

Management and the corporate culture

CORPORATE CULTURE
The shared experiences, stories, beliefs, and norms that characterize a firm.

Just as every individual has a unique personality, every company has a unique identity. This is its **corporate culture**—the shared experiences, stories, beliefs, and norms that characterize it. The opening case provides several examples of corporate cultures. Here are some more:

▶ Magna International, a large Canadian producer of auto parts, is a firm with a strong culture. Its founder, Frank Stronach, is well known for his views about employees, working conditions, daycare centres, unions, the free enterprise system, and profit distribution.[23]

▶ Four Seasons Hotels and Resorts has a different, but equally strong, culture. Managers are judged by deeds, not words, and act as role models; employees take their cues from the managers.[24]

▶ At Toyota's Cambridge, Ontario, plant the corporate culture stresses values, principles, and trust. The culture is one of continuous improvement.[25]

- At WestJet Airlines the corporate culture emphasizes profit maximization. Most of the employees own shares in the company, and all of them get to keep some of the profits. This is a powerful incentive for them to work productively.[26]

In 2008, executives at 340 Canadian companies participated in the Waterstone Human Capital corporate culture survey and expressed the following views:[27]

- Eighty-two percent said that culture has a strong or very strong impact on corporate performance (but only 36 percent of executives felt that the culture of their company was strong).
- Three-year average revenue growth for the top 10 firms on the list was 63 percent higher than that of the 60 largest public companies in Canada that are listed on the S&P/TSX.
- Fifty-three percent felt that a strong culture reduced turnover, and 57 percent felt that a strong culture gave employees a sense of belonging. This finding is important, since an online survey conducted by Ipsos-Reid found that many workers feel that they don't fit in well at work.[28]

A strong corporate culture guides everyone to work toward the same goals and helps newcomers learn accepted behaviours. Cameron Herold—a Vancouver entrepreneur who has had a string of successes in franchising, including College Pro Painters, Boyd Autobody, and 1-800-GOT-JUNK—says that a cult-like culture is crucial for attracting great employees. He says what's needed is a culture that is "more than a business and slightly less than a religion."[29]

In a strong culture where financial success is the key issue, newcomers quickly learn that they are expected to work long, hard hours and that the "winner" is the one who brings in the most revenue. But if quality of life is more fundamental to the culture, newcomers learn that it's acceptable to balance work and non-work activities.

A business's founder or CEO plays a major role in shaping the company's culture. For example, Apple co-founder and CEO Steve Jobs helped establish an informal and laidback culture at the company. Casual business attire and an open-door policy help him maintain that same culture today. And that culture, in turn, helps Apple continue to attract and retain talented people.

Communicating the culture and managing change

Managers must carefully consider the kind of culture they want for their organization, then work to nourish that culture by communicating with everyone who works there. Walmart, for example, assigns veteran managers to lead employees in new territories. As we saw in the opening case, Starbucks Coffee surveys employees every 18 months regarding several aspects of its culture. Royal Bank of Canada and Four Seasons Hotels and Resorts also survey their employees to determine how well they are progressing toward their corporate culture goals.[30]

Communicating the culture

To use its culture to full advantage, managers must accomplish several tasks, all of which hinge on effective communication. First, managers themselves must have a clear understanding of the culture. Second, they must transmit the culture to others in the organization. Communication is thus one aim in training and orienting newcomers. A clear and meaningful statement of the organization's mission is also a valuable communication tool. Finally, managers can maintain the culture by rewarding and promoting those who understand it and work toward maintaining it.

Managing change

An organization may experience difficulty when trying to change its culture. For example, CIBC historically had an aggressive, deal-making culture that caused it to compete head to head with large Wall Street companies in the U.S. But after several major failures in the U.S., CIBC tried to become much more conservative.[31] But as the commercial paper crisis unfolded in 2007, it became clear that CIBC was going to incur billions of dollars of losses because of its exposure to subprime mortgages in the U.S. This happened in spite of CIBC's supposed shift to a low-risk culture.[32]

In 2006, the Brazilian mining company Vale bought Inco, one of Canada's most famous companies. But frictions soon arose because the cultures of the two companies were quite different. Inco had a culture that encouraged the exchange of ideas and a decentralized decision-making structure, while Vale had a much more centralized decision-making structure. Vale executives imposed their culture on Inco executives, who were now expected to obey orders. One former Inco manager noted that many Inco managers left the company after Vale took charge.[33]

Summary of Learning Objectives

1. **Describe the four activities that constitute the *management process*.** *Management* is the process of planning, organizing, leading, and controlling an organization's financial, physical, human, and information resources to achieve the organization's goals. *Planning* means determining what the company needs to do and how best to get it done. *Organizing* means determining how best to arrange a business's resources and the necessary jobs into an overall structure. *Leading* means guiding and motivating employees to meet the firm's objectives. *Controlling* means monitoring the firm's performance to ensure that it is meeting its goals.

2. **Identify *types of managers* by level and area.** Managers can be differentiated in two ways: by level and by area. By level, *top managers* set policies, formulate strategies, and approve decisions. *Middle managers* implement policies, strategies, and decisions. *First-line managers* usually work with and supervise employees. By area, managers focus on marketing, finance, operations, human resource, and information. Managers at all levels may be found in every area of a company.

3. **Describe the five basic *management skills*.** Most managers agree that five basic management skills are necessary for success. *Technical skills* are needed to perform specialized tasks ranging from typing to auditing. *Human relations skills* are needed to understand and get along with other people. *Conceptual skills* allow managers to think in the abstract, to diagnose and analyze various situations, and to see beyond present circumstances. *Decision-making skills* allow managers to define problems and to select the best course of action. *Time management* skills refer to managers' ability to make productive use of the time available to them.

4. **Explain the importance of *goal setting and strategic management* in organizational success.** *Goals*—the performance targets of an organization—can be *long term*, *intermediate*, and *short term*. They provide direction for managers, they help managers decide how to allocate limited resources, they define the corporate culture, and they help managers assess performance. *Strategic management* involves three major activities: setting strategic goals, analyzing the organization and its environment, and matching the organization and its environment. The strategies that are decided upon are then translated into *strategic, tactical,* and *operational plans*.

5. **Discuss *contingency planning* and *crisis management* in today's business world.** To deal with crises or major environmental changes, companies develop *contingency plans* and plans for *crisis management*. *Contingency planning* tries to identify in advance the important aspects of a business or its markets that might change, and how the company will respond if such changes actually occur. *Crisis*

management means developing methods and actions for dealing with an emergency that requires an immediate response. To prepare for such emergencies, organizations develop crisis plans.

6. **Explain the idea of corporate *culture* and why it is important.** *Corporate culture* is the shared experiences, stories, beliefs, and norms that characterize an organization. A strong, well-defined culture can help a business reach its goals and can influence management styles. Culture is determined by several factors, including top management, the organization's history, stories and legends, and behavioural norms. If carefully communicated and flexible enough to accommodate change, corporate culture can be managed for the betterment of the organization.

Questions and Exercises

Questions for Analysis

1. How are the five basic management *skills* related to the four *functions* of management? Give several specific examples.

2. What is the relationship between Mintzberg's *roles* of management and the more traditional *functions* of management? Use examples to clarify your answer.

3. Identify the managers by level and area at your college or university.

4. Can you identify any organizations where the technical skills of top managers are more important than human relations or conceptual skills? Can you identify organizations where conceptual skills are not important?

5. What differences might you expect to find in the corporate cultures of a 100-year-old manufacturing firm based in Winnipeg and a five-year-old e-commerce firm based in Ottawa?

6. Consider the various corporate-level strategies discussed in the text (concentration, growth, integration, diversification, investment reduction). What is the relationship between these various strategies? Are they mutually exclusive? Are they complementary? Defend your answer.

Application Exercises

7. Interview an administrator at your college or university. Ask the administrator to give his or her views on the college or university's strengths and weaknesses, and on the threats and opportunities the school is facing. Then use this information to write up a SWOT analysis for the school.

8. Review the example of the decisions made by Airbus and Boeing regarding new large aircraft. Then research the most current information on the status of the two planes. Which company seems to have made the better decision?

9. Choose two companies in the same industry—for example, fast food, electronics, retailing—and compare and contrast the corporate cultures of the two companies.

10. Select any group of which you are a member (your company, your family, your church, or a club). Explain the relevance of the management functions of planning, organizing, directing, and controlling for that group.

Team Exercises

Building Your Business Skillls

SPEAKING WITH POWER

Goal

To encourage students to appreciate effective speaking as a critical human relations skill.

Background

A manager's ability to understand and get along with supervisors, peers, and subordinates is a critical human relations skill. At the heart of this skill, says Harvard University professor of education Sarah McGinty, is the ability to speak with power and control. McGinty defines "powerful speech" in terms of the following characteristics:

- The ability to speak at length and in complete sentences
- The ability to set a conversational agenda
- The ability to deter interruption
- The ability to argue openly and to express strong opinions about ideas, not people
- The ability to make statements that offer solutions rather than pose questions
- The ability to express humour

Taken together, says McGinty, "all this creates a sense of confidence in listeners."

Method

Step 1 Working alone, compare your own personal speaking style with McGinty's description of powerful speech by taping yourself as you speak during a meeting with classmates or during a phone conversation. (Tape both sides of the conversation only if the person to whom you are speaking gives permission.) Listen for the following problems:

- Unfinished sentences
- An absence of solutions
- Too many disclaimers ("I'm not sure I have enough information to say this, but . . .")
- The habit of seeking support from others instead of making definitive statements of personal conviction (saying, "As Emily stated in her report, I recommend consolidating the medical and fitness functions," instead of, "I recommend consolidating the medical and fitness functions.")
- Language fillers (saying, "you know," "like," and "um" when you are unsure of your facts or uneasy about expressing your opinion)

Step 2 Join with three or four other classmates to evaluate each other's speaking styles.

- Have a 10-minute group discussion on the importance of human relations skills in business.
- Listen to other group members, and take notes on the "power" content of what you hear.
- Offer constructive criticism by focusing on what speakers say rather than on personal characteristics (say, "Bob, you sympathized with Paul's position, but I still don't know what you think," instead of, "Bob, you sounded like a weakling.").

Follow-Up Questions

1. How do you think the power content of speech affects a manager's ability to communicate? Evaluate some of the ways in which effects may differ among supervisors, peers, and subordinates.
2. How do you evaluate yourself and group members in terms of powerful and powerless speech? List the strengths and weaknesses of the group.
3. Do you agree or disagree with McGinty that business success depends on gaining insight into your own language habits? Explain your answer.

4. In our age of computers and email, why do you think personal presentation continues to be important in management?
5. McGinty believes that power language differs from company to company and that it is linked to the corporate culture. Do you agree, or do you believe that people express themselves in similar ways no matter where they are?

Exercising Your Ethics

Clean Up Now, or Clean Up Later?

THE SITUATION

The top management team of a medium-sized manufacturing company is on a strategic planning "retreat" where it is formulating ideas and plans for spurring new growth in the company. As one part of this activity, the team, working with the assistance of a consultant, has conducted a SWOT analysis. During this activity, an interesting and complex situation has been identified. Next year, the federal government will be issuing new—and much more stringent—pollution standards for the company's industry. The management team sees this as a potential threat in that the company will have to buy new equipment and change some of its manufacturing methods in order to comply with the new standards.

THE DILEMMA

One member of the team, James Smith, has posed an interesting option—not complying. His logic can be summarized as follows:

1. The firm has already developed its capital budgets for the next two years. Any additional capital expenditures will cause major problems with the company's cash flow and budget allocations.
2. The company has a large uncommitted capital budget entry available in three years; those funds could be used to upgrade pollution control systems at that time.
3. Because the company has a spotless environmental record so far, James Smith argues that if the company does not buy the equipment for three years, the most likely outcomes will be (a) a warning in year 1; (b) a small fine in year 2; and (c) a substantial fine in year 3. However, the total amounts of the years 2 and 3 fines will be much lower than the cost of redoing the company budgets and complying with the new law next year.

TEAM ACTIVITY

Assemble a group of four students and assign each group member to one of the following roles:

- Management team member
- Lower-level employee at the company
- Company customer
- Company investor

ACTION STEPS

1. Before hearing any of your group's comments on this situation, and from the perspective of your assigned role, decide whether James Smith's suggestion regarding ignoring pollution standards is a good one. Write down the reasons for your position.
2. Before hearing any of your group's comments on this situation, and from the perspective of your assigned role, decide what are the underlying ethical issues in this situation. Write down the issues.
3. Gather your group together and reveal, in turn, each member's comments on James Smith's suggestion. Next, reveal the ethical issues listed by each member.
4. Appoint someone to record main points of agreement and disagreement within the group. How do you explain the results? What accounts for any disagreement?
5. From an ethical standpoint, what does your group conclude is the most appropriate action that should be taken by the company in this situation?
6. Develop a group response to the following question: What are the respective roles of profits, obligations to customers, and obligations to the community for the firm in this situation?

Business Case 6

The Business of Bagging Customers

Coach Inc. started out in 1941 making virtually indestructible, high-quality handbags. In the 1970s it was bought by Sara Lee Corp., a big company that was pursuing a strategy of diversification. Because Coach was just one of literally dozens of businesses owned by Sara Lee, it suffered from the lack of focused management attention. Coach's CEO, Lew Frankfort, knew that his company's success depended on finding the right industry niche. In 2000, he convinced Sara Lee to spin off Coach as an independent company.

By 2007, Coach had sales of $2.6 billion, and the company's net income growth had averaged 51 percent per year for the previous five years. In spite of the recession that started in 2008, the company planned to open many new stores in North America and in China. And it had big plans to compete with the best-known brand names in the industry. For example, just a few years ago in China, Louis Vuitton had the largest market share (33 percent), followed by Gucci and Prada (more than 10 percent each). Coach had only 2 percent. But by 2007, Coach's market share had increased to 12 percent, Louis Vuitton's share had dropped to 27 percent, and Gucci and Prada had less than 10 percent each.

These successes have come in the high-fashion business, where fickle customers and rapid changes make planning difficult. Most fashion designers—Ralph Lauren, Donna Karan, Prada, Gucci, Fendi—have adopted a design-driven business model, in which the designer dictates style to the customers. Coach, however, has taken a different approach. The company asks the customers what they want and then provides it. Coach's customer focus has created a competitive advantage for the firm, which annually sells $865 of merchandise for every square foot of store space, compared to an industry average of $200–$300.

Frankfort introduced many new analytical tools for tracking market trends, evaluating effectiveness, and managing risk. The firm's leaders look at sales data for each store and each product type on a daily basis (several times a day during busy seasons). But extensive and intensive customer research remains the cornerstone of his planning. Indeed, the company spends $2 million per year on surveys. The surveys are supplemented with one-on-one interviews with customers from locations around the world, to quiz them on everything from appearance and quality to the correct length for a shoulder strap.

"The tremendous amount of testing they do differentiates them from a lot of other fashion companies," says industry analyst Robert Ohmes. Analyst Bob Drbul says, "Their execution and business planning is in the league of a Walmart or a Target" (two much larger firms known for their effective business planning). To test new products, Coach shows them to selected buyers in 12 worldwide markets to gauge initial customer reaction. An initial demand forecast is then made, and six months before introduction, they are tested in another 12 markets. At launch time, sales are monitored closely and adjustments made quickly.

For example, when an unexpected spike in sales was investigated, managers found that buying by Hispanic customers was on the increase. Within a week, the firm had moved up the opening date of a South Miami store and began advertising in Spanish for the first time. Frankfort understands that, to be effective, plans must be translated into appropriate actions. "Not only do you need to know your business and your customers . . . you also need to be nimble to adapt," he says.

A host of other changes have also aided Coach in its rapid rise. Lew Frankfort hired a former Tommy Hilfiger designer, Reed Krakoff, to update the firm's classic but clunky styles. "Something was missing," says Krakoff. "I had to take these ideas and make them fun—young in spirit." Instead of introducing new products twice a year (which is a common practice in the fashion industry), Coach releases new styles monthly. Customers now have a reason to visit the stores more often. Outsourcing the production function allowed the company to increase gross profit margins by 24 percent over five years. The firm has diversified into many other related lines of business, including shoes, jewellery, furniture, and more. There is even a Coach car, a co-branded Lexus, with a Coach leather interior.

Women's Wear Daily, the bible of the fashion industry, recently named Coach as the "most splurge-worthy luxury brand." Customers agree. Investors too like Coach. The firm's share price rose an astonishing 900 percent during its first four years as an independent firm. Krakoff gives the credit for the firm's achievements to Frankfort's planning skills, saying, "The key to Lew's success . . . is his ability to orchestrate a decision-making process that is both inclusive and incisive."

QUESTIONS FOR DISCUSSION
1. Describe examples of each of the management functions illustrated in this case.
2. Which management skills seem to be most exemplified in Lew Frankfort?
3. Explain the role of goals and strategy in the success of Coach.
4. What corporate culture issues might exist when a former division of a big company is spun off?

Notes

1. Chris Knight, "McDonald's New Recipe for Success; The Golden Arches Has Fought Its Way Back, Not with the Burger, but with Coffee, Snack Wraps, and a Restaurant Facelift," *National Post*, September 5, 2009, FP1.
2. Grant Buckler, "Workplace Wheel of Fortune," *The Globe and Mail*, December 18, 2007, B8.
3. *Hoover's Handbook of American Business 2006* (Austin: Hoover's Business Press, 2006).
4. Alex Taylor III, "How a Top Boss Manages His Day," *Fortune*, June 19, 1989, 95–100.
5. Harvey Schachter, "Turning a Company Inside Out," *The Globe and Mail*, May 18, 2009, B4.
6. "2009 All-Star Execs," *Canadian Business*, November 23, 2009, 59.
7. Roma Luciw, "No. 1 Employee Not Always Your No. 1 Manager," *The Globe and Mail*, February 17, 2007, B10.
8. The experiences of these and other bosses are described in a CBS television series entitled "Undercover Boss" that premiered in 2010. It depicts the experiences business executives have when working with entry-level employees (who

don't know they are working with the president). The program summarizes the lessons the CEOs learned. Another series, the "Big Switcheroo" on CBC, portrays situations where bosses trade jobs with lower-level workers.
9. www.cbc.ca/money/story/2010/01/04/ executive-compensation-average-salary-ceo. html#ixzz0lroe33Ns.
10. Rick Spence, "As a Leader, Are You a Cop or a Coach? Top Secret Meet Reveals Great Coaches Are Rare," *National Post*, July 21, 2009, FP11.
11. Jerry Useem, "Boeing vs. Boeing," *Fortune*, October 2, 2000, 148–160; "Airbus Prepares to 'Bet the Company' as It Builds a Huge New Jet," *The Wall Street Journal*, November 3, 1999, A1, A10.
12. Charles P. Wallace, "Adidas—Back in the Game," *Fortune*, August 18, 1997, 176–182.
13. Barry M. Staw and Jerry Ross, "Good Money after Bad," *Psychology Today*, February 1988: 30–33.
14. Gerry McNamara and Philip Bromiley, "Risk and Return in Organizational Decision

Making," *Academy of Management Journal*, Vol. 42 (1999): 330–339.

15. Brian O'Reilly, "What It Takes to Start a Startup," *Fortune*, June 7, 1999, 135–140.

16. Sinclair Stewart and Derek DeCloet, "It's Mr. Focus v. Mr. Diversification," *The Globe and Mail*, June 3, 2006, B4.

17. Michael Porter, *Competitive Strategy: Techniques for Analyzing Industries and Competitors* (New York: The Free Press, 1980).

18. Bertrand Marotte, "Gildan Takes T-Shirt Making to the Cutting-Edge of Casual Apparel," *The Globe and Mail*, July 3, 2004, B3.

19. "Cruise-Ship Delays Leave Guests High and Dry," *The Wall Street Journal*, October 24, 1997, B1, B10; *Hoover's Handbook of American Business 2000* (Austin: Hoover's Business Press, 2000), 1512–1513.

20. Any Hoffman, "Potash Strike Leaves Slippery Side Effects," *The Globe and Mail*, November 17, 2008, B1.

21. Steve Ladurantaye, "Maple Leaf Battered by Meat Recall Costs," *The Globe and Mail*, October 30, 2008, B3.

22. Kristine Owram, "Maple Leaf Claims 'Progress' after Recall," *The Globe and Mail*, February 25, 2009, B5.

23. Ric Dolphin, "His Race, His Rules," *Canadian Business*, May 1988, 32.

24. Isadore Sharp, "Quality for All Seasons," *Canadian Business Review*, Spring 1990: 21–23.

25. Bruce McDougall, "The Thinking Man's Assembly Line," *Canadian Business*, November 1991, 40–44.

26. Peter Verburg, "Prepare for Takeoff," *Canadian Business*, December 25, 2000, 95–99.

27. Sanam Islam, "Execs See Link to Bottom Line: Gap Is Closing; More Firms Keen to Be Seen as Best Corporate Culture," *National Post*, November 12, 2008, FP16.

28. Wallace Immen, "Half of Workers Don't Fit In," *The Globe and Mail*, October 22, 2008, C2.

29. Derek Sankey, "Cult-Like Culture Is Key," *The Financial Post*, July 28, 2008, www.nationalpost.com/story-printer. html?id=684225.

30. "Golden Rule Is Measure of Success: 10 Most Admired Corporate Cultures," *National Post*, December 3, 2008, FP16; Calvin Leung, "Culture Club," *Canadian Business*, October 9–22, 2006, 115, 116, 118, 120.

31. Sinclair Stewart and Andrew Willis, "Hunkin Is De-Risking the Place," *The Globe and Mail*, December 11, 2004, B4.

32. Carrie Tait, "CIBC Shuffles the Deck," *National Post*, January 8, 2008, www.nationalpost.com/story.

33. Bernard Simon and Jonathan Wehatley, "Heading in Opposite Directions," *Financial Times*, March 11, 2010, 10.

chapter 12

The Global Context of Business

Tim Hortons USA: Exporting
A Strategic Model
Is No Easy Task

When you think of Tim Hortons, what images come to mind? Students typically use the following words: hockey, Timbits, maple, Canada, doughnuts, coffee, Sidney Crosby, inexpensive. Tim Hortons is very successful in Canada, and its doughnuts have become the Canadian equivalent of American apple pie or the Big Mac. The company has worked hard to create a warm, homegrown image in the minds of the Canadian consumer. Its low-cost/high-volume approach, its tremendous channel domination, and its unapologetic links to Canadian symbols are all sources of competitive advantage for Tim Hortons in Canada. According to the website, Tim Hortons is the fourth largest quick-service restaurant chain in North America. It is the largest in Canada with over 3000 stores. To put this figure into perspective, McDonald's has approximately 1400 stores in Canada. But can Tim Hortons successfully export its business model to the U.S.?

The Challenge

The first U.S. Tim Hortons opened in Buffalo, New York, in 1984, and there are now 563 stores in 12 northern U.S. states. Recently the company announced plans to open 300 new U.S. stores, and it now seems ready for a more concentrated push into the U.S. But what approach should be used? Should the same standardized approach that has worked in Canada be used or will the model have to be adapted for the U.S. market? For obvious

reasons, Tim Hortons has not focused on hockey and Canadian symbols to sell its doughnuts and coffee in the U.S. It might try to replace hockey with baseball, but Dunkin' Donuts already has strong grassroots links to that sport. It could wrap itself in the U.S. flag, but that would leave it open to charges of being fake, and that approach might also confuse or upset Canadians who visit the U.S. Another problem: Tim Hortons cannot rely on a large marketing channel advantage in the United States. In Canada, there is one Tim Hortons for every 11 000 consumers, but this is not the case across the border. In the U.S., there are thousands of local coffee shops in addition to major players like Dunkin' Donuts,

---

After reading this chapter, you should be able to:

> Describe the rise of international business and identify the *major world marketplaces*. p. 370

> Explain *import–export balances, exchange rates*, and *foreign competition determine how countries* and businesses respond to the international environment. p. 373

> Discuss the factors involved in conducting business internationally and in selecting the *appropriate levels of international involvement and organizational structure*. p. 377

> Describe some of the ways in which *social, cultural, economic, legal, and political differences* act as barriers to international trade. p. 383

> Explain how *free trade agreements* assist world trade. p. 388

Whether you see yourself living abroad, working for a big company, or starting your own business, the global economy will affect you in some way. Exchange rates for different currencies and global markets for buying and selling affect everyone, regardless of their role or perspective. The material in this chapter will help you to (1) understand how global forces impact you as a *customer*, (2) understand how globalization affects you as an *employee*, and (3) assess how global opportunities and challenges can affect you as a business owner and as an *investor*.

Starbucks, and even McDonald's (especially with its recent McCafé push). In the U.S., these companies have the sort of market penetration that Tim Hortons enjoys in Canada.

So, what can be done? Until now, Tim Hortons' central message in the United States has focused on value and freshness. This was not a very original idea, but at least it was an honest approach. Unfortunately, this hasn't differentiated Tim Hortons from its competitors. Something else is needed. But what? The company is now pursuing several strategies, including the acquisition of prime locations, co-branding, and going upscale.

Acquiring Prime Locations

In 2009, Tim Hortons opened its first outlets in New York City after reaching an agreement with a former Dunkin' Donuts franchisee who owned 12 prime locations in Manhattan and Brooklyn. This gave Tim Hortons a great opportunity to develop its brand and gain exposure in this key market because prime locations are difficult to find, especially in New York City. The fact that people were already accustomed to going to these particular locations for their coffee fix should also help. As a result of this deal, Tim Hortons has some much-needed exposure, including a location in Madison Square Garden.

Co-Branding

Also in 2009, Tim Hortons and Kahala Corporation, owner of the Cold Stone Creamery—an ice cream parlour franchise—announced a co-branding agreement that would see the development of up to 100 combined stores in the U.S. At the same time, approximately 60 outlets across Canada were converted to test this new co-branded format. This should help Tim Hortons to get noticed and to improve its competitive position in the U.S. market.

Going Upscale

In 2010, Tim Hortons announced that it was planning to create upscale café/bake shops with a different menu that would include pastries baked onsite. These new stores were scheduled to open in existing markets such as New York and Michigan. The announcement raised several new questions. Could a high-end Tim Hortons work? How would the company manage the traditional stores alongside the new outlets? Would there be a sub-brand created or would it eventually transform all U.S. locations? This strategy should help relieve some of the stress of the rising food costs that have recently been squeezing low-cost food providers like Tim Hortons. But can the company manage the brand and not confuse consumers? Time will tell.

Tim Hortons is taking a concept that has worked in Canada and is trying to make it work in a foreign market. In order to succeed, Tim Hortons must develop a clear strategy that U.S. consumers can identify with. That approach is what made the company successful in Canada. Succeeding in new markets is not easy!

The contemporary
global economy

The total volume of world trade today is immense—around $8 trillion each year. As more firms engage in international business, the world economy is fast becoming a single interdependent system—a process called **globalization**. Even so, we often take for granted the diversity of goods and services available as a result of international trade. Your television set, your shoes, and even the roast lamb on your dinner table may all be **imports**—that is, products made or grown abroad but sold in Canada. At the same time, the success of many Canadian firms depends on **exports**—products made or grown domestically and shipped abroad.

In early 2010, China officially passed Germany as the world's top merchandise exporter; this was a clear sign of the importance of international trade.[1] However, trade between nations can be traced back at least as far as 2000 BCE, when North African tribes took dates and clothing to Assyria and Babylonia in the Middle East and traded them for olive oil and spices. International business is nothing new. But international trade has become increasingly central to the fortunes of most nations of the world, as well as businesses. Whereas in the past many nations followed strict policies to protect domestic companies, today more and more countries are aggressively encouraging international trade. They are opening their borders to foreign businesses, offering incentives for their own domestic businesses to expand internationally, and making it easier for foreign firms to partner with local firms through various alliances.

Several forces have combined to spark and sustain globalization. For one thing, governments and businesses have simply become more aware of the benefits of globalization to their countries and stockholders. For another, new technologies have made international travel, communication, and commerce easier, faster, and cheaper than ever before. Overseas phone calls and seaborne shipping costs per tonne have both declined sharply over the last several decades. Likewise, transatlantic travel once required several days aboard a ship. Today, conventional transatlantic travel takes less than a day. The internet has also torn down barriers for large and small companies. Finally, there are competitive pressures: sometimes, a firm simply must enter foreign markets just to keep up with its competitors.

Globalization is not without its critics, who charge that it allows businesses to exploit workers in less developed countries and bypass domestic environmental and tax regulations. They also charge that globalization leads to the loss of cultural heritages and often benefits the rich more than the poor. As a result, many international gatherings of global economic leaders—including the G8 and G20 meetings in Toronto in 2010—have been marked by protests and demonstrations. But despite fears and apprehensions, globalization is part of our existence and there are some interesting trends emerging. A *Globe and Mail* article listed five key trends based on a report from McKinsey: (1) the economic centre of gravity will shift away from North America/Europe/Japan to Asia and Latin America, (2) the productivity imperative (improved productivity is essential to compete in the highly competitive marketplace), (3) the global grid (increasing complex global networks of people and capital), (4) environmental sustainability will take on even more importance, and (5) there will be increased controls on businesses and markets as governments try to cope with the financial crisis.[2]

GLOBALIZATION
Process by which the world economy is becoming a single interdependent system.

IMPORT
Product made or grown abroad but sold domestically.

EXPORT
Product made or grown domestically but shipped and sold abroad.

Advocates of globalization argue that increased international commerce benefits all sectors of society and should be actively encouraged. But critics, like these protestors, argue that globalization benefits only big business and is eroding distinctive national cultures.

The major world marketplaces

PER-CAPITA INCOME
The average income per person of a country.

The World Bank, an agency of the United Nations, uses **per-capita income**—average income per person—to make distinctions among countries. Its current classification\method consists of four categories of countries:[3]

1. *High-income countries:* have an annual per-capita income greater than U.S. $11 906. They include Canada, the United States, most countries in Europe, Australia, New Zealand, Japan, South Korea, Kuwait, the United Arab Emirates, Israel, Singapore, and Oman.

2. *Upper middle-income countries:* have an annual per-capita income between U.S. $3856 and U.S. $11 905. This group includes Columbia, Peru, Lebanon, Hungary, Poland, Turkey, Mexico, Argentina, and South Africa.

3. *Low middle-income countries:* have an annual per-capita income between U.S. $976 and U.S. $3855. This group includes Côte d'Ivoire, Guatemala, Samoa, and Thailand.

4. *Low-income countries* (often called *developing countries*): have an annual per-capita income of U.S. $975 or less. Benin, Ethiopia, Haiti, and Vietnam are among the countries in this group. Due to low literacy rates, weak infrastructures, unstable governments, and related problems, these countries are less attractive for international business. For example, the East African nation of Somalia is plagued by drought, civil war, and starvation, and plays virtually no role in the world economy.

Geographic clusters

The world economy revolves around three major marketplaces: North America, Europe, and Asia. These clusters include relatively more of the upper-middle and high-income nations, but relatively few low- and low-middle-income countries. For instance, because Africa consists primarily of low- and low-middle-income countries, it is not generally seen as a major marketplace. The three geographic regions that do warrant this designation are home to most of the world's largest economies, biggest corporations, most influential financial markets, and highest-income consumers.

North America The United States dominates the North American business region. It is the single largest marketplace and still enjoys the most stable economy in the world. Canada also plays a major role in the global economy. Moreover, the United States and Canada are each other's largest trading partner. Many U.S. firms, such as General Motors and Procter & Gamble, have maintained successful Canadian operations for decades, and many Canadian firms, such as Research In Motion and Scotiabank, are also major international competitors.

Mexico has become a major manufacturing centre, especially along the U.S. border, where cheap labour and low transportation costs have encouraged many firms from the United States and other countries to build factories. The auto industry has been especially active, with Daimler, General Motors, Volkswagen, Nissan, and Ford all running large assembly plants in the region. Several major suppliers have also built facilities in the area. But Mexico's role as a low-cost manufacturing centre may be usurped by China as companies begin shifting production from Mexico to China.[4]

Europe Europe is often seen as two regions—Western and Eastern. Western Europe, dominated by Germany, the United Kingdom, France, Spain, and Italy, has long been a mature but fragmented marketplace. But the transformation of this region via the European Union (EU) (discussed later in this chapter) into an integrated economic system has further increased its importance. Major international firms, such as Unilever, Renault, Royal Dutch/Shell, Michelin, Siemens, and Nestlé, are headquartered in Western Europe.

E-commerce and technology have also become increasingly important in this region. There has been a surge in internet start-ups in southeastern England, the Netherlands, and the Scandinavian countries, and Ireland is now one of the world's largest exporters of software. Strasbourg, France, is a major centre for biotech start-ups; Barcelona, Spain, has many flourishing software and internet companies; and the Frankfurt region of Germany is dotted with both software and biotech start-ups.

Eastern Europe, once primarily Communist, has also gained importance, both as a marketplace and as a producer. Multinational corporations such as Nestlé, General Motors, and ABB Asea Brown Boveri have all set up operations in Poland. Ford, General Motors, Suzuki, and Volkswagen have all built new factories in Hungary. On the other hand, governmental instability has hampered development in Bulgaria, Albania, Romania, and other countries.

Pacific Asia Pacific Asia consists of Japan, China, Thailand, Malaysia, Singapore, Indonesia, South Korea, Taiwan, the Philippines, and Australia (which is technically not in Asia but is included because of proximity). Some experts still distinguish Hong Kong, though now part of China, as a part of the region, and others include Vietnam. Fuelled by strong entries in the automobile, electronics, and banking industries, the economies of these countries grew rapidly in the past three decades. A currency crisis in the late 1990s slowed growth in virtually every country of the region, but that crisis ran its course, and most of these countries, especially Japan and China, have since flourished.

As the trends indicate, Pacific Asia is a growing force in the world economy and a major source of competition for North American companies. The Japanese dominate the region, led by firms such as Toyota, Toshiba, and Nippon Steel. However, South Korea (with major manufacturers Samsung and

The growth in international commerce has led to the emergence of several major marketplaces. Much of the international commerce in these marketplaces, in turn, is managed from major cities. Traditional centres of international commerce include New York, London, Paris, Brussels, and Tokyo. In recent years, though, cities like Shanghai, Beijing, Hong Kong, Dubai, Vancouver, Bangalore, and Kuala Lumpur have taken on increased importance. For example, international business now defines the glittering skyline of Shanghai.

Hyundai), Taiwan (with Chinese Petroleum and manufacturing for foreign firms), and Hong Kong (a major financial centre) are also successful players in the global economy. China, the world's most densely populated country, has emerged as an important market and now boasts the world's third-largest economy behind that of the United States and only slightly behind that of Japan.[5]

As in North America and Europe, technology is playing an increasingly important role in the future of this region. In some parts of Asia, however, the emergence of technology firms has been hampered by poorly developed electronic infrastructures, slower adoption of computers and information technology, and a higher percentage of lower-income consumers.

The rising power of emerging markets: The role of BRIC

BRIC
A term used to describe four important and powerful emerging markets in the business world: Brazil, Russia, India, and China.

BRIC is the term that is often used in international trade magazines and newspapers to describe the increasing importance of four specific nations in global trade: *B*razil, *R*ussia, *I*ndia, and *C*hina. The BRIC concept was first used by Goldman Sachs in 2001; since that time BRIC investment funds have become an important group for money managers and international analysts. These four nations have even begun to act like a unit, and an unofficial BRIC meeting took place in 2009.

The status of these four nations has risen in international trade for different reasons. Brazil is strong in commodities and agriculture, Russia is a powerful energy supplier, and China is a major hub of manufacturing activity. India has become a leading service provider at various levels ranging from basic customer service call centres to engineering solutions providers. The growth and quick market development of the consumer market in these four nations is also providing tremendous sales opportunities for foreign companies in many industries, including car manufacturing and high-end clothing brands.[6]

The old international trading patterns and activities are changing. Once upon a time, Western companies used less developed markets to acquire natural resources supplies and to carry out simple assembly tasks. But these four nations now demonstrate relationships that are much more complex. A clear signal of this shift was evident a couple of years ago, when Indian car maker Tata acquired Jaguar and Land Rover from Ford. Earlier that year, Tata Steel bought the Anglo Dutch steel maker Corus Group LLC for US$12.1 billion. This was not quite business as usual.[7]

Of the four countries, Russia has encountered the most profound troubles in recent years. Some analysts have even called for the exclusion of Russia from this supergroup. Among the reasons cited were corruption and excessive levels of bureaucratic red tape. For example, in 10 years in the Russian market, IKEA had been able to open only 11 stores despite major efforts to expand. Frustrated by the red tape, IKEA put further investment in Russia on hold.[8]

While China, India, and Russia have had most of the attention, it is Brazil that is now at the front of the pack in terms of optimism and opportunity. In the first quarter of 2010, Brazil's economy expanded by an impressive 9 percent, which continued a positive trend despite the world economic crisis; the growth rate averaged 10 percent for the previous three quarters as well. This was based on positive domestic demand and high levels of investment. According to Transparency International, Brazil is the least corrupt of the four BRIC nations. Brazil's rich natural resources and momentum from World Cup 2014 should help propel it for years to come.[9]

While the BRIC nations have received a lot of publicity, there are tremendous opportunities and stories of development in many nations, including South Africa, Thailand, Indonesia, and Ukraine, to name just a few. A new world order is slowly emerging, and "old" economic powers like the U.S., Japan, Germany, and even Canada are going to have to adapt.

The balance of trade

A country's **balance of trade** is the difference in value between its total exports and its total imports. A country that exports more than it imports has a *favourable* balance of trade, or a **surplus**. A country that imports more than it exports has an *unfavourable* balance of trade, or a **deficit**. Canada has enjoyed a favourable balance of merchandise trade for many years, but in 2009, we had a trade deficit of $4.8 billion. The United States is by far the largest trading partner Canada has, and our overall trade balance has been generally favourable only because Canada exports so much more to the United States than it imports from it. But this is changing, partly due to the higher Canadian dollar. For years, economists had warned against Canada's dependence on the United States. Canada's nearly $47 billion surplus in 2008 turned into a deficit in large part because of a major decline in exports to the U.S. In addition, we import more from the countries of the European Union and Japan than we export to those countries, and we also import more than we export from all other countries as well (see Table 12.1).

The balance of payments

Even if a country has a favourable balance of trade, it can still have an unfavourable **balance of payments**. A country's balance of payments is the difference between money flowing into the country and money flowing out of the country as a result of trade and other transactions. An unfavourable

BALANCE OF TRADE
The economic value of all the products that a country exports minus the economic value of all the products it imports.

SURPLUS
Situation in which a country exports more than it imports, creating a favourable balance of trade.

DEFICIT
Situation in which a country's imports exceed its exports, creating a negative balance of trade.

BALANCE OF PAYMENTS
Flow of all money into or out of a country.

Table 12.1 Canadian exports to and Imports from Selected Countries, 2009

COUNTRY	EXPORTS TO (IN BILLIONS OF $)	IMPORTS FROM (IN BILLIONS OF $)
United States	271.2	236.5
European Union	32.1	38.7
Japan	8.8	9.3
All Others	57.4	89.6

ATTRIBUTES OF NATIONAL
COMPETITIVE ADVANTAGE

Key 12.1

Strategies, Structures, and Rivalries

Factor Conditions

Demand Conditions

Related and Supporting Industries

balance means more money is flowing out than in. For Canada to have a favourable balance of payments for a given year, the total of our exports, foreign-tourist spending in this country, foreign investments here, and earnings from overseas investments must be greater than the total of our imports, Canadian-tourist spending overseas, our foreign aid grants, our military spending abroad, the investments made by Canadian firms abroad, and the earnings of foreigners from their investments in this country. Canada has had an unfavourable balance of payments for the last two decades, but it is slowly improving. In 1999, for example, $142 billion more flowed out of Canada than flowed in, but in 2009, that amount was $103 billion.[10]

Exchange rates

An **exchange rate** is the rate at which the currency of one nation can be exchanged for another.[11] For example, if the exchange rate between Canadian dollars and British pounds is 1 to 1.55, this means that it costs $1.55 in Canadian dollars to "buy" one British pound. Alternatively, it would cost only 0.65 of a British pound to "buy" one Canadian dollar. This exchange rate means that 0.65 of a British pound and one Canadian dollar should have exactly the same purchasing power.

The value of one country's currency relative to that of another country varies with market conditions. For example, when many English citizens want to spend pounds to buy Canadian dollars (or goods), the value of the dollar relative to the pound increases, or becomes "stronger"; *demand* for the Canadian dollar is high. It is also "strong" when there is high demand for goods manufactured in Canada. Thus, the value of the Canadian dollar rises with the demand for Canadian goods. Exchange rates typically fluctuate by very small amounts on a daily basis. More significant variations usually occur over greater spans of time.

Fluctuation in exchange rates can have an important impact on the balance of trade. Suppose, for example, that you wanted to buy some English tea for 10 British pounds per box. At an exchange rate of 1.55 Canadian dollars to the British pound, a box will cost you $15.50 (10 pounds × 1.55 = 15.50). But what if the pound gets stronger? At an exchange rate of, say, 2.1 Canadian dollars to the pound, the same box of tea would cost you $21.00 (10 pounds × 2.1 = $21.00).

Changes in the exchange rate affect more than just the price of tea. If instead the Canadian dollar gets stronger in relation to the British pound, the prices of all Canadian-made products would rise in England and the prices of all English-made products would fall in Canada. As a result, the English would buy fewer Canadian-made products, and Canadians would spend more on English-made products. The result could conceivably be a Canadian trade deficit with England. This is why the recent increase in the value of the Canadian dollar has Canadian exporters very concerned.

One of the most significant developments in foreign exchange has been the introduction of the **euro**—a common currency among 16 members of the European Union (Denmark, Sweden, and the United Kingdom do not participate). The euro was officially introduced back in 2002. The Euro has quickly become as important as the U.S. dollar and the Japanese yen in international commerce. The euro has risen in value against the U.S. and Canadian dollars since its inception. It actually stood as high as $1.73 against the Canadian dollar in 2008; however, there was a sharp drop in the Euro currency in 2010—to $1.25. This raised fears about the stability of the Eurozone (see the Managing in Turbulent Times boxed feature entitled "The Crisis in Europe").

Exchange rates and competition

Companies that conduct international operations must watch exchange-rate fluctuations closely because these changes affect overseas demand for their products and can be a major factor in international competition. In general, when the value of a country's domestic currency rises—becomes "stronger"— companies based there find it harder to export products to foreign markets and easier for foreign companies to enter local markets. It also makes it more cost-efficient for domestic companies to move production operations to lower-cost sites in foreign countries. When the value of a country's currency declines— becomes "weaker"—just the opposite patterns occur. Thus, as the value of a country's currency falls, its balance of trade should improve because domestic companies should experience a boost in exports. There should also be a

The Crisis in Europe: Let the Name Calling Begin

P-I-I-G-S! You would expect to hear this sort of language in an elementary school playground. Lately, however, this acronym is used by reporters to identify the primary sources of the economic crisis that threatens the European Union. The villains are *P*ortugal, *I*reland, *I*taly, *G*reece, and *S*pain.

Why are they villains? The governments of these countries have been spending far more money than they have been taking in. In 2010, most of the headlines focused on Greece as the leading culprit. This small European nation was particularly guilty of overspending and not living up to commitments it made when it entered the Eurozone. In 2009, Greece's annual deficit was 13 percent of GDP, which is far above the Eurozone's self-imposed limit of 3 percent. When an individual has too much debt and not enough income, bankruptcy is often the only solution. Default, the national equivalent, became a very real possibility for Greece. The country's financial situation had become very bad; partially because of U.S.-based Goldman Sachs' role as an enabler (it shielded some of Greece's debt with off-balance-sheet currency swaps).

But Greece was not alone. A key measure of economic stability is the debt-to-GDP ratio. A country's debt is the accumulation of all previous deficits (total obligations) and GDP measures total goods and services produced by a nation (which relates to its ability to pay). The PIIGS had the following ratios at the beginning of 2010: Greece 125 percent, Italy 117 percent, Portugal 85 percent, Ireland 83 percent, and Spain 66 percent. While Spain was in the best shape in terms of this particular ratio, its jobless rate stood at approximately 20 percent. These scary numbers raised many questions. How should the European Union deal with the problem nations? Should it allow Greece to default on its debt? If so, would that create a domino effect, with other nations following? Should the EU bail out Greece and reward its bad behaviour? Should the EU allow one of its nations to seek help from the International Monetary Fund (IMF)?

The initial reaction to the Greek crisis by the other EU countries was to say no to any sort of bailout or support. But for countries like Germany, that have large trade surpluses within the Eurozone, it was also in their interest to support the union and not risk its potential collapse. Pressure was therefore put on the Greek government to reduce its spending and to freeze the wages of government workers. But such actions will take time to have an effect, and in the meantime, the euro was taking a major hit on currency markets. The solidarity of the Eurozone was being severely tested for the first time. After months of debate, the European Union and the IMF stepped up with a EUR$750 billion support plan (EUR$500 from the EU and EUR$250 from the IMF). But this was not the end. The situation was dangerous for the union and had major implications for the world economy.

Critical Thinking Questions

1. Should the Eurozone partners allow one of their members to face the consequences of its economic problems on their own? Debate the pros and cons.

2. Should the Eurozone partners expel members from the EU who do not meet the financial criteria set out by the EU? Explain.

corresponding decrease in the incentives for foreign companies to ship products into the domestic market.

A good case in point is the fluctuation in the Canadian dollar relative to the American dollar. About a decade ago, as we entered the new millennium, Canadians had grown accustomed to a weak dollar—in the 65–70 cent range against the U.S. dollar. The thought of a dollar at parity with the American dollar was almost unthinkable. Yet seven years later, on November 9, 2007, the dollar reached US$1.09, a level that had not been seen for decades. That movement and strength encouraged Canadians to cross the U.S. border and purchase everything from clothing to cars. Over the next few years the dollar retreated a bit, but a new era was upon Canadians. In mid-2010, the dollar was once again flirting with parity.[12]

These dollar fluctuations have also had a huge impact on businesses. Canadian companies are finding it harder to compete internationally, since they can no longer rely on a cheap dollar to make their products more affordable across the border and abroad. But after the initial shock, companies are learning to cope. According to chairman and CEO of Clearwater Seafoods Income Fund, "The way you deal with the stronger Canadian dollar is to increase the efficiency of your operations."[13] Other companies, like Nova Scotia–based High Liner Foods, which buys most of its raw fish on the world markets in U.S. dollars, has seen a net benefit. The rise in the Canadian dollar helped the company increase profits by 40 percent in 2009.[14]

International business management

Wherever a firm is located, its success depends largely on how well it is managed. International business is challenging because the basic management responsibilities—planning, organizing, leading, and controlling—are much more difficult to carry out when a business operates in several markets scattered around the globe.

Managing means making decisions. In this section, we examine the three most basic decisions that a company's management must make when faced with the prospect of globalization. The first decision is whether to "go international" at all. Often that decision is made because a company feels it has to shift its production to a low-cost foreign country in order to remain competitive. Once that decision has been made, managers must decide on the company's level of international involvement and on the organizational structure that will best meet its global needs.

"Going international"

The world economy is becoming globalized, and more and more firms are conducting international operations. As Key 12.2 shows, several factors enter into the decision to go international. One overriding factor is the business climate in other nations. Even experienced firms have encountered cultural, legal, and economic roadblocks, as we shall see later in this chapter. In considering international expansion, a company

While Toyota markets five sport-utility vehicle models in Canada (manufacturing the RAV4 in Woodstock, Ontario, and exporting the other models to Canada), it sells only its two smallest ones at home in Japan, where crowded roads, narrow driveways, and scarce parking spaces make larger vehicles impractical.

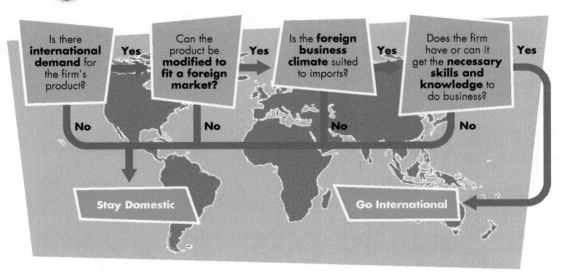

should also consider at least two other questions: Is there a demand for its products abroad? If so, must those products be adapted for international consumption? As we saw in the opening case, these decisions can be quite complicated.

Gauging international demand

Products that are seen as vital in one country may be useless in another. Snowmobiles are popular for transportation and recreation in Canada and the northern United States, and they revolutionized reindeer herding in Lapland. But there would be no demand at all for this product in Central America. Although this is an extreme example, the point is quite basic to the decision to go international: namely, that foreign demand for a company's product may be greater than, the same as, or weaker than domestic demand. Even when there is demand, advertising may still need to be adjusted. For instance, in Canada, bicycles and small motorcycles are mainly used for recreation, but in many parts of Asia they are seen as transportation. Market research and/or the prior market entry of competitors may indicate whether there's an international demand for a firm's products. New Brunswick–based McCain Foods has worked hard to build market share in South Africa. It even developed single-sized portions of frozen vegetables to serve customers who do not have proper refrigeration. There are now 2000 McCain employees in South Africa serving eight African nations.[15]

Some products—like smart phones, Hollywood movies, and video games—are popular all over the world. Movies like *Avatar* and *Twilight* earn significant revenues in North America but generate even more revenues overseas.

Adapting to customer needs

If there is international demand for its product, a firm must consider whether and how to adapt that product to meet the special demands and

Epic Entrepreneurs: Have Camera, Will Travel

Help wanted: Dynamic and innovative company seeks staff who are adventurous, love to travel, and are willing to spend most of the year in some of the world's most exotic locations, many of them very warm! Sounds like a dream job, right? Well, while there's sure to be other mandatory criteria, jobseekers interested in working for EPIC Newsgroup Inc. must meet the above demands. EPIC was started in 2004 by two young Vancouverites, Sabrina Heinekey and Tiffany Steeves. While travelling on foreign assignment, the duo realized that many countries and their respective tourism boards, corporations, ministries, and so on were not using television as a promotional medium. They decided the gap was worth pursuing, and thus their agency was launched.

EPIC is a production and media placement company that creates segments for broadcast on various channels throughout Europe, North America, Africa, the Middle East, and Asia. Generally, each year Heinekey and Steeves select up to five countries that they believe have some form of potential for international interest (e.g., developing a brand, misconception of a brand, international mystique), and they prepare a thoroughly researched media package. As an example, EPIC produced a video for Jordan's tourism board. According to Steeves, "People often lump the Middle East together as a war-torn area. Well, Jordan isn't like that at all. It's a safe, peaceful country." So sometimes their work is to help countries reposition and/or realign themselves in the international marketplace. Many of EPIC's clients were previously working under the perception that television production as a form of media exposure was difficult and out of reach; EPIC provides a solution. However, in doing so, Heinekey and Steeves haven't always found the exotic, international locations easy to navigate themselves.

The pair learned early on that young women don't often play a role in the business environment of some countries. Heinekey and Steeves state, "In some countries, for example, we've had to disprove local attitudes towards working with two women. . . . " The cultural differences regarding television as an appropriate medium have also required that they "take potential clients through a learning process." What has been their guiding philosophy in navigating these unfamiliar waters? According to Heinekey, it's their sensitivity to cultural differences and their focus on professionalism and preparation that have helped open doors for them around the globe.

"We're really doing well," says Steeves. In 2007, the Business Development Bank of Canada (BDC) applauded their success and bestowed upon them the Young Entrepreneur Award for British Columbia. In 2008, *Chatelaine* magazine named the two co-founders in an issue that profiled "80 amazing women to watch." According to BDC president and CEO Jean-René Halde, "They took an interesting concept, developed a novel product, and turned it into a thriving global enterprise."

Critical Thinking Questions

1. The decision to "go international" requires a high degree of analysis and examination of factors both internal and external to the business. Assess EPIC's form of competitive advantage, level of involvement in international business, and various barriers to international trade.

expectations of foreign customers. Movies, for example, have to be dubbed into foreign languages. Likewise, McDonald's restaurants sell wine in France, beer in Germany, and meatless sandwiches in India to accommodate local tastes and preferences. Ford products must have their steering wheels mounted on the right if they are to be sold in England and Japan. When Toyota launches upscale cars at home, it retains the Toyota nameplate; those same cars are sold under the Lexus nameplate in Canada because the firm has concluded that Canadian consumers will not pay a premium price for a "Toyota." BlackBerry smart phones may originate in Waterloo, Ontario, but Research In Motion has sold over 1.2 million smart phones in Indonesia; in Jakarta, a BlackBerry is an important symbol of success. To succeed in this market, RIM adapted its approach by creating prepaid scratch cards. This enables the consumer to pay a set amount for data and email service each week or month.[16] The boxed insert entitled "Epic Entrepreneurs" describes one company's experience in going international.

Levels of involvement in international business

After a firm decides to go international, it must decide on the level of its international involvement. Several options are available. At the most basic level, a firm may act as an *exporter* or *importer*, organize as an *international firm*, or operate as a *multinational firm*. Most of the world's largest industrial firms are multinationals.

Exporters and importers

EXPORTER
Firm that distributes and sells products to one or more foreign countries.

An **exporter** is a firm that makes products in one country and then distributes and sells them in others. An **importer** buys products in foreign markets and then imports them for resale in its home country. Exporters and importers tend to conduct most of their business in their home nations. Both enterprises entail the lowest level of involvement in international operations and are excellent ways to learn the fine points of global business.

IMPORTER
Firm that buys products in foreign markets and then imports them for resale in its home country.

Exporting is not limited to multinationals. Small firms also export products and services. For example, Lingo Media Inc. is the largest supplier of English-language textbooks in China's primary school system. Now this Toronto-based company has created speak2me.cn, a learning solution website that uses voice recognition. The site was created to solve a major problem in China: there is a shortage of teachers who speak English properly. The company registered 1 million users on the site in the first year alone.[17]

International firms

INTERNATIONAL FIRM
Firm that conducts a significant portion of its business in foreign countries.

As firms gain experience and success as exporters and importers, they may move to the next level of involvement. An **international firm** conducts a significant portion of its business abroad. International firms also maintain manufacturing facilities overseas but their primary focus remains on their domestic market.

Multinational firms

MULTINATIONAL FIRM
Firm that designs, produces, and markets products in many nations.

Most **multinational firms** do not ordinarily think of themselves as having domestic and international divisions. Instead, planning and decision making are geared toward global markets.[18] The locations of headquarters are almost irrelevant. Royal Dutch/Shell, Nestlé, IBM, and Ford are well-known multinationals.

The economic importance of multinational firms should not be underestimated. Consider, for example, the economic impact of the 500 largest multinational corporations. In 2009, Royal Dutch/Shell ranked number one in the Fortune Global 500 rankings with over 102 000 employees and US$458 billion in sales. Exxon was second with 105 000 employees and US$443 billion in sales. Walmart ranked third with US$405 billion in sales and 2.1 million employees (with 700 000 international employees in its 4000 international outlets). Multinationals employ millions of people; buy supplies, parts, equipment, and materials from thousands of other firms; and pay billions of dollars in taxes. Moreover, their activities and products affect the lives of hundreds of millions of consumers, competitors, and investors (sometimes not in a very positive way).[19] Organized protests against the activities of multinational corporations have become quite common.

International organizational structures

Different levels of involvement in international business require different kinds of organizational structure. For example, a structure that would help coordinate an exporter's activities would be inadequate for the activities of a multinational firm. In this section, we briefly consider the spectrum of international organizational strategies, including *independent agents*, *licensing arrangements*, *branch offices*, *strategic alliances*, and *foreign direct investment*.

Independent agents

An **independent agent** is a foreign individual or organization that agrees to represent an exporter's interests in foreign markets. Independent agents often act as sales representatives: they sell the exporter's products, collect payment, and ensure that customers are satisfied. Independent agents often represent several firms at once and usually do not specialize in a particular product or market. Levi Strauss uses agents to market clothing products in many small countries in Africa, Asia, and South America.

Licensing arrangements

Canadian companies seeking more substantial involvement in international business may opt for **licensing arrangements**. Firms give individuals or companies in a foreign country the exclusive right to manufacture or market their products in that area. In return, the exporter typically receives a fee plus ongoing payments called **royalties**.[20] Royalties are usually calculated as a percentage of the licence holder's sales. For example, Can-Eng Manufacturing, Canada's largest supplier of industrial furnaces, exports its furnaces under licensing arrangements with Japan, Brazil, Germany, Korea, Taiwan, and Mexico.

Franchising is a special form of licensing that is also very popular.[21] McDonald's and Pizza Hut franchise around the world. Similarly, Accor SA, a French hotel chain, franchises its Ibis, Sofitel, and Novotel hotels.

Branch offices

Instead of developing relationships with foreign companies or independent agents, a firm may simply send some of its own managers to overseas branch offices. A company has more direct control over branch managers than over agents or licence holders. **Branch offices** also give a company a more visible public presence in foreign countries. Potential customers tend to feel more secure when a business has branch offices in their country.

When a business operates branches, plants, or subsidiaries in several countries, it may assign one plant or subsidiary the responsibility for researching, developing, manufacturing, and marketing one product or line of products. This is known as **world product mandating**.

INDEPENDENT AGENT Foreign individual or organization that agrees to represent an exporter's interests.

LICENSING ARRANGEMENT Arrangement in which firms choose foreign individuals or organizations to manufacture or market their products in another country.

ROYALTIES Fees that an exporter receives for allowing a company in a foreign country to manufacture or market the exporter's products.

BRANCH OFFICE A location that an exporting firm establishes in a foreign country to sell its products more effectively.

WORLD PRODUCT MANDATING The assignment by a multinational of a product responsibility to a particular branch.

Strategic alliances

In international business, it means that a company finds a partner in a foreign country where it would like to conduct business. Each party agrees to invest resources and capital in a new business or else to cooperate in some way for mutual benefit. This new business—the alliance—is then owned by the partners, which divide its profits. For example, Canadian publisher Lingo Media Inc. is involved in a strategic alliance with the state-owned People's Education Press, which is the market leader in providing textbooks to Chinese schools.[22]

The number of strategic alliances among major companies has increased significantly over the last decade and is likely to grow even more. In many countries, including Mexico, India, and China, laws make alliances virtually the only way to do business within their borders.[23]

In addition to easing the way into new markets, alliances give firms greater control over their foreign activities than independent agents and licensing arrangements. (All partners in an alliance retain some say in its decisions.) Perhaps most important, alliances allow firms to benefit from the knowledge and expertise of their foreign partners. In India, Walmart partnered with Bharti Enterprises to build 10–15 large cash-and-carry stores. Walmart wanted to capture a share of the booming retail market without angering the local mom-and-pop merchants and middlemen that dominate the industry.[24]

Foreign direct investment

FOREIGN DIRECT INVESTMENT (FDI)
Buying or establishing tangible assets in another country.

The term **foreign direct investment (FDI)** means buying or establishing tangible assets in another country.[25] For example, Dell recently built new assembly plants in Europe and Brazil, and Volkswagen built factories in Mexico and Brazil. The establishment of branch offices in foreign countries is also a type of foreign direct investment.

As we've seen, many Canadian firms export goods and services to foreign countries, and they also set up manufacturing operations in other countries. Bombardier recently landed a $4 billion deal in China, for the sale of 80 high-speed trains. This deal was made possible because of years of direct investments and a Bombardier/China joint venture group called Bombardier Sifang (Qingdao).[26] However, a debate has been going on for many years about how FDI by foreign firms in Canada affects Canadians. The **Foreign Investment Review Agency** was established in 1973 to ensure that FDI benefited Canadians. In 1985, FIRA became **Investment Canada** and the mandate was changed to focus on attracting foreign investment. Since the late 1980s, foreign ownership of Canadian industry has again been on the rise, and now stands at approximately 30 percent.[27]

FOREIGN INVESTMENT REVIEW AGENCY (FIRA)
Established in 1973 to screen new foreign direct investment in Canada; supposed to ensure that significant benefits accrued to Canada.

Recently, foreign buyouts of major firms like Inco, Four Seasons Hotels, and Alcan have caused some Canadian business leaders to express renewed fears about FDI in Canada. A study by Secor Consulting concluded that Canada is the easiest country in the world for foreigners to come into and take over a business. It also found that only three countries in the world were net sellers of their companies: Canada, the United States, and Great Britain.[28] The most general concern is that foreign buyouts of Canadian firms will damage the economy because the head offices will move to foreign countries and major decisions will be made there, not in Canada.

Another concern is that foreign takeovers will mean large job losses. But a Statistics Canada study showed that between 1999 and 2005, foreign companies were responsible for creating *all* of the new head offices that were created in Canada and about two-thirds of the jobs in those new head offices.[29] Another survey of 150 senior Canadian executives showed that the issue of foreign ownership ranked low on their list of perceived economic challenges.[30]

Table 12.2 Top 10 Foreign-controlled companies in Canada, 2009

COMPANY	ANNUAL REVENUES (IN BILLIONS OF $)
1. Imperial Oil	21.3
2. Walmart Canada Corp.	17.5
3. Husky Energy Inc.	15.1
4. Novelis Inc.	11.5
5. Costco Wholesale Canada	10.9
6. Direct Energy Marketing Ltd.	10.8
7. Honda Canada Inc.	9.4
8. Ford Motor Co. of Canada	9.1
9. Ultramar Ltd.	7.3
10. Canada Safeway Ltd.	6.7

Many experts argue that placing limitations on foreign investment in Canada essentially shields companies from competition and makes them less efficient.[31] Table 12.2 lists the top 10 foreign-owned companies in Canada.

Barriers to international trade

Whether a business is selling to just a few foreign markets or is a true multinational, a number of differences between countries will affect its international operations. How a firm responds to and manages social, economic, and political issues will go a long way toward determining its success.

Social and cultural differences

Any firm involved in international business needs to understand something about the society and culture in the countries it plans to operate in. Unless a firm understands these cultural differences—either itself or by acquiring a partner that does—it will probably not be successful in its international business activities.

Some differences are relatively obvious. Language barriers can cause inappropriate naming of products. In addition, the physical stature of people in different countries can make a difference. For example, the Japanese and French are slimmer and shorter on average than Canadians, an important consideration for firms that intend to sell clothes in these markets. Differences in the average age of the local population can also have ramifications for product development and marketing. Countries with growing populations tend to have a high percentage of young people. Thus, electronics and fashionable clothing would likely do well. Countries with stable or declining populations tend to have more old people. Generic pharmaceuticals might be more successful in such markets.

In addition to such obvious differences, a wide range of subtle value differences can have an important impact. For example, many Europeans shop daily. To Canadians used to weekly trips to the supermarket, the European pattern may seem like a waste of time. But for Europeans, shopping is not just "buying food." It is also meeting friends, exchanging political views, gossiping, and socializing.

What implications does this kind of shopping have for firms selling in European markets? First, those who go shopping each day do not need the large refrigerators and freezers common in North America. Second, the large supermarkets one sees in Canada are not an appropriate retail outlet in Europe. Finally, the kinds of food Europeans buy differ from those Canadians buy. While in Canada prepared and frozen foods are important, Europeans often prefer to buy fresh ingredients to do their own food preparation "from scratch." These differences are gradually disappearing, however, so firms need to be on the lookout for future opportunities as they emerge.

Even more subtle behavioural differences that can influence business activity exist. For example, crossing your legs in a business meeting in Saudi Arabia is inappropriate, because showing the sole of your foot is viewed as an insult to the other people in the room. In Portugal, it is considered rude to discuss business during dinner, and in Taiwan, tapping your fingers on the table is a sign of appreciation for a meal. In China, don't give a businessman a green hat and don't wrap a gift in white or black (a green hat on a Chinese man is said to indicate that his wife is unfaithful, and black and white are associated with death). Deals can be lost based on inadvertent cultural insults. Knowledge of local dos and don'ts is important in international business activity. Do your homework.[32]

Economic differences

Although cultural differences are often subtle, economic differences can be fairly pronounced. In dealing with economies like those of France and Sweden, firms must be aware of when—and to what extent—the government is involved in a given industry. The French government is heavily involved in all aspects of airplane design and manufacturing.

Similarly, a foreign firm doing business in a command economy must understand the unfamiliar relationship of government to business, including a host of idiosyncratic practices. General Motors, which entered a US$100 million joint venture to build pickup trucks in China, found itself faced with an economic system that favoured state-owned companies over foreign investors. So, while its Chinese suppliers passed on inflation-based price increases for steel and energy, GM could not in turn pass increases on to Chinese consumers. With subsidized state-owned automakers charging considerably less per truck, GM had no choice but to hold its own prices—and lose money on each sale. Despite such problems, however, not all companies have had entirely negative experiences. For example, when Motorola opened a factory in China to manufacture communication devices, it involved Chinese technicians in the production process. Chinese designers and engineers played key roles in creating an operation that integrated manufacturing, sales, research, and development.

Legal and political differences

Legal and political differences are often closely linked to the structure of the economic systems in different countries. These issues include *tariffs* and *quotas*, *local-content laws*, and *business-practice laws*.

Quotas, tariffs, and subsidies

Even free-market economies often use some form of quota and/or tariff that affects the prices and quantities of foreign-made products in those nations. A **quota** restricts the total number of certain products that can be imported into a country. It indirectly raises the prices of those imports by reducing their supply. The ultimate form of quota is an **embargo**, a government order forbidding exportation and/or importation of a particular product—or even all the products—of a particular country. For example, many countries control bacteria and disease by banning certain plants and agricultural products.

In contrast, a **tariff** is a tax charged on imported products. Tariffs directly affect the prices of products, effectively raising the price of imports to consumers, who must pay not only for the products but also for the tariff. Tariffs may take either of two forms. A **revenue tariff** is imposed strictly to raise money for the government. Most tariffs in effect today, however, are **protectionist tariffs** meant to discourage the import of a particular product. A few years ago, the Canadian government placed a 34.6 percent tariff on barbecues made in China after complaints were received that Chinese companies were unfairly subsidizing their production.[33]

Governments impose quotas and tariffs for a wide variety of reasons. For example, the U.S. government restricts the number of Japanese automobiles that can be imported into that country. Italy imposes high tariffs on imported electronic goods, thus making them more expensive. Canada also imposes tariffs on many imported goods.

Back in 2002, the U.S. Commerce Department imposed a 29 percent tariff on softwood lumber exported from Canada to the United States (84 percent of Canadian lumber is exported to the United States). Ottawa immediately appealed the decision under the provisions of both the North American Free Trade Agreement (NAFTA) and the World Trade Organization (WTO). During 2002 and 2003, both the WTO and NAFTA ruled against the United States on various points in the appeal and said that duties on Canadian lumber must be cut drastically. In spite of these rulings, the United States continued to impose the duties. The Canadian lumber industry paid over $5.3 billion in duties to the United States.[34] A tentative resolution was reached in 2006, when the United States agreed to pay back 78 percent of the duties imposed on Canadian lumber, on the condition that Canada agree that its share of the U.S. lumber

QUOTA
A restriction by one nation on the total number of products of a certain type that can be imported from another nation.

EMBARGO
A government order forbidding exportation and/or importation of a particular product.

TARIFF
A tax levied on imported products.

REVENUE TARIFF
A tariff imposed solely to raise money for the government that imposes it.

PROTECTIONIST TARIFF
A tariff imposed at least in part to discourage imports of a particular product.

The long-standing softwood lumber dispute between the United States and Canada hurt Canadian companies in the forestry industry. The dispute was settled in 2006, but much unhappiness is still evident, and critics have charged that the Conservative government caved in to American pressure.

market would be capped at 34 percent.[35] Several Canadian lumber companies said that they weren't happy with that, but an agreement was eventually reached that went into effect in October 2006.[36]

A **subsidy** is a government payment given to a domestic business to help it compete with foreign firms. Bombardier has received subsidies from both federal and provincial governments. These funds and low-interest loans have helped the company compete and develop its major projects. Bombardier and its main rival, Brazil-based Embraer, have accused each other of receiving excessive unfair government support, which has led to disputes at the WTO. The end-of-chapter case addresses this dispute.

When the government of a country pays subsidies to one of its domestic companies or industries, this can have a negative effect on producers in other countries. For example, the WTO ruled that the U.S. government's subsidies to its cotton growers broke trade rules, depressed world cotton prices, and hurt Brazilian cotton producers.[37] These subsidies also hurt small cotton farmers in Africa because they caused highly productive U.S. farmers to produce a lot of cotton, which drove down the price African farmers received.[38] Canada's supply management system, which restricts imports and guarantees markets for producers of chickens, turkeys, eggs, and milk, could also come under fire since the WTO views the system as an unfair subsidy to producers.[39] More information about the WTO is available at the end of the chapter.

SUBSIDY
A government payment to help domestic business compete with foreign firms.

PROTECTIONISM
Protecting domestic business at the expense of free market competition.

LOCAL-CONTENT LAWS
Laws requiring that products sold in a particular country be at least partly made in that country.

Protectionism—the practice of protecting domestic business at the expense of free market competition—has advocates and critics. Supporters argue that tariffs and quotas protect domestic firms and jobs. In particular, they protect new industries until they are able to compete internationally. Some claim they are necessary because other nations have such measures. Still others justify protectionism in the name of national security and argue that advanced technology should not be sold to potential enemies.

But opponents of protectionism are equally vocal. They note that protectionism reduces competition and drives up prices. They cite it as a cause of friction between nations. They maintain that while jobs in some industries would be lost if protectionism ceased, jobs in other industries would expand if all countries abolished tariffs and quotas.

Protectionism sometimes takes on almost comic proportions. Neither Europe nor the United States grows bananas, but both European and U.S. firms buy and sell bananas in foreign markets. Problems arose when the EU put a quota on bananas imported from Latin America—a market dominated by two U.S. firms, Chiquita and Dole—in order to help firms based in current and former European colonies in the Caribbean. The United States retaliated and imposed a 100 percent tariff on certain luxury products imported from Europe, including Louis Vuitton handbags, Scottish cashmere sweaters, and Parma ham.[40]

Subsidies are designed to support domestic companies; however, in this free-trade era, governments are increasingly generous with foreign firms that can help develop local industries and provide local jobs. Warner Bros. is opening up a new studio to develop high-end video games in Montreal. Local talent, reputation, and knowledge were key factors in the decision, but government funding helped close the deal. The Quebec government provided $7.5 million to get the studio off the ground. Speed Racer is one of the games produced by Warner Bros. Interactive.

Local-content laws

A country can affect how a foreign firm does business there by enacting **local-content laws** that require products sold in a particular country be at least partly made in that country. These laws typically mean that firms seeking to do business in a country must either invest directly or have a local joint-venture partner. In this way, some of the profits in a foreign country are shared with the people who live there. Many countries have local-content laws. In a fairly extreme case, Venezuela forbids the import of any product if a similar product is made in Venezuela. Back in 2005, Venezuela's president said he would cancel all mining licences and stop issuing new ones to foreign companies. This move was designed to protect the many small, local miners. Oil and gas licences held by foreign companies had already been cancelled. These actions make foreign companies reluctant to invest in Venezuela.[41]

Local-content laws may even exist within a country; when they do, they act just like trade barriers. In Canada, for example, a low bid on a bridge in British Columbia was rejected because the company that made the bid was from Alberta. The job was given to a B.C. company. A window manufacturer from New Brunswick lost a contract in Nova Scotia despite having made the lowest bid, and the job went to a company in Nova Scotia.

The Agreement on Internal Trade (AIT) requires all 10 Canadian provinces to remove barriers to agricultural trade. But when Quebec—which has a strong dairy lobby—prohibited margarine coloured to look like butter, it was in violation of the agreement.[42] Unilever Canada Ltd. challenged the legality of the ban on coloured margarine in 2002, but it was not until 2008 that the province of Quebec repealed the law.[43] In another case, Prince Edward Island ignored a dispute panel ruling that stated P.E.I.'s milk import restrictions also violated the AIT.[44] A third case involves the question of who is allowed to audit the financial statements of public companies. At present, only chartered accountants (CAs) are allowed to do this in Quebec. This rule is being challenged by the certified general accountants (CGAs), who have auditing rights in most other provinces.[45] If provincial governments do not honour their obligations, the AIT will become meaningless.

Business-practice laws

Many businesses entering new markets encounter problems in complying with stringent regulations and bureaucratic obstacles. Such practices are affected by the **business-practice laws** that host countries use to govern business practices within their jurisdictions. Walmart left Germany and South Korea because it did not effectively adapt to local tastes and was unable to achieve economies of scale.[46] In Germany, for example, Walmart had to stop refunding price differences on items sold for less by other stores because the practice is illegal in Germany. In an example closer to home, mixed martial arts UFC events have been held in Montreal, Vancouver, and the U.S., but until recently they were banned in Ontario.[47]

Paying bribes to government officials to get business is another problem area. The Canadian Corruption of Foreign Public Officials Act prohibits bribery of foreign officials, but as more Canadian companies do business abroad, they find themselves competing against companies that are not reluctant to pay bribes to get business. As a result, some Canadian companies are losing business.[48] In an attempt to create fairer competition among multinational companies, ministers from the Organisation for Economic Co-operation and Development (OECD) agreed in 1997 to criminalize bribery of foreign public officials.[49] Recently, four employees of the mining giant Rio Tinto pled guilty to bribery charges in China. Mr. Stern Hu, a top executive in charge of iron ore, was sentenced to 10 years in prison for accepting a bribe of US$146 000.[50]

Transparency International (TI), an organization devoted to stamping out global corruption, says that companies from Belgium and Canada are least likely to pay bribes to win business in foreign countries; Russian firms are most likely to pay bribes.[51] TI publishes a Corruption Perceptions Index, which ranks

BUSINESS-PRACTICE LAW
Law or regulation governing business practices in given countries.

countries based on the amount of corruption that is perceived to exist, based on ratings by business people, academics, and risk analysts. The 2009 index showed that the least corrupt countries are New Zealand, Denmark, and Singapore, while the most corrupt countries are Myanmar, Afghanistan, and Somalia. Canada was tied for eighth least corrupt with Iceland and Australia, and the United States was nineteenth.[52]

CARTEL
Any association of producers whose purpose is to control supply of and prices for a given product.

Cartels and Dumping A cartel is an association of producers whose purpose is to control the supply and price of a commodity. The most famous cartel is the Organization of the Petroleum Exporting Countries (OPEC). It has given oil-producing countries considerable power in the last 25 years. At various times, other cartels have been evident in diamonds, shipping, and coffee. While nothing much can be done when governments form a cartel like OPEC, private-sector businesses can be prosecuted for doing so. In 2008 alone, the European Union imposed fines on importers of Dole and Del Monte bananas (who were fined US$95.5 million), on makers of car glass (fined $2 billion), and on makers of paraffin wax used in paper plates and cups (fined $1 billion).[53] Canada is involved in a potash cartel with Belarus and Russia (these three nations account for almost 80 percent of production); the price has quadrupled in just a few years.[54]

DUMPING
Selling a product for less abroad than in the producing nation.

Many countries forbid dumping—selling a product abroad for less than the comparable price charged in the home country. Antidumping legislation typically defines dumping as occurring if products are being sold at prices less than fair value, or if the result unfairly harms domestic industry. Recently, the U.S. imposed duties of 10.36 to 15.78 percent on steel pipes produced in China. China denounced the U.S. protectionist approach.[55] However, the U.S. is not alone in its concerns; India has accused China of dumping products on the Indian market that it can't sell elsewhere.[56]

Overcoming barriers to trade

Despite the barriers to trade described so far, international trade is flourishing. This is because both organizations and free-trade treaties exist to promote international trade. The most significant of these are the General Agreement on Tariffs and Trade (GATT), the World Trade Organization (WTO), the European Union (EU), and the North American Free Trade Agreement (NAFTA).

General Agreement on Tariffs and Trade (GATT)

GENERAL AGREEMENT ON TARIFFS AND TRADE (GATT)
International trade agreement to encourage the multilateral reduction or elimination of trade barriers.

Governments typically view exports as good (because they create jobs in the country) and imports as bad (because they cause job losses in the country). Because of this, governments may be tempted to erect trade barriers to discourage imports. But if every country does this, international trade is stifled. To overcome this tendency, the **General Agreement on Tariffs and Trade (GATT)**—which was often humorously referred to as the General Agreement to Talk and Talk—was signed after the Second World War. Its purpose was to reduce or eliminate trade barriers, such as tariffs and quotas. It did so by encouraging nations to protect domestic industries within agreed-upon limits and to engage in multilateral negotiations. While 92 countries signed GATT, not all complied with its rules. The United States was one of the worst offenders. A revision of GATT went into effect in 1994, but many issues remained unresolved—for example, the opening of foreign markets to most financial services.

World Trade Organization

On January 1, 1995, the **World Trade Organization (WTO)** came into existence as the successor to GATT. The 153 member countries are required to open markets to international trade, and the WTO is empowered to pursue three goals:

1. Promote trade by encouraging members to adopt fair trade practices.
2. Reduce trade barriers by promoting multilateral negotiations.
3. Establish fair procedures for resolving disputes among members.

The WTO is overseeing reductions in import duties on thousands of products that are traded between countries. Canada, the United States, and the European Union are founding members of the WTO.[57] Unlike GATT, the WTO's decisions are binding, and many people feared that it would make sweeping decisions and boss countries around. These fears were a bit overstated.[58] The WTO has served in its role as a ruling body but appeals can often drag on for years. For example, in 2010, Boeing won a ruling against Airbus because it received US$4.1 billion in loans from European governments while developing its A380 jets. Despite the ruling, there appears to be even more money being given to Airbus for development of the new A350. It has been five years since the case was first presented and it could be years before Boeing sees any rewards from the ruling.[59] The WTO also recently ruled against China and its practice of controlling access to distribution of films. China allows only 70 foreign films to be distributed in that country per year. The WTO ordered China to open distribution channels; this is seen as a big win for North American movie, music, and print distributors.[60]

The WTO has had significant trouble dealing with the issue of agricultural subsidies. Many attempts have been made during the last few years to resolve this problem (the so-called Doha Round of trade talks). The general idea was that developing countries would lower their tariffs on industrial goods, and European and American governments would lower subsidies on agricultural products. In 2008, however, these efforts collapsed, with negotiators from China and India blaming the United States, and negotiators from the United States blaming China and India.[61] In addition, WTO talks on trade liberalization have often been disrupted by protestors who resent the power of the WTO and who are concerned about what world trade is doing to both the environment and the developing countries.[62] Protestors include labour unions (which regard Third World imports as unfair), environmentalists (who are concerned about business activity harming the environment), social activists (who are concerned about poor working conditions in developing countries), and farmers (who are concerned about the effect of free trade on grain prices).

The European Union

Originally called the Common Market, the **European Union (EU)** initially included only the principal Western European nations like Italy, Germany, France, and the United Kingdom. But by 2010, 27 countries belonged to the EU (see Key 12.3). Other countries are in the process of applying for membership, including Croatia and Turkey. The EU has eliminated most quotas and set uniform tariff levels on products imported and exported within its group. The EU is the largest free marketplace in the world and produces nearly one-quarter of total global wealth.[63]

WORLD TRADE ORGANIZATION (WTO) Organization through which member nations negotiate trading agreements and resolve disputes about trade policies and practices.

EUROPEAN UNION (EU) Agreement among major Western European nations to eliminate or make uniform most trade barriers affecting group members.

The North American Free Trade Agreement

NORTH AMERICAN FREE TRADE AGREEMENT (NAFTA)
Agreement to gradually eliminate tariffs and other trade barriers among the United States, Canada, and Mexico.

On January 1, 1994, the **North American Free Trade Agreement (NAFTA)** took effect. The objective of NAFTA was to create a free trade area for Canada, the United States, and Mexico. It eliminates trade barriers, promotes fair competition, and increases investment opportunities.

Surveys conducted during the early 1990s showed that the majority of Canadians were opposed to NAFTA. They feared that jobs would be lost to other countries or that Canada's sovereignty would be threatened, and that Canada would be flooded with products manufactured in Mexico, where wages are much lower. Supporters of NAFTA argued that the agreement would open up U.S. markets for Canadian products and thereby create more employment in Canada, that the agreement would not threaten Canada's sovereignty, and that NAFTA would create more employment possibilities for women.

THE NATIONS OF THE EUROPEAN UNION

What has actually happened since NAFTA took effect? A group of economists at the Canadian Economics Association concluded that free trade has not been as good for Canada as predicted by its supporters, nor as bad for Canada as predicted by its detractors.[64] Several specific effects are noticeable:

NAFTA has created a much more active North American market.

▶ Direct foreign investment has increased in Canada.

▶ U.S. imports from (and exports to) Mexico have increased.

▶ Canada has become an exporting powerhouse.

▶ Trade between the United States and Canada has risen sharply, and Canada still enjoys a large trade surplus with the United States.

In the last few years, there is evidence that the benefits of NAFTA are slowly being eroded by ever-increasing delays at border crossings, caused mostly by heavy U.S. border security as a result of the terrorist attacks in 2001. Studies by the Conference Board of Canada and the Canadian and U.S. chambers of commerce show that companies are having difficulty taking advantage of the efficiencies of integrated supply chains because there are so many cross-border delays. Those delays are forcing companies to spend extra time and money just trying to ensure that their deliveries will get through to customers on time.[65] On the positive side, there is now an extensive Canadian presence in Mexico in everything from mining to auto parts to banking. For example, Scotiabank, the most international Canadian bank, has made great inroads in Mexico with over two million Mexican clients.[66]

Other free trade agreements in the Americas

While NAFTA has been the most publicized trade agreement in the Americas, there has been a flurry of activity among other countries as well. On January 1, 1995, a free trade agreement known as Mercosur went into effect between Argentina, Brazil, Uruguay, and Paraguay. Venezuela was awaiting final approval to become the fifth member in 2010. Within the first decade of its existence, tariffs had been eliminated on 80 percent of the goods traded between the original members. Brazil has proposed enlarging Mercosur into a South American Free Trade Area (SAFTA), which might eventually negotiate with NAFTA to form an Americas Free Trade Area (AFTA).

Free trade agreements elsewhere

Around the world, groups of nations are banding together to form regional trade associations for their own benefit. Some examples include

▶ the ASEAN Free Trade Area (see Key 12.4)

▶ the Asia-Pacific Economic Cooperation (many nations of the Pacific Rim, as well as the United States, Canada, and Mexico)

THE NATIONS OF THE ASSOCIATIONS OF
SOUTHEAST ASIAN NATIONS (ASENA)

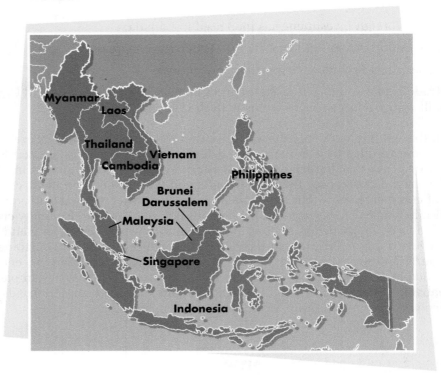

► the Economic Community of Central African States (many nations in equatorial Africa)

► the Gulf Cooperation Council (Bahrain, Kuwait, Oman, Qatar, Saudi Arabia, and United Arab Emirates

PEARSON
mybusinesslab 🏃

To improve your grade, visit the MyBusinessLab website at **www.pearsoned.ca/ mybusinesslab.** This online homework and tutorial system allows you to test your understanding and generates a personalized study plan just for you. It provides you with study and practice tools directly related to this chapter's content. MyBusinessLab puts you in control of your own learning! Test yourself on the material for this chapter at **www.pearsoned.ca/mybusinesslab.**

Summary of Learning Objectives

1. **Describe the rise of international business and identify the** *major world marketplaces.* More and more business firms are engaged in international business. The global economy is characterized by a rapid growth in the exchange of information and trade in services. The three major marketplaces for international business are *North America, Europe,* and *Asia–Pacific.*

2. **Explain how different forms of** *competitive advantage, import–export balances, exchange rates,* **and** *foreign competition* **determine how countries and businesses respond to the international environment.** With an *absolute advantage,* a country engages in international trade because it can produce a good or service more efficiently than any other nation. Countries usually trade because they enjoy *comparative advantages;* they can produce some items more efficiently than they can produce other items. A country that exports more than it imports has a *favourable balance of trade,* while a country that imports more than it exports has an *unfavourable balance of trade.* If the exchange rate decreases, our exports become less expensive for other countries, so they will buy more of what we produce. The reverse happens if the value of the Canadian dollar increases. Changes in the exchange rate therefore have a strong impact on our international competitiveness.

3. **Discuss the factors involved in conducting business internationally and in selecting the** *appropriate levels of international involvement and international organizational structure.* In deciding whether to do business internationally, a firm must determine whether a market for its product exists abroad and whether the firm has the skills and knowledge to manage such a business. Firms must also assess the business climates in other nations and the preferred level of international involvement: (1) *exporter* or *importer,* (2) *international firm,* or (3) *multinational firm.* The choice will influence the organizational structure of its international operations, specifically, its use of *independent agents, licensing arrangements, branch offices, strategic alliances,* and *direct investment.*

4. **Describe some of the ways in which** *social, cultural, economic, legal, and political differences* **act as barriers to international trade.** *Social* and *cultural differences* that can serve as barriers to trade include language, social values, and traditional buying patterns. Differences in economic systems may force businesses to establish close relationships with foreign governments before they are permitted to do business abroad. *Quotas, tariffs, subsidies,* and *local-content laws* offer protection to local industries. Differences in *business-practice laws* can make standard business practices in one nation illegal in another.

5. **Explain how** *free trade agreements* **assist world trade.** Several *trade agreements* have attempted to eliminate restrictions on free trade internationally. The *General Agreement on Tariffs and Trade (GATT)*

was instituted to eliminate tariffs and other trade barriers among participating nations. The *European Union (EU)* has eliminated virtually all trade barriers among the 27 member nations. The *North American Free Trade Agreement (NAFTA)* eliminates many of the barriers to free trade among the United States, Canada, and Mexico.

Questions and Exercises

Questions for Analysis

1. Explain how the economic system of a country affects foreign firms interested in doing business there.

2. Assume that you are the manager of a small firm seeking to enter the international arena. What information would you need about the market that you're thinking of entering?

3. Do you think that a firm operating internationally is better advised to adopt a single standard of ethical conduct or to adapt to local conditions? Under what conditions might each approach be preferable?

4. Explain how it is possible for a country to have a positive balance of trade and a negative balance of payments.

5. Is NAFTA good or bad for Canada? Give supporting reasons for your answer.

6. The EU includes most of the Western European countries, but some (such as Switzerland) have chosen not to join. Why might that be? What are the implications for countries that do not join?

Application Exercises

7. Interview the manager of a local firm that does at least some business internationally. Identify reasons why the company decided to "go international," as well as the level of the firm's involvement and the organizational structure it uses for its international operations.

8. Select a familiar product. Using library references, learn something about the culture of India and identify the problems that might arise in trying to market this product to India's citizens.

9. What attributes of your province or region (cultural, geographical, economic, etc.) would be of interest to a foreign firm thinking about locating there? Visit provincial government sites and find resources that are available for businesses to help them invest in your province. Identify a company that has recently invested in your province. What reasons did it give for its decision?

10. Visit the website of a major global company such as Coca-Cola and enter some of its international sites. Make sure to choose countries from different parts of the world. What are some of the differences that you see in the websites? Identify some of the similar themes and report your findings.

Team Exercises

Building Your Business Skills

PUTTING YOURSELF IN YOUR PLACE

Goal

To encourage students to apply global business strategies to a small-business situation.

Situation

Some people might say that Yolanda Lang is a bit too confident. Others might say that she needs confidence—and more—to succeed in the business she's chosen. But one thing is certain: Lang is determined to grow INDE, her handbag design company, into a global enterprise. At only 28 years of age, she has time on her side—if she makes the right business moves now.

These days, Lang spends most of her time in Milan, Italy. Backed by $50 000 of her parents' personal savings, she is trying to compete with Gucci, Fendi, and other high-end handbag makers. Her target market is women willing to spend $400 on a purse. Ironically, Lang was forced to set up shop in Italy because of the snobbishness of these customers, who buy high-end bags only if they're European-made. "Strangely enough," she muses, "I need to be in Europe to sell in North America."

To succeed, she must first find ways to keep production costs down—a tough task for a woman in a male-dominated business culture. Her fluent Italian is an advantage, but she's often forced to turn down inappropriate dinner invitations. She also has to figure out how to get her 22-bag collection into stores worldwide. Retailers are showing her bags in Italy and Japan, but she's had little luck in the United States. "I intend to be a global company," says Lang. The question is how to succeed first as a small business.

Method

Step 1 Join together with three or four other students to discuss the steps that Lang has taken so far to break into the U.S. retail market. These steps include:

- buying a mailing list of 5000 shoppers from high-end department store Neiman Marcus and selling directly to these customers; and
- linking with a manufacturer's representative to sell her line in major U.S. cities while she herself concentrates on Europe.

Step 2 Based on what you learned in this chapter, suggest other strategies that might help Lang grow her business. Working with group members, consider whether the following options would help or hurt Lang's business. Explain why a strategy is likely to work or likely to fail.

- Lang could relocate to the United States and sell abroad through an independent agent.
- Lang could relocate to the United States and set up a branch office in Italy.
- Lang could find a partner in Italy and form a strategic alliance that would allow her to build her business on both continents.

Step 3 Working alone, create a written marketing plan for INDE. What steps would you recommend that Lang take to reach her goal of becoming a global company? Compare your written response with those of other group members.

Follow-Up Questions

1. What are the most promising steps that Lang can take to grow her business? What are the least promising?
2. Lang thinks that her trouble breaking into the U.S. retail market stems from the fact that her company is unknown. How would this circumstance affect the strategies suggested in Steps 1 and 2?
3. When Lang deals with Italian manufacturers, she is a young, attractive woman in a man's world. Often, she must convince men that her purpose is business and nothing else. How should Lang handle personal invitations that get in the way of business? How can she say no while still maintaining business relationships? Why is it often difficult for women to do business in male-dominated cultures?
4. The American consulate has given Lang little business help because her products are made in Italy. Do you think the consulate's treatment of an American businessperson is fair or unfair? Explain your answer.
5. Do you think Lang's relocation to Italy will pay off? Why or why not?
6. With Lang's goals of creating a global company, can INDE continue to be a one-person operation?

Exercising Your Ethics

Weighing the Tradeoffs

THE SITUATION

There is a small bank that is headquartered in western Canada. The firm is privately owned and all the managers own stock in the bank. The company's senior managers (and majority owners) have decided to sell the bank to a major international banking company within the next two to three years. But, the bank needs to trim its expenses in order to make it more attractive to a potential buyer.

THE DILEMMA

Because the bank corporation has been a locally owned and operated enterprise it has maintained a full slate of operations within the local market. For instance, its corporate offices, many banking outlets, and all of its support activities are housed locally. The latter category includes a large call centre—a staff of 30 people who handle most customer calls involving questions about their accounts.

There has been a growing trend in banking to outsource call centres to foreign countries (e.g., India). Such markets have an abundance of English-speaking employees, excellent technology, and low wages. One senior manager has argued that they should outsource the call centre immediately. This would enable the firm to lower its costs. When confronted with the prospect of cutting 30 jobs, the manager acknowledges that it will be tough but reasons that any buyer will eventually do the same.

Another vocal senior manager is opposed to this idea. This person argues that because the bank corporation was started locally and has strong ties to the local community, it should maintain its current operations until the bank is sold. He argues, if a new owner decides to cut jobs, "it will be on their conscience, not ours."

TEAM ACTIVITY

Assemble a group of four students and assign each group member to one of the following roles:

- Senior manager (majority owner) of the bank
- Call centre employee
- Bank customer
- Bank corporation investor

ACTION STEPS

1. Before discussing the situation with your group, and from the perspective of your assigned role, decide whether the call centre should be outsourced immediately. Write down the reasons for your position.

2. Before discussing the situation with your group, and from the perspective of your assigned role, decide what underlying ethical issues, if any, there are in this situation. Write down the issues.

3. Gather your group together and reveal, in turn, each member's comments on whether the call centre should be outsourced immediately. Next, reveal the ethical issues listed by each member.

4. Appoint someone to record the main points of agreement and disagreement within the group. How do you explain the results? What accounts for any disagreement?

5. From an ethical standpoint, what does your group conclude is the most appropriate action for the bank to take in this situation?

6. Develop a group response to the following question: Can your team identify other solutions that might help satisfy both senior managers' views?

Business Case 5

Bombardier's Global Strategy

Montreal-based Bombardier Inc. is a diversified Canadian company that specializes in transportation solutions, from commercial and business jets to rail transportation equipment and services. Bombardier was founded in 1942 to manufacture a now-classic Canadian product—tracked vehicles for transportation across snow-covered terrain. Many of the Bombardier snowmobiles that were manufactured decades ago can still be seen in various areas of Canada. One such half-track sits on the windswept shores of Yathkyed Lake in Nunavut, hundreds of kilometres from any town. It is a mute reminder of the important role Bombardier played in opening up Canada's remote North.

Bombardier's headquarters are in Montreal, but its employees also work in the United States, Mexico, Europe, and the Middle East. More than 90 percent of company revenues come from outside Canada. Bombardier's strategy is to achieve accelerated growth in foreign markets, so it is continually refining its strategy to find new business opportunities in global markets.

Bombardier has historically been very successful in the commercial airplane market with its regional jets, which seat 50–90 passengers. But competition is fierce. In the mid-1990s, Bombardier held two-thirds of the market; then Brazilian rival Embraer entered the market and became a strong competitor. In 2007, Embraer finally overtook Bombardier to become the market leader in regional jets. Along the way, Bombardier had complained to the World Trade Organization that the Brazilian government was unfairly subsidizing Embraer by giving it large sums of money. But the Canadian government was also giving loans to Bombardier's customers to help them purchase Bombardier's planes.

Irrespective of how the competitive wars in the regional jet market turn out, an inescapable fact is that the regional jet market is declining because airline companies want jets with longer ranges, lower operating costs, and wider cabins. Bombardier planners reasoned that if they did not develop a new jet, they would gradually be forced out of the commercial airplane business. In 2008, at the famous Farnborough

A photo of Bombardier's new CSeries plane. After getting an initial order from Lufthansa Bombardier began the process to produce its long awaited CSeries plane.

(Photo courtesy of Bombardier Inc. and used under license.)

International Airshow near London, England, the company announced that it would go ahead with its new transcontinental CSeries commercial jet, a plane that will seat 110–130 passengers and which is designed for transcontinental flights. The plane will be more fuel efficient than current models and much quieter due to technological improvements in the new engines. Bombardier also announced that Deutsche Lufthansa AG had signed a letter of intent (LOI) for 30 of the planes, as well as an option for 30 more. As of November 2010, Bombardier had recorded firm orders for 90 CSeries aircraft and options from Lufthansa, Lease Corporation International Group, and Republic Airways. Qatar Airways has also expressed strong interest in the plane.

The introduction of the CSeries aircraft means Bombardier will be going head to head with global giants Airbus and Boeing. That strategy is risky, but if it succeeds, it will mean huge sales revenues and profits for Bombardier. It will also mean that Canada is one of only three countries in the world that produce intercontinental commercial jet aircraft. Market research suggests that the market for commercial jets like the CSeries will be 5000–6000 units over the next 20 years, and Bombardier hopes to get 50 percent of that market. The price of each plane is about $59 million, so if the company achieves its market share goal, it could receive approximately $190 *billion* in revenues over the next 20 years.

That sounds impressive, but there are three areas of risk associated with Bombardier's strategy. First, there may (or may not) be competing products from other airplane manufacturers. Here, Bombardier may get lucky. There is little evidence that Airbus or Boeing is planning to develop a plane that will compete directly with the CSeries aircraft. That's because there are large order backlogs (four to five years) for both the Airbus A320 and the Boeing 737, and the companies are fully engaged trying to fill those orders. However, Embraer may be developing a jet to compete with the CSeries aircraft.

Second, there is some risk associated with Bombardier's alleged "cozy" relationship with the Canadian government. In the past, the federal government has loaned money to Bombardier's customers so they can purchase the planes and trains the company manufactures. But will the government decide to stop handing out money? When he was Opposition leader, Stephen Harper said he wanted to end this type of support to private-sector companies, but as prime minister he has now reversed his position. Industry Minister Jim Prentice says that Canada wants to maintain its position as a global supplier in the airplane business. The Liberal industry critic, Scott Brison, says the Canadian government doesn't have an industrial strategy and is just making ad hoc decisions based on which way the political winds are blowing. But given the uncertain economic times, it appears that government loans are likely to continue.

Third, there is a risk that Boeing, Airbus, and Embraer will argue at the World Trade Organization that Canada is illegally subsidizing Bombardier. There is a long and contentious history between Bombardier and Embraer about government subsidies, and each company has claimed at various times in the past that the other is being illegally subsidized by its government. The outcome of any legal action by other airplane manufacturers against Bombardier is very uncertain.

Bombardier's strategy also includes shifting some of the risk of the CSeries aircraft to suppliers and to government. The overall development cost and capital investment of the CSeries aircraft program are projected to total $3.4 billion, of which Bombardier is providing $2 billion, including $700 million in capital expenditures and $1.3 billion in non-recurring costs. The remaining $1.4 billion in CSeries aircraft program costs will be split between the government of Canada, the province of Quebec, the government of the United Kingdom (where the wings of the CSeries aircraft will be built), and suppliers. The various governments will be paid a royalty on each plane that is sold. The project will create 3500 high-paying jobs in Quebec and about 800 jobs in the United Kingdom.

QUESTIONS FOR DISCUSSION

1. How does Bombardier's development of the CSeries aircraft highlight the challenges and opportunities of globalization?
2. What role will governments play in the success and failure of the CSeries aircraft? Identify the role of subsidies and debate the concept of free trade and protectionism as it relates to this case.
3. How does this case help demonstrate the important role of the WTO in the international business arena?
4. Do you think that Bombardier will be successful in its move to capture a share of this new growing market? Explain your answer. If yes, what are some of the long-term obstacles?

Notes

1. John W. Miller and Marcus Walker, "China Passes Germany as Top Exporter," *The Globe and Mail*, January 6, 2010, B8.

2. Jiri Maly, "Five Trends That Will Shape the Global Economy," *The Globe and Mail*, June 7, 2010, B5.

3. World Bank website, http://web.worldbank.org/WBSITE/EXTERNAL/DATASTATISTICS/0,contentMDK:20420458~menuPK:64133156~pagePK:64133150~piPK:64133175~theSitePK:239419,00.html, accessed March 21, 2010; Ricky Griffin and Michael W. Pustay, *International Business: A Managerial Perspective*, 5th ed. (Upper Saddle River, NJ: Prentice Hall, 2007).

4. Thomas Friedman, *The World Is Flat* (New York: Farrar, Straus, and Giroux, 2005).

5. Barrie McKenna, "China, India Crowd G7 in Driver's Seat," *The Globe and Mail*, July 19, 2006, B11; Andrew Batson, "China's Rise as Auto-Parts Power Reflects New Manufacturing Edge," *The Wall Street Journal*, August 1, 2006, A1, A6.

6. Paul Brent, "A Few BRICS Short of a Load," *Canadian Business*, November 23, 2009, 21; Courtland L. Bovee, John V. Thill, and George Dracopoulos, *Business in Action,* 2nd ed. (Don Mills, ON: Pearson Education, 2008), Chapter 2; Shirley Won, "BRIC May Cure Any Resource Sector Ills," *The Globe and Mail*, November 22, 2007, B17; Andrew Mills, "The Face of Brazil's Ascent," *The Globe and Mail*, March 12, 2010, B11.

7. Tom Krishner, "Indian Car Maker May Land Jaguar, Land Rover," *The Globe and Mail*, January 4, 2008, B3.

8. Jason Bush, "Ikea in Russia: Enough Is Enough," *BusinessWeek*, July 13, 2009, 33.

9. Tavia Grant and Brian Milner, "Why Brazil Stands Out," *The Globe and Mail*, June 10, 2010, B1, B6.

10. Bank of Canada website, http://test.bankofcanada.ca/pdf/bfs.pdf, Table J2, *Bank of Canada Banking and Financial Statistics* (March 2010): S-112, accessed March 28, 2010.

11. Karl E. Case and Ray C. Fair, *Principles of Economics*, 5th ed. (Upper Saddle River, NJ: Prentice Hall, 1999), 818–821.

12. Jeremy Torobin, "Dollar at Par: The New Normal," *The Globe and Mail*, March 18, 2010, B1, B6; Bank of Canada website, www.bankofcan-ada.ca/cgi-bin/famecgi_fdps, accessed March 27, 2010.

13. LuAnn LaSalle, "Clearwater Eyes Productivity to Offset High Loonie," *The Globe and Mail*, March 24, 2010, B1.

14. Gordon Pitts, "How Captain High Liner Beat the Dollar Odds," *The Globe and Mail*, March 16, 2010, B1–B4.

15. Geoffrey York, "McCain Laying Down Its Chips on African Strategy," *The Globe and Mail*, December 22, 2009, B3.

16. Mark MacKinnon, "RIM's Indonesian Bonanza," *The Globe and Mail*, March 25, 2010, B1.

17. Diane Francis, "China Learns the Lingo," *The National Post*, January 16, 2010, FP2; Shirley Won, "Small Firms Beating a Path to the Middle Kingdom," *The Globe and Mail*, August 31, 2004, B7.

18. Ray August, *International Business Law: Text, Cases, and Readings*, 3rd ed. (Upper Saddle River, NJ: Prentice Hall, 2000), 192–197.

19. Fortune 500 website, Global 500 Rankings, http://money.cnn.com/magazines/fortune/global500/2009/index.html, accessed March 28, 2010.

20. Warren J. Keegan, *Global Marketing Management*, 6th ed. (Upper Saddle River, NJ: Prentice Hall, 1999), 290–292; Ricky W. Griffin and Michael W. Pustay, *International Business: A Managerial Perspective*, 2nd ed. (Reading, MA: Addison-Wesley, 1999), 427–431; John J. Wild, Kenneth L. Wild, and Jerry C.Y. Han, *International Business: An Integrated Approach* (Upper Saddle River, NJ: Prentice Hall, 2000), 454–456.

21. Ricky W. Griffin and Michael W. Pustay, *International Business: A Managerial Perspective*, 2nd ed. (Reading, MA: Addison-Wesley, 1999), 431–433; John J. Wild, Kenneth L. Wild, and Jerry C.Y. Han, *International Business: An Integrated Approach* (Upper Saddle River, NJ: Prentice Hall, 2000), 456–458.

22. Shirley Won, "Small Firms Beating a Path to the Middle Kingdom," *The Globe and Mail*, August 31, 2004, B7.

23. Shirley Won, "Small Firms Beating a Path to the Middle Kingdom," *The Globe and Mail*, August 31, 2004, B7.

24. Gaurav Raghuvanshi and Eric Bellman, "Wal-Mart Tiptoes into India's Marketplace," *The Globe and Mail*, February 21, 2010, B13.

25. John J. Wild, Kenneth L. Wild, and Jerry C.Y. Han, *International Business: An Integrated Approach* (Upper Saddle River, NJ: Prentice Hall, 2000), Chapter 7; Ricky W. Griffin and Michael W. Pustay, *International Business: A Managerial Perspective*, 2nd ed. (Reading, MA: Addison-Wesley, 1999), 436–439.

26. Carolynne Wheeler, "Bombardier Laid Track Long Ago for Deal in China," *The Globe and Mail*, October 1, 2009, B1; Bertrand Marotte, "Bombardier Speeds Ahead in China," *The Globe and Mail*, September 29, 2009, B1.

27. Eric Beauchesne, "Foreign Control of Economy Hits 30-Year High," *Winnipeg Free Press*, November 19, 2005, B7.

28. Janet McFarland, "Corporate Canada Easy Prey for Foreign Buyers, *The Globe and Mail*, February 27, 2008, B1–B2.

29. Roma Luciw, "Hollowed Out Fears? Relax, Foreigners Lead on Hiring," *The Globe and Mail*, July 14, 2006, B1–B2.

30. Gordon Pitts, "Mixed Messages on Danger of Foreign Takeovers," *The Globe and Mail*, September 18, 2006, B1, B3. For an extensive analysis of the effect of foreign takeovers of Canadian business firms, see Roger Martin and Gordon Nixon, "Who, Canada," *The Globe and Mail*, July 2, 2007, B1–B3.

31. John Partridge, "Foreign Takeover Fears Played Down," *The Globe and Mail*, August 22, 2007, B3.

32. Marcus Gee, "Green Hats and Other Ways to Blow a Deal in China," *The Globe and Mail*, August 27, 2007, B1.

33. Steven Chase, "Canada Slaps Duties on Chinese-Made Barbecues," *The Globe and Mail*, August 28, 2004, B2.

34. Peter Kennedy, "Softwood Decision Gets Mixed Reviews," *The Globe and Mail*, December 8, 2005, B6.

35. Jennifer Ditchburn, "Canada, U.S. Pen Deal to End Lumber Dispute," *The Winnipeg Free Press*, July 2, 2006, A6.

36. Paul Veira, "Emerson Warns Lumber Leaders of 'Consequences,'" *The Financial Post*, August 1, 2006, FP1, FP5; also Steve Merti, "Lumber Exporters Taste Sting of Softwood Deal," *The Winnipeg Free Press*, September 22, 2006, B5.

37. "WTO Strikes Down U.S. Cotton Subsidy Appeal," *The Globe and Mail*, March 4, 2005, B10.

38. Scott Kilman and Roger Thurow, "To Soothe Anger over Subsidies, U.S. Cotton Tries Wooing Africa," *The Wall Street Journal*, August 5, 2005, A1, A6.

39. Simon Tuck, "Farmers to WTO: If It Ain't Broke . . . ," *The Globe and Mail*, August 9, 2004, B1–B2.

40. Anthony DePalma, "Chiquita Sues Europeans, Citing Banana Quota Losses," *The New York Times*, January 26, 2001, C5; Brian Lavery, "Trade Feud on Bananas Not as Clear as It Looks," *The New York Times*, February 7, 2001, W1; David E. Sanger, "Miffed at Europe, U.S. Raises Tariffs for Luxury Goods," *The New York Times*, March 4, 1999, A1, A5.

41. Wendy Stueck, "Mining Firms Hit Again by Chavez Threat," *The Globe and Mail*, September 23, 2005, B4; also Barrie McKenna, "A Nation of Big Riches, Bigger Risks," *The Globe and Mail*, September 24, 2005, B4.

42. Konrad Yakabuski, "Quebec Courts Margarine War," *The Globe and Mail*, October 14, 1997, B1, B4.

43. Kevin Doherty, "Yellow Margarine Ban to Be Lifted in Quebec," *Montreal Gazette*, July 8, 2008, B1; Bertrand Marotte, "Ontario Calls for Dispute Panel in Quebec Margarine Battle," *The Globe and Mail*, March 26, 2002, B10.

44. Neville Nankivell, "Spilled Milk over Provincial Trade," *National Post*, April 24, 2000, C9.

45. Gerry Stobo, "Cross-Border Mobility," *CGA*, May–June 2005: 13–16.

46. Gary McWilliams, "Wal-Mart Era Wanes Amid Big Shifts in Retail," *The Wall Street Journal*, October 3, 2007, A1, A17.

47. Thestar.com website, "UFC May Have Long Wait to Crack Ontario Market," www.thestar. com/sports/wrestling/ufc/article/783892—ufc-may-have-long-wait-to-crack-ontario-market, accessed July 9, 2010.

48. Dawn Walton, "Builders Most Likely to Bribe, Report Finds," *The Globe and Mail*, January 21, 2000, B5.

49. Nicholas Bray, "OECD Ministers Agree to Ban Bribery as Means for Companies to Win Business," *The Wall Street Journal*, May 27, 1997, A2.

50. Elaine Kurtenbach, "Rio Workers Get Harsh Sentences," *The Globe and Mail*, March 29, 2010, B1: Elaine Kurtenbach, "Rio Tinto Exec Admits to Some Bribery Charges," *The Globe and Mail*, March 23, 2010, B12.

51. "Canada Ties for First in List of Countries Resistant to Corrupt Business," *National Post*, December 10, 2008, FP2; "Russian Firms Most Prone to Bribery, Survey Finds," *The Globe and Mail*, December 10, 2008, B14.

52. Transparency International website, www. transparency.org/policy_research/surveys_ indices/cpi/2009, accessed May 25, 2010.

53. "EU Fines Banana Importers for Cartel Actions," *The Globe and Mail*, October 16, 2008, B11; "EU Imposes Highest Fine over

Auto Glass Cartel," *The Globe and Mail*, November 13, 2008, B9; "Oil Companies Fined by EU over 'Paraffin Mafia' Cartel," *The Globe and Mail*, October 2, 2008, B7.

54. Toby Heaps, "Potash Politics," *Corporate Knights*, Winter 2009, 19–23.

55. Canadian Press, "China Decries U.S. Duties on Steel Pipes," *The Globe and Mail*, January 1, 2010, B4.

56. Peter Wonacott, "Downturn Heightens China–India Tension on Trade," *The Wall Street Journal*, March 20, 2009, A8.

57. Peter Wonacott, "Downturn Heightens China–India Tension on Trade," *The Wall Street Journal*, March 20, 2009, A8.

58. "New Global Trade Regulator Starts Operations Tomorrow," *Winnipeg Free Press*, December 31, 1994, A5.

59. Barrie McKenna, "Boeing's WTO Win May Prove a Hollow Victory," *The Globe and Mail*, September 5, 2009, B5.

60. "US Hails WTO Victory over China," *The Globe and Mail*, December 22, 2009, B5.

61. John Miller, "Global Trade Talks Fail as New Giants Flex Muscle," *The Wall Street Journal*, July 30, 2008, A1, A12.

62. Michelle MacAfee, "Trade Protest Turns Violent," *Winnipeg Free Press*, July 29, 2003, A9.

63. Europa website, http://europa.eu/index_en.htm, accessed March 23, 2010.

64. Bruce Little, "Free-Trade Pact Gets Mixed Reviews," *The Globe and Mail*, June 7, 2004, B3.

65. Barrie McKenna, "Dead End for Free Trade," *The Globe and Mail*, May 17, 2008, B4–B5.

66. Rachel Pulfer, "NAFTA's Third Amigo," *Canadian Business*, June 15, 2009, 27.

GLOSSARY

A Corporate-Level Strategy Identifies the various businesses that a company will be in, and how these businesses will relate to each other.

Acquisition The purchase of a company by another, larger firm, which absorbs the smaller company into its operations.

Acronym A word formed from the first letters of a series of words created to help you remember the series.

Aggregate Output Total quantity of goods and services produced by an economic system during a given period.

Applied R&D Focusing specifically on how a technological innovation can be put to use in the making of a product or service that can be sold in the marketplace.

Argument A set of connected ideas, supported by examples, made by a writer to prove or disprove a point.

Assumption A judgment, generalization, or bias influenced by experience and values.

Balance of Payments Flow of all money into or out of a country.

Balance of Trade The economic value of all the products that a country exports minus the economic value of all the products it imports.

Balance of Trade The total of a country's exports (sales to other countries) minus its imports (purchases from other countries).

Basic (or Pure) R&D Improving knowledge in an area without a primary focus on whether any discoveries that might occur are immediately marketable.

Bias A preference or inclination, especially one that prevents even-handed judgment.

Board of Directors A group of individuals elected by a firm's shareholders and charged with overseeing, and taking legal responsibility for, the firm's actions.

Bootstrapping Doing more with less.

Brainstorming Letting your mind wander to come up with different ideas or answers.

Branch Office A location that an exporting firm establishes in a foreign country to sell its products more effectively.

Bric A term used to describe four important and powerful emerging markets in the business world: Brazil, Russia, India, China.

Budget Deficits The result of the government spending more in one year than it takes in during that year.

Business An organization that seeks to earn profits by providing goods and services.

Business Cycle Pattern of short-term ups and downs (expansions and contractions) in an economy.

Business Plan Document in which the entrepreneur summarizes her or his business strategy for the proposed new venture and how that strategy will be implemented.

Business Process Management Approach by which firms move away from department-oriented organization and toward process-oriented team structures that cut across old departmental boundaries.

Business-Level (Competitive) Strategy Identifies the ways a business will compete in its chosen line of products or services.

Business-Practice Law Law or regulation governing business practices in given countries.

Canada Water ACT Controls water quality in fresh and marine waters of Canada.

Canadian Radio-television and Telecommunications Commission (CRTC) Regulates and supervises all aspects of the Canadian broadcasting system.

Canadian Wheat Board Regulates the price farmers receive for their wheat.

Capitalism An economic system in which markets decide what, when, and for whom to produce.

Cartel Any association of producers whose purpose is to control supply of and prices for a given product.

Chief Executive Officer (CEO) The highest ranking executive in a company or organization.

Chunking Placing disconnected information into smaller units that are easier to remember.

Co-operative An organization that is formed to benefit its owners in the form of reduced prices and/ or the distribution of surpluses at year-end.

Collateral Assets that a borrower uses to secure a loan or other credit, and that are subject to seizure by the lender if the loan isn't repaid according to the specified repayment terms.

Command Economy An economic system in which government controls all or most factors of production and makes all or most production decisions.

Common Stock Shares whose owners usually have last claim on the corporation's assets (after creditors and owners of preferred stock) but who have voting rights in the firm.

Communism A type of command economy in which the government owns and operates all industries.

Competition The vying among businesses in a particular market or industry best satisfy consumer demands and earn profits.

Concentration Strategy Involves focusing the company on one product or product line.

Conceptual Skills Abilities to think in the abstract, diagnose and analyze various situations, and see beyond the present situation.

Conglomerate Merger A merger of two firms in completely unrelated businesses.

Consumer Price Index (CPI) Measure of the prices of typical products purchased by consumers living in urban areas.

Contingency Planning Identifying aspects of a business or its environment that might require changes in strategy.

Controlling That portion of a manager's job concerned with monitoring the firm's performance and, if necessary, acting to bring it in line with the firm's goals.

Core Competencies Skills and resources with which an organization competes best and creates the most value for owners.

Corporate Culture The shared experiences, stories, beliefs, and norms that characterize a firm.

Corporation A business considered by law to be a legal entity separate from its owners with many of the legal rights and privileges of a person; a form of business organization in which the liability of the owners is limited to their investment in the firm.

Cost Leadership Becoming the low-cost leader in an industry.

Crisis Management An organization's methods for dealing with emergencies.

Decision-Making Skills Skills in defining problems and selecting the best courses of action.

Deficit Situation in which a country's imports exceed its exports, creating a negative balance of trade.

Deflation A period of generally falling prices.

Demand and Supply Schedule Assessment of the relationships between different levels of demand and supply at different price levels.

Demand Curve Graph showing how many units of a product will be demanded (bought) at different prices.

Demand The willingness and ability of buyers to purchase a product or service.

Deregulation A reduction in the number of laws affecting business activity.

Differentiation Strategy A firm seeks to be unique in its industry along some dimension that is valued by buyers.

Diversification Expanding into related or unrelated products or market segments.

Divestiture Occurs when a company sells part of its existing business operations to another company.

Dividends The amount of money, normally a portion of the profits, that is distributed to the shareholders.

Double Taxation A corporation must pay income taxes on its profits, and then shareholders must also pay personal income taxes on the dividends they receive from the corporation.

Dumping Selling a product for less abroad than in the producing nation.

Economic Environment Conditions of the economic system in which an organization operates.

Economic System The way in which a nation allocates its resources among its citizens.

Effectiveness Achieving set organizational goals.

Efficiency Achieving the greatest level of output with a given amount of input.

Embargo A government order forbidding exportation and/ or importation of a particular product.

Employee Stock Ownership Plans An arrangement whereby a corporation buys its own stock with loaned funds and holds it in trust for its employees. Employees "earn" the stock based on some condition such as seniority. Employees control the stock's voting rights immediately, even though they may not take physical possession of the stock until specified conditions are met.

Entrepreneur A business person who accepts both the risks and the opportunities involved in creating and operating a new business venture.

Entrepreneur An entrepreneur is someone who assumes the risk of creating, organizing, and operating a business and who directs all the businessresources.

Entrepreneurship The process of identifying an opportunity in the marketplace and accessing the resources needed to capitalize on it.

Environmental Analysis The process of scanning the environment for threats and opportunities.

Environmental Contaminants ACT Establishes regulations for airborne substances that are a danger to human health or to the environment.

Escalation of Commitment Condition in which a decision maker becomes so committed to a course of action that he or she stays with it even when there is evidence that the decision was wrong.

Euro A common currency shared among most of the members of the European Union (excluding Denmark, Sweden, and the United Kingdom).

European Union (EU) Agreement among major Western European nations to eliminate or make uniform most trade barriers affecting group members.

Evidence Facts, statistics, and other materials that are presented in support of an argument.

Exchange rate Rate at which the currency of one nation can be exchanged for the currency of another nation.

Export Product made or grown domestically but shipped and sold abroad.

Exporter Firm that distributes and sells products to one or more foreign countries.

External Environment Everything outside an organization's boundaries that might affect it.

Factors of Production The factors of production are the resources used to produce goods and services.

Financial Capital Financial capital is money used to facilitate a business enterprise.

Financial Managers Those managers responsible for planning and overseeing the financial resources of a firm.

First-line Managers Those managers responsible for supervising the work of employees.

Fisheries ACT Regulates the discharge of harmful substances into water.

Focus Strategy Selecting a market segment and serving the customers in that market niche better than competitors.

Food and Drug ACT Prohibits the sale of food unfit for human consumption and regulates food advertising.

Foreign Direct Investment (FDI) Buying or establishing tangible assets in another country.

Foreign Investment Review Agency (FIRA) Established in 1973 to screen new foreign direct investment in Canada; supposed to ensure that significant benefits accrued to Canada.

Formulas General facts, rules, or principles usually expressed in mathematical symbols.

Franchise An arrangement that gives franchisees (buyers) the right to sell the product of the franchiser (the seller).

Franchising Agreement Stipulates the duties and responsibilities of the franchisee and the franchiser.

Friendly Takeover An acquisition in which the management of the acquired company welcomes the firm's buyout by another company.

Functional Areas Functional areas in businesses are often separate departments where business activities are grouped by similar tasks or skills.

Functional Strategies Identify the basic courses of action that each department in the firm will pursue so that it contributes to the attainment of the business's overall goals.

Gdp Per Capita Gross domestic product per person.

General Agreement on Tariffs and Trade (GATT) International trade agreement to encourage the multilateral reduction or elimination of trade barriers.

General Education Requirements Courses required for graduation in a variety of academic fields, including the humanities, social sciences, math, and science.

General Partner A partner who is actively involved in managing the firm and has unlimited liability.

General Partnership A type of partnership in which all partners are jointly liable for the obligations of the business.

Geographic Expansion Expanding operations in new geographic areas or countries.

Globalization Process by which the world economy is becoming a single interdependent system.

Goal An end toward which you direct your efforts.

Goods Goods are any physical products offered by a business.

Gross Domestic Product (GDP) Total value of all goods and services produced within a given period by a national economy through domestic factors of production.

Gross National Product (GNP) Total value of all goods and services produced by a national economy within a given period regardless of where the factors of production are located

Horizontal Integration Acquiring control of competitors in the same or similar markets with the same or similar products.

Horizontal Merger A merger of two firms that have previously been direct competitors in the same industry.

Hostile Takeover An acquisition in which the management of the acquired company fights the firm's buyout by another company.

Human Relations Skills Skills in understanding and getting along with people.

Human Resource Managers Those managers responsible for hiring, training, evaluating, and compensating employees.

Import Product made or grown abroad but sold domestically.

Importer Firm that buys products in foreign markets and then imports them for resale in its home country.

Income trust A structure allowing companies to avoid paying corporate income tax if they distribute all or most of their earnings to investors.

Incubators Facilities that support small businesses during their early growth phase by providing basic services, office space, legal advice and more.

Independent Agent Foreign individual or organization that agrees to represent an exporter's interests.

Inflation Occurrence of widespread price increases throughout an economic system.

Information and Knowledge Information and knowledge are quickly becoming the key factors of production as the new competitive business environment places a premium on these factors.

Information Managers Those managers responsible for the design and implementation of systems to gather, process, and disseminate information.

Initial Public Offering (IPO) Selling shares of stock in a company for the first time to a general investing public.

Input Market Firms buy resources that they need in the production of goods and services.

Inside Directors Members of a corporation's board of directors who are also full-time employees of the corporation.

Intelligence As defined by Howard Gardner, an ability to solve problems or create products that are of value in a culture.

Intermediate Goals Goals set for a period of one to five years.

International Firm Firm that conducts a significant portion of its business in foreign countries.

Internships Temporary work programs in which a student can gain supervised practical experience in a job and career area.

Intrapreneurs   People who create something new within an existing large firm or organization.

Intuition   An innate belief about something, often without conscious consideration.

Investment Reduction   Reducing the company's investment in one or more of its lines of business.

Labour   Labour is the human resource that refers to any physical or intellectual work people contribute to business production.

Law of Demand   The principle that buyers will purchase (demand) more of a product as price drops.

Law of Supply   The principle that producers will offer (supply) more of a product as price rises.

Leading   That portion of a manager's job concerned with guiding and motivating employees to meet the firm's objectives.

Learning Style   A particular way in which the mind receives and processes information.

Licensing Arrangement   Arrangement in which firms choose foreign individuals or organizations to manufacture or market their products in another country.

Limited Liability   Investor liability is limited to their personal investments in the corporation; courts cannot touch the personal assets of investors in the event that the corporation goes bankrupt.

Limited Partner   A partner who generally does not participate actively in the business, and whose liability is limited to the amount invested in the partnership.

Limited Partnership   A type of partnership with at least one general partner (who has unlimited liability) and one or more limited partners. The limited partners can not participate in the day-to-day management of the business or they risk the loss of their limited liability status.

Listening   A process that involves sensing, interpreting, evaluating, and reacting to spoken messages.

Lobbyist   A person hired by a company or an industry to represent its interests with government officials.

Local-Content Laws   Laws requiring that products sold in a particular country be at least partly made in that country.

Long-term Goals   Goals set for extended periods of time, typically five years or more into the future.

Long-Term Memory   The brain's permanent information storehouse, from which information can be retrieved.

Major or Concentration   An academic subject area chosen as a field of specialization, requiring a specific course of study.

Management   The process of planning, organizing, leading, and controlling a business's financial, physical, human, and information resources in order to achieve its goals.

Market   An exchange process between buyers and sellers of a particular good or service.

Market Economy   An economic system in which individuals control all or most factors of production and make all or most production decisions.

Market Penetration   Boosting sales of present products by more aggressive selling in the firm's current markets.

Market Price (Equilibrium Price)   Profit-maximizing price at which the quantity of goods demanded and the quantity of goods supplied are equal.

Marketing Managers   Those managers responsible for developing, pricing, promoting, and distributing goods and services to buyers.

Master Note Set   A complete, integrated note set that contains both class and text notes.

Merger   The union of two companies to form a single new business.

Middle Managers   Those managers responsible for implementing the decisions made by top managers.

Mission Statement   An organization's statement of how it will achieve its purpose in the environment in which it conducts its business.

Mixed Market Economy   An economic system with elements of both a command economy and a market economy; in practice, typical of most nations' economies.

Mnemonic Devices   Memory techniques that use vivid associations and acronyms to link new information to what you already know.

Monopolistic Competition A market or industry characterized by a large number of firms supplying products that are similar but distinctive enough from one another to give firms some ability to influence price.

Monopoly A market or industry with only one producer, who can set the price of its product and/or resources.

Multinational Firm Firm that designs, produces, and markets products in many nations.

Nascent Entrepreneurs People who are trying to start a business from scratch.

National Debt The total amount of money that a country owes its creditors.

Nationalization The transfer of activities from private firms to the government.

Natural Monopolies A market or industry in which having only one producer is most efficient because it can meet all of consumers' demand for the product.

Natural Resources Natural resources are the raw materials provided by nature and used to produce goods and services.

New Venture A recently formed commercial organization that provides goods and/ or services for sale.

Nominal GDP GDP measured in current dollars or with all components valued at current prices.

Non-Profit and Voluntary Sector The non-profit and voluntary sector includes non-governmental, nonprofit organizations that receive support from individual Canadians, governments, and businesses.

North American Free Trade Agreement (NAFTA) Agreement to gradually eliminate tariffs and other trade barriers among the United States, Canada,and Mexico.

Not-for-profit Organization An organization that provides goods and services to customers, but does not seek to make a profit while doing so.

Oligopoly A market or industry characterized by a small number of very large firms that have the power to influence the price of their product and/or resources.

Operational Plans Plans setting short-term targets for daily, weekly, or monthly performance.

Operations Managers Those managers responsible for controlling production, inventory, and quality of a firm's products.

Organizational Analysis The process of analyzing a firm's strengths and weaknesses.

Organizational Boundary That which separates the organization from its environment.

Organizational Politics The actions that people take as they try to get what they want.

Organizing That portion of a manager's job concerned with mobilizing the necessary resources to complete a particular task.

Output Market Firms supply goods and services in response to demand on the part of consumers.

Outside Directors Members of a corporation's board of directors who are not also employees of the corporation on a day-to-day basis.

Outsourcing Strategy of paying suppliers and distributors to perform certain business processes or to provide needed materials or services.

Parent Corporation A corporation that owns a subsidiary.

Partnership A business with two or more owners who share in the operation of the firm and in financial responsibility for the firm's debts.

Per-capita Income The average income per person of a country.

Perfect Competition A market or industry characterized by a very large number of small firms producing an identical product so that none of the firms has any ability to influence price.

Perspective A characteristic way of thinking about people, situations, events, and ideas.

Planning That portion of a manager's job concerned with determining what the business needs to do and the best way to achieve it.

Poison Pill A defence that management adopts to make a firm less attractive to an actual or potential hostile suitor in a takeover attempt.

Potentials Abilities that may be developed.

Primary Sources Original documents, including academic journal articles and scientific studies.

Prioritize To arrange or deal with in order of importance.

Private Business Sector   The private business sector includes goods and services produced and delivered by private individuals or groups as a means of enterprise for profit.

Private Corporation   A business whose stock is held by a small group of individuals and is not usually available for sale to the general public.

Private Enterprise   An economic system characterized by private property rights, freedom of choice, profits, and competition.

Private Equity Firms   Companies that buy publicly traded companies and then make them private.

Private Sector   The part of the economy that is made up of companies and organizations that are not owned or controlled by the government.

Privatization   The transfer of activities from the government to the private sector.

Process   Any activity that adds value to some input, transforming it into an output for a customer (whether external or internal).

Procrastination   The act of putting off a task until another time.

Product Development   Developing improved products for current markets.

Productivity   Measure of economic growth that compares how much a system produces with the resources needed to produce it.

Products ACT   Regulates banned products and products that can be sold but must be labelled hazardous.

Profit   What remains (if anything) after a business's expenses are subtracted from its sales revenues.

Progressive Revenue Taxes   Taxes levied at a higher rate on higherincome taxpayers and at a lower rate on lower-income taxpayers.

Protectionism   Protecting domestic business at the expense of free market competition.

Protectionist Tariff   A tariff imposed at least inpart to discourage imports of a particular product.

Public Business Sector   The public business sector includes goods and services produced, delivered, and allocated by the government and public

sector organization (publicly controlled government business enterprises).

Public Corporation   A business whose stock is widely held and available for sale to the general public.

Purchasing Power Parity   Principle that exchange rates are set so that the prices of similar products in different countries are about the same.

Quota   A restriction by one nation on the total number of products of a certain type that can be imported from another nation.

Real Capital   Real capital refers to the physical facilities used to produce goods and services.

Real GDP   GDP calculated to account for changes in currency values and price changes.

Regressive Revenue Taxes   Taxes that cause poorer people to pay a higher percentage of income than richer people pay.

Research and Development (R&D)   Those activities that are necessary to provide new products, services, and processes.

Restrictive Taxes   Taxes levied to control certain activities that legislators believe should be controlled.

Revenue Tariff   A tariff imposed solely to raise money for the government that imposes it.

Revenue Taxes   Taxes whose main purpose is to fund government services and programs.

Risk Propensity   Extent to which a decision maker is willing to gamble when making a decision.

Royalties   Fees that an exporter receives for allowing a company in a foreign country to manufacture or market the exporter's products.

Sales Forecast   An estimate of how much of a product or service will be purchased by prospective customers over a specific period.

Scanning   Reading material in an investigative way to search for specific information.

Secondary Sources   Other writers' interpretations of primary source documents.

Sensory Register   Brain filters through which sensory information enters the brain and is sent to short-term memory.

Services Services refer to intangible products that are bought or sold.

Short-term Goals Goals set for the very near future, typically less than one year.

Short-term Memory The brain's temporary information storehouse, in which information remains for a limited time (from a few seconds to half a minute).

Shortage Situation in which quantity demanded exceeds quantity supplied.

Shorthand A system of rapid handwriting that employs symbols, abbreviations, and shortened words to represent words and phrases.

Skimming Rapid, superficial reading of material to determine central ideas and main elements.

Small Business An independently owned and managed business that does not dominate its market.

Smart Goals Goals that are Specific, Measurable, Achievable, Realistic, and Time-framed.

Socialism A kind of command economy in which the government owns and operates the main industries, while individuals own and operate less crucial industries.

Sole Proprietorship Business owned and usually operated by one person who is responsible for all of its debts.

Spinoff Strategy of setting up one or more corporate units as new, independent corporations.

Stability Condition in an economic system in which the amount of money available and the quantity of goods and services produced are growing at about the same rate.

Standard of Living Total quantity and quality of goods and services that a country's citizens can purchase with the currency used in their economic system.

Stock A share of ownership in a corporation.

Stockholders Investors who buy shares of ownership in the form of stock.

Strategic Alliance An enterprise in which two or more persons or companies temporarily join forces to undertake a particular project.

Strategic Goals Long-term goals derived directly from the firm's mission statement.

Strategic Management The process of helping an organization maintain an effective alignment with its environment.

Strategic Plans Plans that reflect decisions about resource allocations, company priorities, and steps needed to meet strategic goals.

Strategy Formulation Creation of a broad program for defining and meeting an organization's goals.

Strategy The broad set of organizational plans for implementing the decisions made for achieving organizational goals.

Stress Physical or mental strain or tension produced in reaction to pressure.

Subsidiary Corporation One that is owned by another corporation.

Subsidy A government payment to help domestic business compete with foreign firms.

Supply Curve Graph showing how many units of a product will be supplied (offered for sale) at different prices.

Supply The willingness and ability of buyers to purchase a product or service.

Surplus Situation in which a country exports more than it imports, creating a favourable balance of trade.

Surplus Situation in which quantity supplied exceeds quantity demanded.

SWOT Analysis Identification and analysis of organizational strengths and weaknesses and environmental opportunities and threats as part of strategy formulation.

Tactical Plans Generally, short-range plans concerned with implementing specific aspects of a company's strategic plans.

Tariff A tax levied on imported products.

Technical Skills Skills associated with performing specialized tasks within a firm.

Technology All the ways firms create value for their constituents.

Technology Technology includes human knowledge, work methods, physical equipment, electronics and telecommunications, and various processing systems used to perform business activities.

Technology Transfer The process of getting a new technology out of the lab and into the marketplace.

Textile Labelling ACT Regulates the labelling, sale, importation, and advertising of consumer textile articles.

Time Management Skills Skills associated with the productive use of time.

Tobacco ACT Prohibits cigarette advertising on billboards and in retail stores, and assigns financial penalties to violators.

Top Managers Those managers responsible for a firm's overall performance and effectiveness and for developing long-range plans for the company.

Topic Sentence A one- or two-sentence statement describing the main idea of a paragraph.

Trade Association An organization dedicated to promoting the interests and assisting the members of a particular industry.

Typology A systematic classification or study of types.

Unemployment The level of joblessness among people actively seeking work in an economic system.

Unlimited Liability A person who invests in a business is liable for all debts incurred by the business; personal possessions can be taken to pay debts.

Values Principles or qualities that you consider important.

Verbal Signposts Spoken words or phrases that call attention to information that follows.

Vertical Integration Owning or controlling the inputs to the firm's processes and/ or the channels through which the products or services are distributed.

Vertical Merger A merger of two firms that have previously had a buyer– seller relationship.

Viral Marketing Strategy of using the internet and word-of-mouth marketing to spread product information.

Vision (or Purpose) A statement indicating why an organization exists and what kind of organization it wants to be.

Weights and Measures ACT Sets standards of accuracy for weighing and measuring devices.

World Product Mandating The assignment by a multinational of a product responsibility to a particular branch.

World Trade Organization (WTO) Organization through which member nations negotiate trading agreements and resolve disputes about trade policies and practices.